CW01368054

Early Medieval Settlement in Upland Perthshire: Excavations at Lair, Glen Shee 2012-17

Early Medieval Settlement in Upland Perthshire: Excavations at Lair, Glen Shee 2012-17

David Strachan, David Sneddon and Richard Tipping

with contributions by

Łukasz Banaszeck, Steven Black, Ewan Campbell, Ann Clarke, David Cowley,
Derek Hall, Stratford Halliday, Derek Hamilton, Catherine Johnson,
Anthony Krus, Dawn McLaren, Peter McNiven, Peter Morris,
Daniël Postma, Danny Paterson, Susan Ramsay,
Catherine Smith and Dene Wright

ARCHAEOPRESS ARCHAEOLOGY

Archaeopress Publishing Ltd
Summertown Pavilion
18-24 Middle Way
Summertown
Oxford OX2 7LG

www.archaeopress.com

ISBN 978-1-78969-315-7
ISBN 978-1-78969-316-4 (e-Pdf)

© the individual authors and Archaeopress 2019

Front Cover: An oblique aerial view of the Pitcarmick buildings at Ashintully, Cnoc an Daimh, looking east (Canmore ID29451: NO 1084 6249): the earthwork remains of this 25m long building are picked out by a low bank. To the left (north) the faint outline of an earlier building is visible and both are surrounded by later cultivation remains (© Crown Copyright: HES DP226073).

Back Cover: One of the many later stone and turf buildings at Lair which share some of the characteristics of the Pitcarmick buildings, with Mount Blair in the background (D. Strachan: 2011).

This work is licensed under a Creative Commons Attribution 4.0 International License.

Printed in England by P2D

This book is available direct from Archaeopress or from our website www.archaeopress.com

Cairns and circles similar to those described are to be seen in other hills of this parish...The elevated situation and cold exposure in which these ruins lie, have preserved them from being ever disturbed by the plough, which has effaced, and probably destroyed ruins of the same kind in other places.

The Reverend Allan Stewart, 1795
(*The Statistical Account of Scotland*, Kirkmichael, Perth, Vol. 15, page 520).

Contents

List of Figures v

List of Tables viii

Acknowledgements ix

List of Contributors x

Notes xi

1. Introduction 1
Strachan and Tipping

    1.1 Background to the project 1
    1.2 North-west European turf and timber houses: an international context for the excavations at Lair 3
        Daniël Postma
        Cultural connections across the North Sea 3
        Elements of societal development 3
        A north-west European building tradition? 3
    1.3 The archaeological setting 4
        Prehistoric and early medieval archaeology in the region 4
        The archaeology of Glen Shee and Strathardle 7
    1.4 Pollen-analytical evidence for land-use change in and around Glen Shee 12
    1.5 Historical and political contexts 13
    1.6 The Pictish language and place-names in and around Glen Shee 14
        Peter McNiven
    1.7 The catchment of the Allt Corra-lairige: geology, topography, soils and climate 16
    1.8 Mapping of the field remains 19
        Łukasz Banaszek and David Cowley
        Source data and survey methodology 20
        Land use and the (in)visibility of archaeological features 21
        Survey results 22
        A palimpsest on the 'high-tide' mark 23
    1.9 Key sites in the study area 24
    1.10 Research objectives 25

2. Results of Archaeological Fieldwork, Radiocarbon Dating, Peat-Stratigraphic and Pollen Analyses 28
Sneddon, Strachan and Tipping

    2.1 Introduction 28
    2.2 Topographic and geophysical survey 28
        Geophysics by Peter Morris
        Results: areas of burning 30
        Cultivation remains 30
        Metallic debris 30
    2.3 Excavation 31
        David Sneddon and Steven Black
        Linear burnt feature 31
        Building 1 33
        Building 2 37
        Building 3 41
        Building 3: the annexe 48
        Building 3: the external platform 50
        Building 4 50
        Building 5 51
        Building 6 and enclosures 51
        Building 7 and enclosure 52
        Structure 4, cairns and other structures 55

2.4 Geo-archaeological analyses 56
2.5 Radiocarbon dating 56
    Anthony Krus and Derek Hamilton
    Bayesian modelling methodological approach...56
    Samples and the models 57
    Building 1...57
    Building 2...59
    Building 3...61
    Other dated contexts 61
    Bayesian models and results..62
    Sensitivity analysis: an alternative Bayesian model..62
    Conclusions..65
2.6 Peat-stratigraphic and pollen-analytical evidence for environmental and land-use change 66
    Danny Paterson and Richard Tipping
    Introduction 66
    Holocene peatland evolution on the lower slopes of Allt Corra-lairige 66
    Pollen analyses from borehole A1, Basin 2 70
        Methods 70
        The pollen source area and its relation to the archaeological structures 70
        Interpretations 70
2.7 Charcoal analysis 76
    Susan Ramsay
    Introduction and methodology 76
    Results 76

3. The Small Finds 78
Strachan and Sneddon

3.1 Introduction 78
3.2 Lithics 78
    Dene Wright
    Contexts 79
    Primary technology...79
    Secondary technology 79
    Discussion 80
3.3 Stone tools 80
    Ann Clarke
    Cobble tools and ground stones 80
    Whetstones, anvil/whetstone and anvil 80
    Rotary grinders 81
    Rotary quern 82
    Ground/structural slab 82
    Lamp/mortar..83
    Slab with hollow 83
    Distribution 84
    Comparison with other sites...84
3.4 A decorated stone spindle whorl 85
    Catherine Johnson
    The decoration and markings...85
    Discussion 86
    Additional note on decorated spindle whorl SF33 87
    Ann Clarke
3.5 The iron objects 87
    Dawn McLaren
    Introduction and methodology 87
    Knives 88
        Catalogue 88
    Other tools 89
        Catalogue 91

        Security equipment 91
            Catalogue 93
        Household equipment 93
            Catalogue 93
        Fittings 93
        Dress accessories 94
            Catalogue 95
        Miscellaneous 96
            Catalogue 96
        Distribution 96
        Discussion 97
    3.6 The vitrified material 98
        Dawn McLaren
        Ferrous metal-working waste 98
        Plano-convex slag cakes 98
        Tapped slag 99
        Unclassified iron slag 99
        Hearth lining 99
        Diagnostic micro-debris: hammerscale 99
        Other vitrified material 99
        Distribution 101
        Ironworking at Lair and beyond 101
    3.7 The pottery 102
        Derek Hall
            Catalogue 102
        Prehistoric sherds 102
        Medieval sherds 103
        Daub 103
        Discussion 103
    3.8 The glass bead 103
        Ewan Campbell
        Description 103
    3.9 Animal bone 104
        Catherine Smith
        Introduction and methodology 104
        Results 105
        Discussion 106

4. Discussion 107
Strachan, Tipping and Sneddon

    4.1 Introduction 107
    4.2 Archaeological and pollen-analytical evidence for later prehistoric settlement and use of the uplands 107
    4.3. A Late Iron Age–early medieval settlement continuum? 108
    4.4 Lair immediately prior to the construction of the Pitcarmick buildings 110
    4.5 Chronology and sequence of the buildings at Lair 110
    4.6 The buildings at Lair: form and function 111
        Buildings 1 and 2 111
        Buildings 3-5 112
        Building 3 112
        Buildings 4 and 5 114
        Building 6 114
        Buildings 7 and 8 116
    4.7 The buildings at Lair: turf, stone, timber and thatch 119
        Sources of turf 119
        The use of stone 119
        Turf wall construction 120
        Wood and thatch: the superstructure 121
    4.8 The buildings at Lair: spatial patterning 122

4.9 Re-visiting the morphology of Pitcarmick buildings 123
    with Stratford Halliday
        Elongation and scale 127
        Rounded ends 127
        Bowed walls, width differentiation and sloping construction 127
        Partially sunken interiors 128
        Entrances 128
        Annexes 128
        Pitcarmick-type group 129
4.10 Early medieval buildings in the North Sea area 129
    Daniël Postma
        Previous research on turf-walled buildings 129
        Typological comparison 129
        Use of space 130
        Building technology 130
        Concluding remarks on the international context of Pitcarmick buildings 131
4.11 The socio-political context and geographic patterns of Pitcarmick buildings in north-east Perthshire 132
    with Stratford Halliday
4.12 The rural economy at Lair AD 600-660 to AD 975-1025: palynological evidence and implications 137
4.13 The wider context of 7th century AD agrarian expansion 140
    with Stratford Halliday
4.14 The function of Pitcarmick buildings..143
    with Daniël Postma
4.15 The social status of 'Pitcarmick' communities 146
4.16 After the 'Pitcarmicks' 147
    with a contribution from Łukasz Banaszek and David Cowley

5. Conclusions 150
5.1 Introduction 150
5.2 Threats to the resource 150
5.3 The impact of the Glenshee Archaeology Project 150
5.4 Lessons learned 152
5.5 Potential for future research 152

References 154

Appendix A 171

Index 178

List of Figures

1. Introduction
Figure 1.1 The location of the site at Lair, Glen Shee, Perth and Kinross. 2
Figure 1.2 Community engagement and the outdoor classroom. 2
Figure 1.3 Selected archaeological and pollen sites mentioned in the text. 5
Figure 1.4 Pont's late 16th century map showing the crannog on Loch Beanie: '[th]e duelling of [th]e cheef man of Glen Chy and StraArdle' (Reproduced by permission of the National Library of Scotland). 7
Figure 1.5 The Early Bronze Age ring-cairn at Lair in the foreground, with glacial deposits behind and Mount Blair beyond (D. Strachan: 2013). 9
Figure 1.6 Aerial view of the multi-period site at Wester Peathaugh (ID31021), including clearance cairns, roundhouses, Dalrulzion-type roundhouses, Pitcarmick buildings and cultivation remains (D. Strachan: 2001). 9
Figure 1.7 The extensive township at Easter Bleaton on the glen floor *c*. 5 km south of Lair (D. Strachan: 2007). 10
Figure 1.8 The upland township of Corra-lairig (E. Martin: 2014). 11
Figure 1.9 Pre-improvement field-systems at Glenkilrie (D. Strachan: 2007). 11
Figure 1.10 The wider region showing early medieval power-centres and the known distribution of Pitcarmick buildings. 13
Figure 1.11: Pictish and Gaelic place-names mentioned in Section 1.6 that appear on current OS maps. 17
Figure 1.12 The catchment of the Allt Corra-lairige showing the topography, bedrock and superficial geology and soils. 18
Figure 1.13: The lower catchment of the Allt Corra-lairige. 19
Figure 1.14 A low-level aerial view, looking south-east, of the setting of the excavations, showing the afforested Torr Lochaidh to the left, the splash of close-cropped grassland bordered by dry *Calluna* heath, the glacial morainic mounds that 'protect' the Allt Corra-lairige, and Glen Shee (E. Martin: 2014). 20
Figure 1.15 Orthophotograph documenting current land use and showing the extent of ALS data (© Historic Environment Scotland (Source: orthophotographs (2008) licensed to Historic Environment Scotland for PGA, through Next Perspectives™)). 21
Figure 1.16 Features mapped from aerial photographs and Airborne Laser Scanning data (© Historic Environment Scotland (Source: contour data derived from DTM (2018) © Bluesky International Limited & Getmapping Plc.)). 23
Figure 1.17 An aerial view of Lair from 1978 showing the main group of Pitcarmick buildings and related buildings beside the ring-cairn (© Crown Copyright: HES A55314). 25
Figure 1.18 One of the smaller buildings at Lair (Building 7) with associated enclosures (D. Strachan: 2011)...........26
Figure 1.19 A larger building (Building 1), closest to the ring-cairn, with stones robbed from the cairn kerb and incorporated into the rounded end (D. Strachan: 2011). 26

2. Results of Archaeological Fieldwork, Radiocarbon Dating, Peat-Stratigraphic and Pollen Analyses
Figure 2.1 Topographic survey showing upstanding archaeology and positions of trenches. 29
Figure 2.2 Magnetic gradiometer survey: see Figure 2.1 for location (Peter Morris: 2014). 30
Figure 2.3 East facing section through linear burning: Trench 3 in 2012 (scale = 2 m). 31
Figure 2.4 Buildings 1 and 2 prior to excavation showing earthworks and trench plan. 32
Figure 2.5 Building 1 excavation plan. 34
Figure 2.6 Building 1: lower turf wall (C21) and location of section B-B' (Figure 2.5) in 2012 (Horizontal scale = 1 m). 35
Figure 2.7 Building 1 and 2 selected sections. 36
Figure 2.8 Building 2 excavation plan. 38
Figure 2.9 A vertical aerial photograph of the south-eastern end of Building 2 partially excavated (E. Martin: 2014). 39
Figure 2.10 Oblique view of the ring-cairn and the south-eastern end of Building 2 (E. Martin: 2014). 40
Figure 2.11 Oblique aerial view of Buildings 3-5, evaluation trenches and earthworks (E. Martin: 2015). 41
Figure 2.12 Buildings 3-5 before excavation showing earthworks and trench plan. 42
Figure 2.13 Building 3 excavation plan. 43
Figure 2.14 Building 3: the hearth C235 and stone infill C157/C166 showing gradient at north-western end in 2016 (scales = 1 m). 44
Figure 2.15 South-west facing section through Buildings 3 and 5. 45
Figure 2.16 Building 3: hearth and selected pit/post-hole sections. 46
Figure 2.17 Building 3: post-hole C169 during excavation at base of stone infill C157/C166 in 2016. 47

Figure 2.18 Building 3: entrances showing stone slab steps leading into the sunken part of the building (foreground) and the three large post-holes (C317, C319 and C321) behind in 2017 (large scales = 1 m). 48
Figure 2.19 Building 3/4: gully and sunken floor in 2016 (horizontal scale = 1 m)..49
Figure 2.20 Building 3 annexe during excavation in 2016. 50
Figure 2.21: Building 6: east-facing section. 52
Figure 2.22 Vertical view of Building 7 during excavation (K. Ward: 2017)..53
Figure 2.23 Building 7: wall within evaluation trench and earthwork in 2014 (scales = 1 m)................................53
Figure 2.24 Building 7: curved wall at the western end in 2017 (scales = 1 m)...54
Figure 2.25 The west facing section through the wall of Building 7..55
Figure 2.26 Structure 4 and nearby cairn in 2013 (scales = 1 m). 55
Figure 2.27 Calibrated radiocarbon dates. Calibrations were calculated using the terrestrial calibration curve (IntCal13) of Reimer *et al.* (2013) and the probability method of Stuiver and Reimer (1993) with OxCal v4.3 (Bronk Ramsey 2017). Radiocarbon dates are grouped into their corresponding contexts.....................60
Figure 2.28 Results and structure of the primary Bayesian model. For each of the radiocarbon measurements two distributions have been plotted, one in outline, which is the result of simple radiocarbon calibration, and a solid one, which is based on the chronological model use. The other distributions correspond to aspects of the model. The large square 'brackets' along with the OxCal keywords define the overall model exactly. 63
Figure 2.29 Results and structure of the alternative Bayesian model. The brackets and keywords define the model structure. The format is as described in Figure 2.28..64
Figure 2.30 Estimated spans of activity from the primary and alternative models..65
Figure 2.31 Oblique aerial photograph looking south over the peats (dark brown) of Basin 1 in the foreground and the northern edge of Basin 2 in the background, separated by improved pasture displaying cultivation traces. Both basin peats have been heavily cut which has created fen peat around them. The position of the pollen site in the fen of Basin 2 is marked by the cross (© Crown Copyright: HES DP226321). 67
Figure 2.32 Sediment-stratigraphic transect across the peats of Basin 2 with inferred phases of peatland development from AMS ^{14}C dating: (Phase 1) a blanket of wood peat shortly before 3372-3628 BC; (Phase 2) herb peat accumulates over wood peat until *c.* 1000 AD; (Phase 3) conjectured surface of the basins shortly before AD 1190-1283 with peat-cutting in the south-westerly basin; (Phase 4) formation of Cyperaceae (sedge) peat after abandonment of peat-cutting shortly before AD 1190-1283, save for a new bank cut in the surface of herb peat at the south-west...68
Figure 2.33 Complete percentage-based pollen diagram at borehole A1, Basin 2 with depth (mm) and with age (cal BP)..72
Figure 2.33 continued, Complete percentage-based pollen diagram at borehole A1, Basin 2 with depth (mm) and with age (cal BP)..73

3. The Small Finds

Figure 3.1 Flint artefacts: Cat 1, 10, 28 and 36. 79
Figure 3.2 The faceted smoother (SF39), grinder/smoother (SF29), lamp/mortar (SF30), and whetstone (SF54). 81
Figure 3.3 The anvil/whetstone (SF58) and whetstone (SF76). 82
Figure 3.4 Rotary grinders SF55 (top) and SF86 (bottom). 83
Figure 3.5 Spindle whorl (SF33): image extracted from RTI and incisions described in the text (RTI courtesy of H. Christie and S. Jeffrey of Glasgow School of Art)...85
Figure 3.6 Selected iron objects. 90
Figure 3.7 The barb-spring padlock (Cat 9) after conservation (© AOC Archaeology Ltd). 92
Figure 3.8 A schematic of the barb-spring padlock and bolt. 92
Figure 3.9 The segmented bead showing colour variation (M. Bell: 2018). 103
Figure 3.10 The bead indicating scale..103

4. Discussion

Figure 4.1 The alignment of Buildings 1 and 2 with the ring-cairn and showing later cultivation remains to the south. The re-use of stone from the cairn in Building 2 may suggest re-use of the cairn or a reverential act of acknowledgement of the structure...109
Figure 4.2 Reconstruction of Buildings 1 and 2 and the ring-cairn (A. Braby and G. McSwan: 2014). 112
Figure 4.3 The distribution of small finds by material in Buildings 3. 113
Figure 4.4 Reconstruction plan of Building 3. 113
Figure 4.5 Schematic sections across Building 3 showing a) rigid A-frame 'caber' roof option, b) the same with loft space, and c) a roof supported by lighter-weight round wood poles under tension and with loft space (C. Mitchell: 2018). 114

Figure 4.6 Schematic longitudinal sections through Building 3 illustrating the noticeable slope of the domestic area (left) compared with the byre on the right hand side, below shows the loft space option (C. Mitchell: 2018). 115

Figure 4.7 Artists' reconstruction of Building 3 as a byre-house over-wintering cattle (C. Mitchell: 2018). 116

Figure 4.8 The Weaver's house at the Highland Folk Museum shows how the wall footings of Building 7 may have looked; the roofs at Lair were probably lower due to their exposed location and high altitude (D. Strachan: 2013). 117

Figure 4.9 The probable broad phasing of the visible remains at Lair: early medieval Buildings 1-2, 3-5; probably 12-13, and possibly 14 (© Historic Environment Scotland (Source: contour data derived from DTM (2018) © Bluesky International Limited & Getmapping Plc.)). 118

Figure 4.10 Icelandic turf wall construction: herring-bone facades of *klambra* or 'clamped block', and alternate courses of *strengur*, with an earthen/turf core on a dwarf foundation wall (D. Strachan: 2013). 120

Figure 4.11 A rounded corner from Tyrfingsstaoir, Iceland, with a herring bone pattern of *klambra* blocks and a stone foundation, both interspersed with *strengur* strip turves (D. Strachan: 2013). 121

Figure 4.12 A selection of comparative plans of unexcavated Pitcarmick-type and related buildings showing variation in scale and morphology (based on RCAHMS: 1990; Cowley: 1997 and MacGregor 2010). 125

Figure 4.13 Comparative plans of the excavated Pitcarmick-type buildings from Lair (1) and Pitcarmick (2, based on Carver et al. 2012), and 'related' buildings at Lair (3 and 4) and Bunrannoch (5, based on MacGregor 2010). 126

Figure 4.14 The numbers of Pitcarmick buildings at increasing distance (5 km units) along a straight line north-west of the Blairgowrie-Alyth axis. 134

Figure 4.15 The distance from Pitcarmick buildings to the nearest well-drained strath terraces. 134

Figure 4.16 Graph showing (a) relative heights of Pitcarmick buildings above the nearest strath; (b) relative heights of Pitcarmick buildings ordered from lowest to highest. 135

Figure 4.17 The distribution of known Pitcarmick buildings with soil types. 136

Figure 4.18 Aspects of known Pitcarmick buildings. 137

Figure 4.19 Graph showing percentages of Pitcarmick buildings in 50.0 x 50.0 m cells (defined by OS grid references on the X-axis) in the area surveyed by RCAHMS (1990) in ten arbitrarily defined equal-width bands of solar irradiance. 139

Figure 4.20 The location of pollen sites in Table 4.1 and Figure 4.21. 141

Figure 4.21 Patterns of economic 'recession' or 'recovery' in the pollen records. 142

Figure 4.22 Stobie's map of 1783 [sheet 5SE] (Reproduced by permission of the National Library of Scotland). 148

Figure 4.23 The well-preserved stretch of military road at Lair, dating from *c.* 1750 (D. Strachan: 2012). 149

List of Tables

2. Results of Archaeological Fieldwork, Radiocarbon Dating, Peat-Stratigraphic and Pollen Analyses

Table 2.1 Radiocarbon data. 58
Table 2.1 continued, Radiocarbon data. 59
Table 2.2 Probability matrix that event τ_1 occurred before event τ_2 in the primary model. 66
Table 2.3 Probability matrix that event τ_1 occurred before event τ_2 in the alternative model. 66
Table 2.4 AMS ^{14}C assays on peat in Basin 1. 67
Table 2.5 Sediment description of borehole A1 in Basin 2. 69
Table 2.6 AMS ^{14}C assays on peat in Basin 2. 69
Table 2.7 Size measurements and possible identification of Poaceae pollen grains with a-axes >35 μm: Key to columns: (a) depth of sample (mm); (b) length (a-axis: μm); (c) width (b-axis: μm); (d) annulus diameter (μm); (e) annulus boundary; (f) annulus: exine thickness ratio; (g) Andersen (1979) Group................71
Table 2.8 Charcoal identification from sample of linear burning (C14). 77
Table 2.9 Charcoal identification from sample of lower hearth fill (C248). 77

3. The Small Finds

Table 3.1 Characteristics of the lithic assemblage. 78
Table 3.2 Analysis of recovery locations by context and sub-analysed between primary and secondary technologies. 79
Table 3.3 Stone artefacts. 80
Table 3.4 Rotary grinders from selected Scottish medieval sites. 83
Table 3.5 Stone artefacts from stratified Building 3 contexts. 84
Table 3.6 The range of vitrified material recovered during excavation. 98
Table 3.7 Distribution of vitrified and heat-affected materials across the excavated area by type and weight. The key to the abbreviations used in the table above can be found in Table 3.6. 100

4. Discussion

Table 4.1 Pollen sites considered in Section 4.13. 138
Table 4.1 continued, Pollen sites considered in Section 4.13. 139

Acknowledgements

Both the excavations at Lair and the subsequent programme of post-excavation research and publication is the result of considerable input from a wide a variety of individuals and organisations. The authors are indebted to them all and hereby acknowledge their contributions. The on-site archaeology team over 2012-17 included staff from Northlight Heritage, then part of York Archaeological Trust: Steve Black (site supervisor), Charlotte Francoz (survey), Clark Innes (palaeobotany) and Katy Firth, and from Perth and Kinross Heritage Trust: Sarah Malone, Sophie Nicol and Gavin Lindsay (who supervised our programme of school engagement). We are indebted to Peter Morris for geophysical survey throughout the project and to Carol Pudsey for her advice on geology. Low-level aerial photography, captured by drone, was a useful addition to our toolkit and was provided by Eddie Martin (2012-16) and Ken Ward (2017). Our attempts to carry out geoarchaeological analyses were undertaken by Paul Adderley and Dennis Dring of the University of Stirling, and by Vanessa Rees, then of the University of Aberdeen.

The excavations could not have taken place without the input of the volunteers who contributed so much each year. They came from the local community and further afield, and were joined annually by archaeology students from the Universities of Glasgow, Aberdeen, Edinburgh and the Highlands and Islands. Special thanks are due to these who attended all six seasons of excavations: Anthea and Deryck Deane, Barbara Hogarth, and Diana MacIntyre, and to those who attended in multiple years: Elspeth Reid, (the late) Tony Simpson, Juliette Mitchell, John Robb, Roy Marsden, Tom Sneddon, Ali Constable, Mike Ballantine, Isobel Morrison, Elizabeth Robertson, Katie South, Anemay Jack, Steve Ponsonby, Alison Selwa, Lauren Davidson, Mark Seaborne and Kerry Gray. The schools that participated included Kirkmichael Primary (2012-13 and 2017), Blairgowrie High (2012 and 2014), Breadalbane Academy (2016), Kettins Primary (2017) and Meigle Primary (2017): we would like to thank all those involved. Many other parts of the local community contributed to the success of the project, and our thanks in particular are extended to the landowner, David Houston, who accommodated with interest our fieldwork over six years and the Clan MacThomas Society, who made available the car park at their gathering place, Clach na Coileach, the Stone of the Cockerel. We would also like to thank Mount Blair Community Council, The Glenshee Pottery (latterly the Wee House of Glenshee), Gulabin Lodge Outdoor Centre Glenshee, and the Eco-camp Glenshee for their support and hospitality.

The excavations at Lair were funded by a number of organisations over the years. In addition to the significant contributions made by both Perth and Kinross Heritage Trust and Northlight Heritage, the main funders were The Heritage Lottery Fund (2013-14), The Gannochy Trust (2014-16), and Historic Environment Scotland (2015-17), with smaller contributions from the Cairngorms National Park (2012-13), Scottish Hydro Drumderg Community Benefit Fund (2012), the Society of Antiquaries of Scotland (2012 and 2015), The Strathmartine Trust (2017), and the Hunter Archaeological and Historical Trust (2013). This publication has been supported by Perth and Kinross Heritage Trust, The Strathmartine Trust, and has been grant-aided by Historic Environment Scotland.

Richard Tipping and Danny Paterson would like to thank David Strachan (Perth and Kinross Heritage Trust) for inviting the opportunity to work at Lair, Julia Campbell (University of Stirling) who assisted in securing funding, which was given by the Scottish Funding Council and Perth and Kinross Heritage Trust. Aden Beresford and Wishart Mitchell helped in fieldwork, and the Division of Biological and Environmental Sciences at Stirling University provided facilities and accommodated the work: Bob McCulloch is thanked for facilitating laboratory work.

In the production of this publication we would also like to thank all of the specialists who have contributed, and those who illustrated their work: Leeanne Whitelaw (line drawings of flint, stone and bead); Woody Clarke (photography of the rotary grinders); Mike Bell (bead photography); Sam O'Leary of AOC Archaeology (metal-work illustrations); Heather Christie and Stuart Jeffrey of Glasgow School of Art (scanning and RTI illustrations of the spindle whorl); and Ingrid Shearer and Peta Glew of Northlight Heritage. Special thanks to our reconstruction artists Alan Braby, Gillian McSwan and Chris Mitchell. Finally we would like to thank David Davison of Archaeopress for his patience, and the numerous colleagues who provided advice and support both on site and in the production of this publication: Martin Carver, Strat Halliday, Piers Dixon, Karen Milek, Oskar Sveinbjarnarson, Þór Hjaltalin, Bryndís Zoega and Guðný Zoega. Our special thanks go to Althea Davies (University of St Andrews) who reviewed the palynological aspects of the text, and to Strat Halliday who kindly reviewed the entire text and helped us re-think aspects of both on site interpretation and wider context.

List of Contributors

Łukasz Banaszeck, Historic Environment Scotland

Steven Black, Northlight Heritage

Ewan Campbell, University of Glasgow

Ann Clarke, freelance lithic specialist

David Cowley, Historic Environment Scotland

Derek Hall, freelance archaeologist and ceramic specialist

Stratford Halliday, independent archaeological researcher

Derek Hamilton, SUERC Radiocarbon Dating Laboratory

Catherine Johnson, University of Glasgow

Anthony Krus, SUERC Radiocarbon Dating Laboratory

Dawn McLaren, AOC Archaeology Group

Peter McNiven, University of Glasgow

Peter Morris, Blairgowrie Geoscience

Daniël Postma, Archaeo Build

Danny Paterson, University of Stirling

Susan Ramsay, freelance archaeobotanical specialist

Catherine Smith, Alder Archaeology Ltd

David Sneddon, Northlight Heritage

David Strachan, Perth and Kinross Heritage Trust

Richard Tipping, University of Stirling

Dene Wright, University of Glasgow

(As at time of writing).

Notes

Chronology, terminology and building dimensions

Throughout, and in line with the Scotland's Archaeological Periods and Ages (ScAPA) project (www.scottishheritagehub.com/content/scapa) we use the following chronological definitions: Bronze Age (2500-800 BC); Iron Age (800 BC-AD 500); early medieval (AD 500-1000); medieval (AD 1000-1600) and post-medieval (after AD 1600) as defined by the ScAPA thesaurus (http://purl.org/heritagedata/schemes/scapa). The Scottish Monument Type Thesaurus (http://purl.org/heritagedata/schemes/1) has been used throughout to describe monument types, and individual sites mentioned are identified by their Canmore ID (e.g. ID1234, see https://canmore.org.uk/).

All radiocarbon (^{14}C) dates mentioned in the text are calibrated (cal) unless otherwise stated.

While RCAHMS (1990) used the term 'Pitcarmick-type building', the thesaurus (above) uses 'Pitcarmick building' and so this is the term commonly adopted within. It is also used in preference to 'longhouse' because it is interpretatively neutral and makes no functional assumptions. Milek (2007: 2-3), notes two definitions of the term 'longhouse'. The first originates with Trier (1969) as cited by Hermanns-Auðardóttir (1989) and is defined as a residential building with a length-to-width ratio of at least 1:2. The second, more commonly used definition, denotes an elongated dwelling with residential space at one end and a byre at the other (cf. Crawford 1987: 145; Fenton 1982). The latter usage is sometimes ambiguous, however, and Milek, for instance, notes that 'longhouse' is commonly used to describe Viking Age houses in Iceland even though they are not, in general, byre-houses (2007: 3).

Building dimensions given in Chapters 1 and 2 relate to the field remains and are taken from the top of the bank defining the feature to the top of the opposite bank. In Chapter 4 estimated internal dimensions are given, and are based on the assumption that turf walls were around 1 m in width and that the top of the bank represents the centre of the original wall line. All should be considered approximate given the nature of collapse and degradation and, unless otherwise stated, all measurements are derived from survey and excavation and may not match dimensions cited in other publications.

Image copyright

Unless otherwise indicated all images are copyright of Perth and Kinross Heritage Trust.

Geographical terms

Sites within Perth and Kinross are accompanied by a locating place-name, and outwith are given their modern local authority area. Occasionally the historic term Perthshire is used when describing the upland zone of what is now Perth and Kinross.

1. Introduction

Strachan and Tipping

with contributions by Postma, McNiven, Banaszek and Cowley

1.1 Background to the project

Glen Shee and Strathardle are broadly north-south oriented valleys straddling the Highland Boundary Fault east of the River Tay, and share many of the heavily glaciated characteristics of the Angus Glens to their east (Figure 1.1). As early as the 1860s the hut-circles in the Strathardle hills had attracted John Stuart's excavations at Balnabroich and Ardlebank (Stuart 1866), one of the earliest attempts to explore these sorts of monuments, and the complex landscapes that surround them, anywhere in Scotland. Glen Shee, while described as 'one of the most interesting glens in the Highlands... once thickly populated and... rich in legendary and traditional lore' (Smith 1895: 96), did not see archaeological research until the 1930s, when Wallace Thorneycroft followed up Stuart's work with his excavations at the roundhouses at Dalrulzion (1933; 1946). His fieldwork and that a little later of Margaret Stewart (1962) was eventually consolidated by the Ordnance Survey in the early 1970s (Thoms and Halliday 2014: 13-15).

The true range and extent of the well-preserved upland archaeology in Glen Shee and Strathardle, however, only emerged following the first systematic survey by the Royal Commission on the Ancient and Historical Monuments of Scotland (RCAHMS) in the late 1980s. Integrating aerial photographic and ground survey, this was published as *North-east Perth: an archaeological landscape* (RCAHMS 1990). A major achievement of the survey was the identification of a new settlement type, the Pitcarmick-type building, though of precisely what date was then uncertain. Two overlay hut-circles, suggesting that they post-dated roundhouse settlement, representing an expansion in the settlement record that 'may follow closely on from the hut-circles, but equally may belong firmly in the medieval period' (RCAHMS 1990: 12). Subsequent excavation at Pitcarmick in the 1990s, by John Barrett and Jane Downes, then of Glasgow University, established a mid-1st to early 2nd millennia AD date range for these distinctive turf and stone buildings: however, these important results remained unpublished until 2012 (Carver *et al.* 2012).

The Glenshee Archaeology Project, resulting in the present publication, was developed in response to the largely untapped archaeological potential of these uplands, and the publication of the Pitcarmick excavations in 2012. The overall aim of the project was to enhance understanding of 'everyday' life and economy for a period in which archaeological study in Scotland has almost exclusively focused on high status monuments and structures: mainly forts and other power-centres (e.g. Alcock and Alcock 1987; Alcock *et al.* 1989; Cook 2013b; Laing and Longley 2006; Lane and Campbell 2000; Mitchell and Noble 2017; Noble *et al.* 2013; SERF 2010), ecclesiastical sites (e.g. Carver 2008; Carver and Spall 2004; Lowe 2006, 2008) and Pictish carved stones (Henderson and Henderson 2004).

Excavation and environmental reconstruction focused on the site of Lair (Figure 1.1), a microcosm of the archaeology of the glen, which comprises several dispersed turf buildings within an assemblage of hut-circles, small cairns and a ring-cairn, probably variously dating from the Iron Age back to the Early Bronze Age. The RCAHMS survey identified Lair as significant, with the ground-plan of one group suggesting a possible sequence of three successive Pitcarmick-type buildings that might be revealed by further work (RCAHMS 1990: 12). This group is partly the focus of the excavations reported within.

Led by Perth and Kinross Heritage Trust, the project was developed as a programme of community archaeology. While none of the sites in the study area are Scheduled Monuments, the excavations were conceived in terms of large-scale evaluation rather than complete investigation of all surviving deposits, thus preserving the greater part of each site for future research. The project was delivered in partnership with Northlight Heritage and the University of Stirling, and funded by a variety of local and national organisations. Public engagement objectives focused on the principle of the outdoor classroom (Figure 1.2), providing learning opportunities for students in primary, secondary, and tertiary education, and for life-long learners. Training in excavation and survey was provided to volunteers from the local area and wider region, while participating undergraduate archaeology students from across Scotland provided near-to-peer training for primary and secondary school pupils. The project also sought to support sustainable tourist initiatives around the 100 km Cateran Trail, and its outreach products included a bespoke website and promotional leaflet, *Explore the Archaeology of Glenshee*; community posters and talks; and in 2014 a 'living history' fair in Blairgowrie. The fair

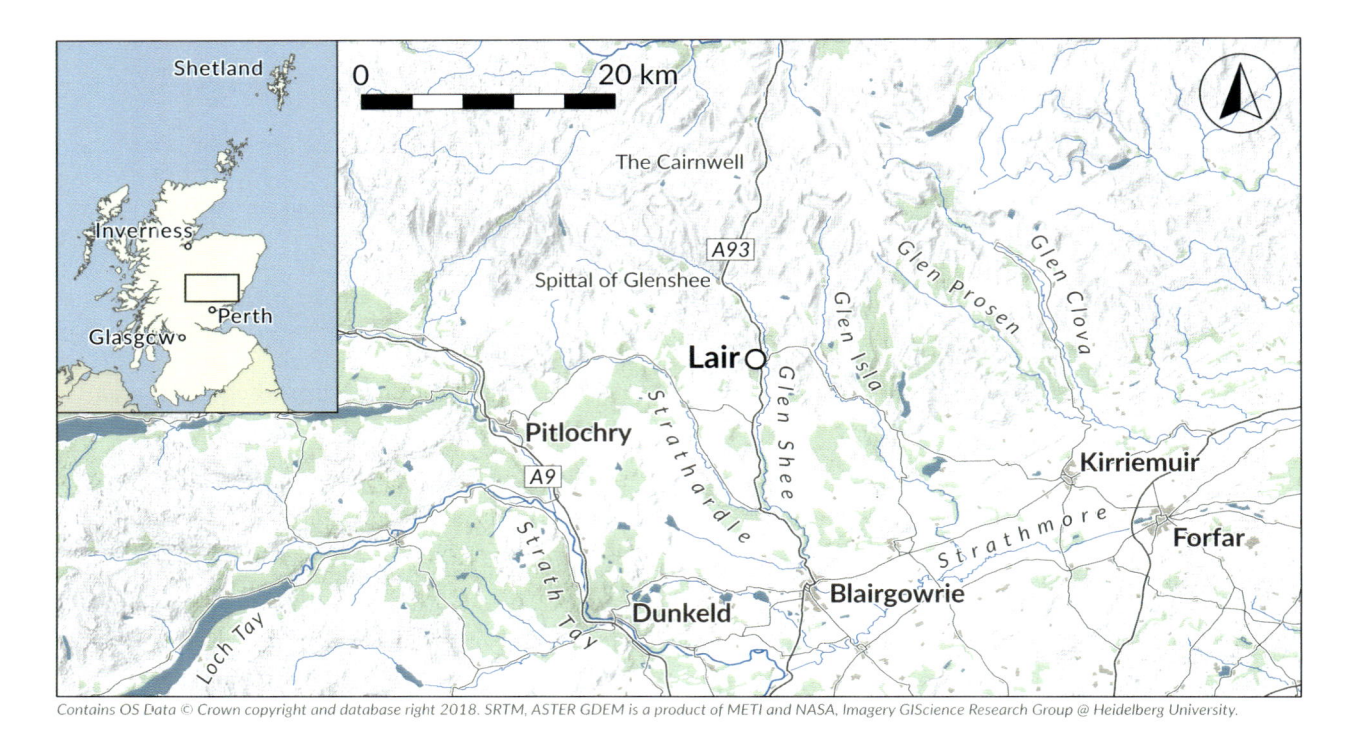

Figure 1.1 The location of the site at Lair, Glen Shee, Perth and Kinross.

Figure 1.2 Community engagement and the outdoor classroom.

saw re-enactments and craft demonstrations, including turf-wall construction, and wood-working and metal-working, the last reproducing excavated blades and buckles and displaying these beside the original items. The excavations employed an open policy for visitors, with site tours being provided, while guided walks of the wider landscape were also undertaken as part of the annual Perthshire Archaeology Month programme.

1.2 North-west European turf and timber houses: an international context for the excavations at Lair

Daniël Postma

Cultural connections across the North Sea

Given the relative isolation of Glen Shee, maritime connections may appear irrelevant to the development of settlements such as Lair, however their potential influence can be better appreciated when the area is viewed from the perspective of a 'maritime cultural landscape'. This broad concept encompasses not only water-based components such as waterways, ships and harbours but also their role in driving large scale overseas undertakings covering themes such as political power, religious ideology and agricultural, as well as artisan and industrial production (Westerdahl 1992, 2014; cf. Crumlin-Pedersen 2010).

Cultural connections across the North Sea became increasingly significant in the early medieval period; with Anglo-Saxon migrations to what is now England in the late 4th and 5th centuries (Morris 2015; Nieuwhof 2011). Cultural connections were maintained as petty kingdoms developed throughout the North Sea's coastal regions, in periods and sub-regions variously labelled Merovingian, Carolingian, Viking and Norse. As Myhre notes 'The sea and ships bound together the Germanic kingdoms, leaders and peoples of the regions; the North Sea became a Germanic North Sea.' (2000: 47–48). Initial Anglo-Saxon colonisation did not emerge from a single, uniform culture, but rather a 'close network of economic, socio-political, cultural and ideological relations across the southern North Sea,' often described as a 'North Sea Culture' (Nicolay 2014: 14; Myhre 2000: 54). Against this liberal approach to what is 'maritime' and the extent of cultural boundaries, it is perhaps not a question of *whether* Lair could have been influenced by this North Sea Culture but rather *to what extent* it actually was.

Elements of societal development

The early medieval societies in this North Sea Culture witnessed increased centralisation of both political power and landed wealth, of which the mid-8th to 9th century manorial estates are one of the more enigmatic materialisations (Verhulst 2002: 33–34; Carver 2019: 207 ff.). It has been suggested that in Scotland such early estates are reflected in the later, historic land units known as *thanages*. As Ralston and Armit note (2003: 222), 'the formation of such holdings will have provided the building blocks for the establishment of extensive kingdoms in the mid-first millennium AD' and debate is ongoing as to whether these elements of early state formation were a product of regional, indigenous developments or adopted from political or monastic land management models in place in the southern North Sea regions at that time.

The challenge of distinguishing between these options is in the difficulty to demonstrate causal effects between scarce archaeological evidence and the complex and changing economic, political and ideological constructs which they may reflect. Elsewhere in the North Sea area, elite gift-exchange and the later establishment of market trading centres known as *emporia*, left sufficient material traces to allow reconstructions of early medieval regional kingdoms to be made (e.g. Nicolay 2014, 2015). In Scotland, however, historical sources and place-name studies refer to a particularly complex mix of Britons, Picts and Scots, noted in archaeology for their remarkably scant material legacy. Further, it has been noted that it is 'difficult to correlate the Early Historic kingdoms […] straightforwardly with the archaeological evidence of structures and of the more mundane material culture' (Ralston and Armit 2003: 221). How, then, may we reconstruct the extent of Glen Shee's cultural connections across the North Sea?

A north-west European building tradition?

The increased number of surveyed and excavated early medieval buildings in north-west Europe is allowing new avenues of research into cultural developments and connections. Building types thought to be indicative of the northward expansion of Anglo-Saxons are timber halls and sunken-featured buildings, which appeared in Northumbria from the 6th century and south Scotland in the 7th century (Carver 2019: 193; Ralston and Armit 2003: 227–29). The Pitcarmick buildings demonstrate that rectilinear buildings were also in use north of the Tay, but their design differed considerably from their southern counterparts; instead of post-built, angular, short and byre-less buildings, they were turf-walled, round-ended, long and fitted with an internal byre. Further, their appearance differs even more from the preceding local house design of post-built roundhouses (Carver 2019: 184–85, 195). It is therefore understandable that Carver, in considering the 'first encounter with a genre […] that has yet to be comprehensively addressed' leant heavily towards a connection with longhouses on the continent (2012: 189–95).

It is probable that the cultural origins of the Pitcarmick buildings are as complex as they are interesting. The typological similarities of ground plans across the North Sea are without doubt an important focal point for further analyses. However, the functional use of these buildings is equally important, and specifically the relationship between buildings incorporating byres and those with separate byres. For example, the occurrence of short-houses in Anglo-Saxon England has historically been considered to be at odds with longhouses on the continent (Hamerow 1999). On the coast of the northern and western Netherlands, however, it would appear that at the time of Anglo-Saxon migration the dominant building design was in fact also of separate houses and byres (Postma 2015). The difference between buildings of the continent and Anglo-Saxon England may not have been as different as was previously thought. From this perspective, while the Pitcarmick buildings may appear more similar to their continental counterparts, they may equally reflect an upland variation of Anglo-Saxon buildings to the south.

A different view could be offered, from a technological perspective, through the suggested use of cuppills ('crucks') in roundhouse construction. This may suggest a closer relationship between circular and rectilinear buildings than typological or use of space analyses might suggest (Walker 2008; see also Strachan 2013) – effectively a practical rearrangement of an indigenous internal timber structure.

In summary, to place the Pitcarmick buildings of eastern Scotland in their wider cultural context, we must first understand how these buildings functioned in terms of their typology, use of space, technology and structural design: we must construct a *functional typology*. First attempts at developing such an interpretative framework for early medieval and later medieval turf longhouses in the Netherlands successfully demonstrate how variations in building length, presence and absence of byre areas, choice of walling material and design of the timber structure (including cuppills), can be charted and explained in a structured and meaningful manner (for the early medieval see Postma 2015; for later medieval see Nicolay and Postma 2018).

1.3 The archaeological setting

Prehistoric and early medieval archaeology in the region

The uplands of Perth and Kinross east of the rivers Tay and Garry (Figure 1.3) contain well-preserved and diverse settlement remains from at least the Middle Bronze Age to the 19th century. Recorded by ground and aerial survey, the earlier settlements typically comprise groups of roundhouse, some of them remarkably extensive and often occurring with field-systems, enclosures and cairn-fields (Harris 1985; Hooper 2002; RCAHMS 1990 and 1994 *passim*). Indeed, this part of Perth and Kinross contains one of the densest concentrations of this type of settlement known anywhere in Scotland. The roundhouses are both dispersed and in clusters, and commonly found between 300-400 m OD (Ordnance Datum: above sea level) and less frequently between 400-500 m OD (Harris 1985; Hooper 2002; RCAHMS 1990: 2).

While some roundhouses are apparently in isolation, by far the majority are juxtaposed to combinations of 'clearance' cairns, lynchets and stone dykes, covering areas from *c.* 2 ha to 20 ha, with most between 8 ha and 14 ha; these ephemeral agricultural systems, which rarely include coherent traces of field enclosures, mainly fall between 210 and 420 m OD (Harris 1985). The chronology and variety of form of the roundhouses is illustrated by the eight excavated from a large group at Carn Dubh (ID26422; Figure 1.3: 28; Rideout: 1995) above Pitlochry at 300-400 m OD. They included the double-walled roundhouses, a distinctive regional site-type found throughout north-east Perth and Kinross and into neighbouring Angus, and named after Thorneycroft's site at Dalrulzion (ID29060; Figure 1.3: 11; Thorneycroft 1933). The excavations confirmed a Late Bronze Age date for these, and revealed a single-walled roundhouse of Early Iron Age which had been reconfigured in the early medieval period. Ard marks were also found beneath the Late Bronze Age buildings.

Forts east of the River Tay are relatively few and far between, their distribution primarily lying along the Sidlaw Hills (RCAHMS 1994: 51) and apparently avoiding the hinterland of Strathmore north of the Highland Boundary Fault. The exceptions, which lie on this natural boundary, are the King's Seat (ID27172; Figure 1.3: 31), on a craggy hill with a commanding position on the north side of the river above Dunkeld, and Barry Hill, overlooking the mouth of Glen Isla and dominating Strathmore at Alyth (ID31061; Figure 1.3: 14; RCAHMS 1990: 5, 27-9). Both are multi-phased: the former has been mooted as potentially early medieval in date (Alcock *et al.* 1989: illus 12 and 209) and the early results of ongoing research would appear to confirm this (Strachan 2017). Of other small forts known in Strathmore, that at Inchtuthil (ID28598; Figure 1.3: 33) is notable for the Roman masonry incorporated into its rampart, which perhaps indicates a minor early medieval caput contemporary with the barrows (ID28599; Winlow 2010) that overlie the Roman fortress.

The upland settlement evidence west of the River Tay has not seen recent survey and publication comparable to north-east and south-east Perth and Kinross (RCAHMS 1990 and 1994). The evidence is similarly varied but also different, including a concentration of massive-walled roundhouses, with a long history of study, and variously called 'circular forts' (Watson 1913), 'ring-forts' (Stewart 1969), 'homesteads' (Taylor 1990) and most recently 'monumental roundhouses' (Strachan 2013). Of around 60 known, six have been excavated: Borenich (ID25880; Watson 1915), Litigan (ID24945) and Queen's View (ID25844; Taylor 1990), two

1. INTRODUCTION

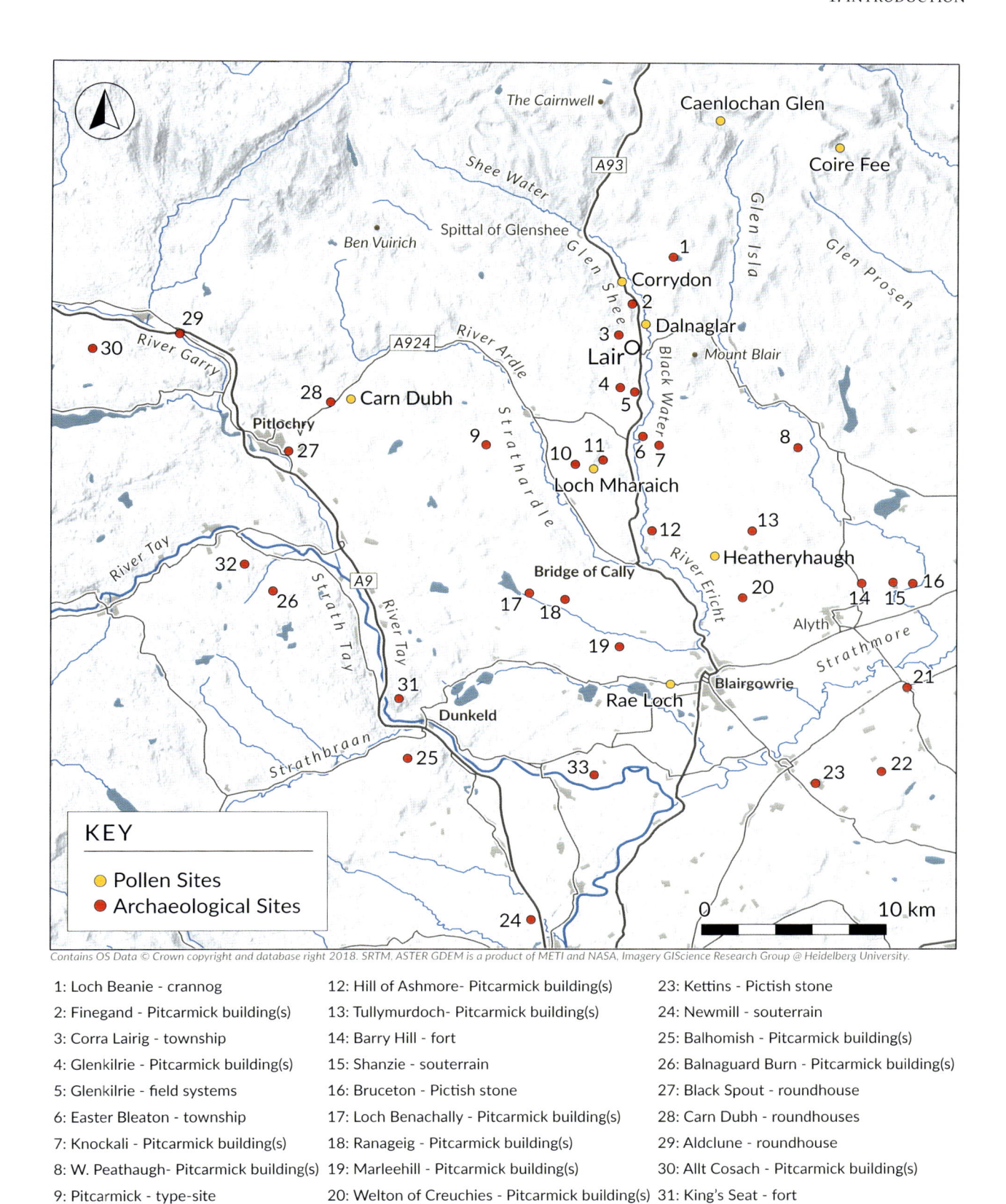

1: Loch Beanie - crannog
2: Finegand - Pitcarmick building(s)
3: Corra Lairig - township
4: Glenkilrie - Pitcarmick building(s)
5: Glenkilrie - field systems
6: Easter Bleaton - township
7: Knockali - Pitcarmick building(s)
8: W. Peathaugh - Pitcarmick building(s)
9: Pitcarmick - type-site
10: Balnabroich - Pitcarmick building(s)
11: Dalrulzion - roundhouses
12: Hill of Ashmore - Pitcarmick building(s)
13: Tullymurdoch - Pitcarmick building(s)
14: Barry Hill - fort
15: Shanzie - souterrain
16: Bruceton - Pictish stone
17: Loch Benachally - Pitcarmick building(s)
18: Ranageig - Pitcarmick building(s)
19: Marleehill - Pitcarmick building(s)
20: Welton of Creuchies - Pitcarmick building(s)
21: Meigle - Pictish stones
22: Keillor - Pictish stone
23: Kettins - Pictish stone
24: Newmill - souterrain
25: Balhomish - Pitcarmick building(s)
26: Balnaguard Burn - Pitcarmick building(s)
27: Black Spout - roundhouse
28: Carn Dubh - roundhouses
29: Aldclune - roundhouse
30: Allt Cosach - Pitcarmick building(s)
31: King's Seat - fort
32: Castle Dow - fort
33: Inchtuthil - fort

Figure 1.3 Selected archaeological and pollen sites mentioned in the text.

sites at Aldclune (ID25822; Hingley *et al.* 1997; Figure 1.3: 29) and the Black Spout (ID26267; Strachan 2013; Figure 1.3: 27). While Stewart (1969) and Taylor (1990) suggested an early medieval date for these from limited radiocarbon assays and a small number of finds, the Aldclune and Black Spout excavations have confirmed these as Late Iron Age constructions, albeit with some early medieval re-use. Litigan and Queen's View have been suggested as part of a wider array of ring-forts in the early medieval (Carver *et al.* 2012: 190-191; Noble *et al.* 2013: 1142); however, the evidence for re-occupation at either of these sites in this period is not clear.

There are also a number of larger forts in the uplands of Strath Tay, in contrast to the upland east of the Tay as outlined above. While some, such as Castle Dow (ID26356; Figure 1.3: 32) overlooking Strath Tay at Grandtully (Hutcheson 1889: 366-7, Figure 7) are likely to be Iron Age in date, Dundurn (ID24873) at the east end of Loch Earn remains the definitive early medieval fort of the area. Excavation here (Alcock *et al.* 1989) established a complicated building sequence spanning the 6-9th centuries AD with high status artefacts including ceramic and glass imports, bronze-working and locally produced leather and iron objects, including an important assemblage of nails and fragments of two barbed-bolt padlocks. The Annals of Ulster record a siege there in AD 683 and the Scottish Regnal Lists state that Girg, son of Dungal, died there in *c.* 889 AD, the latter suggesting that Dundurn was still regarded as a royal seat of the Scots at least in the decades preceding Kenneth MacAlpin's (Cináed mac Ailpin) amalgamation of the Southern Picts and Scots (see Section 1.5).

Another early medieval contender is Caisteal Mac Tuathal (ID24911) on Drummond Hill above Kenmore. With a controlling position overlooking the River Tay in the Appin of Dull, its Gaelic name is said to be connected to Tuathal, the Abbot of Dunkeld in the 9th century AD; the Annals of Ulster record that 'Tuathal son of Artgus, chief bishop of Fortriu and Abbot of Dunkeld' died in AD 865 (Watson 1926: 238). While unexcavated, both its form and controlling location over an important terrestrial pass are reminiscent of both Dundurn and the King's Seat, Dunkeld. Also in the uplands west of the Rivers Tay and Garry, Pictish and Early Christian carved stones are associated with important early ecclesiastical sites at Fortingall (ID24976; Robertson 1997), Dull (ID25617; Macdonald and Laing 1973) and Dunkeld (RCAHMS 1994: 89), and may indicate others at Logierait (ID26339 and 26341), Dunfallandy (ID26295), Old Faskally (ID26439) and Struan (ID25819).

In the lowlands, the cropmark record for Strathmore also features an extensive array of unenclosed roundhouses of probable Bronze Age and Iron Age date, again expressed in a variety of forms (RCAHMS 1994: 43, 45-8). They are frequently found in association with souterrains (Armit 1999; RCAHMS 1994: 63-68; Wainwright 1963). In two instances, at Shanzie Farm, Alyth (ID183018; Coleman and Hunter 2002; Figure 1.3: 15) and Newmill, Bankfoot (ID27007; Watkins 1980) souterrains associated with Late Iron Age settlement produced evidence of early medieval activity. There are also numerous larger cropmark enclosures of probable Iron Age date throughout the lowland zone. At Upper Gothens (ID28912) near Blairgowrie, however, excavation of a sub-circular enclosure of *c.* 60 m in diameter revealed a ditch and internal palisade, and a complex of palisade slots defining an inner area that produced a tinned iron buckle and evidence of metal-working with radiocarbon dates suggesting use from *c.* 885-1024 AD and *c.* 1040-1259 AD (Barclay 2001).

Crannogs are a frequent form of settlement in the uplands west of the River Tay, and particularly on Loch Tay, which has one of the densest concentrations in Scotland (Dixon 2004: illus 1). To the east of the Tay, examples are recorded on Stormont Loch (ID72061) and Loch Clunie (ID28959), the latter occupied by a late medieval tower-house, and in Glen Shee on Loch Beanie (ID29261), near the Spittal of Glenshee, where an island dwelling is depicted and intriguingly annotated on Timothy Pont's late 16th century map as '*Loch Sesatur sumtyms [th]e duelling of [th]e cheef man of Glen Chy and StraArdle*' (Figure 1.3: 1; Figure 1.4). While their known distribution is dictated by the availability of suitable waterbodies, the drainage of bogs and minor lochans in the lowlands during the 18th and 19th centuries may have destroyed others (Stratigos 2016).

While in the upland east of the Tay there are no Pictish symbol stones, the lower end of Strathmore has several Class 1 examples, unworked stones with incised symbols dating from the 6-8th centuries AD. These include Bruceton, which bears an arch and 'Pictish beast' and stands upright on the valley floor of the River Isla (ID31054; Figure 1.3: 16) in an area with antiquarian records of the discovery of human remains and cists (RCAHMS 1990: 87-8). It may be one of the few *in situ* Pictish stones in the area (Clarke 2007). The Keillor Class 1 stone (ID30545; Figure 1.3: 22) stands on the opposite side of the strath, and having been re-erected in the mid-19th century, it is not clear whether it was originally erected on the probably prehistoric grass-covered cairn on which it now stands. A pillar-like stone, Keillor bears three symbols, with a wolf at the top above a double disc and Z-rod and a mirror below, and is possibly of 7th century AD date (RCAHMS 1994: 5, 95). Later Pictish stones in Strathmore include a small rough cross-slab from Alyth (ID30756), a fine cross-slab of probable 8th or 9th century date at Kettins (ID30552; Figure 1.3: 23; RCAHMS 1994: 5, 97) and on the floor of the valley the remarkable collection of sculptured stones from Meigle (Figure 1.3: 21; RCAHMS 1994: 3-5, 98-102), which forms one of the most important

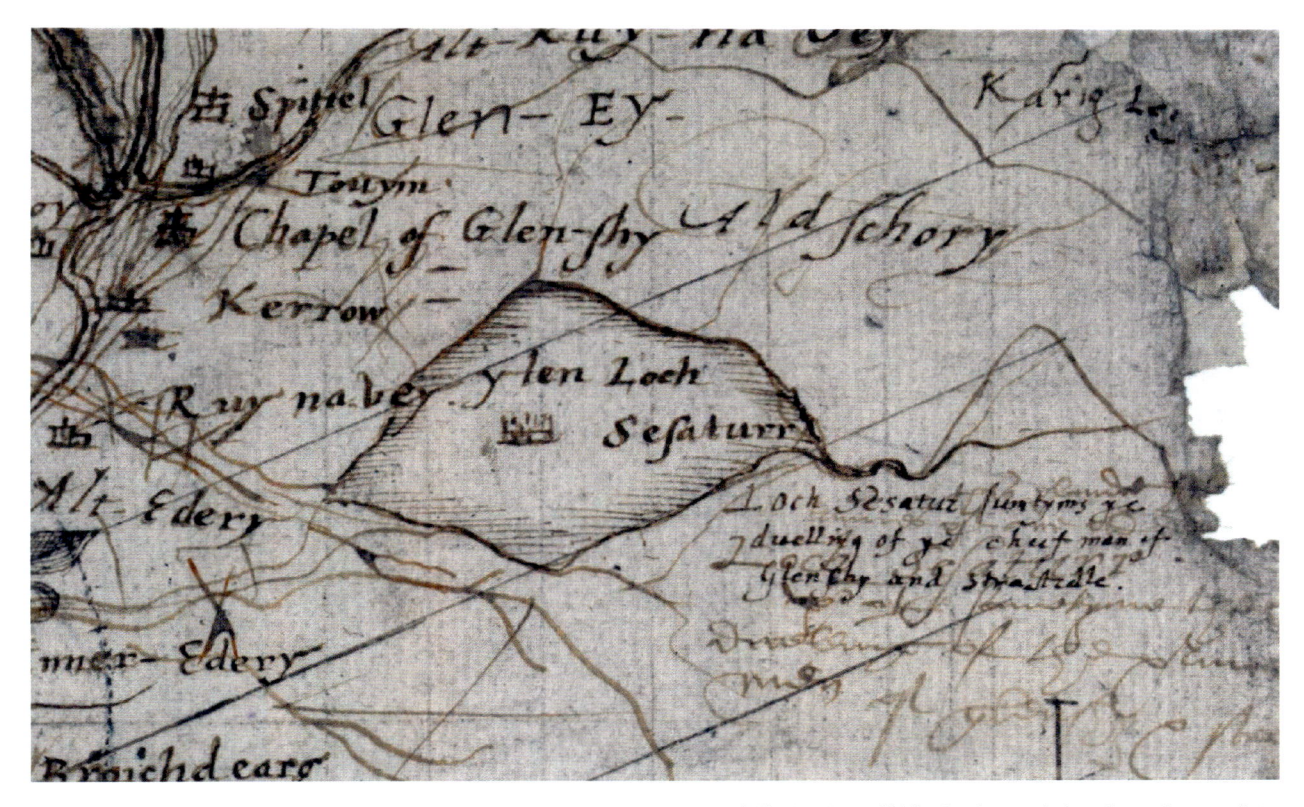

Figure 1.4 Pont's late 16th century map showing the crannog on Loch Beanie: '[th]e duelling of [th]e cheef man of Glen Chy and StraArdle' (Reproduced by permission of the National Library of Scotland).

collections of Pictish sculpture in eastern Scotland. While none of the 30 or so carved stones from Meigle are likely to pre-date *c*. 800 AD, the nature and scale of the assemblage suggest an important early medieval ecclesiastical centre from around that date (Ritchie 1995). Further south at the head of the Tay estuary, Scone was to emerge as the principal royal site *c*. 900 AD supplanting earlier power-centres that included Forteviot and Abernethy in Strathearn and Bertha just to the north of Perth (Driscoll 1998; Driscoll *et al.* 2010; Strachan 2011: 8-11).

Pitcarmick buildings, the principal subject of this report, are discussed below in the context of a more detailed review of the archaeology of Glen Shee and Strathardle, where the majority of the known examples are located. While others have been recorded by aerial photography and ground survey in the neighbouring hills of Angus, only a few possible examples have been identified west of the Tay (Bailey 2014: 22-24; Cowley 1997; Figures 1.3 and 1.10).

The archaeology of Glen Shee and Strathardle

From the gently undulating, agriculturally rich floor of Strathmore and the valley floors of the Isla and Tay, the hills rise steeply north-west across the geological faults that make up the Highland Boundary Fault. These separate the lowland Old Red Sandstone from upland Dalradian metamorphosed mudstones, sandstones and limestones. The hills rise to extensive plateau surfaces of till (boulder clay) and acid metamorphic rocks from around 400 m OD to between 900 m and 1000 m OD on the summits at the top of Glen Shee. Immediately east of Bridge of Cally the River Ardle, draining Strathardle to the north-west, and the Black Water (known as the Shee Water north of Lair) from Glen Shee, come together to form the River Ericht, which has cut a narrow gorge through the lower reaches of Glen Shee to debouch through the Highland Boundary Fault escarpment at Blairgowrie.

The floor of Strathardle is a 20 km long, 0.5 km wide, continuous alluvial 'strath' (floodplain) before climbing to a col at Carn Dubh at *c*. 400 m OD above Pitlochry. Glen Shee extends in a series of more isolated glaciofluvial and alluvial basins to the Spittal of Glenshee (*c*. 350 m OD), from which the modern road (A93) to Braemar turns steeply up Gleann Beag to make the pass below The Cairnwell, some 25 km north from Blairgowrie (Figure 1.1).

The RCAHMS survey (1990) revealed a wealth of archaeological sites surviving as earthworks, including prehistoric, medieval and later, pre-improvement settlements and cultivation remains. The nature of earlier prehistoric sites in Glen Shee and neighbouring Strathardle again appears to differ from Strath Tay to the west, notably in that Neolithic round barrows or chambered long cairns are apparently absent, though an antiquarian excavation of the Grey Cairn at Balnabroich claimed to find a passage leading towards the centre (Stuart 1866: 405-6). A scatter of cup-and-ring marked stones are potentially of this date, but the first significant exploitation of this landscape is revealed by the wealth of Bronze Age funerary and ceremonial monuments, which include round cairns, standing stones and stone circles. Amongst them is a group of five ring-cairns, including an example at Lair (ID29510; Figure 1.5) which is by far the largest of this compact geographical group (RCAHMS 1990: 2).

The area hosts one of the densest concentrations of prehistoric settlement in Scotland, with over 845 roundhouses in the area surveyed, and many others extending across the hills into the fringes of Strath Tay. Unusually amongst such settlements, the roundhouses display a wide range of morphological variation (Figure 1.6) and, as we have seen, survive at high altitudes within the range 300-500 m OD. The conspicuous absence of forts has also been noted above, the exception being Barry Hill, placed on the boundary between the lowland and upland zones, while other later prehistoric sites include 23 burnt mounds, some of which are at similar altitudes to the roundhouses (RCAHMS 1990: 5).

Two monument types are peculiar to the area and remain amongst the most distinctive forms in the region. One is the little studied Dalrulzion-type double-walled roundhouse (Thorneycroft 1933), the second, the 'Pitcarmick-type building' first presented by the RCAHMS (1990). The latter range between c. 10 and 30 m in length, with rounded ends and frequently curved or bowed sides and their interiors are often wider at one end, tapering into a narrower sunken-floored area; around half show signs of a partially sunken floor. The primary building material is turf though one or two are faced externally with a low kerb of boulders. They commonly share locations with prehistoric roundhouse settlements, and are rarely found near pre-improvement farmsteads and townships.

RCAHMS suggested the Pitcarmick buildings were byre-houses, post-dating roundhouses, but, without conclusive dating evidence, it remained uncertain whether they were of early medieval or medieval date (1990: 12). The question for one group of Pitcarmick buildings was resolved with the excavations at the type-site of Pitcarmick (IDs27250 and 27264; Figure 1.3: 9) in Strathardle. Situated at 420 m OD on two ridges (north and south) which descend east towards the River Ardle on either side of a shallow boggy valley, excavations were undertaken by Glasgow University over 1993-5 (Barrett and Downes 1993, 1994), although not published until 2012 (Carver et al. 2012). Later prehistoric roundhouses, Pitcarmick buildings and rectangular buildings had been recorded amongst clearance cairns, field boundaries and cultivation remains (RCAHMS 1990: 75-8). Five areas were excavated: the space around an assumed Bronze Age burial cairn (A); a pair of roundhouses (B); a clearance cairn and field boundary (D); and two Pitcarmick buildings (C and E) (Carver et al. 2012: passim, illus 6). A hearth belonging to a stone and turf-built roundhouse was ^{14}C dated to 1398-920 BC.

Of the Pitcarmick buildings excavated, Building C was only partially examined by two trenches (Carver et al. 2012: illus 13) and while Building E was opened fully in plan (Carver et al. 2012: illus 21), there was a reluctance to excavate to depth and establish natural deposits at both buildings (Carver pers comm). Both buildings were interpreted as byre-houses, with south-facing entrances at the junction of dwelling and byre, offering access to a domestic west end centred around a large hearth, or a byre at the east end with stalls on either side of a drainage gully (Carver et al. 2012: 184). The walls were interpreted as being constructed with turf-and-rubble layers. They broadly dated to the period AD 700-850, but had been reused c. 1000-1200 AD. Subsequently they were subjected to an episode of later medieval or post-medieval ploughing.

The smaller building (C1) measured 22 m by 7.5 m externally and 18 m by 4 m internally, with 2 m wide turf walls, a large hearth and post-pits at each end and in the centre. The paved entrance lay on the south side and was accessed through a porch (Carver et al. 2012: 159-60). It was interpreted by Carver as 'one of the earliest byre-houses yet defined in Britain' (Carver et al. 2012: 163) with an 8 m long dwelling area and 10 m byre with animal stalls. It was occupied in two phases, with construction in the late 7th or early 8th centuries AD, with two ^{14}C dates of AD 680–880, and re-occupation in the 11-12th century AD, through a single ^{14}C date of AD 1020-1180 from the final floor deposit (Carver et al. 2012: 184-185).

The larger building (E) was found to consist of two superimposed structures, a sub-square stone building (E2) overlying the west end of a narrower turf and stone building with a round east end (E1). Building E1 was incompletely excavated and E2 was left in place (Carver et al. 2012: 165). E1 measured 27.5 m by 7.5 m externally, 22.5 m by 4.5 m internally, and was similar in layout to C1 with a domestic west end including a 1 m long rectangular hearth and a paved entrance with 'large flat stones' on the south side; large post-pits at each end, and smaller post-pits along the centre of each wall-line and around the hearth (Carver et al. 2012: illus 22). The walls were interpreted as being constructed in layers of turf and stone, with post-holes at the base of the walls holding 'vertical posts or crucks to support a roof' (Carver et al. 2012: 168) and the large pits at either end interpreted as 'end crucks', with the

Figure 1.5 The Early Bronze Age ring-cairn at Lair in the foreground, with glacial deposits behind and Mount Blair beyond (D. Strachan: 2013).

Figure 1.6 Aerial view of the multi-period site at Wester Peathaugh (ID31021), including clearance cairns, roundhouses, Dalrulzion-type roundhouses, Pitcarmick buildings and cultivation remains (D. Strachan: 2001).

reconstructions at Newtonmore being suggested as a potential comparator. Along the centre of the east end of E1 a stone-capped shallow gully *c.* 1.2 m wide was suggested to be a well-used animal path consolidated with stones, presumably for drainage (Carver *et al.* 2012: 171). Building E1 was assigned to the 7-9th centuries AD, with three ^{14}C dates with a combined age-range of AD 640–890, and the smaller building E2 from the 11-12th centuries AD, with two ^{14}C dates spanning AD 1020-1160 from the floor layer (Carver *et al.* 2012: 184-185), while ploughing had occurred between the dates for each building (Carver *et al.* 2012: 168).

In the overall interpretation Carver suggested that the Pitcarmick buildings were associated with 'husbandry of sheep and possibly cattle, and perhaps...part of the land under cultivation' (Carver *et al.* 2012: 185), although even with a third suggested 'longhouse', it was suggested the group 'does not amount to a village' but rather a 'zone of dispersed farmsteads' (Carver *et al.* 2012: 184-185).

The importance of the Pitcarmick buildings has been established in the literature (e.g. Alcock 2003; Dalgleish 2012; Foster 2004; Govan 2003) and the rarity of settlement structures in early medieval Scotland acknowledged in the Scottish Archaeological Research Framework, with fewer than ten domestic structures known on the mainland (ScARF 2012: Medieval Panel Section 1.42). Away from the uplands of Perth and Kinross, and Angus, Norse settlement in the Northern and Western Isles perhaps provides some of the best parallels as early medieval buildings in Scotland (ScARF 2012: 36), but importantly the buildings at Pitcarmick were constructed long before any recorded Norse activity in Scotland during the very late 8th century AD, or indeed incursion into the region during the reign of Kenneth MacAlpin (AD 843-58).

RCAHMS (1990: 5-6) noted three zones of subsequent medieval and post-medieval settlement. The first, or primary settlement, took in the floors and lower slopes of the main valleys and the mouths of the main tributary valleys, and represents the areas where the main estate centres and principal settlements shown on 18th-century maps occur, though the remains of relatively few of them were still visible on the ground. The second, a zone of secondary settlement locations, extended higher up the hills and further back along the tributaries and, having reverted to moorland, contained a mass of permanent townships and rigged fields, interspersed with the remains of seasonally occupied shielings. Beyond this, high up into the heads of the glens, the third zone contains only shieling activity. The townships range considerably in scale and location. Easter Bleaton (ID29063; Figure 1.3: 6 and Figure 1.7) situated on the valley floor of Glen Shee at *c.* 260 m OD extends over 800 m and consists of at least 52 buildings, a series of enclosures, four kilns and a line of five retting ponds (RCAHMS 1990: 114). Corra-lairig (ID29511; Figure 1.3: 3 and Figure 1.8) high in the tributary glen above Lair at 420 m OD comprises nine buildings, a corn-drying kiln, several small

Figure 1.7 The extensive township at Easter Bleaton on the glen floor c. 5 km south of Lair (D. Strachan: 2007).

enclosures and numerous large fields. The townships were abandoned by or in the 19th century, and many of those in the primary settlement zone were replaced with improved farms.

Critically, monument visibility in these uplands is dependent on the impacts of subsequent phases of agriculture, with each phase of exploitation from the Bronze Age onwards destroying or at least modifying the remains of previous activities (RCAHMS 1990: 1). The three zones of preservation identified by the RCAHMS were: firstly, areas under modern cultivation where preservation is poor; secondly, areas where medieval and post-medieval cultivation traces (broad rig or rig-and-furrow) survive, essentially representing the secondary medieval and later settlement zone; and thirdly, the heather moorlands which were cultivated rarely and which for much of the Middle Ages were given over to cattle and sheep, either through specialist pastoral farms or through shielings. Many of the roundhouses and Pitcarmick buildings survive in this third zone, and though there are often traces of cultivation rigs

Figure 1.8 The upland township of Corra-lairig (E. Martin: 2014).

Figure 1.9 Pre-improvement field-systems at Glenkilrie (D. Strachan: 2007).

around them, the episodes of ploughing, as at Pitcarmick (above), have been relatively light and/or brief, thus allowing visible remains of the earlier settlements to survive. The mosaic of settlement and preservation zones, however, is complex and interwoven, and boundaries between them are seldom clear. The remarkably intact post-medieval landscape of settlement and cultivation remains in the glens above the Spittal of Glenshee (RCAHMS 1990: Figure 278 1A-B), for example, transcend all three settlement zones, but virtually every trace of any earlier remains have been obliterated. However, behind Glenkilrie, c. 3 km south of Lair (RCAHMS 1990: Figure 272.1; Figure 1.3: 5 and Figure 1.9) post-medieval and prehistoric settlement and cultivation remains are closely interwoven and there are not only at least two Pitcarmick buildings, but also other large buildings of unknown date. The archaeological sites at Lair lie on the margin of the secondary settlement zone, where there is certainly evidence of post-medieval cultivation, but probably as no more than outfields and the ploughing has certainly not been sufficiently intense to erase the assemblage of hut-circles, Pitcarmick buildings and scattered small cairns.

1.4 Pollen-analytical evidence for land-use change in and around Glen Shee

The primary woodland that clothed the dry slopes of the hills prior to c. 4000 BC was of *Betula* (birch) and *Corylus* (hazel), with a closed canopy, and with varying proportions of elm (*Ulmus*), particularly on base-rich soils as at Dalnaglar (Figure 1.3) across the glen from Lair (Durno 1962), oak (*Quercus*), rowan (*Sorbus*) and ash (*Fraxinus*), with alder (*Alnus*) and willow (*Salix*) on the valley floors and wetter soils (Bennett 1989, 1996; Caseldine 1979; Tipping 1994, 1995a; Walker 1977). The dry woodland reached altitudes close to the mountain summits in the north of Glen Shee, with Scot's pine (*Pinus*) displacing *Quercus* at these altitudes (Huntley 1994).

The earliest recorded pollen-analytical anthropogenic modifications are seen c. 3700 BC. In the hills at Carn Dubh on the southern slope of Ben Vrackie (Figure 1.3), several pulses of rapid, though only partial, woodland loss occurred between c. 3700-3500 BC and again from c. 2700-2300 BC, probably through sustained grazing by domestic livestock (Tipping 1995a, 2013; Tipping in Rideout 1995). *Calluna* (ling heather) was established within grassland from c. 3000 BC. Caseldine's (1979) pollen analyses from plateau surfaces at Loch Mharaich and Heatheryhaugh (Figure 1.3) are undated but can be interrogated using regionally synchronous pollen-stratigraphic events (Birks 1989) and assigning to the early Neolithic *Ulmus* decline a date of c. 3700 BC, ^{14}C dated at Carn Dubh (Tipping 1995a). Woodland around Loch Mharaich and Heatheryhaugh may have been disturbed by people before the Neolithic, but clearer evidence for anthropogenic woodland clearance at these sites is seen after c. 3300 BC.

Late Neolithic and Early Bronze Age grazing pressures sharply reduced *Corylus* trees around Loch Mharaich after c. 2500 BC, then more gradually until c. 2000 BC when all trees were impacted (Caseldine 1979). Grazing pressures were intensified at Carn Dubh after c. 2200 BC (Tipping 1995a) and at an estimated c. 2400 BC, for perhaps two centuries or so, at Durno's (1962) undated pollen analyses at Dalnaglar. Yet at Heatheryhaugh, woodland regenerated after c. 2250 BC (Caseldine 1979). Single pollen grains of cereal type are recorded at Loch Mharaich and Heatheryhaugh at an estimated c. 2500 BC (Caseldine 1979) but are not defined more closely (cf. Andersen 1979). They are not strong evidence for upland crop cultivation, as Tipping concluded at Carn Dubh after re-assessing his pollen record there in 2013. Caseldine's (1979) records at Heatheryhaugh and Loch Mharaich are truncated within the Bronze Age.

On the highest ground, between 500 m and 700 m OD, woodland remained barely altered until c. 900 BC when slight grazing pressures (or the effects of climatic deterioration) encouraged grassland and heath (Huntley 1981). Trees were poorly represented at Carn Dubh after c. 650 BC at the end of a phase of woodland loss (Tipping 1995a). On the valley floor at Dalnaglar, the first substantive woodland loss is estimated to have begun c. 700 BC (Durno 1962).

Pollen analyses by Durno (1962) and Huntley (1981) are too sparse in the last two millennia to warrant further dissection. The Carn Dubh pollen record (Tipping 1995a, 1995b, 2013) is much the best description of later prehistoric and early medieval upland land-use change in the Perthshire hills, and highly relevant to the landscape at Lair. The Carn Dubh record is resolved at c. 100 year intervals between c. 650 BC and c. 350 AD and at c. 50 year intervals between c. 350-750 AD, though with only two dating controls in the last c. 2400 years. The landscape in the 1st millennium AD was sharply differentiated into areas of valley floor peat and acid mineral soils. Re-assessing this period in more detail than in 1995 and 2013, woodland recovery after c. 150 AD was followed by short-lived assaults by people on trees at c. 300 AD, when a pulse of eroded soil was pushed across the peat. A final reduction of dryland trees is directly ^{14}C dated to AD 630-840. Trees probably still grew after this on peat and wetland soils filling the valley floor, but away from the peat, grassland dominated, though pastoral indicator herbs were not common. A single cereal type pollen grain is recorded after AD 630-840 but no significance is placed on this. The pollen record at Carn Dubh is probably truncated at some time after c. 1000 AD.

1. Introduction

In the lowlands, the late prehistoric and early medieval pollen record at Rae Loch (Edwards and Whittington 1998; Edwards *pers comm*: Figure 1.3) is highly resolved and ^{14}C dated, but assays have large laboratory errors and one demonstrable age 'reversal'. The beginning of a major decline in woodland is directly dated to 1681-1231 BC and its end interpolated at 160 BC-AD 300, the lowest abundance of tree taxa in the last *c.* 3000 years. Clearance was initially for pasture but sustained representation of cereal type pollen commenced at an interpolated 100 BC-AD 210. Partial woodland regeneration occurred AD 33-542. Though grazed grassland was lost then, proportions of cereal type pollen were maintained. Later, directly but imprecisely dated to *c.* 91-600 AD there was major and very rapid deforestation as both cereal cultivation and grazed grassland expanded.

1.5 Historical and political contexts

To define a political history of the uplands of the region in the second half of the 1st millennium AD is not possible: data sources are far too few and too disparate, and concerned only with political and military elites. Our account relies almost totally on the recent in-depth analyses of Fraser (2009) and Woolf (2007), which both focus on penetrating critiques of the sources in reconstructing their narratives.

Pictishness, Fraser points out, was a Roman idea and not one that contemporary natives might have recognised. Several peoples merged in the 7th century AD to form a unified southern Pictland. By *c.* 700 AD Adomnán recognised people in both southern Pictland and Fortriu all as Picts and that southern Pictland may have had a single king by that time (Márkus 2017: 103). Prestige goods flowed from the near-continent to northern British leaders at Clatchard Craig and Dundurn (Alcock 2003: 84-87). Some regions established kingdoms, while others remained 'farmer republics' as late as the Norse period, 'small, self-governing areas ... held in varying degrees of subjection, central places to their inhabitants, no doubt, but all but unnoticed in surviving texts' (Fraser 2009: 348).

Atholl (*Athflotla*), probably in the middle course of the River Tay (Figure 1.10) had a king in the 8th century AD and may have had 'pride of place among the southern

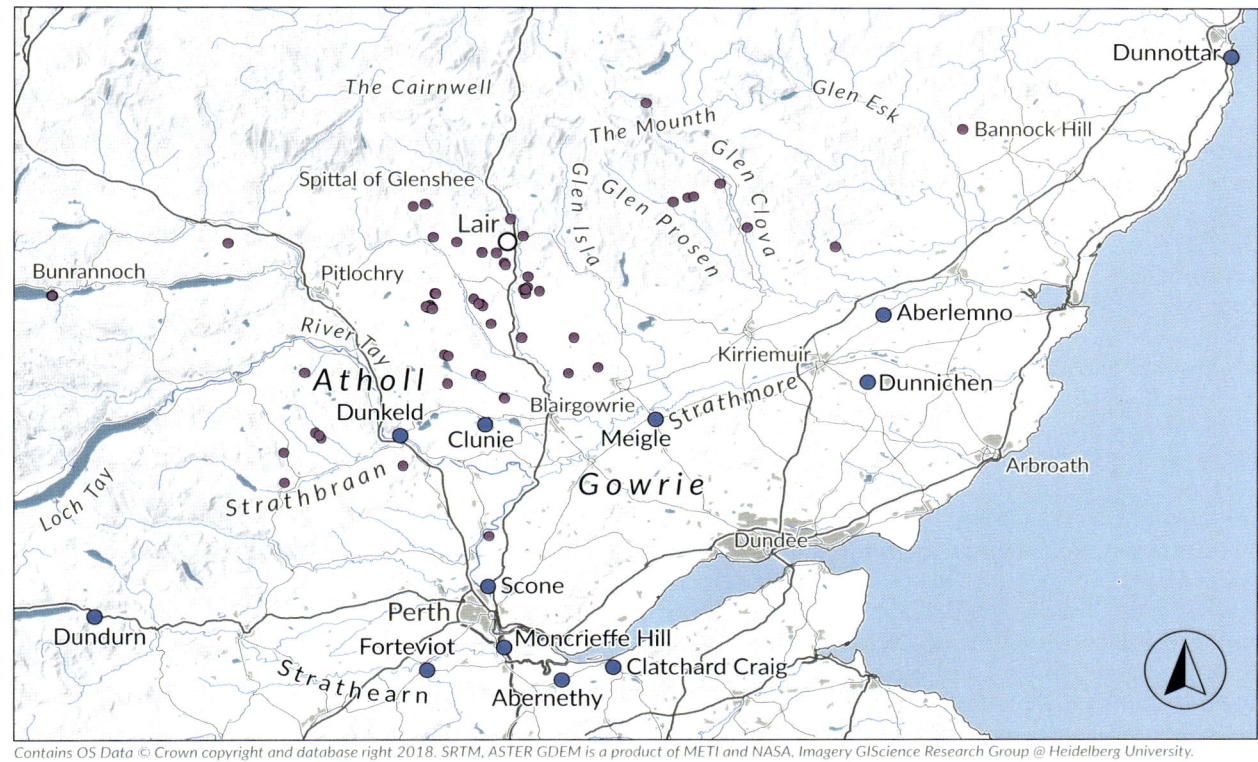

Figure 1.10 The wider region showing early medieval power-centres and the known distribution of Pitcarmick buildings.

Pictish regions' (Fraser 2009: 102). Borders fluctuated bewilderingly, in reality and in different historians' reconstructions. Brown (2012: 40) defined the kingdom of Fortriu in the 8th century AD as 'stretching from Strathearn (if not the Forth) to the Mounth and including Gowrie and Angus' while Woolf (2007) has argued that it lay north of the Mounth. Control of southern Pictland swung from Pictish to Northumbrian until Bridei, an expansionist king, pushed into Fife and Manau (Fraser 2009: 254), lay siege in AD 680 to Dunnottar on the North Sea coast, perhaps the northern edge of the southern Pictish zone, and in AD 682 to Dundurn at its south-western extremity, and wrested control from Northumbrian paramountcy in AD 685 at Dún Nechtáin. Though Woolf (2006) locates this battle on the River Spey, Fraser (2006, 2009: 216) and Cruickshank (2012) maintain the traditional link with Dunnichen, in Angus, around 25 km east of Glen Shee, and near to the Aberlemno symbol stone which has been interpreted as depicting the battle (Figure 1.10).

Bridei's empire, 'Pictavia', was of many parts and never a single, centralised kingdom (Fraser 2009: 262). It began to be dismantled after AD 717, though with little evidence in southern Pictland of political instability. Onuist, probably a native of the Mearns, his power-centre at Dunnottar, ousted Elphin at Moncreiffe Hill, near Perth, in AD 728 and then at *Castellum Credi*, perhaps Scone (Fraser 2009: 288), pushing back the Atholl and Fortriu kings to become *rex Pictorum* in AD 732. By AD 789 Pictavia was split into northern and southern halves, and 'sharply disunited' (Fraser 2009: 329).

Viking raids had probably begun by AD 793 (Woolf 2007) and with its wealthy church-settlements, including Meigle, south of Alyth (Figure 1.10), which may also have had a royal hall, Pictavia might have been expected to have been targeted. Few such attacks are chronicled, though, perhaps because Pictish interests do not feature in surviving sources. Graham-Campbell and Batey (1998: 102) list four Viking incursions in southern Pictland in the 9th century AD, recorded in the *Old Scottish Chronicle*, but this source is of doubtful merit (Woolf 2007: 88-93). Woolf (2007: 340) argued for 'ceaseless Scandinavian attacks on the heartland of the kingdom', the Tay basin, and for southern Pictish kings 'fighting for their very survival in the heartland of their own kingdom' (Woolf 2007: 341), with the demand for man-power impacting on agricultural production. Márkus has suggested that the impact of the Dublin Norse, and of Haálfdan's great army from the south, probably brought Pictland close to collapse during the 870s AD (2017: 273).

Áed (r. AD 876-878) was the last king described as *rex Pictorum* in the Irish chronicles and subsequent kings were styled *ri Albain* in Gaelic and kings of the Scottas in Old English. Domnall acceded in AD 889, and in the 11 years separating these kings, Pictland and its Alpínid dynasty 'suffered a political takeover by a Gaelic-speaking group but retained its integrity' (Woolf 2007: 321), a top-down 'regime change' – and linguistic change – with Gaelic dominant by the 12th century AD. Áed's killing may well have been a *coup d'état* by a Gaelic faction driven east from Dál Riata, running from Norse raids in the west. Márkus (2017: 108-9) argues for the systematic absorption of powerful Gaelic leaders into the Pictish body-politic, so controlling to an extent the twin threats of inter-marriage and land grants to Gaels. Religious reform (Woolf 2007: 315) and losses of their estates to secular lords (Woolf 2007: 318) made church-settlements like Meigle all but disappear from the historical record by the 11th century AD.

The 'men of Alba' under Constantin son of Áed were defeated in battle at Corbridge in northern England in AD 918 by the Norse led by Ragnall, but Constantin maintained control of Alba until AD 934 when the English king, Athelstan, penetrated Alba as far as Dunnottar and the Mounth. Constantin, pragmatically, submitted to Athelstan but in AD 937 in alliance with the Dublin Norse invaded England, only to be defeated by the English at Brunanburh. It has been observed that 'early medieval battles almost never happened on borders' (Woolf 2007: 237), and these battles may suggest stability in the Tay heartland, reconstructed from royal itineraries around a 'central transit zone' of Dunkeld, Scone and St Andrews, together with Forteviot and Abernethy in Strathearn, and Clunie, c. 5 km west of Blairgowrie (Figure 1.10). Royal familiarity with Glen Shee might be suggested by the death of one king at, perhaps, Kirkmichael in Strathardle (Woolf 2007: 203). Mael Coluim, who succeeded Constantin around AD 943, was killed 'by the men of the Mearns at Fetteresso' (Woolf 2007: 191), close to Dunnottar, but our understanding of 10th century AD geography is such that 'we cannot tell if the Mearns (Kincardineshire) was a marginal part of the kingdom or part of its heartland' (Woolf 2007: 192): Alcock (2003: 46) saw in this an inland penetration of coastal communities being harried by Norse raids, thus weakening Pictish power. Weakening power is also seen after AD 962 when five Alban kings reigned in quick succession, all but one killed by his own people as past loyalties broke down, and Alba turned in the years around AD 990 to embrace its Gaelic, Scottish identity.

1.6 The Pictish language and place-names in and around Glen Shee

Peter McNiven

This section is based on recent research between Strathardle in eastern Perth and Kinross and Glen Isla in western Angus (McNiven 2014, 2017a and 2017b): place-names in italics are not on current mapping and so are historic. The toponymic, or place-name, evidence for Pictish words can be problematic, but what we have suggests that Pictish is a dialectal variation within 'a greater Brittonic continuum', sharing elements with British south of the Forth and Welsh (Forsyth 2005: 9). Pictish was the most widely spoken language in the 9th century AD in what is now modern Scotland (the other languages being Gaelic, British, Norse and Old English), and yet it was the one that disappeared (Forsyth 2005: 32). In eastern Perth and Kinross, the Pictish language is generally thought to have died out by *c.* 900 AD, to be replaced by Gaelic, which in turn was replaced by Scots from the 18th century AD. It is not entirely clear why Gaelic replaced Pictish (Woolf 2007: 322-340): surviving documentary evidence written in Scotland starts after the disappearance of Pictish and when Gaelic was at its peak. Whether through the influence of a Gaelic-speaking church, or the fact that Pictish was not written, at least not in the manner of its contemporaries, Old Irish and Old English, or whether through the replacement of the royal dynasty after the defeat of the Picts by the Norse in AD 839, a new Gaelic ascendency arose by AD 900. As outlined, from that date a new style of describing the ruler north of the Forth emerged, not *rex Pictorum* 'king of the Picts', but *rí Alban* 'king of Alba', and with it, gradually perhaps, the Pictish language was abandoned (Forsyth 2005: 32; Márkus 2017: 264; see Section 1.5).

Place-name evidence for the presence of the Picts in Glen Shee is conspicuous by its absence. However, within the wider landscape of eastern Perth and Kinross, there are about 12 place-names that give an indication of its extent. The place-names suggested to be Pictish or Pictish-influenced are: Alyth; Cally (as in Bridge of Cally); Cammock; Cochrage; Doldy; Dollasbank; Formal; Forter; The Keith; Mount Blair; Rochallie and Strathardle. The details and early forms of these can be found in McNiven (2017a) and while some may have been coined by Gaelic speakers, and so may be Gaelic place-names, many of the elements seem to have been borrowed into Gaelic from Pictish. Gaelic predominates in the area between Strathardle and Glen Isla. Not only is it the original language of most of the settlement names, but it is the language of the majority of relief features such as hill and river-names. Pictish, or at least Pictish influence, is only present in a few, though important, settlement names (Figure 1.11).

The element *pit*, or more properly *pett*, is shared, at the very least, by 350 place-names in eastern Scotland between the Firth of Forth and Moray Firth, including Pitlochry, Pittodrie, Pittenweem, Pittentaggart and Pittendreich. Their general distribution almost matches the distribution of Pictish symbol stones (Wainwright 1962: 117). While there are no *pett*-names in Glen Shee itself, within the wider area are Pitcarmick in Strathardle, Pitlochry in Glen Isla, Pitdrey near Alyth, and Balvarran in Strathardle, which was originally a *pett*-name – *Petverren* in 1641. Pitcarmick, from which the building form takes its name, means 'Cormac's share or portion' (Nicolaisen 2001: 196; Watson 1926: 409). We do not know who Cormac was, but this old Gaelic personal-name appears early in the written history of Scotland: a holy man called Cormac is the subject of a story in Adomnan's *Life of Columba*, written *c.* 700 AD (Anderson and Anderson 1961: 440-47). However, while the element *pett* does indeed have a Pictish provenance, most of the second, or specific, elements are Gaelic. Therefore, just like the Scots language has borrowed Gaelic elements such as *loch* and *glen* to make *Scots* place-names, so Pictish *pett* was borrowed into Gaelic to make *Gaelic* place-names. *Pett*-names, then, are probably best seen not as the settlements of Pictish-speakers but rather as the 'extent of Gaelic-speakers in the 10th century as Alba is beginning to expand out with its core lands between the Dornoch Firth in the north and the Firth of Forth in the south' (Taylor 2011: 79). However, since *pett* must have been part of the Pictish vocabulary relating to the politics and economics of land-management, as Broun has pointed out, 'the existence of a *pett* name with a Pictish second element (e.g. Pitpointie in Angus) suggests that they were first coined when the Pictish language was still spoken' (2015: 53, note 206). The borrowing of *pett* into Gaelic suggests there was continuity of these practices from the Pictish- to Gaelic-speaking eras (Márkus 2017: 270; for more on *pett*-names see *PNF* 5: 217-225 and Broun 2015: 53-55). Some apparently Gaelic names may have been borrowed into Gaelic from Pictish or show Pictish influence (Taylor 2011). The survival of these names may be due to their continuing importance or distinctiveness.

The vast majority of Gaelic 'agricultural' place-names in Glen Shee are of a pastoral nature. Indeed, only five of the 23 names indicating agricultural use have a distinctly arable component. Drumturn may contain Gaelic ('G') *sòrn* 'kiln' as its specific, meaning in this case a corn-drying kiln. Drumfork contains G *coirce* 'oats' and must be an area of arable land and has Mill of Drumturn nearby which could have processed that grain. Milton Knowe, just south of Ashintully Castle, indicates the existence of a former mill, *Moulinuarie* (probably containing G *muileann* 'mill') just west of Milton Knowe. Mills were an important source of baronial income and were often resented by the local populace (Smout 1969: 120). The other agricultural place-names indicate areas of grazing or some other aspect of animal husbandry, and most have either the names of animals or names containing grazing specifics. One that does not, however, is Creag a' Chaise, 'crag of the cheese'. This indicates an area of cheese production and in certain parts of the Highlands cheese was used as part of the rent or tribute in the Middle Ages (Duncan 1975: 152-53). Milking of cows probably took place at Cnoc na Cuinneige 'hillock of the milking pail'. Domesticated animals that can be found in the place-names of Glen Shee include calves at Bad an Lòin (earlier *laoigh* 'calf') and Coire an Laoigh, and 'goat' at Coire Goibhre, a reminder that goats were important as a source of dairy produce, meat and wool before the now ubiquitous Blackface sheep was introduced into the Highlands in the 18th and 19th centuries.

Grazing was an important aspect of agriculture in Glen Shee and we can differentiate between grazing near the townships and grazing as part of the system of transhumance at shielings. Along the Shee/Black Water there are a number of place-names beginning with the element Dal-; these derive from G *dail* 'water-meadow, haugh'. These floodplains are enriched by nutrients, making them suitable for grazing or growing hay for winter feed. In Glen Shee a number of these became settlements: at Dalhenzean; Dalmunzie; Dalnoid; Dalrulzion; Dalnaglar and Dunmay (*Dalmaya* in 1512). The main shieling region in the study area, based on place-names, seems to have been in the area between Glen Shee and Strathardle. Ruigh a' Chaorainn, Ruigh Chonnuill, and Ruigh Dubh are all to be found here. On the eastern side of the Shee Water is Meall an Ruighe 'round lumpy hill of the shieling'. G *ruighe* is the usual term for shieling in this part of Perthshire, but in southwest Perthshire (Strathearn and Menteith) the usual term is *àirigh*, and the reason may have much to do with the perception of ruggedness of the slopes. According to Bil (1992), *airigh* conveyed several meanings in Perthshire Gaelic: a shieling or hill pasture, a mountain hut, a shepherd's cottage or a green grove (Armstrong 1825: 15). This last usage was acquired from the green appearance of the grazed pasture, the effect of long-term manuring of small areas of ground around the huts occupied during the summer. *Ruighe*, on the other hand, 'was used to describe a shepherd's house, a hut, a hill pasture where cattle were grazed in the summer months, as well as a shieling' (Armstrong 1825: 475-6). *Ruighe* also meant literally the human arm, or more precisely the fore-arm, and from this possibly originated the meaning of a spreading lower slope on a hill (Bil 1992: 388, 390). One of the places where the livestock might have grazed in this area is Coire a' Blàrain 'corry of the little muir or field'. G *blàr* is common in Scotland, and is usually anglicised as 'blair', and in the lowlands can apply to large open stretches of land (*PNF* 5: 298), and presumably this is how Blair in Atholl and Gowrie were perceived. However, in highland glens *blàr* might apply to a small area of grazing land (see McNiven 2011: 110-16 for *blàr* in Menteith).

The most numerous Gaelic habitative element in Glen Shee is G *baile* 'land-holding, farm, vill', the Gaelic equivalent of Sc *toun*, and currently exists in five place-names in Glen Shee – Balnoe, Balnauld, Sheanval, and Coire a' Bhaile and Blacklunans. Stobie shows a number of others including three *Balinaulds* (containing G *allt* 'burn') between Sheanval and Broughdearg, *Balneton* near Spittal of Glenshee, and *Balriach* (containing G *riabhach* 'brindled, speckled or variegated'), north-west of Lair. Sheanval is in G *seann bhaile* 'old farm', and is on record from 1686, but it is not known why or when the epithet 'old' came to be applied to it unless it was replaced by Spittal of Glenshee on record from 1542. Blacklunans was *Bawclownane* in 1460 (*C.A. Rental* i, 131) and *Balclunas* in 1506 (*Dunkeld Rent.* 76); the specific element appears to be G *cluan* 'meadow' and names on the Ordnance Survey '6 inch' 1st Edition suggest something of the organisation that made up a township. The name applies to an area of arable land on the east bank of the Shee Water/Black Water and contained the farms of Westertown, Burnside, Tomlia, *Croydon*, *Coldrach*, Drumour, *Hillyhouse*, Boreland, *Hillocks of Boreland*, Whitehouse, *Dounie*, Millton and *Wynd*. Boreland was a farm that provided for the landowner of an area; the produce from that farm went directly to his table, in this case the bishop of Dunkeld. Kerrow, near Spittal of Glenshee, is an indication of land or settlement division, deriving from G *ceathramh* meaning 'quarter', Watson stating that it might mean the 'fourth part of a davoch' (Watson 1926: 236). A davoch (G *dabhach*), with a basic meaning of 'vat, tub', is a unit of land measurement and assessment of variable area. Each davoch possessed the 'necessary resources for a group of people to survive throughout the year' (Ross 2006: 66), and was a mixture of arable and pastoral land. It was also the basic unit of assessment for army service and was one of the building blocks of the parish north of the Forth (*PNF* 5, 348). There are no *davoch*-names in Glen Shee and Kerrow is only an indicator that this unit of measurement might have been in place here. Pictish and Gaelic place-names mentioned in the text that appear on current OS maps are show in Figure 1.11.

1.7 The catchment of the Allt Corra-lairige: geology, topography, soils and climate

The catchment of the Allt Corra-lairige above its confluence with the Shee Water is around 3.5 km² in area (Figure 1.12). It faces east, sheltered from dominant westerly winds by a ridge rising to the west to over 500 m OD between Cnoc Feanndaige, Lamh Dearg and Meall Easganan. The steeper gradient hills in the west above 450-500 m OD are underlain by quartz-rich (and so nutrient-poor) Duchray Hill Gneiss, the lower ground by the equally quartz-rich Mount Blair Psammite and Semipelite Formation. Till smears the rounded summits of the watershed above 380 m OD. The north side of the catchment is punctured by a series of broadly parallel sub-glacial meltwater channels from the north, several emerging from the afforested Torr Lochaidh to flow east. The south side of the catchment is punctured by one such channel along the Allt an Lair (Figure 1.13).

Figure 1.13 focuses on the agricultural remains on lower ground (see also Banaszek and Cowley: Section 1.8) where till forms low stream-lined 'whale-back' morainic ridges and comparatively poorly-drained soils

1. INTRODUCTION

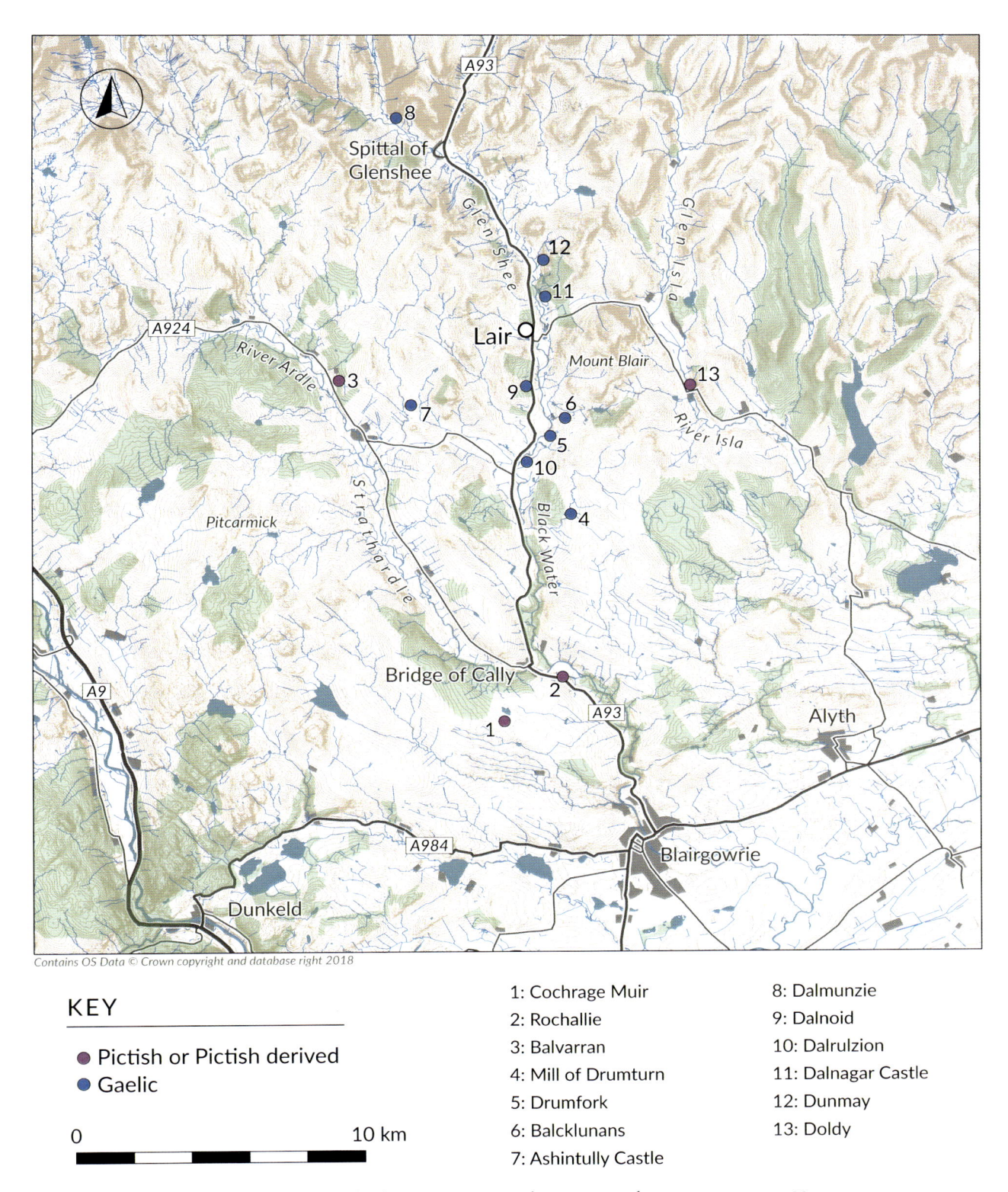

KEY

● Pictish or Pictish derived
● Gaelic

0   10 km

1: Cochrage Muir	8: Dalmunzie
2: Rochallie	9: Dalnoid
3: Balvarran	10: Dalrulzion
4: Mill of Drumturn	11: Dalnagar Castle
5: Drumfork	12: Dunmay
6: Balcklunans	13: Doldy
7: Ashintully Castle	

Figure 1.11: Pictish and Gaelic place-names mentioned in Section 1.6 that appear on current OS maps.

covered by heather (*Calluna*), immediately west of the A93. Till also forms a pair of enormous glacial mounds that almost block the valley, an end-moraine created at a late stage of deglaciation (Figure 1.14). Trains of weakly developed glaciofluvial terraces on the south side of the catchment give rise to thin, nutrient-poor but well drained podsolic soil also covered by *Calluna*.

The gentle lower slopes in the centre of the catchment at 380-390 m OD carry two extensive masses of peat, Basins 1 and 2, both confined basins set below till surfaces. The Allt Corra-lairige is a small 2nd Order stream which falls east over 3.3 km from 550 m OD on Meall Easganan to the Shee Water at 290 m OD (Figure 1.12). Its upper reach on Meall Easganan is initially

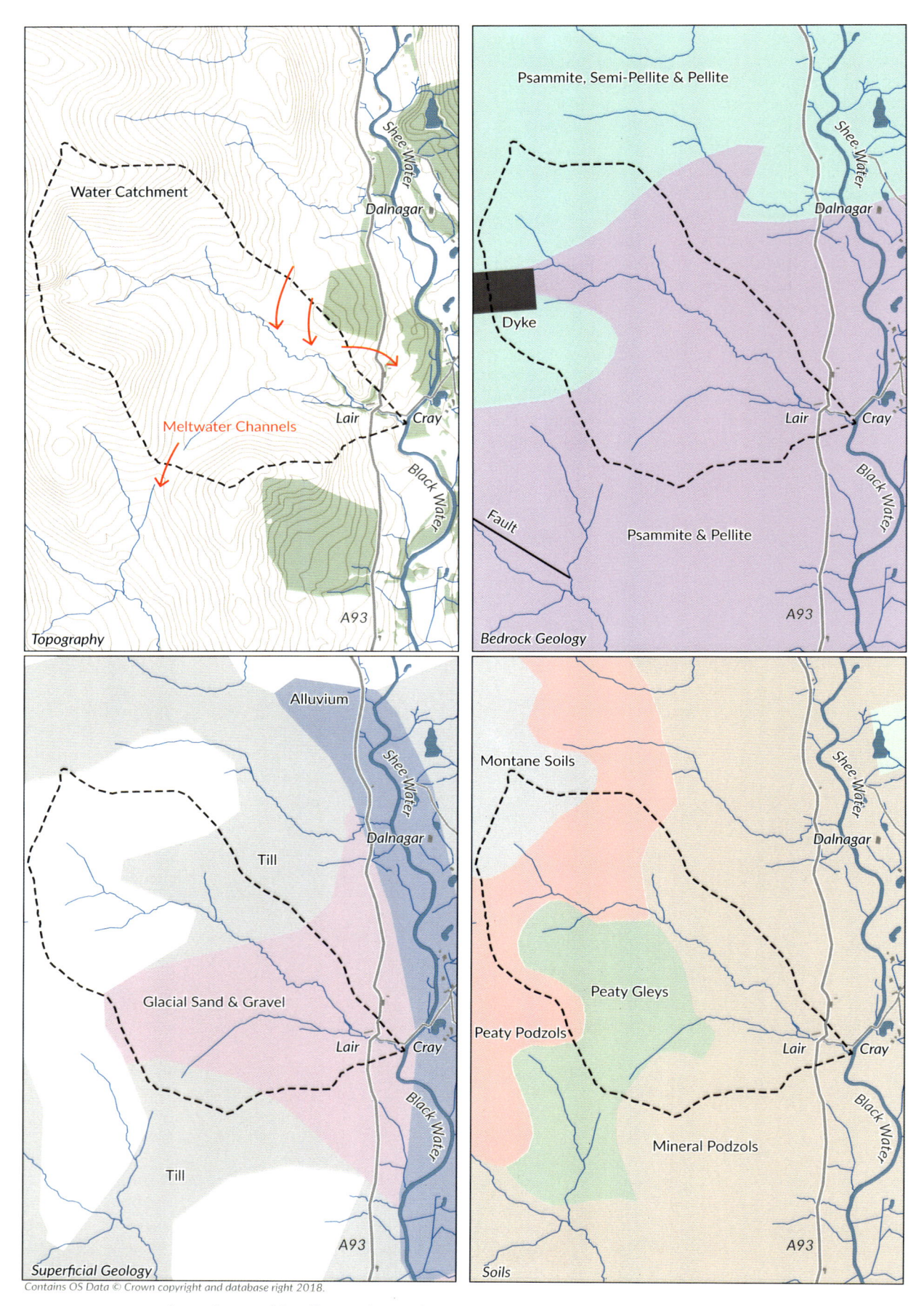

Early Medieval Settlement in Upland Perthshire: Excavations at Lair, Glen Shee 2012-17

Figure 1.12 The catchment of the Allt Corra-lairige showing the topography, bedrock and superficial geology and soils.

steep with a gradient of *c.* 11 %, becoming gentler below 450 m OD (gradient 1.5 %) before falling into a steep and incised gorge (gradient 10 %) below 370 m OD cut during deglaciation. Relict channels now filled with peat almost encircle Basin 2. Though the natural drainage is eastward, the shallow stream course now flows west and south to join the Allt Corra-lairige. The flow directions of the wet peat-choked stream courses and mires are shown in Figure 1.13. Much drainage takes place through peat pipes, not over the surface. The only locality where a minerogenic floodplain has formed is above the incised gorge. The Allt an Lair is the only tributary.

The heather-clad lower slopes of the catchment between the Allt Corra-lairige and the Allt an Lair are today burnt for grouse. Conifer forest covers the Torr Lochaidh. Birch (*Betula*) and alder (*Alnus*) trees line the incised gorge above Lair Farm. Elsewhere (Figure 1.13) are areas of rough, species-impoverished *Nardus* grassland, and improved pasture on well-drained soils, probably heavily grazed in the recent past by cattle on summer pastures (Section 1.6) and now close-cropped by sheep.

Mean annual temperatures over high ground are less than 6 °C. January is the coldest month when temperatures lower than -2 °C are common. Braemar, 15 km north of Lair and at a similar altitude, has the UK record for low temperature, -27.2 °C in 1982. The mean temperature at Braemar in January is 0.6 °C. Conversely, in the lee of high ground when warm south or south-westerly airstreams are crossing Scotland, winter temperatures can on occasion reach 15 °C. Snowfall is normally confined to the months from November to April. July is the warmest month, with mean daily maximum temperatures at low altitudes approaching 20 °C. At Braemar the mean July temperature is 12.7 °C with an average 175 hours of sunshine between May and July. This is the wettest area in eastern Scotland with mean annual rainfall >1500 mm, though dry compared with >4000 mm in the western Scottish Highlands (McClatchey 1996).

1.8 Mapping of the field remains

Łukasz Banaszek and David Cowley

The detail of the various themes outlined above can be seen in play in the landscape at Lair. Here, the visible archaeological remains, extending from the banks of the Shee Water to the top of the Allt Corra-lairige, range in date from at least the Early Bronze Age to the late 18th century and also span the various zones of settlement and preservation. Thus, the excavated buildings lie within a complex relict archaeological landscape in which traces of multiple periods of occupation and activity are interwoven. First recorded in outline by the

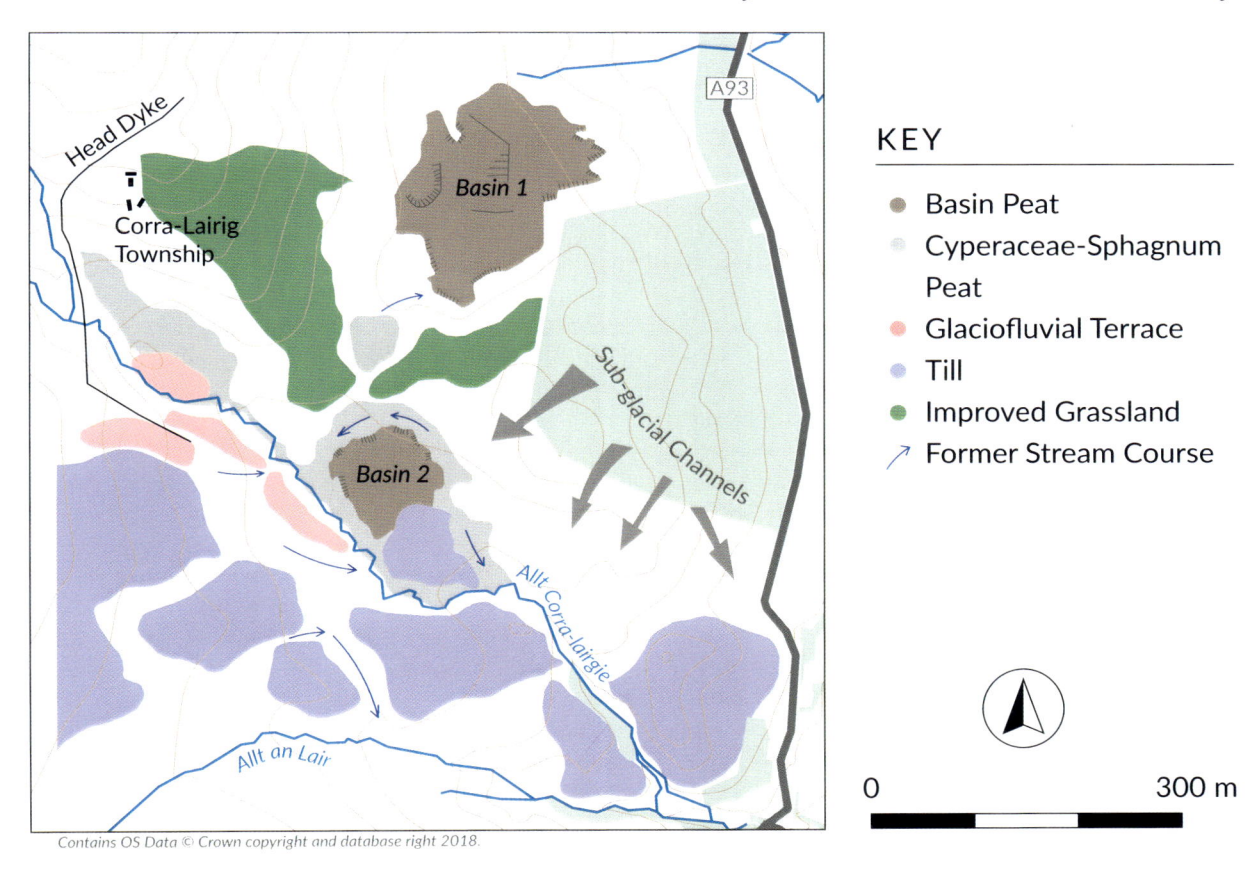

Figure 1.13: The lower catchment of the Allt Corra-lairige.

Figure 1.14 A low-level aerial view, looking south-east, of the setting of the excavations, showing the afforested Torr Lochaidh to the left, the splash of close-cropped grassland bordered by dry Calluna *heath, the glacial morainic mounds that 'protect' the Allt Corra-lairige, and Glen Shee (E. Martin: 2014).*

RCAHMS survey in 1987-8, these have been re-mapped in detail by Historic Environment Scotland (HES) to better understand the field remains and in particular the character of the extensive cultivation traces only patchily visible on the ground.

Source data and survey methodology

The mapping presented here was completed in 2018, and draws on remote sensing (RS) data, informed by both the RCAHMS survey (1990) and topographic mapping while the excavations were ongoing (Section 2.2). Two RS dataset types, Airborne Laser Scanning (ALS) (Scottish Remote Sensing Portal 2018, https://remotesensingdata.gov.scot/) and aerial imagery were used, producing an outline plan, aspects of which were explored during a field visit in April 2018. The ALS data was collected between March 2011 and May 2012, commissioned collectively by the Scottish Government, Scottish Environmental Protection Agency and Scottish Water (available under Open Government licence v3.0). With a last echo density of 1.49 pts/m^2, which provides a point spacing of 0.82 m, the ALS data are not high-resolution, and is available for only part of the mapped area (Figure 1.15). The ALS point cloud was processed to produce a digital terrain model (DTM) with a 1 m spatial resolution. Thereafter, the Relief Visualisation Toolbox (Kokalj *et al.* 2011; Zakšek *et al.* 2011) was used to produce visualisations for interpretation and mapping in a Geographical Information System (GIS) environment, drawing on recent experience gained by HES in working with ALS-derived visualisations during survey of Arran (Banaszek *et al.* 2018). The aerial imagery comprises orthophotographs taken in 2008 and 2011 and supplied to HES through a Service Level Agreement administered by the Scottish Government, and oblique aerial photographs taken by RCAHMS in 1987-8 and by HES in 2015-6. The orthophotographs comprise tiled imagery at 25 cm ground sampling distance. Selected oblique images from 2015-6 were rectified for mapping purposes, while the 1987-8 images were used primarily to inform interpretation. The desk-based mapping raised some detailed questions of interpretation that required field assessment, undertaken in early 2018. Field observation concentrated on the topographic and chronological relationships between certain buildings and the cultivation remains, as these offered an opportunity to establish any phasing visible in the field remains.

Land use and the (in)visibility of archaeological features

In broad terms, the surveyed area can be divided into three general land-use types (cf. Section 1.6; Figure 1.15), the disposition of which conditions both differing patterns of archaeological visibility, and different patterns of potential for preservation of archaeological remains. The first land-use type area, lying to the east of the A93 (Figure 1.15: A), where the ground falls to the Shee Water, has been enclosed since at least the early 19th century and is under a mixture of improved and semi-improved pasture. There are also patches of what was once managed woodland along the river. Second, the area west of the A93 (Figure 1.15: B) is predominantly rough grazing heath, mainly ling heather (*Calluna*), and characterised by a patchwork of different ages of heather cover and rough grass. The northern edge of the area falls under the third type of land use, a dense coniferous plantation established in the 20th century (Figure 1.15: C), clothing the upper slopes and summit of the hillock known as Torr Lochaidh. Whereas visibility in the unenclosed ground is moderate or good for the heathland, and perfect for the improved pastures, the plantation has not been subject to ground observation and the specification of the general purpose ALS survey did not produce an archaeologically useful DTM under the dense canopy. With the exception of the plantation, this broad pattern of land use persists at least from the 19th century, as shown on Sheet XXXIII of the 1st Edition of the Ordnance Survey 6-inch map (Perthshire 1865-7).

As outlined above, the pattern of historic and modern land use has had a significant impact on the survival and visibility of archaeological remains. A fourth zone of preservation can be added to those identified already (RCAHMS 1990: 1; Stevenson 1975). This is the forestry plantation, the planting of which is not only catastrophically destructive but has proved impenetrable to the survey techniques deployed to date. Thereafter the same three zones of preservation can be traced out. Firstly, there are areas that have been under cultivation in the last 50 years, characterised by smooth surfaces, and where any earlier remains have been ploughed flat. These areas all lie in the main valley east of the A93, and generally represent the poorest zone for visibility of medieval and earlier archaeological features. Being largely under permanent pasture, there is no real scope for the discovery of buried features through vegetation proxies on aerial photographs. Secondly, there is a zone of surviving medieval and post-medieval rig-and-furrow (sometimes of multiple phases), field banks and clearance cairns. This lies partly on the slopes east of the A93, where the continuity of the 19th century and more recent cultivation breaks up northwards into discrete patches, and partly in

Figure 1.15 Orthophotograph documenting current land use and showing the extent of ALS data (© Historic Environment Scotland (Source: orthophotographs (2008) licensed to Historic Environment Scotland for PGA, through Next Perspectives™)).

the heather moorland to the west. Below the A93 the RS data offer an exceptionally clear view of the archaeological features, with little noise from irregular vegetation, allowing even the slightest topographic anomalies to stand out in the ALS derivatives. In the heather moorland to the west of the A93, however, the definition of the results is softened by the character of the vegetation. While the traces of cultivation in this zone must have obliterated visible traces of many early features, remarkably, fragments of a group of roundhouses survive amongst the cultivation rigs on terraces overlooking the Shee Water. As with the survival of the Pitcarmick buildings to the west of the A93, their survival as earthwork features depends on the intensity of later cultivation. The third zone of unimproved heather moorland beyond the rigged zone theoretically has the highest potential for preservation of visible prehistoric remains, and indeed for structures of early medieval date. However, in practice this pattern is blurred at Lair by varying intensities of later cultivation and the survival of so many earlier features in the rigged zone.

A further factor that needs to be taken into account is that visibility itself is not even across the heather moorland, it varying with the pattern of management, in which the heather growth is burnt back in rotation over a period of years to create a complex mosaic of bare ground, short young growth and mature bushes. This is evident when comparing the oblique aerial photographs taken in 1987-8 to those from 2015-6. In effect, this type of heather management creates a parallel mosaic of differential archaeological visibility that changes from year to year. This is most likely to have an impact on the extent to which shallow furrows of cultivation and slight remains of buildings can be observed, either in the RS data or in the field, and should be kept in mind as a commentary on the extent of the mapped archaeological remains, particularly around the upper margins of the rigged zone.

Survey results

The HES mapping attempted to account for all archaeological remains identified during earlier survey by RCAHMS and the Glenshee Archaeology Project. It also identified additional, previously undocumented features (below), providing mapping of individual rigs, banks and clearance cairns for the first time. This illustrates the cumulative nature of survey and how the results depend on the specification of the survey and the prevailing conditions on the ground. This is underlined by the discovery of previously undocumented remains in an area that has already been subject to a relatively systematic survey on the ground in 1987-8. These new monuments include the remains of several buildings (Figure 1.16: 17 and 19) within the main scatter of features, while a few possible shieling huts (Figure 1.16: 25-27) were also detected on the south-western edge of the study area. There are, however, a handful of small cairns noted during the earlier survey that it has not been possible to account for, and some other known features were barely visible in the RS data (e.g. Figure 1.16: 16) and confidence in their interpretation depended on the field visit.

Nevertheless, the new mapping confirms the broad patterning of remains previously documented by RCAHMS (1990). The ring-cairn is assumed to be of Early Bronze Age date and the roundhouses may be Middle Bronze Age or Iron Age in date (Cook and Dunbar 2008; Rideout 1995). The rectangular buildings within the survey area include structures that can comfortably be classified as Pitcarmick buildings (Figure 1.16: 3-5 and 12, 14, 20), with others that are round-ended but less clearly belong to that group (Figure 1.16: 1-2, 6, 7-8, 9, 10). This conforms to a broader pattern of generally sub-rectangular buildings of medieval and post-medieval date in similar upland areas (Atkinson 2016; Cowley and Harrison 2001). The scatters of small cairns have often been assumed to be of prehistoric date, but in reality clearance on stony soils is a timeless function of agriculture and individual heaps may date from any period from the Late Neolithic to the post-medieval (e.g. McIntyre 1998). Indeed, what we perceive as groups of cairns may have been formed piecemeal through field clearance at different periods. The same may be true of the disarticulated lengths of field banks, though some form small enclosures adjacent to buildings and presumably formed small yards within discrete farmsteads (Figure 1.16: around 6 and 7-8). None of the rig in the study area is well developed, and is characterised by a flat profile separated by shallow furrows. In some cases, close inspection reveals a pattern of alternating deeper and shallower furrows, suggesting that broader rigs some 3-5 m across have been split into narrower strips. This is a pattern that can also be recognised widely and is identifiably a medieval and later phenomenon (Cowley and Harrison 2001; Halliday 2001).

The HES mapping was stimulated by the question of whether any of the field remains, in particular the rig, could be of early medieval date and related to the periods of occupation revealed by the excavated buildings (Section 2.4) or activity identified in the pollen analyses (Section 2.6). There are general reasons to demand a high standard of proof when identifying early medieval or prehistoric cultivated surfaces. The character of any field surface is inherently fragile and prone to radical modification by re-cultivation in later periods. Indeed, pragmatic decisions by farmers will tend to selectively seek out areas that have been 'improved' by earlier cultivation. On one hand this is witnessed by the incidence of rigs woven through the cairns and banks around many hut-circle groups in north-east Perth

1. INTRODUCTION

and Kinross (e.g. Drumturn Burn - ID29005; RCAHMS 1990: 47-9), and on the other by the identification of split rigs in many post-medieval rig-systems. In principle, there is nothing in the character of the rigs here to distinguish them from those in systems around post-medieval townships and farmsteads elsewhere. Furthermore, the interpretation of the ALS data and targeted field observation, confirmed also by the excavations, demonstrates that the rigs overlie all the buildings with which they are juxtaposed (Figure 1.16: 1, 2 and 12). On balance, there are no grounds to suggest that the rig-system here is other than post-medieval in date. The more general context for its cultivation is probably as outfields expanding out of the main valley as the population grew prior to the reorganisation that created the pattern of modern farms. Elsewhere, this sort of expansion carried more permanent settlement onto shieling grounds, represented by the secondary settlement zone discussed above and also seen in the place-names of some deserted townships, such as Cro na h-Airighe in Gleann Beag above the Spittal of Glenshee (ID29611; RCAHMS 1990: 119-20, no. 14). The presence of possible shieling huts at Lair is probably evidence of a similar history. At Lair, the process of expansion eventually leap-frogged these outfields to found a new farmstead by AD 1700 at Corra-lairig (ID29511), only for this to be abandoned by the mid-19th century (RCAHMS 1990: 151-2, no.16).

A palimpsest on the 'high-tide' mark

The buildings at Lair sit in a landscape littered with the remains of human activity over many millennia, a locale that has been visited and revisited at intervals over time producing a sometimes chaotic palimpsest of archaeological features (these are described in greater detail in Section 1.9). Today this landscape lies beyond the upper altitudinal limit of intensive arable land use, though obviously vulnerable to silviculture. However, in preceding centuries it lay on a 'high-tide' mark for settlement and land use, evidenced by the surviving remains of several visible periods of prehistoric, early medieval and later occupation. Whether this was continuous or episodic is difficult to demonstrate conclusively (see Sections 4.2 and 4.3), but is perhaps most likely to represent a margin exploited at varying intensities as differing patterns of land use or increases in population demanded. Pressure from increasing population was clearly a factor in the post-medieval period, and perhaps when it was colonised in the early medieval period too (Sections 4.5 and 4.12). The rash of undated buildings and enclosures, however, raises the possibility that these were just two of a series of times when attempts were made to take this area into more permanent occupation. In this context, the landscape at Lair is far from unique and is representative of extensive areas of surviving relict, multi-phased,

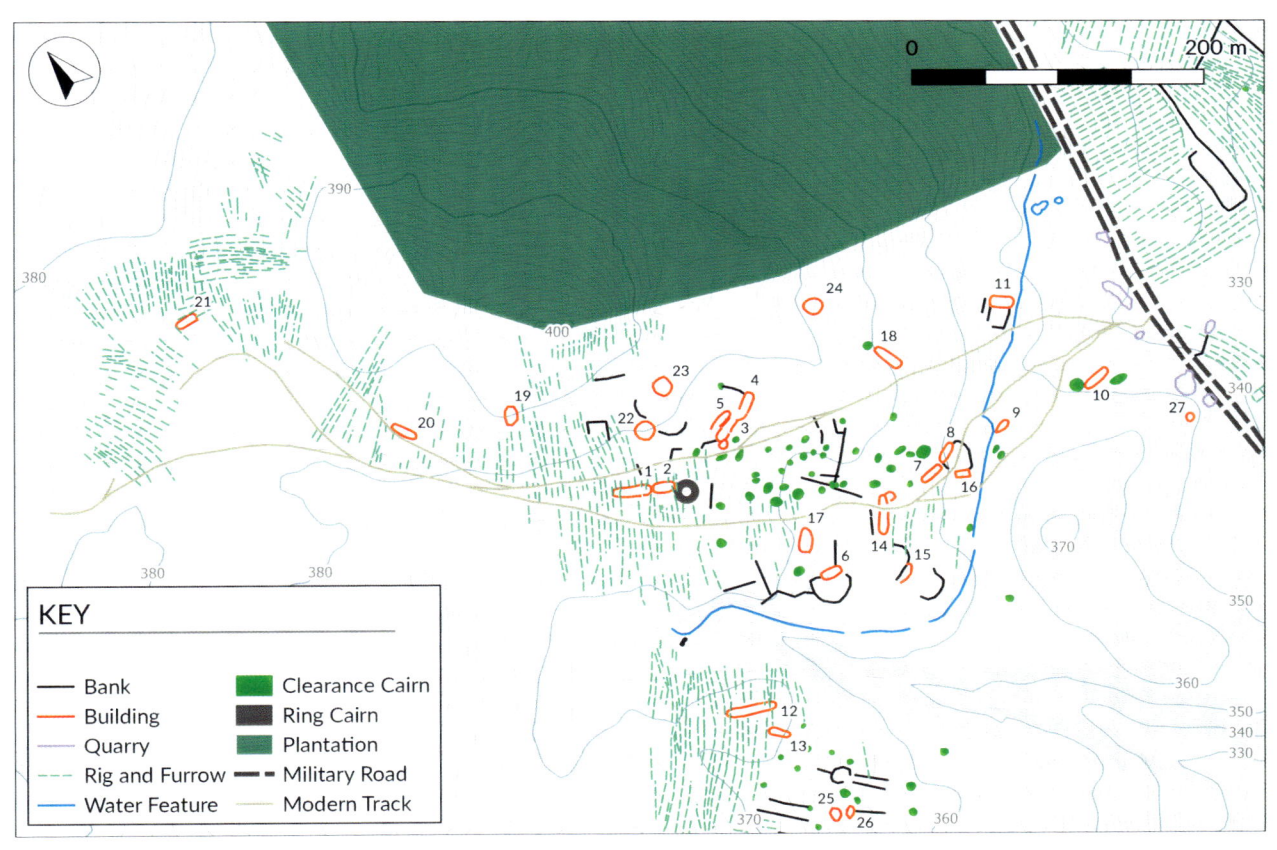

Figure 1.16 Features mapped from aerial photographs and Airborne Laser Scanning data (© Historic Environment Scotland (Source: contour data derived from DTM (2018) © Bluesky International Limited & Getmapping Plc.)).

palimpsest landscapes not only in Glen Shee and Strathardle, but across eastern and central Scotland (Carver *et al.* 2012; Cowley 1997; RCAHMS 1990). These all have in common the recurrent juxtaposition of prehistoric, early medieval and post-medieval remains, in landscapes characterised by successive overprinting and reuse, with consequent implications for long-term processes that drive variable survival, visibility and selective destruction.

1.9 Key sites in the study area

Prior to the Glenshee Archaeology Project, the complex of extant remains at Lair (Figure 1.16) was recognised as an important example of many other multi-period sites in the glen (RCAHMS 1990 *passim*). It extends from the valley floor on the west bank of the Shee Water at NO 145 635, and rises west some 300 m upslope to the small township, or *fermtoun*, of Corra-lairig (ID29511) at *c*. 430 m OD, skirting around the east and south flanks of Torr Lochaidh, the largely afforested hill north-west of Lair steading (NO 142 633). The assemblage of monuments that make up the complex includes at least two notable early prehistoric cairns, the most impressive being the ring-cairn (ID29510) built on the edge of a narrow terrace at *c*. 370 m OD and overlooking lower ground to the south and west, but overlooked from the north and east. The cairn (Figure 1.5) is roughly circular, *c*. 15 m in diameter over an outer kerb of boulders, a section of which on the north-west has been robbed and incorporated into one of the later buildings (ID29509). At least 26 stones of the kerb survive *in situ*, the largest measuring up to 1.2 m in length: the inner court, however, which lies eccentric to the outer kerb is *c*. 4 m in diameter, and less well defined with only one boulder clearly *in situ*, suggesting the centre of the cairn may have been excavated at some time. The second cairn (ID29505), which is *c*. 10 m in diameter and defined by an arc of seven surviving kerb-stones, is situated upslope at *c*. 410 m OD on a south-east facing slope *c*. 200 m south-east of Corra-lairig township.

The other prehistoric component of the complex is represented by roundhouse settlement and probably by some of the small cairns scattered around them. Within Glen Shee itself, on the east flank of Torr Lochaidh, within a group of seven roundhouses (ID29514) and a burnt mound (ID29523), several are just above the glen floor at *c*. 320m OD and represent a rare survival in this topographical setting. Six are 7-9 m in internal diameter, while one is *c*. 11 m. Another three are situated on the southern flank of Torr Lochaidh (ID29508; Figure 1.16: 22-4), two lying to the north of the ring-cairn and occupying a west-facing slope on a low rise; one is *c*. 9.5 m in internal diameter, the other *c*. 12 m, the latter partially levelled into the slope with a south-east entrance. The third lies *c*. 130 m to the east of these and is located on a narrow terrace on an east-facing slope, it is *c*. 9 m in internal diameter. Cairn-fields, comprising small cairns *c*. 3-4 m in diameter, are recorded both north (ID29499) and south (ID29508) of the Allt Corra-lairige.

Two important groups of Pitcarmick buildings at Lair have been identified (Figure 1.16). The first is the complex of three buildings (ID29437; RCAHMS 1990: 150) defined by low, stony banks, *c*. 30 m east of the ring-cairn, at 370 m OD (Figure 1.16: 3-5). The best-preserved is *c*. 23 m in overall length and varies in width from up to 6.5 m at the west end to *c*. 4.5 m at the east end. Its interior was found to be slightly scooped with possible opposed entrances and a small D-shaped enclosure attached to its south-west corner (see Chapter 2: Building 3). It was interpreted as overlying the building to the north, which measured *c*. 23 m by *c*. 5 m overall (Chapter 2: Building 5), and was set end-on to the third building (Chapter 2: Building 4), which measured *c*. 17 m by up to 5 m overall.

The second group (ID29495), on a low knoll on the south-west side of the Allt Corra-lairige (Figure 1.16: 12-13), also comprises three buildings defined by low banks enclosing shallow depressions. Two are set end-on to each other, although their stratigraphic relationship was unclear (RCAHMS 1990: 149). The larger, to the south-east, measures *c*. 19 m by 6 m overall, and that on the north-west *c*. 15 m by 6 m (Chapter 2: Building 12). The third building, 15 m to the south-west, is *c*. 14 m long and *c*. 4.5 m wide (Chapter 2: Building 13).

These two groups, however, are not the only Pitcarmick buildings identified in the catchment. One (ID29513; Figure 1.16: 20) measuring *c*. 18 m by 5 m lies on a low terrace overlooking poorly-drained ground to the south with another possible smaller example to the north-west (Figure 1.16: 21). Another lies on an east-facing slope on the far side of the catchment *c*. 750 m west-south-west of the ring-cairn(ID29446); it measures *c*. 19 m in length by *c*. 6 m in width overall, and there are seven clearance cairns nearby.

In addition to the Pitcarmick buildings, the original RCAHMS survey recorded a wide range of other buildings in the area, most of which were interpreted as townships, farmsteads and shieling huts, and assumed to be of later date (1990: 150). The most obvious of these is the township of Easter Lair (ID29436) just above the valley floor at 300 m OD, and comprising at least 20 buildings with enclosures, pens and two kilns, but there were also smaller examples, such the township of Corra-lairig (ID29511) contrastingly set at 420 m OD in a slight hollow in the southern flank of the spur forming the northern boundary of the catchment (Figure 1.8).

In their abandoned states, these townships were clearly part of the post-medieval settlement pattern, but there were also other buildings which could not be attributed dates with any such confidence. The first of these lay directly to the north-west of the ring-cairn (Figure 1.16: 1-2), comprising the poorly-defined remains of two buildings (ID29509), aligned north-west to south-east and set end-on to each other. That nearest the cairn (Figure 1.17; Chapter 2: Building 2), the upper of the two on the gentle slope, measures *c.* 14 m by up to 6 m overall with its south-east end being particularly well-defined by a row of boulders robbed from the kerb of the ring-cairn. The lower structure (Figure 19; Chapter 2: Building 1) measures *c.* 26 m by up to 6.5 m over ill-defined banks. Entrances in the south-west side were noted on both buildings. Rather more shadowy as field monuments were a possible building crossed by the track leading up from the road *c.* 125 m south-east from the ring-cairn (Figure 1.16: 14; Chapter 2: Building 14), and a second possibly with a slightly sunken interior on a terrace on the east flank of the southern spur of Torr Lochaidh (Figure 1.16: 18).

Other buildings could be more conventionally classed as elements of farmsteads, which in the RCAHMS terminology were defined as having between one and five buildings with at least one attendant enclosure. One of these farmsteads (Figure 1.16: 7-8, 16) lies adjacent to the track, *c.* 160 m south-east of the ring-cairn, at *c.* 360 m OD (ID29498) and comprises three buildings with an irregularly-shaped enclosure. The best-preserved of these (Figure 1.18; Chapter 2: Building 7) 'superficially resembles' a Pitcarmick building (RCAHMS 1990: 151) in the sense that it has rounded ends and measures overall *c.* 15.5 m by up to 4.5 m, although in contrast to most other Pitcarmick buildings it appeared to have a stone faced wall-footing. The second building is levelled into the south-facing slope, measures *c.* 14 m by up to 5 m overall and adjoins a roughly rectangular enclosure that may include a third building on its south-west side. This farmstead, however, is only one of three or four in the vicinity, though most of the others comprise only a single building and enclosure (Figure 1.16: 6, 11 and 15).

The buildings vary considerably in scale and morphology, as do the enclosures. One single compartment building (ID29496) with a rounded west end and entrance in the south wall, measures *c.* 8 m by 4 m (Figure 1.16: 6; Chapter 2: Building 6), and adjoins to the south a sub-circular enclosure measuring *c.* 23 m by 18 m internally. Another single compartment building (ID29502) is clearly more rectangular and measures *c.* 14.5 m by 4.5 m overall (Chapter 2: Building 11). It adjoins a rectangular enclosure measuring *c.* 15 m by 12 m internally, which lies immediately adjacent the lade that traverses the east flank of Torr Lochaidh, though the stratigraphic relationship between the two cannot be determined.

In addition to these other features are post-medieval shieling huts and bothies, as well as fragments of several field banks and more extensive traces of rig and furrow. The rig on the lower slopes of Torr Lochaidh appears largely unenclosed, but the rig-system around Corra-lairig includes a head-dyke and several other boundary dykes.

Finally while for much of its route, Caulfeild's military road through Glen Shee, built over 1748-50, is beneath the modern A93, it does occasionally survive as an earthwork as in the well preserved stretch at Lair, which includes a number of small quarries (Figure 1.16).

1.10 Research objectives

The overarching research aim of the project was to better understand the development of the Pitcarmick building tradition and further explore the function of the buildings in the context of their landscape, environmental and economic settings. A multi-disciplinary team was engaged with a series of defined targets: to excavate and interpret the archaeological evidence (Sneddon and Strachan: Chapter 2); investigate environmental and economic change (Paterson and Tipping: Chapter 2); apply new techniques to further explore the landscape archaeology at Lair (Banaszek and Cowley above); date the excavated sites by AMS ^{14}C dating and refine their chronology by Bayesian modelling (Krus and Hamilton: Chapter 2); analyse the recovered artefactual and eco-factual remains to understand human activities and building functions (Campbell; Clarke; Hall; Johnson; McLaren; Smith; Wright: Chapter 3) and provide a place-name history (McNiven: Section 1.6). While annual research objectives were developed to guide the excavation

Figure 1.17 An aerial view of Lair from 1978 showing the main group of Pitcarmick buildings and related buildings beside the ring-cairn (© Crown Copyright: HES A55314).

Figure 1.18 One of the smaller buildings at Lair (Building 7) with associated enclosures (D. Strachan: 2011).

Figure 1.19 A larger building (Building 1), closest to the ring-cairn, with stones robbed from the cairn kerb and incorporated into the rounded end (D. Strachan: 2011).

of specific structures, the strategic objectives for the project were explored under eight general headings with a series of dependent questions:

1. The chronology, phasing and sequence of construction of Pitcarmick buildings at Lair and establish any temporal relationship between them. Are the groups of buildings contemporary or do they represent sequences of construction over time and, if so, can these be defined? Do groups of Pitcarmick buildings at Lair represent single farm units or do they represent a collection of farm units comparable to the townships of the pre-improvement period?

2. The nature and function of individual buildings. Are differences in size and form indicative of function? Could domestic activity be identified? Did some buildings have specialist functions (e.g. smithing or craft production)? Were Pitcarmick buildings at Lair byre-houses? And what might these factors imply about the origin of this tradition?

3. Evidence for reconstruction, repair, maintenance and abandonment. Were individual structures rebuilt? Did they have longevity? Were they deliberately destroyed or did they decay through neglect? And when were the Pitcarmick buildings at Lair abandoned and why?

4. The relationship of the archaeological structures to their wider landscape context. Is there evidence for the agricultural economy beyond the archaeological structures themselves? Can this be related to the evidence for field-systems, clearance cairns and land boundaries?

5. The relation of the Pitcarmick buildings at Lair to contemporary developments in the lowlands, and their toponymic, political and socio-economic contexts.

6. The relation of the Pitcarmick buildings at Lair to those at Pitcarmick (Carver *et al.* 2012).

7. The relationship of the Pitcarmick buildings at Lair to the archaeological remains of earlier periods. Why was this location chosen for re-occupation in the early medieval period? Is there evidence of continuity of settlement?

8. The social and cultural context of Pitcarmick buildings. Do they represent particular ways of living, or a cultural tradition which is distinct from other parts of Scotland in the 1st millennium AD? Are biases in preservation or exploration in other regions biasing our perception of this tradition?

2. Results of Archaeological Fieldwork, Radiocarbon Dating, Peat-Stratigraphic and Pollen Analyses

Sneddon, Strachan and Tipping
with contributions by Morris, Black, Krus, Hamilton, Paterson and Ramsay

2.1 Introduction

The archaeological investigations at Lair concentrated on a parcel of land to the west of the A93 and south of the area of commercial forestry on Torr Lochaidh. As outlined in sections 1.8 and 1.9, the south-east facing heather- and grass-covered slopes contained a variety of visible surface features, including a prehistoric ring-cairn, three probable prehistoric roundhouses, at least six Pitcarmick buildings (Figure 2.1: Buildings 3-5 and 12-14) and 11 other elongated buildings (Figure 2.1: Buildings 1-2, 6-11), a lade and likely related features, several small quarries alongside Caulfeild's military road, scattered small cairns, a series of enclosures, and extensive ridged cultivation remains (Figures 1.16 and 2.1). In general these features appear as indistinct grass- and heather-covered banks and mounds although several of the buildings and the ring-cairn were more prominent.

The core fieldwork comprised detailed topographic and geophysical survey between 2011 and 2014 (Section 2.2), archaeological excavation 2012 to 2017 (Section 2.3), complemented by a programme of radiocarbon (^{14}C) dating and Bayesian modelling (Section 2.5) in 2017-18. Geo-archaeological analyses were planned (Section 2.4) and are in part proceeding, though incomplete and not presented here. Environmental and land-use changes were explored from 2014 to 2016 through a programme to study the peat-stratigraphic and pollen-analytical evidence (Section 2.6). The results of charcoal identification for ^{14}C dating are presented in Section 2.7. The remote sensing mapping reported in Chapter 1 was carried out retrospectively in 2018 (Section 1.8).

2.2 Topographic and geophysical survey

Geophysics by Peter Morris

Between 2012 and 2014 the archaeological features and topography were surveyed using a sub-cm Differential Global Positioning System with GNSS-RTK Network (Leica GS08). The results were processed with CAD and ArcGIS (Figure 2.1).

In addition, between 2011 and 2014 magnetic gradiometry was carried out over roughly 5 ha of ground (Figures 2.1 and 2.2) with readings acquired using a Bartington type 601a magnetic gradiometer over a series of 20 m by 20 m grids. Resistivity measurements were obtained using a TR Systems meter with 0.5 m probe spacing: resistivity measurements were also conducted over Buildings 2 and 7. Ground conditions on site varied and were often challenging, with well-established heather making progress slow and awkward. Despite this the data quality was reasonable. Magnetic anomalies were subsequently targeted by archaeological trenches which have shown this technique to be productive: resistivity data, however, proved to be of limited value.

The metamorphosed Dalradian schists which form the bedrock in the surveyed area are generally only weakly magnetic: there is no significant evidence that they cause local magnetic anomalies. The schists are covered by sandy glacial sediments from which successive inhabitants of the site have extracted rocks to build cairns, houses and walls. Most of the many stones and boulders at Lair tested for magnetic susceptibility proved to be only very weakly magnetic. A small percentage, however, mostly igneous glacial erratics, were strongly magnetic. The magnetic survey shows the walls of roundhouses, the ring-cairn, parts of the buildings, clearance cairns and some enclosure boundaries (Figure 2.2). The survey did not, however, detect walls of buildings and other features constructed largely from turf, though they were clearly visible on the topographic survey. Features on the magnetic survey are those containing a higher than normal percentage of magnetic rocks. Most magnetic anomalies in the survey are in the amplitude range -5 to +5 nT, but there is a set of short wavelength anomalies with amplitudes in the range +5 to +50 nT. Many of the latter may be due to the presence of near-surface magnetic boulders. Positive 'point' anomalies appear much more concentrated in some areas than others, which could indicate zones of more intense human activity.

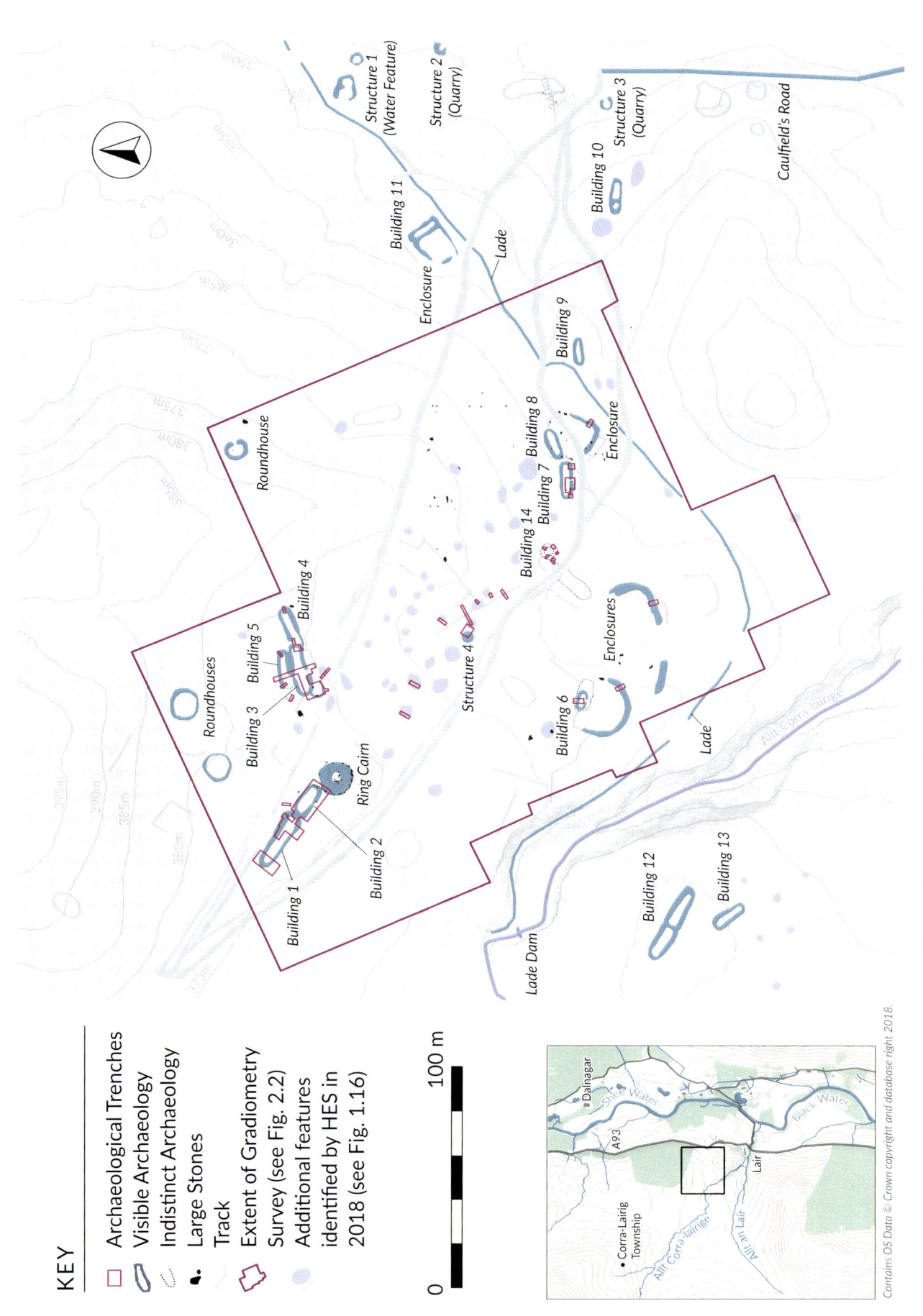

2. Results of Archaeological Fieldwork, Radiocarbon Dating, Peat-Stratigraphic and Pollen Analyses

Figure 2.1 Topographic survey showing upstanding archaeology and positions of trenches.

Results: areas of burning

Strong heating can cause chemical changes to the iron minerals found within a rock or sediment and result in the production of magnetic minerals capable of producing significant magnetic anomalies (heating some pieces of local Dalradian schist in a domestic fire for over an hour produced a tenfold increase in magnetic susceptibility). This suggests that heating could render many local rocks or sediment magnetically detectable. The anomalies over the roundhouses and ring-cairn attributed above to the presence of magnetic boulders could well be enhanced if episodes of burning have taken place. One of the most striking features on Figure 2.2, the linear feature in the top left-hand corner, was excavated and shown to be an area where fire has locally magnetised sandy sediment (Section 2.3: Figure 2.3).

Cultivation remains

A characteristic striped anomaly pattern is often associated with cultivation traces or rig (Section 1.8). Strong north-north-east trending anomalies were recorded around the linear feature and similarly spaced stripes, perpendicular to the first set, occur north-west of Building 6 at co-ordinate 0/150 m (Figure 2.2).

Metallic debris

A very intense anomaly was revealed at the centre of the ring-cairn (Figure 2.2) and is almost certainly due to the presence of metallic iron. Small-scale modern iron debris probably produced further 'point' anomalies in addition to those from magnetic rocks.

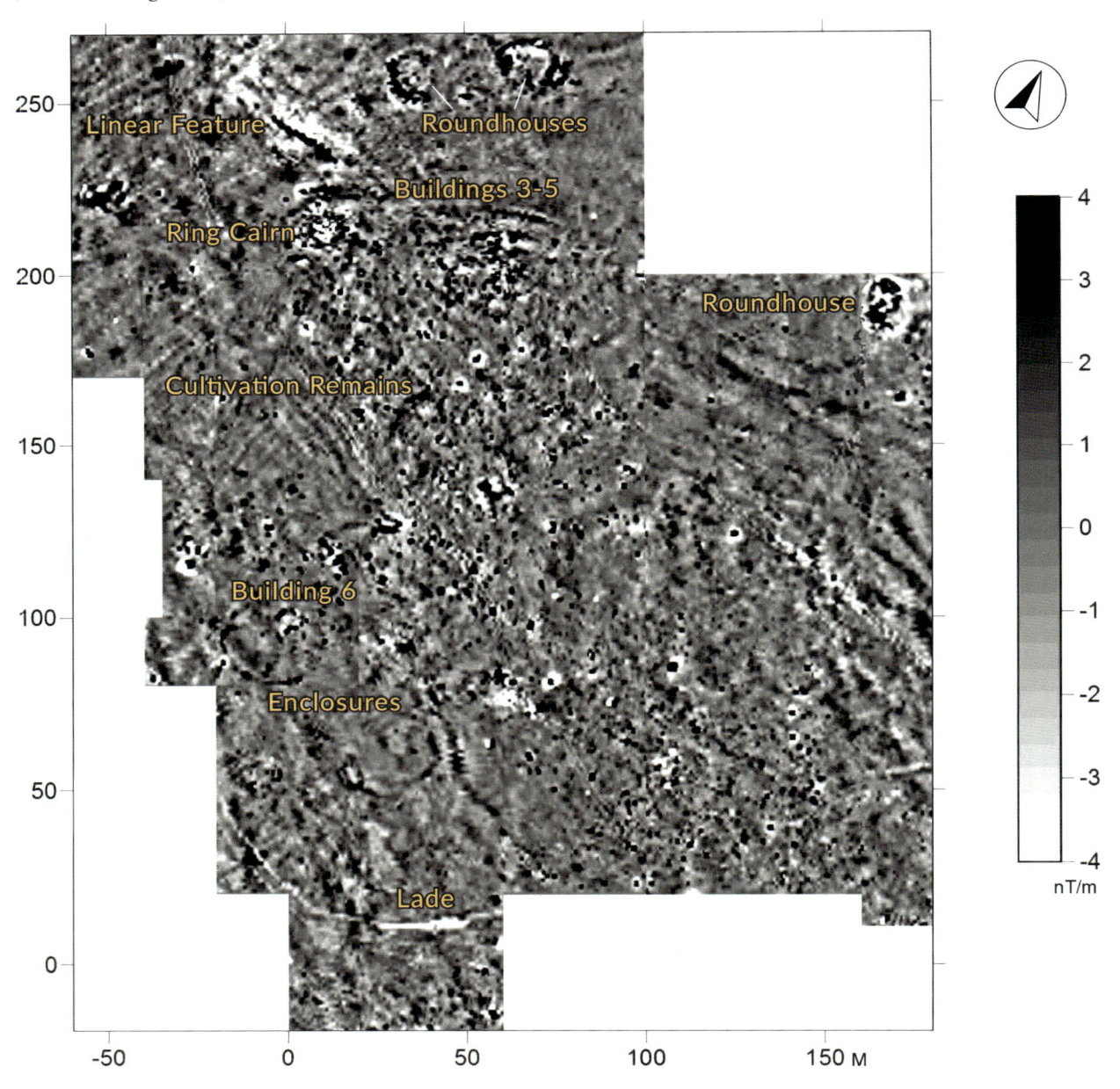

Figure 2.2 Magnetic gradiometer survey: see Figure 2.1 for location (Peter Morris: 2014).

2. Results of Archaeological Fieldwork, Radiocarbon Dating, Peat-Stratigraphic and Pollen Analyses

2.3 Excavation

David Sneddon and Steven Black

Excavation concentrated on Buildings 1-5 adjacent to the ring-cairn (Figure 2.1) and Buildings 6-7, the aim being to investigate potential structural and chronological relationships between them. While none of the buildings were fully excavated, information relating to the construction, function and date of the buildings was recorded. Excavation over more subtle features between Buildings 1-5 and Building 7 also demonstrated that archaeological remains extended beyond the more obvious visible earthworks.

The remains encountered within the 34 trenches can be separated into three broad categories by chronology: those originating in prehistory (nominally those prior to c. 500 AD); those relating to activity in the mid to late 1st millennium AD and very early 2nd millennium AD and those that could not be dated with any degree of confidence. Unsurprisingly, features dating from the second half of the 1st millennium AD were by far the most abundant, as structures thought to be of this period (cf. Carver et al. 2012) were targeted during the project. Numbers prefixed by C in the text refer to unique context numbers issued to features and deposits during the excavation, while those prefixed by SF indicate unique numbers issued to the material culture recovered (Chapter 3).

The grass and heather-covered soil over all trenches was in general relatively shallow, in some places being only 0.05 m in depth, although deeper areas were present. These tended to correspond to the locations of some buildings, suggesting that the decay of the turf used in their construction, in some cases coupled with the effects of later cultivation and bioturbation, had deepened the topsoil. The natural glacial substrate consisted of various mixtures of silt, sand, pebbles and cobbles.

No trenches specifically targeted features thought to be prehistoric. The ring-cairn is of probable Early Bronze Age date (Section 1.9; Figure 1.5) and was exposed only on its north-west margin in the course of the excavation of Building 2 (below). Despite the presence of at least three roundhouses in the immediate vicinity of the ring-cairn, prehistoric material within the trenches was surprisingly limited, confined to occasional pieces of pottery and worked flint and quartz which had found their way into the remains of later buildings. This scarcity might suggest that prehistoric activity did not significantly extend beyond the remains of the roundhouses visible today, while it is also possible that evidence of wider activity has been truncated by later periods of occupation and cultivation. A single prehistoric ^{14}C date was obtained, from a sample in C86 within post-hole C85 (Building 1 or 2: Table 2.1 and below) but is considered residual.

The trenches over Buildings 1-3 formed the most extensive areas excavated and contained some of the most complex archaeological features encountered.

Linear burnt feature

The earliest stratigraphic feature was a 21 m long linear area of burning which corresponded to a magnetic anomaly in the geophysical survey (Section 2.2; Figure 2.2). The feature was excavated in Trench 3 (Figures 2.3 and 2.4) and in three areas beneath the eastern end of Building 1, where it was seen to peter out at westwards as a rough spread of material (C56). The burning, evident as scorching on the natural substrate and as a thin layer of sandy silt containing numerous flecks and chunks of charcoal (C14/24), including some well-preserved roundwood pieces, lay in places within the shallow hollows and undulations (Figure 2.3) of the natural substrate (Figures 2.5 and 7). Virtually all the charcoal present within a bulk sample of C14 consisted of *Betula* (birch), but also included smaller amounts of

Figure 2.3 East facing section through linear burning: Trench 3 in 2012 (scale = 2 m).

Corylus (hazel) and *Salix* (willow) (Section 2.7). A heavily degraded and fractured fragment of iron (Cat 28, SF16), a possible barbed-spring bolt (Cat 8, SF17) and the tip of an iron pin shank (Cat 22, SF18) were recovered from this deposit where it seemed to form the spread of material (C56) beneath and partially mixed with the bank of Building 1.

Most of the burnt material lay within the hollows and undulations, and the remainder of the depressions had been filled with a deposit (C16/23) that appeared to have accumulated naturally, though intentional levelling of the hollows cannot be ruled out. Some charcoal flecks were present at the base of C16/23, possibly the result of either natural mixing or purposeful backfilling. A single flint barbed and tanged arrowhead (Cat 10, SF7) was recovered from the lower levels: it is interpreted as residual.

Where this linear area of burning corresponded to the location of Building 1, it clearly lay beneath the material that formed the bank defining the wall of the building (C3; Figure 2.7), though at its western end, where the burnt material petered out into a rough spread (C56), this relationship was much less distinct and the deposit had been mixed with the lower layers of the bank material (C21).

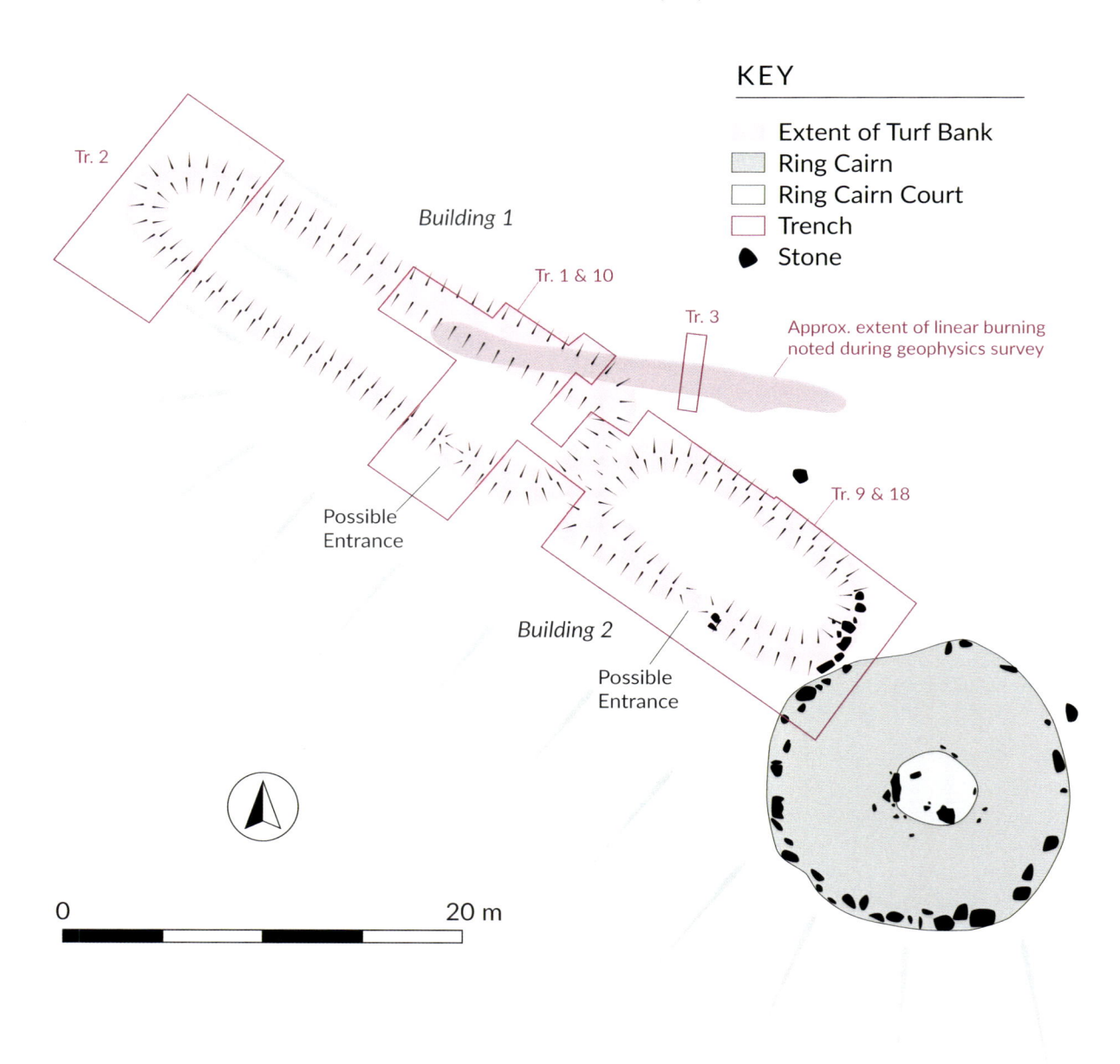

Figure 2.4 Buildings 1 and 2 prior to excavation showing earthworks and trench plan.

2. Results of Archaeological Fieldwork, Radiocarbon Dating, Peat-Stratigraphic and Pollen Analyses

The linear nature of the feature, the presence of large pieces of well-preserved charcoal within it (including roundwood, mostly of birch) and the undulating nature of the natural substrate (not encountered elsewhere) make interpretation difficult given the small areas in which it was exposed. On site interpretation considered this the result of the burning of a fence or felled and burnt trees raked into a rough line, and are not presented with any conviction. The geophysical survey demonstrates that it was the result of a specific and confined event and, at some 21 m in length, there is the distinct possibility that it represents the fugitive remains of yet another building, destroyed by fire and then truncated by turf-stripping to build the walls of the later structures (Stratford Halliday *pers comm*). In this respect, it should be noted that the feature not only contained several iron artefacts (Cat 8, 22 and 28), but also that other artefacts were recovered from the collapsed turf wall of Building 1 (Cat 1, 2, 3, 11, 12, 20, 21, 27 and 29). These latter artefacts may have originated in the earlier building, having been incorporated into the later building within the turves used in its construction.

Lying directly beneath the bank defining Building 1, the linear feature is clearly earlier than the structure, and while the radiocarbon dates from its lower fill (C14: SUERC 42419; 51328) and from the mixed deposit at its west end (C56: SUERC 49666; 51333) span the whole of the second half of the 1st millennium AD, indicating a very mixed origin for these deposits, they also include the earliest early medieval date recovered from the site (SUERC 51328) and one of the latest (SUERC 49666). Although the latter can be modelled to provide a *Terminus Post Quem* (*TPQ*) date range of the late 8th to late 10th centuries AD for the construction of Building 1 (see below and Section 2.5) a true understanding of this feature can only be resolved by further excavation.

Building 1

The low turf bank, representing degraded and slumped former turf and earth walls, indicated that Building 1 was an estimated 26 m in length and up to 6.5 m in width (measured from the top of the bank). During initial survey by the RCAHMS (Section 1.9; ID29509) neither Building 1 nor 2 were identified as Pitcarmick buildings.

Before excavation, the banks were among the slightest seen at Lair and had clearly been disturbed by later ploughing. The north-western end lay on a north-west facing slope (Figure 2.4), with the remainder on more level ground. A slight dip on the southern side near Building 2 was the only indication of a break in the bank. There were no signs of internal features.

Building 1 was the first excavated in the project, selected as a 'pilot' as it appeared to be single phased, while other building groups appeared to be more complex.

Trial excavation trenches focused on both ends and part of the north-eastern side of the building and allowed assessment of the subsoils and preservation of the archaeological features.

The remains of the turf and earth walls at the north-west end were heavily slumped down the slope and were the least defined of any encountered. The slope and later plough traces had spread them across the entire extent of the trench. This was also seen at the south-east end of the building though to a lesser extent because a strip some 3 m wide in the centre of the building remained clear of bank material.

Waterlogging and animal disturbance in the lower lying areas between the banks had resulted in the formation of a shallow silt and sand deposit (C5 and C28) above the bank material. C5 contained a flint awl (Cat 1, SF1) and a burnt flint flake (Cat 2, SF2) that were clearly not *in situ*. Lying immediately beneath the topsoil and these areas of more recent disturbance, the bank consisted of mid-brown silty sand containing only occasional sub-angular gravels, pebbles and cobbles (C2, C3, C6 and C55). At its thickest, generally corresponding to the south-east end of the building where the highest points of the bank were visible on the surface, the deposit was 0.3 m in height, though shallower on the slope at the north-western end. A substantially intact whittle-tanged knife blade (Cat 3, SF15), an intact iron plate buckle (Cat 20, SF8) and an iron bar fragment (Cat 27, SF14), along with fragments of partially charred bark that had no distinguishing features and could not be identified (Susan Ramsay *pers comm*) were recovered from the bank material, all from the eastern end of the building. Although some of the cobbles appeared to be concentrated within parts of bank material, they formed no coherent structure. They were probably part of the original turf and earth wall construction.

Beneath the bank material (C3) on the northern side of Building 1, close to its south-eastern end, the discovery of a deposit (C21) containing a moderate amount of charcoal inclusions (Figure 2.6) suggested that, though generally degraded, a relatively well defined patch of the original turf and earth wall was present. It was 1.7 m in maximum width, lying within a slight hollow (Figure 2.7) over the remains of the linear burnt feature (C14/C56, see above). It contained a higher concentration of stone cobbles compared to other excavated sections of the bank (C2, C3 and C6). Several artefacts were also recovered from this portion of the wall, namely a forged iron buckle hoop and pin (Cat 21, SF9), two pieces of corroded iron, a badly damaged small whittle-tanged knife (Cat 2, SF10), and three fragments of semi-charred *Pinus sylvestris* (Scots pine; Susan Ramsay *pers comm*). If the linear burnt feature C14/56 is interpreted as an earlier building (see above) it raises the possibility that C21 could relate to the earlier building rather than

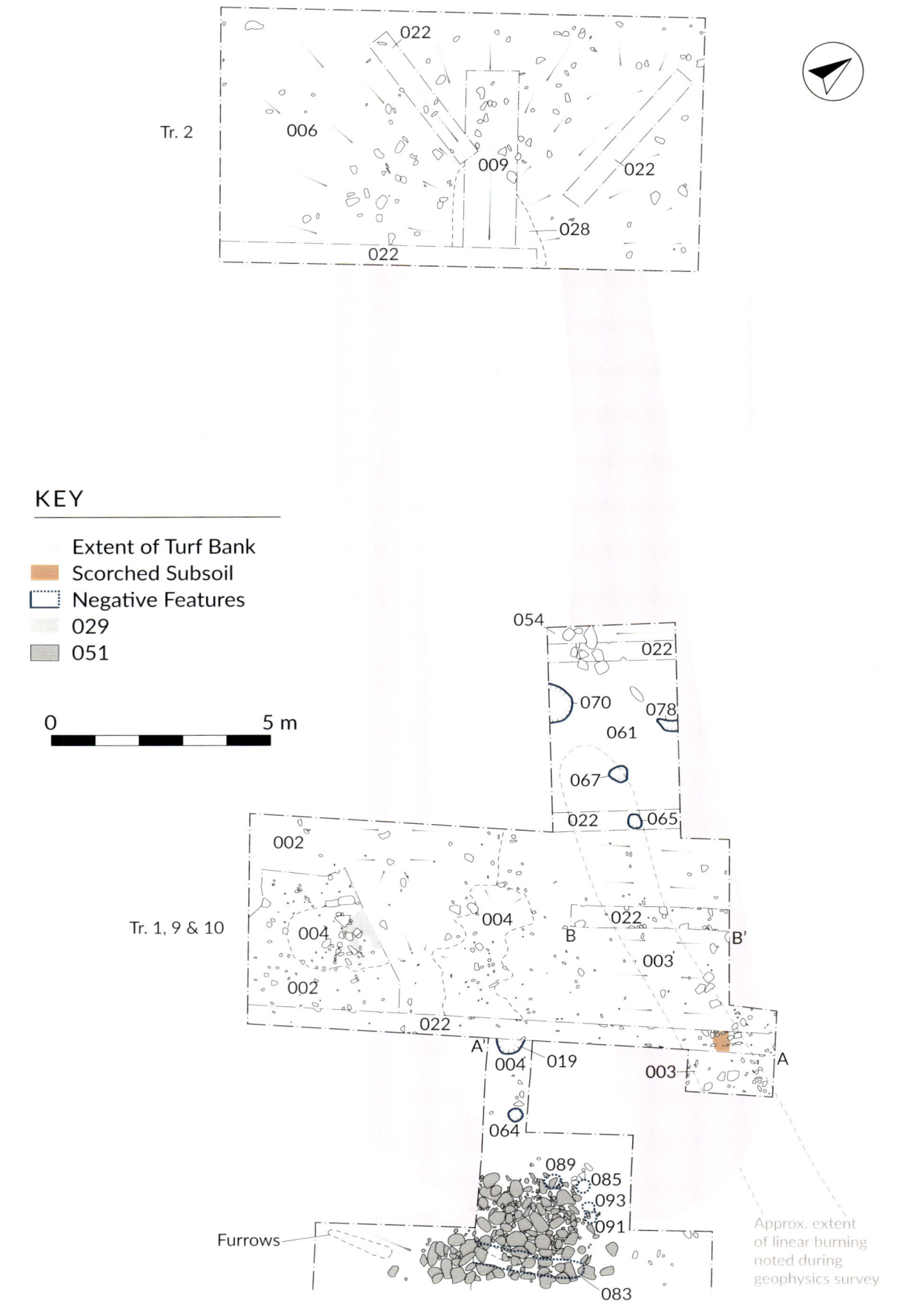

EARLY MEDIEVAL SETTLEMENT IN UPLAND PERTHSHIRE: EXCAVATIONS AT LAIR, GLEN SHEE 2012-17

Figure 2.5 Building 1 excavation plan.

2. Results of Archaeological Fieldwork, Radiocarbon Dating, Peat-Stratigraphic and Pollen Analyses

Figure 2.6 Building 1: lower turf wall (C21) and location of section B-B' (Figure 2.5) in 2012 (Horizontal scale = 1 m).

the later Building 1, although the same deposit was not found elsewhere above the linear feature.

There was no obvious sign of an internal floor layer, although deposit C4, very similar in character to the bank material it lay beneath and only distinguishable from it by being slightly more compact and containing more charcoal flecks, likely represents what would have been the surface over which the building was constructed. It could also represent the level of truncation any earlier buildings were subjected to during construction of Building 1. Gradual slippage on the slope and subsequent cultivation inevitably led to a significant degree of mixing between this and the bank. C4 existed to 0.25 m depth and, in all areas bar those parts investigated on the northern side of the building, in turn lay on top of the natural sterile substrate (C22). A small prehistoric rim sherd (Cat 1, SF6), two small joining sherds of unglazed Scottish White Gritty ware fabric dating to between the 12th and 15th centuries (Hall: Section 3.7) and fragments of partially charred bark similar to that recovered from the bank material (C3), again with no distinguishing features (Susan Ramsay *pers comm*), were recovered from C4. If Building 1 is interpreted as a later structure overlying one or more earlier buildings (see above and Section 2.5) these pot sherds may relate to the latter phases of occupation on the site of Building 1.

Time constraints and wet conditions hampered removal of much of the slumped bank material and the entirety of this surface was not explored within this trench. However, where the bank material was removed several features were uncovered, all confined to the south-eastern trench. Although some were visible on the surface of C4, others only became apparent when the trench was excavated down to the natural sub-soil. This is not to say that C4 overlay these latter features, rather that they only became clearly visible after C4 had been removed, and thus may also have been cut through C4.

In the southern part of the trench, lying on the surface of C4 in the area corresponding to a gap in the bank identified by RCAHMS (1990: Figure 290.3), a relatively thin concentration of pebbles and gravel (C29) was revealed, although not to its full extent (Figure 2.5). Given its location, it would appear to confirm the position of an entrance to Building 1. The pebbles and gravel had been laid in a relatively unstructured manner, presumably to firm up the ground surface. It is notable that, though they did not form any clear structure, more cobbles were found in the bank material here (C2) than elsewhere in the trench, suggesting the turf and earth walls to either side of the entrance may have contained a larger quantity of stone.

At the far south-eastern end of the building a broadly central pit (C19; Figures 2.5 and 2.7) was present. It was roughly circular in shape and held a single homogenous fill (C20) containing a small amount of charcoal. A single sherd of residual coarse prehistoric pottery (Hall: Section 3.7; Cat 3, SF11) and a very small early medieval green segmented glass bead, recovered from soil sample processing, were found within the pit (Campbell: Section 3.8). It is feasible that the pit once held an upright timber supporting the roof although it is also possible that it was utilised for another, unknown purpose.

Lying partly beneath the bank of Building 1 at its eastern end was a dense concentration of cobbles and boulders (C51) within a matrix that appeared to have been derived from collapsed turf and earth walls. Although the majority of this deposit lay beneath Building 2 (see below), and was interpreted on site as a stone foundation for it, there is a possibility that it could instead have related to the construction of Building 1 or formed part of an earlier structure(s) beneath Buildings 1 and 2.

Where the bank material and this concentration of stones were removed at the eastern end of Building 1 a series of five post-holes were uncovered (C64, 85, 89, 91 and 93; Figures 2.5 and 2.8). They were all 0.25-0.4 m in diameter by 0.15-0.25 m in depth and held similar homogenous fills that contained small amounts of burnt bone and charcoal inclusions. The presence of occasional pebbles and cobbles in the upper portions of C89 and C85 may represent packing-stones, but no post-pipes were present, suggesting the posts had been removed. A small extension on the upper eastern side of C89 may relate to either the insertion or removal of the post, while the truncation of C91 by C93 may indicate a post replacement. There was no evidence that any bank material or internal occupation layers had subsided into the upper portions of these post-holes, suggesting they may have been truncated.

Post-hole C64 could conceivably have acted as a support for a larger timber in C19, assuming this pit held such an object. Post-holes C85, 89, 91 and 93, appearing to respect the edge of stone foundation C51, could relate to either Building 1 or 2; however, on balance and presuming stone layer C51 related to Building 1 or 2, it would seem more likely they formed part of Building 2 (see below). There is also the possibility that these post-holes pre-date both Buildings 1 and 2 and relate to an earlier structure, something that is hinted at by the relatively uniform 7th to 8th century AD radiocarbon date ranges obtained from material within these features in the area of Building 1 and 2 (Table 2.1), all being earlier than the late 8th to late 10th century AD modelled *TPQ* date obtained for the construction of Building 1 (Section 2.5), and the suggestion that they had been truncated.

Two pits and two post-holes were also present (Figure 2.5) beneath the turf bank material on the northern side of Building 1. Both pits (C70 and 78) were only partially revealed but had very different characteristics. Pit C70 would have lain inside the building and, where exposed, was oval and contained two fills. The lower fill (C73) was very similar to the natural substrate and was only present on the north-eastern side, possibly representing partial collapse of the pit edge. The remainder of the pit was filled by a deposit containing a small number of stone cobbles and pebbles and a small amount of charcoal, giving little insight into the purpose of the pit. It was not clear whether pit C78 was beneath the turf and earth wall or just on its exterior, meaning it was not possible to conclusively identify its stratigraphic relationship with the turf wall. It was very irregular in both plan and profile, holding a single homogenous fill.

The two post-holes, which were in close proximity to each other (C67 and 65; Figure 2.5), would have lain

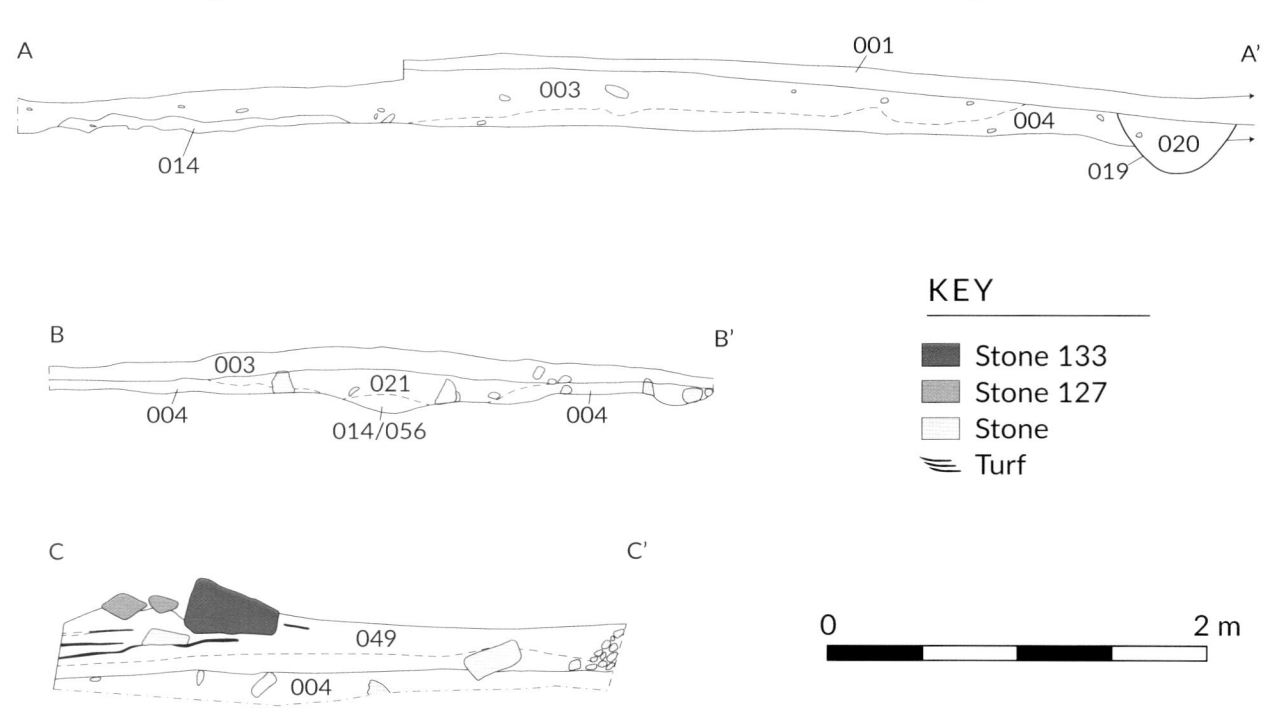

Figure 2.7 Building 1 and 2 selected sections.

beneath the turf and earth wall. They were similar in size, being respectively 0.4 m and 0.35 m in diameter by 0.4 m and 0.15 m in depth. The shallower depth of the latter is because it was not recognised until after the removal of C4, its upper portions potentially having been lost. Post-hole C67 held a series of packing stones in the upper parts of the fill, while the absence of any stone packing in C65 may be the result of truncation. The V shaped profile of C65 may indicate a pointed post, but no post-pipe was visible in either, indicating the posts may have been removed after use.

Whether these posts relate to specific structural elements of Building 1 or pre-date it remains unclear due to the relatively small area explored to this level. Their positions broadly along the suspected line of the turf and earth wall could equally be the result of them relating to structural posts incorporated into, or at the edge of, the walls of Building 1 or them relating to activity pre-dating the wall itself.

Building 2

The full extent of the smaller Building 2 was revealed during excavation and, in contrast to Building 1, more elements of the original structure were identifiable. It lay on a relatively level area of ground and measured 14 m in length and up to 6 m in width (measured from the top of the bank) with a possible entrance indicated by a dip in the crest of the bank in the middle of the southern side (Figure 2.4).

The chronological relationship between Building 1 and 2 was difficult to ascertain on site primarily due to the similarity of the bank material and lack of inter-cutting features. Being end-to-end (although the exact wall lines here were difficult to define), on the same orientation, and broadly the same width, at the very least implied that, even if not directly contemporary, the presence of the one was recognised at the time of construction of the other. The programme of Bayesian chronological modelling (Krus and Hamilton: Section 2.5) has shown that, presuming all excavated features related directly to either Buildings 1 or 2, there is a very high likelihood Building 2 was constructed at a later date than Building 1 but also that the two were contemporary for a reasonable length of time. However, it is likely that the excavation of Buildings 1 and 2 included remains from earlier structures, meaning that the scenario suggested by the modelling is not straightforward. If Building 1 is presumed to be a later addition on top of earlier buildings (represented by the negative cut features and linear burning C14), a modelled *TPQ* date of late 8th to late 10th century AD for the construction of Building 1 seems likely (Section 2.5). If the negative cut features within Building 2 are similarly considered to be from earlier activity the dates obtained from the hearth (C148) provide the only indication of when Building 2 was used. These also range from the late 8th to late 10th centuries AD (Table 2.1).

As with Building 1, immediately beneath the topsoil, the degraded remains of the turf and earth walls (C49) had formed banks up to 0.4 m in height (Figure 2.7). The bank material at the adjoining ends of Buildings 1 and 2 had merged together, resulting in no clear indication of where one ended and the other began. Indeed, the sole evidence that they were separate was a slight dip in the ground surface. In the parts not disturbed by subsequent ploughing, the relatively homogenous bank included occasional darker turf lines, representing compacted remains of turves that once formed the building's walls. An iron tack or horseshoe nail head (Cat 13, SF19) and a partially smoothed and pecked stone (SF21) were recovered from bank material on the southern side of the trench which may represent earlier material incorporated into the walls of Building 2 within the turves they were constructed from.

One of the most striking features of Building 2 was at the south-east end, where seven large boulders (C133) from the kerb of the adjacent ring-cairn had been rolled onto the end of the building (Figures 2.8, 2.9 and 2.10), resulting in a gap in the kerb of the cairn. Whether the re-use of these stones held some significance or whether they were merely a convenient source of large boulders used to define and/or stabilise this end of the building is discussed later (Section 4.3). Nevertheless, it does represent a specific and short-lived event relating to the construction of a turf building that is not seen elsewhere at Lair. They both overlay and sat partly within parts of the bank material (C49), indicating that they were not rolled into place as part of the initial construction of Building 2 but were more likely to have been a later addition. A concentration of cobbles and small boulders (C127) lay along the inside edge of the re-used kerb stones. These probably originated from the main body of the nearby cairn and similarly lay partly within and on top of the bank material (C49), suggesting they also relate to a later phase of Building 2. A stone slab with a natural hollow (SF24) was recovered from this stone deposit.

The presence of the re-used kerb stones had provided a level of protection from later cultivation to the lower courses of the turf and earth wall, in which up to three layers of generally horizontal turf lines (Figure 2.7) were preserved. The preservation was such that individual turf layers were visible, showing they were laid turf side up, although partial degradation prevented individual turves being defined. Occasional stones present within the lower turf layers indicate that the walls were not solely of turf and earth. In contrast the remainder of the building had been afforded no protection from later cultivation,

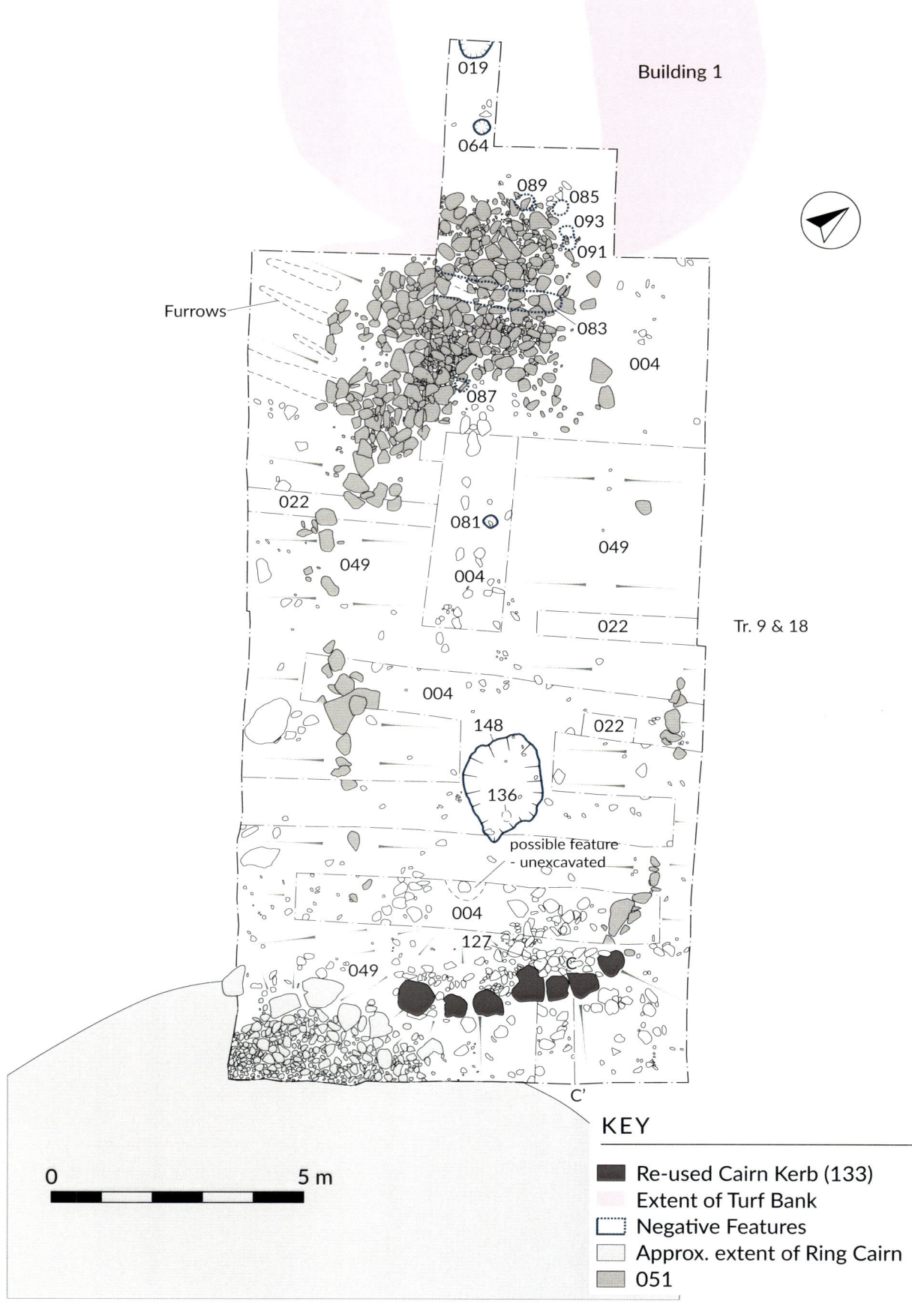

Early Medieval Settlement in Upland Perthshire: Excavations at Lair, Glen Shee 2012-17

Figure 2.8 Building 2 excavation plan.

2. Results of Archaeological Fieldwork, Radiocarbon Dating, Peat-Stratigraphic and Pollen Analyses

Figure 2.9 A vertical aerial photograph of the south-eastern end of Building 2 partially excavated (E. Martin: 2014).

demonstrated by the presence of obvious furrow scores (Figure 2.8); in these sectors of the wall only occasional patches of compressed turf lenses were visible.

The vast majority, if not all, of the cobble and boulder concentration (C51) first detected beneath the eastern end of Building 1 seemed to relate to the western end of Building 2 although the potential they relate to an earlier building cannot be completely ruled out. They created a foundation at most only one to two courses (0.25 m) deep and lay within a matrix of the collapsed turf and earth from the walls, forming an arc corresponding roughly to the north-western end of Building 2 (Figure 2.8). Along the inner edge of this arc, however, there was a distinct area of smaller compacted stones which could relate to an internal area of the building. Stones also extended sporadically along the sides of the building, some of them perhaps derived from the turf and earth walls, and others possibly deliberately placed to define the outer edge of the walls.

As with Building 1 these structural remains lay on top of the upper natural substrate, layer C4, which also formed the interior of the structure and into which a series of negative features were cut. At the north-western end, beneath the stone foundation deposit, part of a linear gully aligned north-east to south-west (C83) was revealed, displaying a very slight curve to the north at its eastern end. A terminal was located at its north-eastern end, while to the south-west the feature continued beneath the possible stone foundation (C51; Figure 2.8). It was up to 0.5 m in width by 0.15 m in depth. The single fill (C84) did not have any diagnostic characteristics so its purpose remains unclear, although ^{14}C dating of samples retrieved from the fill appear broadly contemporary with other dates from the negative cut features in Buildings 1 and 2. The fact that the gully had been filled and was out of use prior to the laying of stone layer C51, which itself pre-dates the turf walls of Building 2, strongly suggests that the gully belongs to an earlier phase of activity on the site.

Figure 2.10 Oblique view of the ring-cairn and the south-eastern end of Building 2 (E. Martin: 2014).

Only two internal post-holes (C81 and C87; Figure 2.8) were identified. They were 0.3 m and 0.22 m in diameter respectively by 0.25 m and 0.18 m in depth. The absence of post-pipes suggest the posts were removed and the relatively homogenous fills, containing occasional charcoal flecks, are likely to be a mixture of the soil dug out when they were cut and other material introduced when the post was removed. The presence of occasional pebbles and cobbles in the upper portions of C81 may represent displaced packing-stones, while the fill of C87 appears to have been entirely packed with earth. Post-hole C87 appeared to respect the internal edge of the stone foundation (Figure 2.8), while C81 lay in a broadly central location on the long-axis of the building. Although the central location of C81 lends itself to interpretation as a roof support or internal division it cannot be discounted that these features relate to an earlier building on the site.

In the south-eastern half of the interior lay a relatively large but shallow central hearth (C148; Figure 2.8). It was cut some 0.1 m into C4 and, given the evidence for later cultivation, is likely to have been at least partially truncated. As with Building 1, however, there was no obvious evidence of an occupation surface within the building. The hearth contained dark sandy silt with frequent flecks of charcoal, nutshells (*Corylus*) and burnt bones (C128). Scorched earth covered its base, while on the surface two concentrations of cobbles were present. Located at the north-western and south-eastern sides respectively, the north-western group created a relatively flat surface. A poorly-defined small oval feature, roughly 0.15 m deep, was present at the south-eastern end of the hearth, but part of its fill had been disturbed by burrowing, not a frequent occurrence across the excavated areas at Lair. Although the lower deposits of the hearth were cut into C4, it formed more of a spread rather than anything more formally defined. In this respect it was reminiscent of an open uncontained fire, which, due to its shallow depth, would have required frequent raking out if used for any great length of time.

Building 3

Around 50 m east of Buildings 1 and 2, the complex of Buildings 3-5 (Figures 2.11 and 2.12) appeared from surface remains alone to be of very different character. RCAHMS survey (1990; ID29437; Sections 1.8 and 1.9) identified these buildings as Pitcarmick buildings. Parts of the banks defining these buildings were noticeably more pronounced than in both Buildings 1 and 2, particularly in the case of Building 3 which also had an oval annexe attached to its south-western corner. The excavation of Building 3 and its related annexe generated the most diverse set of features uncovered during the project.

Building 3 was excavated on a larger scale than either Building 4 or 5. The western half of the building lay on gradually sloping ground with the higher point to the south-west, although internally this was exaggerated by the apparent sunken area at the eastern end. Overall the building measured 23 m in length by up to 6.5 m in width (measured from the top of the bank), with an entrance indicated by a clear dip in the crest of the bank on its southern side. A less distinct dip in the opposed bank on the northern side possibly marked a second entrance leading into the adjacent Building 5 (Figure 2.12). Building 3, at its eastern end, appeared to curve slightly to the south, although it is uncertain to what extent the lines of the banks reflect the original lines of the walls.

If all the features excavated are taken to relate directly to either Buildings 1, 2 or 3, then the ^{14}C dating programme and associated Bayesian modelling (Krus and Hamilton:

Figure 2.11 Oblique aerial view of Buildings 3-5, evaluation trenches and earthworks (E. Martin: 2015).

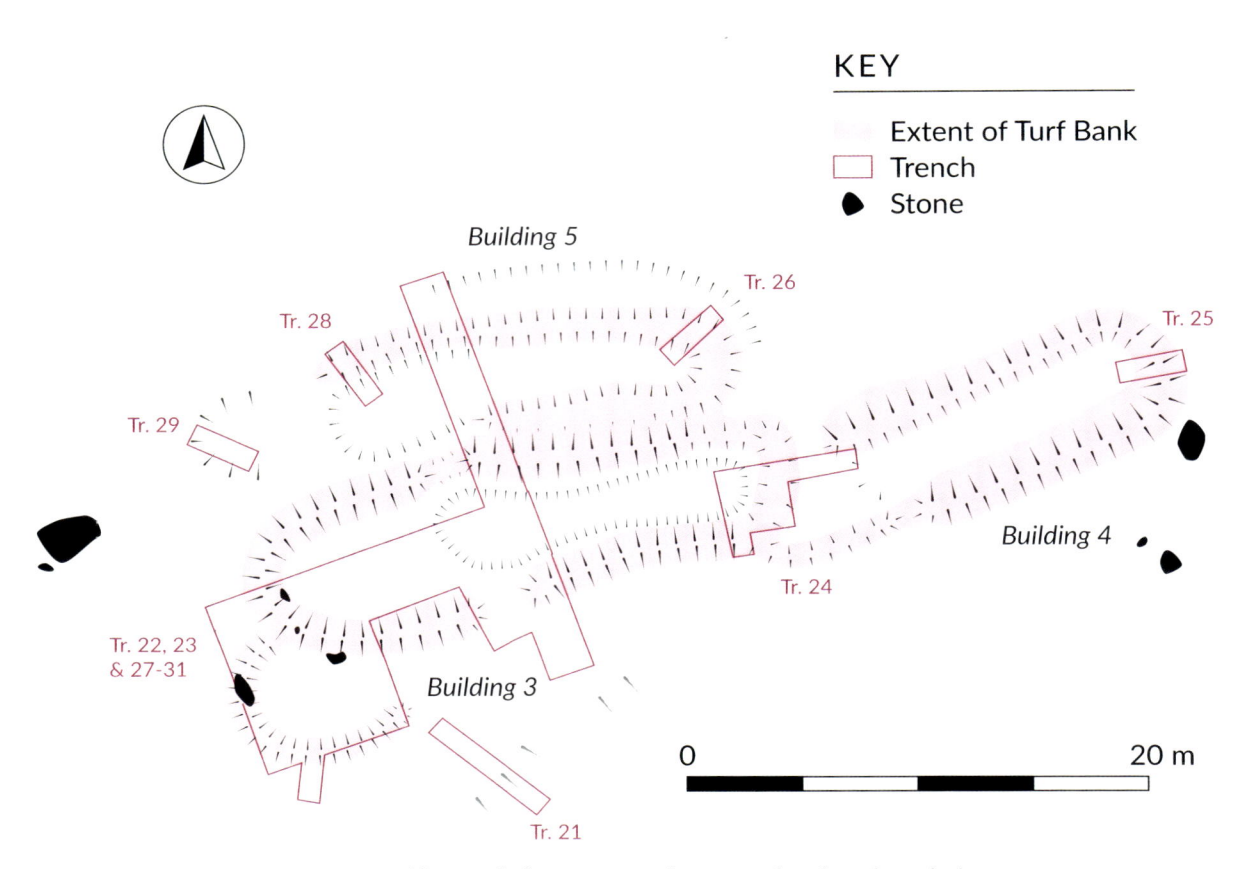

Figure 2.12 Buildings 3-5 before excavation showing earthworks and trench plan.

Section 2.5) show there is a very high likelihood that Building 3 was constructed after Building 2 but that there was a period when Buildings 1, 2 and 3 were all contemporary. They also indicate that Building 2 remained functional after Building 1 and 3 had gone out of use. However, as noted above, it is likely that several features encountered within Buildings 1 and 2 were from earlier structures, suggesting the chronological relationship between the three sites is more complex. This is heightened by the possibility that Buildings 3 to 5 relate to more than one phase.

Immediately beneath the topsoil the degraded remains of the turf and earth walls (C158) had formed banks (Figure 2.12) up to 0.4 m in height and were spread up to 2 m in width. No turf layers were recognisable within the banks of Building 3. They comprised a single homogenous deposit derived from the decay of the earth and turf walls. Cobbles and the occasional more substantial boulder were present in the lower parts of the bank, particularly on the southern side of the building, which could have formed part of the wall structure. They were, however, rare, and not in sufficient abundance to suggest they formed a formal foundation layer. Unlike Buildings 1 and 2, the remains of the walls lay directly on top of the natural glacial substrate (C22), the intermediate deposit seen under the buildings to the west (C4) only being noted around the central hearth (C284, see below). An unfinished stone lamp or mortar (SF30), a whetstone (SF78), an iron pin with ball shaped head (Cat 25, SF77) and a residual small body sherd of prehistoric pottery (Cat 5, SF32) were recovered from the bank material, suggesting they could have derived from earlier occupation, having been incorporated into the walls of Building 3 within the turves used for its construction.

Although very faint traces of two banks could be seen on the surface separating Buildings 3 and 5 (Figure 2.12), no clear stratigraphic separation could be seen in section (Figure 2.15). The bulk of the bank material, however, appeared to belong to Building 3 rather than Building 5 (see below). On the northern side of both the southern and northern banks of Building 3 two shallow features (C207 and C215; Figure 2.15) had been cut into their edges, although they were visible only in section. C215, on the north, was by far the wider and corresponded roughly to the line of the bank of Building 5. Both held a single fill with darker turf lenses at their base. Given the denuded nature of the former turf and earth walls (C158) and the limited extent over which these shallow cuts were revealed, interpretation of their relationship is problematic. It is entirely feasible, however, that they represent the remains of later cultivation furrows that utilised the position of the existing banks. This may also explain the absence of bank material in the south-western portion of Building 5. Beyond the external edge of the bank material, to the west of the Building 3,

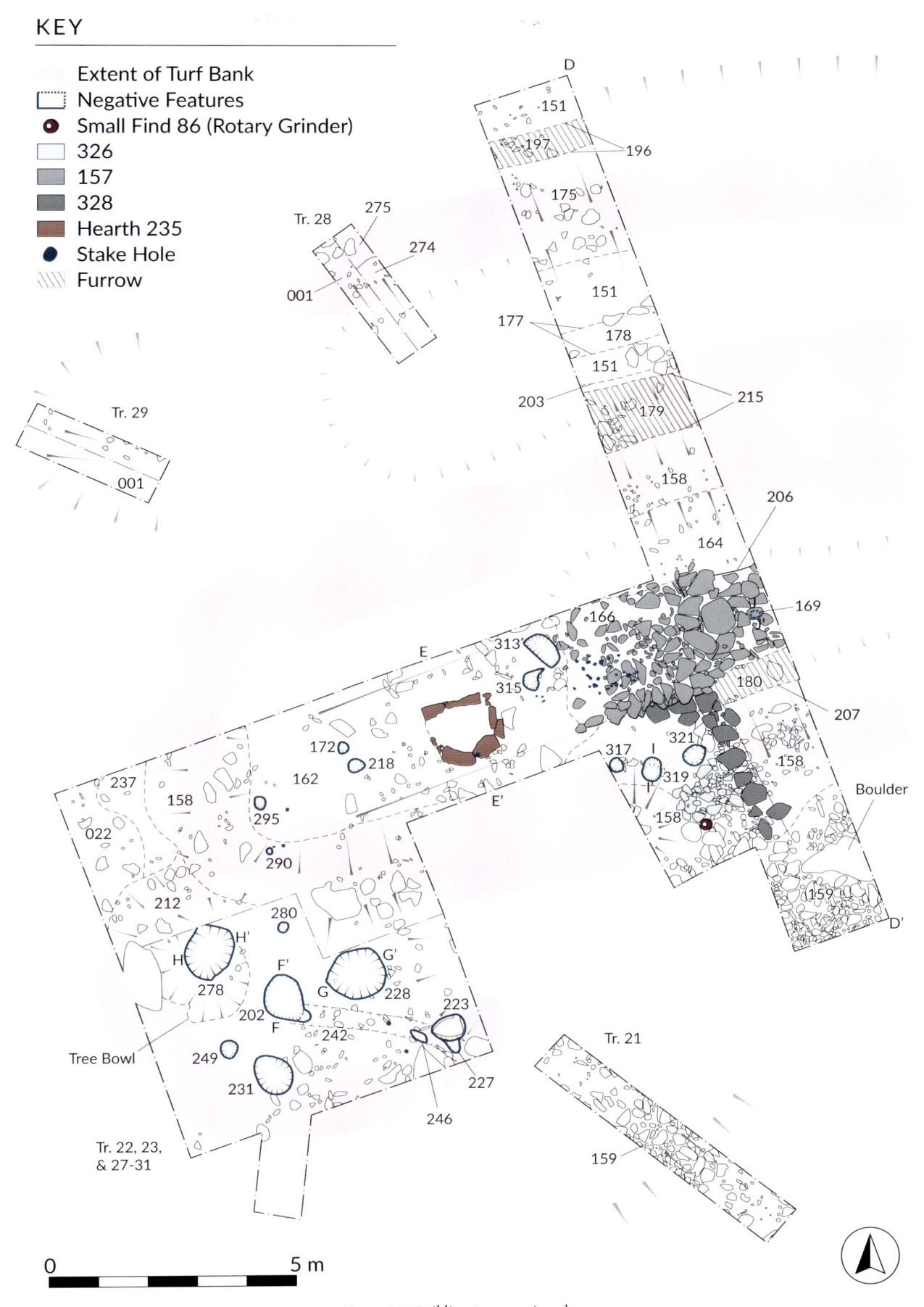

2. Results of Archaeological Fieldwork, Radiocarbon Dating, Peat-Stratigraphic and Pollen Analyses

Figure 2.13 Building 3 excavation plan.

43

Figure 2.14 Building 3: the hearth C235 and stone infill C157/C166 showing gradient at north-western end in 2016 (scales = 1 m).

lay a 0.18 m deep deposit containing occasional patches of lighter soil and clear black lenses (C237), distinctly visible in section and less obvious in plan, that likely represented scorched turves.

Unlike Buildings 1 and 2, which had no distinct internal occupation layers, the interior of Building 3 contained features and deposits relating to its use. The occupation surface at the western end of the building (C162) comprised a thin (up to 0.07 m thick) deposit of dark silty sand containing relatively frequent charcoal flecks and occasional fragments of burnt bone (162). Patches of denser burnt material, some potentially burnt turf layers, and scorched earth were present within this floor deposit, tending to lie nearer the edges of the interior. This deposit contained an abundance of material culture, including a flint core (Cat 25, SF37), two flint sub-angled scrapers (Cat 28, SF42 and Cat 36, SF74), a flint fragment (Cat 29, SF44), unidentified iron fragments (Cat 33, SF36 and Cat 35, SF57), an incomplete iron knife blade (Cat 4, SF40), iron rod fragments (Cat 34, SF45), a probable iron nail head (Cat 16, SF48), a possible iron pot hanger found close to the hearth (Cat 10, SF59), an iron fitting or mount (Cat 17, SF64), a barb-spring padlock (Cat 9, SF67), parts of an iron pin (Cat 24, SF73), part of an iron hook tipped tool (Cat 6, SF43), four fragments of quartz (Cat30/SF46, Cat31/SF47, Cat 32/SF50 and Cat 38/SF80), a faceted stone smoother (SF39), a small quartz pebble with polished face (SF41), a plain hammerstone (SF49), a jasper pebble (SF70), a whetstone (SF76), roughly half of one small slag cake (SF35) and two other intact slag cakes (SF75), a small piece of fired clay or daub (Cat 6, SF27) and a spindle whorl with incised markings (SF33).

The floor of the building at the eastern and lower end of the trench (C206) had been sunk up to 0.3 m into the subsoil, within which was placed a deposit of boulders, cobbles and pebbles (C157) in a sandy silt matrix containing occasional patches of charcoal and scorched

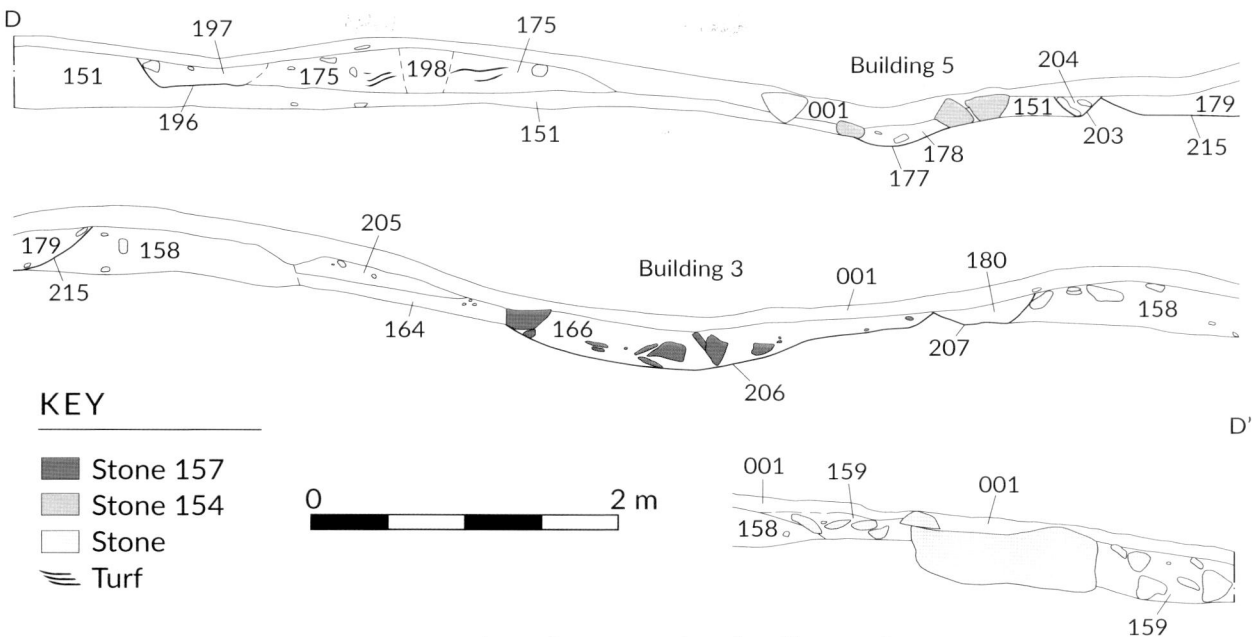

Figure 2.15 South-west facing section through Buildings 3 and 5.

earth (C166; Figures 2.13 and 2.14). The stones appeared to be randomly deposited except for the upper surface stones where some degree of placement had taken place to create a more level surface. The southern side was clearly defined by a line of stones. This deposit likely represents the deliberate infilling of at least part of the sunken end of the interior, thus creating a more level floor, whilst also acting as a drain/sump. Bones from an immature sheep (SF65 and 66), two pieces of flint (Cat 35, SF72 and Cat37, SF79), a fragment of a rotary quern (SF56) and a stone anvil (SF81) had been incorporated into C166 (see Chapter 3).

Beneath the shallower western end of this stone infill lay a concentration of 29 shallow stake-holes (Figure 2.13), which were visible only in the surface of the natural substrate. They were relatively shallow in depth, being only up to 0.1 m deep, and only present in the centre of the building near the edge of the stone infill layer. They are likely to represent some form of internal division, but they were not sufficiently deep to support a free-standing partition, unless they had also been driven through the stone infill (C166).

Immediately to the north of the edge of the stone infill a very distinct layer of burning (C164; Figure 2.15) extended up to and appeared to lie against the turf bank defining the northern wall of the building (C158); the bank at this point retained a steep internal profile which would likely have corresponded to the position of the inner face of the wall. This deposit possibly contained burnt turf layers. The charcoal analysed from a sample of this layer was mixed but the vast majority was of *Corylus* (hazel) possibly derived from an internal hurdle panel, either forming a partition or perhaps lining the wall. The burning was sealed by a shallow layer very similar to that which formed the bank of the wall, and probably collapsed material from its superstructure.

Roughly at the centre of the western end of the building was a stone-lined hearth (C282) oriented with the axis of the interior. Large stones (C235) had been set within a relatively shallow oval cut (Figure 2.16), including one at the north-western corner which was flat-topped and sat proud of the others and the floor surface (C162; Figures 2.13 and 2.14), and would have been suited to resting cooking utensils or similar. The material within the hearth (C248) was rich in *Betula* (birch) charcoal (Section 2.7, Table 2.8) and burnt bone, while it also contained a small amount of fire-cracked stone and a probable iron poker tip (Cat 7, SF60). This hearth material was sealed by shallow silty sand (C236) formed after the hearth had gone out of use. Frequent fine roots from this layer had also penetrated the upper layers of C248. The area around the hearth was the only part of Building 3 where an upper subsoil layer was present (C284), comparable to C4 found in Buildings 1 and 2. The occupation layer C162 lay directly onto C284.

Running down the centre of Building 3 was a series of three post-holes (C169, C218 and C295; Figure 2.13). The easternmost, C169, which was cut into the base of the sunken area beneath the stone infill (Figure 2.17), and C295 at the western end of the building, had nearly vertical sides down to a flat base and were 0.15 m and 0.3 m deep respectively. No trace of the post in C169 was detected in the stone infill layer above it, though whether this was just lost in the coarse aggregate of the fill, or the post-hole belonged to an earlier phase of the structure is not known. The shallow depth of this post-hole could be taken as evidence of either, but this

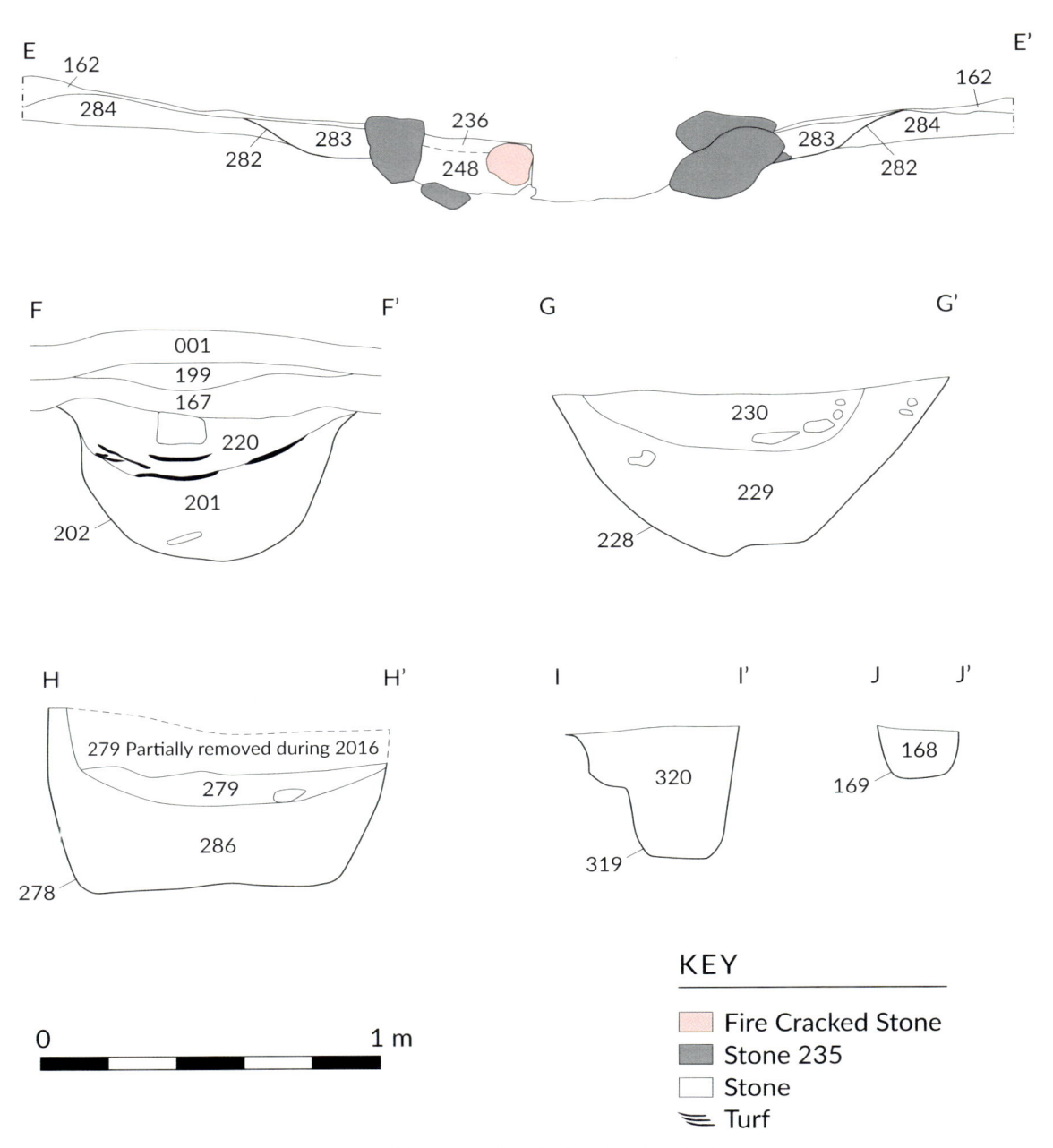

Figure 2.16 Building 3: hearth and selected pit/post-hole sections.

feature is perhaps better accounted for by the erosion of this end of the interior in its earlier phase of use. A slightly smaller post-hole (C172), also with near vertical sides but with its base tapering to a point, suggesting a driven post, lay just to the north-west of the third axial post-hole, the larger C218, which had been partially disturbed by burrowing.

No packing stones or post-pipes were observed in the relatively homogenous fills of any of these post-holes, suggesting that the posts themselves had been removed. The fills, which contained occasional charcoal flecks, presumably comprised the earth used as original packing material mixed with later material introduced when the post was removed, both of which have been subsequently subject to bioturbation. Given their position down the long axis of Building 3, like the stake-holes to the east of the hearth, it is tempting to conclude that they relate to internal divisions within the building or upright posts for roof support. However, it is also feasible that they relate to earlier activity on the site and that they have been truncated by Building 3. These options are further discussed in Section 4.6.

Three stake-holes and another small post-hole (C290) lay at the west end of the interior south of C295, while a larger stake-hole lay beneath the southern side of the hearth stones (C235), all providing further indications that internal structures or divisions of space could have been present in this area of the building.

Figure 2.17 Building 3: post-hole C169 during excavation at base of stone infill C157/C166 in 2016.

In addition to the stakes and post-holes two irregularly-shaped shallow pits (C313 and C315) were found just north-east of the hearth. These were distinct from other cut features in that their fills contained frequent inclusions of charcoal and metal-working residues. For example, pit C313 held a slag cake fragment, iron slag, a probable slag attached to a piece of hearth-lining (all SF84) and hammerscale. This indicates that the pit may be a disturbed metal-working hearth or that material from a metal-working hearth had been dumped within the feature. Either way, it perhaps represents small-scale metal-working within Building 3. Given the lack of truncation evident in this area, it is perhaps unlikely that the two features were originally parts of the same pit.

The gap in the bank identified before excavation as the entrance was uncovered in the south-eastern part of the trench, where there was also clear evidence of structural alterations. One of the clearest features of the entrance was a series of large flat stone slabs (C328; Figures 2.13 and 2.18) leading through the gap and forming steps down into the sunken area of the building. There the slabs appeared to turn to the south-west beside the line of stones marking the edge of stone infill deposit (C157 above), creating a pathway towards the hearth.

Immediately west of these stone steps, corresponding to an area where the bank was lower than around the remainder of the building, was a dense concentration of small boulders and cobbles (C326) covering an area approximately 1.2 m by 1 m. This deposit extended from the end of the higher part of the bank (C158), on the south-west of the entrance, to the edge of the paving stones forming the steps (C328) and seemed to represent a small stone foundation for a short section of turf and earth wall. The presence of a thin compacted layer of pebbles and small cobbles beneath this foundation, coupled with several distinct flat paving slabs immediately to the south and post-holes framing the gap on the inside (below), indicate that this may have been an earlier entrance, subsequently blocked off and moved slightly to the east when the stone steps were inserted. On the southern edge of the small stone foundation (C326), within the area of flat slabs, lay an unusual rotary grinder (SF86) with an offset hole (Chapter 3: Figure 3.4). The stratigraphic relationship between these entrances, however, was not clear, other than that some of the foundation (C326) partly overlay one of the steps, but this relationship could easily be the result of post-occupation disturbance and degradation. While it is therefore possible that there were two contemporary entrances, one leading into the living area and the other into the raised stone floor area, this is considered unlikely. The location of these entrances and the adjacent end of the bank are among the few instances at Lair where the original position of the turf and earth wall can be placed with some certainty. The main mass of bank material here also lies inside this projected line, probably indicating that the bulk of the wall collapsed inwards.

Immediately within the blocked entrance and west of the secondary stone steps lay three large post-holes (C317, C319 and C321). They were all sub-circular in

Figure 2.18 Building 3: entrances showing stone slab steps leading into the sunken part of the building (foreground) and the three large post-holes (C317, C319 and C321) behind in 2017 (large scales = 1 m).

plan, measuring between 0.4 m and 0.5 m in diameter. Two, C319 and C321, framed the earlier gap and had near vertical sides and flat bases. Some 0.4 m and 0.3 m deep respectively, the upper part of C319 also expanded on its northern side, potentially the result of either inserting or removing the large post. The third and westernmost of the three (C317) had slightly less steep sides and a partially rounded base. It was also the shallowest, being no more than 0.26 m in depth. No packing stones or post-pipes were present. All three held similar homogenous fills containing frequent concentrations of charcoal flecks and occasional burnt bone. Located immediately inside the wall line, these substantial posts are likely to have been structural and to relate to one or both of the entrances.

A small trench excavated over the eastern end of Building 3 and the adjacent Building 4 (Figure 2.12: Trench 24) revealed two cut features beneath the remains of the turf, earth and stone walls; on the surface at least, the bulk of the wall material appeared to relate to Building 3. The edge of the sunken part of the interior of Building 3 was identified and here it was 0.15 m deep (C183; Figure 2.19). A short distance to the east, beneath the highest part of the bank, a linear gully (C185) was uncovered; aligned north and south, this continued beyond both sides of the trench. It showed similarities in both size and location to that uncovered at the north-western end of Building 2. Another possible gully feature (C187) was visible in section above C185, although it was very indistinct and not visible in plan. The function of these gullies remains unclear.

Building 3: the annexe

The presence of roughly semi-circular annexes at their broader ends is a recognised characteristic of Pitcarmick buildings (RCAHMS 1990; Section 4.6). The annexe off the south-western end of Building 3 is significant for being the first to be excavated. The bank of this feature was not as pronounced as that of the adjacent building and was not continuous, and a gap was present on its eastern side. Its interior measured roughly 6.5 m east-to-west by 4.25 m transversely. Excavation showed no sign of a turf bank on its northern side indicating as was apparent on the surface, that it was built onto the side of Building 3. A large boulder set at the base of the wall of Building 3 may have served to strengthen it, though it is unclear whether it had been moved here or was *in situ*. Where present the bank defining the annexe was of similar make-up to those elsewhere, suggesting turf and earth walls, but it was much lower than those found in Buildings 1, 2 and 3, indicating that the walls were either less substantial or had slumped more widely; the slope dropping away to the south may have increased the external slumping of the bank.

2. Results of Archaeological Fieldwork, Radiocarbon Dating, Peat-Stratigraphic and Pollen Analyses

Figure 2.19 Building 3/4: gully and sunken floor in 2016 (horizontal scale = 1 m).

At the terminal of the bank on the south side of the gap there were two inter-cutting pits (C227 and C223; Figure 2.13). The smaller (C227) was possibly a shallow post-hole, having very steep sides. C223 was larger and held a flat-topped stone that was the same size as the pit beneath and was level with the floor surface of the annexe (C167, see below): it may have functioned as a post pad.

Spread over the interior of the annexe immediately below the topsoil and above the natural substrate (C22) lay a mixed deposit containing charcoal flecks and burnt bone fragments (C167). Up to 0.15 m in depth, this represented an occupation layer within the structure. Small corroded iron sheet fragments (Cat 32, SF34), a small broken whetstone (SF54) and an anvil/whetstone (SF58) were recovered from this material (see Chapter 3).

Once internal deposit (C167) and any collapsed wall material had been removed, a series of negative features of varying character were visible cut into the natural substrate. Four were large oval pits (C202, C228, C231 and C278) which occupied much of the interior (Figure 2.20). They were all relatively steep-sided, varied in maximum diameter between 0.7 m and 1.2 m, and were generally 0.5 m deep, although C231 was slightly shallower and C202 slightly deeper. All except pit C278 (below) held relatively sterile upper and lower fills, although some charcoal lenses were visible in the upper fill of C228, which also contained hammerscale, and several large cobbles were present at the base of C231. A striking difference in the central pit (C202) were distinct turf lenses separating the upper and lower fills (Figure 2.16), which seemed to indicate the lower fill (C201) had been capped by turves. The upper fill (C220) had then been placed over the turves and capped by a large stone. At some time, the lower fill (C201) and the turf capping had subsided, suggesting the fill was not compacted when placed within the pit. The occupation layer (C167) overlay the pit, but the subsidence was also detectable in its upper surface, where a shallow depression had formed; the fill of this depression comprised a series of very narrow alternating lenses of lighter sands and darker silts (C199), which became clearer after a period of weathering. They may represent a series of thin turves placed in the small hollow. A small pit (C272) extended away from the south-eastern edge of C202, but both contained very similar fills and the relationship between them was not clear.

The westernmost pit (C278) had been cut into the northern side of a large tree bowl (Figure 2.13) and, as seen in the three other large pits, held two fills. The homogenous silty sand primary fill contained a small iron pin (Cat 24, SF63), what appears to be part of an iron fitting represented by a broken narrow strip of iron with four fine holes (Cat 19, SF68) and occasional fragments of bone. The upper fill was similar in composition, but mottled, with a distinctly darker colour, particularly around the edges; this staining was probably either derived from the animal bones found in abundance within this layer, or to organic material associated with them. The bones represented at least three immature or adult cattle, one neonatal calf and a pig (SF83: Section 3.9). Three large flat stones had been placed on the surface of the pit on its northern side.

Three smaller pits (C246, C249 and C280) and two stake-holes were also present, seemingly disposed at random, while a very shallow linear feature (C242) extended away from the south-eastern side of pit C202. It ran broadly eastwards before turning slightly to the south and exiting the trench, and its shallow and uneven profile indicated wear or erosion rather than a cut feature. Little can be gleaned from the linear feature being stratigraphically under the bank material as this could have been the result of collapse and slumping of the bank.

Figure 2.20 Building 3 annexe during excavation in 2016.

To the north of the post-hole/post pad (C223 and C227), at the terminal of the bank, was another hollow up to 0.15m deep (not on plan). Its full extent was not revealed but it continued to the east toward the area thought to be the entrance. It held a very dark deposit containing occasional darker lenses and lighter patches (C241), and gradually increased in depth to the east. The dark lenses appeared to be the remains of turf layers, while the lighter patches could represent redeposited natural substrate or scorched earth. A portion of a large circular rotary grinder (SF55) was recovered from C241.

The presence of these substantial pits contrasts strongly with the interior of Building 3. Together with the smaller volumes of material culture from the annexe and the absence of a hearth or other evidence of burning, this suggests the structure was not lived in. It may have been some form of workshop or processing area related to activities not requiring heat. This is discussed further in Section 4.6.

Building 3: the external platform

Immediately south of the entrance to Building 3 and south-east of the annexe, Trench 21 (Figure 2.13) exposed a dense deposit of cobbles and boulders (C159), which suggests that the level platform visible in front of Building 3 prior to excavation was at least partly artificial. Some of the stones, particularly around the southern edge of the platform, may have been the result of field clearance. Near the entrance to Building 3, where the deposit extended around a very large boulder, it contained more organic material, possibly the remains of turf.

Building 4

Very small trial trenches were placed over Building 4, one at each end (Trench 24 and 25, Figure 2.12), the western at the intersection with Building 3. As with others at Lair, Building 4 was defined by a low heather-covered bank. It measured some 17 m in length and up to 5 m in width (measured from the top of the bank). At the western end, the bank forming the northern side of the building was all but absent, while the southern side was very indistinct although appeared to extend to the edge of Building 3. The trench at this end was designed to test the relationship with Building 3 and to establish whether Building 4 was an addition to Building 3 rather than a stand-alone structure. Near the area where the northern bank disappeared the interior of Building 4 appeared slightly sunken and the banks to either side became more substantial (Figure 2.12).

As we have already seen, although material relating to a collapsed earth and turf wall was uncovered at the western end of the building (C189), there was no clear indication as to whether this related to Building

3, Building 4, or both. The absence of any clear bank relating to Building 4, however, suggests it originated mainly from the wall of Building 3. Beneath this lay the linear feature (C222) already described, which was up to 0.85 m in width but only 0.1 m in depth, and filled by collapsed turf and earth wall material. Interpretation within the confines of such a small trench can only be limited, but it is likely to relate either to the interior of Building 4 or the exterior of Building 3.

At the eastern end of Building 4, beneath the bank material, a linear concentration of irregularly-shaped, but relatively flat, cobbles (C221) ran approximately north-to-south across the western half of the trench. Although disturbed, they formed up to three courses in height and one in width. Again, the limited extent to which they were revealed makes interpretation difficult, but they may relate to the inner face of the wall, being either stone edging or collapse from within its lower courses.

Building 5

On the surface, Building 5 was similar to other buildings at Lair. It had a wall reduced to a low grass- and heather-grown bank enclosing the sunken eastern end of the interior, but the western end (as seen in Building 4) was by comparison poorly defined, marked out by little more than a shallow scoop, giving a maximum length of 23 m by up to 5 m in breadth (measured from the top of the bank). Like its neighbour on the south, Building 3, the interior appears to curve southwards towards the east end.

Although the surface earthworks suggested that Building 5 had a separate wall adjoining Building 3, excavation of a section across both buildings gave no clear indication that this was the case (Figure 2.15), only that the combined banks (C158) were spread wider here than elsewhere. On the northern side of the building the lower section of the wall appeared relatively well preserved and was the only place within any of the trenches at Lair where a section of the original wall appeared to survive *in situ*. Distinct turf lenses formed the outer and inner skins (C175; Figure 2.15) of an earthen cored (C198) wall 1 m thick, all of which sat atop the natural substrate. This chance preservation provides evidence of the original form that the lower parts of most turf and earth walls at Lair are likely to have taken before they degraded to the homogenous deposits found in other trenches.

Reflecting what was seen in Building 3 (C207 and C215, see above), a shallow feature (C196; Figures 2.13 and 2.15) had been cut into the outer edge of the north bank of Building 5, though it was visible only in section. In size it was closer to C207 cut into the southern bank of Building 3 than the larger C215, though the section through the latter also showed that another smaller gully (C203) had been cut into its northern side. C196 did not contain the turf lenses seen in C207 and C215, but it is perhaps too much of a coincidence to believe that three similar features found cutting into the northern sides of the banks of two adjacent buildings are not in some way related. The chronological separation between the gullies and the banks of Building 3 was uncertain (above), but in the case of C196, the preservation of the structure of the original wall conclusively demonstrates that the gully was cut into the tail of the bank that had formed after the wall's collapse. If these three gullies are all related, they probably belong to a single phase of activity that took place long after the buildings had gone out of use and represent the remains of cultivation furrows utilising the existing banks as a form of rig.

The interior of Building 5 showed no clear sign of an occupation deposit, and the floor comprised the surface of the natural substrate (C151). It had been slightly sunken in the centre to create an axial channel (C177), which was sporadically defined on its outer edges by irregular cobbles (C154; Figure 2.15) and filled with clay (C178). While the full extent of this feature was not uncovered, it could represent a roughly built central drain. Part of an iron tack or possible horseshoe nail (Cat 15, SF28) was recovered from the fill. Given both Buildings 3 and 5 were broadly the same size and contained similar sunken areas across the central portion and eastern ends, it could be suggested that, as with Building 3, the main human activity in Building 5 was at the western end. If this was the case it seems plausible that Buildings 3 and 5 were similar in their spatial layouts.

Excavation at the eastern end of Building 5 (Trench 26) uncovered a small post-hole in the interior, covered by the collapsed turf and earth wall. Small concentrations of stones within the bank indicated the walls had a slight stone element. Trenches 28 and 29 at the western end were positioned to investigate areas where the bank was less pronounced or almost absent, but neither was fully excavated. Trench 28 confirmed the presence of a collapsed turf and earth wall containing some stone (C274), and identified a possible shallow turf layer (C275) on top of the outer margin of the bank. Trench 29 did not proceed beyond the removal of the topsoil.

Building 6 and enclosures

The southernmost building investigated during the project was Building 6, which lay a little over 100 m south-south-east and slightly downslope from the ring-cairn. On the surface it appeared small and rectangular, measuring roughly 8 m by 4 m overall, and appeared to have been constructed over a larger building, although no direct evidence of this was found during excavation. At least one associated enclosure was present, while an additional enclosure lay a short distance to the south-east (Figure 2.1). Both the building and the enclosures were defined by low heather-grown banks, but in the case of the building some stones protruding through the surface in the interior.

Trench 15 across the north side of Building 6 revealed a relatively distinct concentration of cobbles and small boulders (C96) beneath a thin layer of heather and topsoil. These stones and the soil matrix around them (C95) corresponded to the bank visible on the surface and represented the remains of the wall. The wall was not well defined, either in plan or section (Figure 2.21), although in places up to two courses of stone were visible. The apparently random positioning of the stones may have resulted from the collapse of a well-constructed turf and stone wall or, perhaps more likely, it was never anything more than a rough foundation. In either case it is unlikely that the surviving portion was more than a footing a few courses in height, although it could have supported a higher wall of turf or turf and stone above. The soil matrix (C95) within and slightly outside the wall may have derived from such a superstructure.

The natural substrate under the wall was itself very stony in places and may have included shattered natural bedrock. Cut into the substrate immediately outside the wall were two shallow linear gullies. The better preserved and probably the later (C121) appears to represent a shallow drainage ditch or drip gully relating to the building. Its fill (C122) contained a single body sherd from a splash-glazed jug in Scottish Redware fabric (Cat 4, SF22) likely to date from the 13th to 15th centuries AD (Hall: Section 3.7). This gully in turn cut the corner of what may have been an earlier gully (C123), located closer to the wall of the building, though this was poorly preserved and visible only in the east-facing section. It contained the slumped material originating from wall C95 suggesting it had been open when the wall collapsed.

The interior of Building 6 was covered in numerous cobbles and small boulders, which lay on and partially within C95. They were also visible protruding through the ground surface of most of the internal area. The uneven nature of the internal surface did not indicate a level floor surface was present, but too little was examined to be sure whether this building was the remains of a bothy, a byre or simply a barn. In addition some of the stones may have been placed within the structure after it had gone out of use, possibly as a result of field clearance.

Trenches 16 and 17 investigated the adjacent enclosures, where in some sectors the banks were clearly defined, but in others less so. In both trenches (Trench 16 being over the western enclosure and 17 over the eastern) the bank material generally consisted of a single homogenous deposit of light brown sandy silt with only occasional stones present; this lay directly on the natural substrate. No associated ditches were found. In Trench 16 this material was up to 0.35 m in depth and was spread to 4.1 m, while in Trench 17 it was of similar depth but had slumped beyond the extent of the 4 m long trench. Although excavation was limited, it appears the enclosure's walls were constructed in earth and turf in a similar manner to those of Buildings 1-5. Any evidence of the inner and outer skins of turf had been lost through slumping and decomposition.

Building 7 and enclosure

Building 7 was the easternmost investigated at Lair, lying adjacent to the track some 140 m south-east from the ring-cairn and 15 m downslope of Buildings 1-5. On the surface it was one of the clearest buildings at Lair, measuring some 15.5 m in overall length by up to 4.5 m in width (measured from the top of the bank), with partly stone faced grass- and heather-grown banks forming the slightly bowed sides and rounded ends. Its morphology and size presented similarities to the group excavated to the north-west, as did the less distinct Building 8 located just to the east (Figure 2.1). An enclosure bank to the south appeared to be related to the buildings, truncated at its northern end by the modern track. RCAHMS survey (1990: 151; ID29498; Section 1.9) noted a third, even less distinct building attached to the enclosure. Traces of this building were not observed in the 2012-2017 fieldwork but were recorded during the subsequent mapping programme undertaken in 2018 (Section 1.8; Figure 1.16).

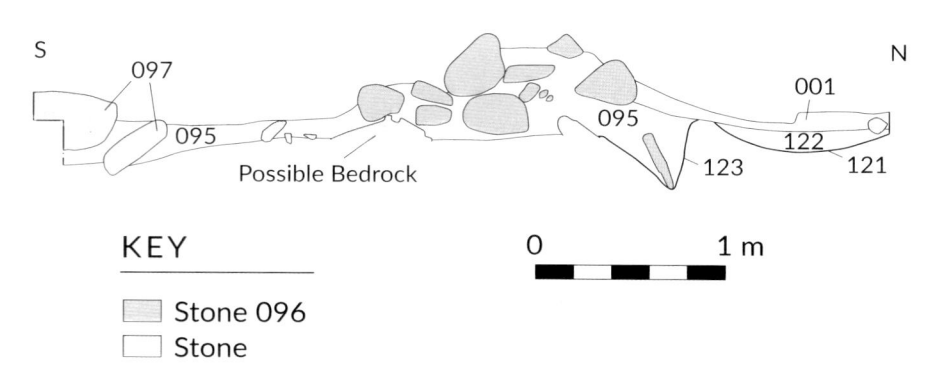

Figure 2.21: Building 6: east-facing section.

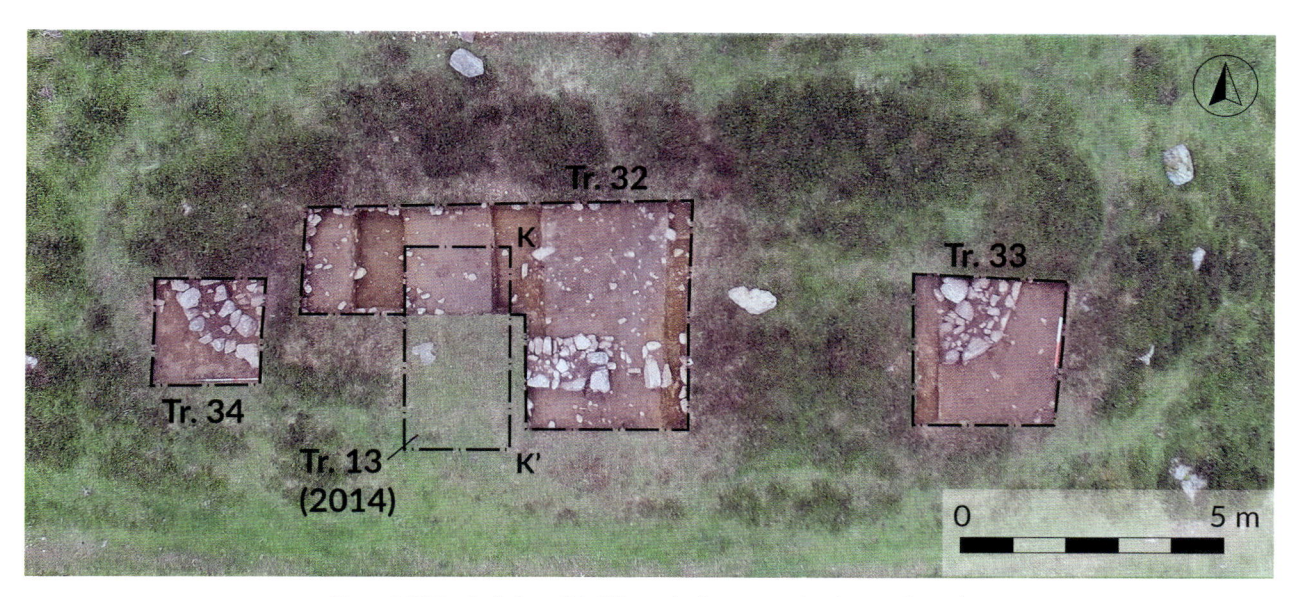

2. Results of Archaeological Fieldwork, Radiocarbon Dating, Peat-Stratigraphic and Pollen Analyses

Figure 2.22 Vertical view of Building 7 during excavation (K. Ward: 2017).

Figure 2.23 Building 7: wall within evaluation trench and earthwork in 2014 (scales = 1 m).

Trenches were opened to cover virtually all the western end of the interior and smaller sections of the wall at each end (Figure 2.22). In contrast to Buildings 1-5, the banks defining Building 7 held a well-preserved low stone wall or footing that consisted of outer and inner skins of stone with an earth and stone core (C104; Figure 2.23). It generally stood to between one and two courses and was of variable thickness, ranging between 0.6 m and 1 m. The thickest point lay adjacent the entrance, which was 0.7 m wide and roughly in the centre of the southern side. The entrance was defined on the exterior by two large boulders, but there was no stone threshold. At the curving western (Figure 2.24) and eastern ends of the building the wall was of similar construction. At the eastern end, however, in Trench 33, the wall thinned southwards to between 0.6 m and

Figure 2.24 Building 7: curved wall at the western end in 2017 (scales = 1 m).

0.7 m where it disappeared into the baulk at the edge of the trench. This narrower section was also constructed of smaller stones and may represent a robbed/damaged area, a section of repair, or possibly a blocked entrance; the correct explanation can only be established with more extensive excavations.

To either side of the footing, though mainly to the exterior and more sporadically on the interior, was a darker deposit containing cobbles and clear turf lenses (C103). This was the remains of the collapsed turf and stone superstructure that had been raised upon the footing. Sections of this collapse, particularly in the interior, were lighter in colour and devoid of turf lenses (C105), and may have incorporated other material gradually accumulating after the building had gone out of use.

Beneath parts of the stone wall (C103) in both the central and eastern trenches there were indications that the stone footing had been constructed on top of an earlier turf and earth structure. This was seen in a layer containing differentially preserved turf lenses and, in some locations, a small bank of earth and stone (C125). A sample retrieved from C125 produced a ^{14}C date of AD 770-970 (SUERC-57553: Section 2.5), providing a *TPQ* not only for the construction of the stone footing, but also the possible structure underneath.

Outside the wall along the southern side and the eastern end there was a small gully (C147; Figure 2.25). This had been partly filled by the collapsed upper wall (C103), and is probably a contemporary drainage channel or drip gully running around the edges of the building.

The floor within the interior was formed by the top of a nearly sterile natural deposit similar to C4 uncovered beneath Buildings 1 and 2, which also extended beneath the walls; it contained occasional charcoal flecks in its upper parts (C106). The area of the interior examined was devoid of archaeological features, other than a thin trampled layer of compacted darker material that extended through the entrance and spread both east and west across the floor. This deposit could have formed during use of the building, but equally may have been formed by the subsequent traffic of sheep and cattle through the entrance after it had gone out of use.

The bank of the enclosure to the south of Buildings 7 and 8 was only faintly visible on the surface, where it formed a curving 'L' shape in plan. Where examined in section on the south-eastern side it formed a homogenous deposit of earth and stone which had slumped up to 6 m in width and was, at its deepest, only 0.25 m. The stones lying in the bank material displayed

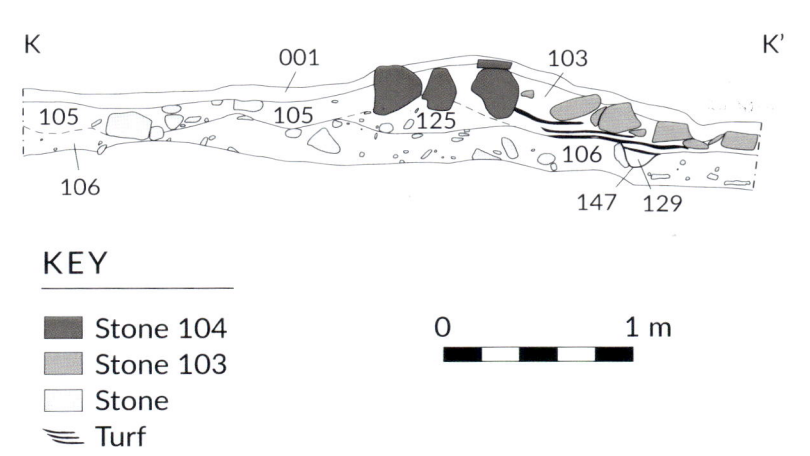

Figure 2.25 The west facing section through the wall of Building 7.

no evidence of its structure, though this can be no more than expected given the degree of slumping. It seems the bank was primarily constructed of turf, earth and some stones and, as with the other examples excavated, no corresponding ditch was found, the bank material lying directly on top of sterile natural substrate.

Structure 4, cairns and other structures

In addition to the buildings investigated at Lair, a series of other features visible on the surface were partly excavated, primarily in the area between Buildings 1-5 and Building 7 (Figure 2.1). Most of them lay in a naturally sheltered and more level area of the hillside.

Situated roughly in the middle of the flatter part of the sheltered area was a small circular structure measuring roughly 6 m diameter and defined by a band of cobbles and boulders only one course high and no more than two courses wide (Structure 4: Figures 2.1 and 2.26). A trench opened over the eastern quadrant showed that the band of stones lay directly on top of the natural substrate, while its slightly raised interior was composed of similar material (C39), but containing occasional flecks of charcoal. Three small pieces of iron slag (SF12) and a possible iron tanged awl (Cat 5, SF13) were recovered from just below the surface of C39 within the structure.

The function of this structure remains unclear. There was no indication that it was used for habitation. It is more likely to have been related to agricultural or craft activities. The single radiocarbon date of AD 660-780 (SUERC-49676, Table 2.1) obtained from a charcoal sample from within the structure has no secure context and merely documents the general period of early medieval activity in the vicinity.

The area around Structure 4 was littered with numerous small mounds which were shown to be small cairns. Assuming that other, unexcavated mounds in this area are similar, they form part of a small cairn-field and are probably the result of field clearance. All the cairns were of similar size, measuring between 3 m and 4 m across. None were strictly circular on plan, most presenting irregular oval shapes, while one uncovered immediately east of Structure 4 had a distinct straight edge on one side (Figure 2.26). All were composed of angular and sub-angular cobbles which sat within a matrix of earth and, where excavated, they

Figure 2.26 Structure 4 and nearby cairn in 2013 (scales = 1 m).

were between 0.15 m and 0.4 m high, lying directly on top of the natural substrate. No evidence of a former ground surface was visible beneath any of the cairns. A few fragments of slag (SF25) were recovered from immediately beneath a cairn north-east of Structure 4, but otherwise they were devoid of material culture.

A longer trench immediately east of Structure 4 and another 24 m to the south-east were positioned to investigate what appeared on the surface to be a linear level area running roughly north-west to south-east, with small sections of bank and alignments of stones appearing to define its edges. No archaeological deposits were found, which suggests that the linear platform was at least in part a natural feature. The banks were composed of material identical to the upper subsoil, and the apparent alignments of stones proved to have no real substance. The presence of tightly packed cobbles and boulders within the south-easternmost trench, and the small cairns identified within small trenches on top of the platform, suggest that the cultivators of the surrounding ground were aware of this feature, which in its turn may have influenced the way they cultivated the ground and disposed of unwanted stones. Thus an essentially natural feature has become emphasised by the deposition of field clearance.

Finally, five small test pits were opened over what may be traces of a building beneath the modern trackway (Building 14; Figure 2.1). Although subsequent remote sensing data indicated a building was present (Section 1.8; Figure 1.16) at the time of excavation nothing more than an unusual quantity of stones exposed by the track indicated archaeology may be present. No conclusive archaeological remains were uncovered here, but several arrangements of stones were noted which may have defined the line of a wall (as seen in Building 2) or been derived from a turf and earth wall. While the limited investigations proved inconclusive, they did not rule out the possibility that a building stood at this location.

2.4 Geo-archaeological analyses

Geo-archaeological analyses were planned at the inception of the project because of the interpretative potentials and challenges that the remains of turf or earth buildings present (Milek and Roberts 2013; Parkin and Adderley 2017). Multi-element mapping of contexts within excavated buildings was one approach proposed (Middleton 2004; Middleton and Price 1996), because, it has been argued, fine-scale spatial differences in key elements on floors can help to distinguish the functions of different areas of the interior. Similarly, fine-scaled enhanced magnetic susceptibility values on internal floors are thought to be one product of fires in buildings (Canti and Linford 2000), and simple measures of optically stimulated luminescence (portable OSL: Sanderson and Murphy 2010) have been used to verify the stratigraphic integrity and relative ages of sediment accumulations (e.g. Kinnaird *et al.* 2017). These plans did not bear fruit.

Soil-micromorphological analyses were also proposed to reconstruct patterns of activity within buildings and the functions of separate rooms or spaces (e.g. Simpson and Adderley 2011), and because it has recently been used to try to distinguish seasonal from all-year occupation in turf buildings (Kupiec *et al.* 2016). Samples have been taken, and results will form part of Vanessa Rees' PhD thesis, supervised by Karen Milek at the University of Durham.

2.5 Radiocarbon dating

Anthony Krus and Derek Hamilton

Thirty-one ^{14}C measurements from archaeological contexts are available from the settlement at Lair. Single-entity samples (Ashmore 1999) of wood charcoal, charred nutshell, and charred grain were submitted to the Scottish Universities Environmental Research Centre (SUERC) Radiocarbon Dating Laboratory. The samples were pre-treated following the protocols described in Dunbar *et al.* (2016). Graphite targets were prepared and measured following Naysmith *et al.* (2010). SUERC maintains rigorous internal quality assurance procedures and participation in international inter-comparisons (Scott 2003; Scott *et al.* 2003, 2007; Scott *et al.* 2010) indicates no laboratory offsets, thus validating the measurement precision quoted for the radiocarbon ages.

Conventional radiocarbon ages (Stuiver and Polach 1977) are presented in Table 2.1, where they are quoted in accordance with the Trondheim convention (Stuiver and Kra 1986). Calibrated date ranges were calculated using the terrestrial calibration curve (IntCal13) of Reimer *et al.* (2013) and OxCal v4.3 (Bronk Ramsey 2017). The date ranges in Table 2.1 have been calculated using the maximum intercept method (Stuiver and Reimer 1986) and quoted with the endpoints rounded outward to 10 years. The probabilities shown in Figure 2.27 were calculated using the probability method of Stuiver and Reimer (1993).

Bayesian modelling methodological approach

A Bayesian approach has been applied to the interpretation of the chronology (Buck *et al.* 1996). Although simple calibrated dates are accurate estimates of the age of samples, this is not usually what archaeologists really wish to know. It is the dates of the archaeological events represented by those samples that are of interest. In this case, for example, it is the

2. Results of Archaeological Fieldwork, Radiocarbon Dating, Peat-Stratigraphic and Pollen Analyses

timing of the activity associated with the construction and use of the buildings, rather than the dates of individual samples. The chronology of this activity can be estimated not only by using the absolute dating derived from the radiocarbon measurements, but also by using the stratigraphic relationships between samples and the relative dating information provided by the archaeological phasing.

Methodology is now available which allows the combination of these different types of information explicitly, to produce realistic estimates of the dates of archaeological interest. It should be emphasised that the posterior density estimates produced by this modelling are not absolute. They are interpretative estimates, which can and will change as further data become available and as other researchers choose to model the existing data from different perspectives. The technique used is a form of Markov Chain Monte Carlo sampling and has been applied using the program OxCal v4.3 (http://c14.arch.ox.ac.uk/). Details of the algorithms employed by this program are available in Bronk Ramsey (1995, 1998, 2001, 2009a) or from the online manual. The algorithm used in the models can be derived from the OxCal keywords and bracket structure shown in Figures 2.27-2.29.

Samples and the models

Specific contexts were targeted for dating to assess activity related to the buildings and other structures, yielding 31 radiocarbon measurements. Bayesian chronological models were used to improve understanding of the precise timing and duration of this activity. Multiple radiocarbon measurements used to date the same archaeological contexts were subjected to chi-square tests to further assess their consistency (Ward and Wilson 1978). Figure 2.27 presents a graphical summary of the calibrated dates. In most instances, the younger of the two measurements used to date a single context is interpreted as the best date, because it is usually more likely that the older date is a residual or offset sample.

Building 1

Building 1 presents an important example of interpreting the radiocarbon dating in light of the archaeological evidence and taphonomic interpretations. In the models presented here, the samples from the pits, post-holes and in and under the turf walls are assumed to date the activity associated with the upstanding feature. However, the lack of a developed occupation surface might suggest an alternative interpretation whereby the bulk of the dated material is derived from an earlier structure that is preserved by remains in pits and post-holes and the overlying soil that would form the turves used in the construction of the upstanding Building 1. The radiocarbon dating cannot be used to determine which of these scenarios is most likely, but the radiocarbon dates can be modelled in a way that enables dates to be extracted for the two possibilities.

Thus the construction of Building 1 appears to have been preceded by ground preparation including de-turfing of the general vicinity to create a solid surface. A linear wooden feature (C14) was originally thought to be a fence, or possibly wood gathered in a linear pile before burning, but it may also relate to a building earlier than Building 1 (above). Two samples of wood charcoal (*Betula* sp.) were submitted for dating from this feature, yielding two radiocarbon measurements (SUERC-42419 and SUERC-51328). It is not feasible that these two samples are the same age, as the measurements do not pass a chi-square test (T=35.2; df=1; T'(0.05)=5.8), suggesting that this context may have formed over a period of some longevity and/or that the dated samples may be residual or suffer from an appreciable old wood offset. The younger of the two radiocarbon measurements (SUERC-42419) provides the best estimate for the date (cal AD 670–880, 95% confidence) of this context (C14), because this measurement is probably the closest in time to the actual date of context formation.

Six additional contexts associated with Building 1 were sampled for dating. A sample of wood charcoal (*Pinus sylvestris*) from within a well-preserved section of turf wall (C21) was submitted for dating, yielding a radiocarbon measurement (SUERC-42420). This measurement is interpreted as a *TPQ* for the construction and use of Building 1, because the dated sample may have been deposited in the turf before construction of the building.

Two samples of wood charcoal (*Betula* sp. and *Alnus*) were submitted for dating from the fill (C20) of a pit/post-hole (C19) within Building 1, yielding two radiocarbon measurements (SUERC-42424 and SUERC-51329). It is not feasible that these two radiocarbon samples are the same age, as the measurements do not pass a chi-square test (T=5.4; df=1; T'(0.05)=3.8), suggesting that this context may have formed over a period of some longevity and/or that the dated samples may be residual or suffer from an appreciable old wood offset. The younger of the two radiocarbon measurements (SUERC-42424) provides the best estimate for the date (cal AD 660–780, 95% confidence) of this context (C20), because this measurement is probably the closest in time to the actual date of context formation.

Samples of charred grain (*Hordeum vulgare* v. *vulgare*) and wood charcoal (*Alnus*) were submitted for dating from the fill (C68) of a post-hole (C67) from within Building 1,

Table 2.1 Radiocarbon data.

Lab ID	Context Description	Material	$\delta^{13}C$ (‰)	Radiocarbon Age (BP)	Calibrated Date (95% confidence)
SUERC-42419	Building 1 (Tr 1): Base (C14) of linear feature.	Wood charcoal (*Betula* sp.)	1247 ± 29	−26.1	AD 670–880
SUERC-51328	Building 1 (Tr 1): Base (C14) of linear feature.	Wood charcoal (*Betula* sp.)	1503 ± 32	−25.2	AD 430–640
SUERC-42420	Building 1 (Tr 1): Well-preserved turf wall, Slot 3 (C21).	Wood charcoal (*Pinus sylvestris*)	1464 ± 29	−25.7	AD 540–650
SUERC-42424	Building 1 (Tr 1): Fill (C20) of pit C19.	Wood charcoal (*Betula* sp.)	1269 ± 29	−25.6	AD 660–780
SUERC-51329	Building 1 (Tr 1): Fill (C20) of pit C19.	Wood charcoal (*Alnus* sp.)	1369 ± 32	−26.9	AD 620–690
SUERC-51333	Building 1 (Tr 10): Thin charcoal-rich deposit (C56) beneath turf bank C55.	Roundwood charcoal (*Corylus*)	1522 ± 32	−25.5	AD 420–610
SUERC-49666	Building 1 (Tr 10): Thin charcoal-rich deposit (C56) beneath turf bank C55.	Wood charcoal (*Betula* sp.)	1104 ± 29	−26.8	AD 880–1020
SUERC-51334	Building 1 (Tr 10): Fill (C68) of post-hole C67.	Charred grain (*Hordeum vulgare* v. *vulgare*)	1312 ± 32	−23.8	AD 650–770
SUERC-49667	Building 1 (Tr 9): Fill (C63) of post-hole C64.	Wood charcoal (*Betula* sp.)	1353 ± 29	−26.7	AD 640–690
SUERC-49671	Building 1 (Tr 10): Fill (C68) of post-hole C67.	Wood charcoal (*Alnus*)	1311 ± 29	−26.2	AD 650–770
SUERC-49672	Building 1 (Tr 10): Fill (C71) of partially excavated pit C70.	Wood charcoal (*Salix* sp.)	1246 ± 29	−27.2	AD 670–880
SUERC-51335	Building 1 (Tr 10): Fill (C79) of a possible small pit C78.	Wood charcoal (*Alnus*)	1366 ± 32	−27.5	AD 630–690
SUERC-51338	Building 2 (Tr 9): Fill (C92) of post-holes C91 and C93.	Wood charcoal (*Salix* sp.)	1305 ± 32	−27.2	AD 650–770
SUERC-51343	Building 2 (Tr 9): Fill (C90) of post-hole C89.	Roundwood charcoal (*Salix* sp.)	1315 ± 32	−27.7	AD 650–770
SUERC-51336	Building 2 (Tr 9): Fill (C82) of post-hole C81.	Wood charcoal (*Betula* sp.)	1211 ± 32	−26.9	AD 690–900
SUERC-49673	Building 2 (Tr 9): Fill (C82) of post-hole C81.	Wood charcoal (*Prunoideae*)	1165 ± 26	−25.6	AD 770–970
SUERC-51337	Building 2 (Tr 9): Fill (C84) of linear gully C83 below stone foundation.	Wood charcoal (*Alnus*)	1342 ± 32	−26.7	AD 640–770
SUERC-49674	Building 2 (Tr 9): Fill (C84) of linear gully C83 below stone foundation.	Wood charcoal (*Betula* sp.)	1353 ± 29	−25.4	AD 640–690
SUERC-51339	Building 2 (Tr 9): Fill (C86) of post-hole C85.	Wood charcoal (*Salix* sp.)	1337 ± 32	−26.4	AD 640–770
SUERC-49675	Building 2 (Tr 9): Fill (C86) of post-hole C85.	Wood charcoal (*Prunoideae*)	3764 ± 27	−26.3	2290–2050 BC
SUERC-57549	Building 2 (Tr 18): Basal fill (C128) of central hearth C148.	Nutshell (*Corylus*)	1180 ± 29	−23.2	AD 760–950
SUERC-57550	Building 2 (Tr 18): Basal fill (C128) of central hearth C148.	Roundwood charcoal (*Corylus*)	1124 ± 29	−27.0	AD 770–990
SUERC-57551	Building 2 (Tr 18): Basal fill (C128) of central hearth C148.	Nutshell (*Corylus*)	1143 ± 28	−25.0	AD 770–990
SUERC-65411	Building 3 (Tr 22): Fill (C168) of possible post-hole C169.	Wood charcoal (*Betula* sp.)	1166 ± 29	−25.9	AD 770–970
SUERC-65410	Building 3 (Tr 22): Large angular cobble filling (C166) within a wide central sunken area of the building.	Roundwood charcoal (*Corylus*)	1243 ± 29	−28.2	AD 670–880
SUERC-65406	Building 3 (Tr 22): Burned layer (C164).	Roundwood charcoal (*Corylus*)	1225 ± 29	−25.5	AD 680–890

Table 2.1 continued, Radiocarbon data.

Lab ID	Context Description	Material	$\delta^{13}C$ (‰)	Radiocarbon Age (BP)	Calibrated Date (95% confidence)
SUERC-74161	Building 3 (Tr 27): Fill (C248) of Hearth (C235).	Roundwood charcoal with bark (*Corylus*)	1195 ± 20	−26.8	AD 760–900
SUERC-74162	Building 3 (Tr 27): Fill (C248) of Hearth (C235).	Roundwood charcoal with bark (*Salix* sp.)	1208 ± 20	−27.5	AD 720–890
SUERC-79014	Building 3 (Tr 30): Upper fill (C279) of pit C278.	Articulated bone (*Bos* sp.)	1259 ± 20	−21.7	AD 670–780
SUERC-57553	Building 7 (Tr 13): Bank of material (C125) beneath the wall C104.	Wood charcoal (*Betula* sp.)	1166 ± 29	−26.9	AD 770–970
SUERC-49676	Structure 4 (Tr 4): Small patch of burnt material (C39) found along with slag SF12.	Wood charcoal (*Alnus*)	1287 ± 29	−28.3	AD 660–780
SUERC-57552	Base of cairn (C137)	Roundwood charcoal (*Corylus*)	1253 ± 29	−28.2	AD 670–870

yielding two radiocarbon measurements (SUERC-51334 and SUERC-49671). It is feasible that these two samples are the same age, as the measurements pass a chi-square test (T=0.0; df=1; T'(0.05)=3.8), suggesting that the samples were deposited over an extremely short-period of time. The radiocarbon measurements from both samples were the same (cal AD 650–770, 95% confidence) which estimates the date of this context. A sample of wood charcoal (*Betula* sp.) from the fill (C63) of a possible post-hole (C64) within Building 1 was also submitted for dating, yielding a radiocarbon measurement (SUERC-49667).

Two pits (C70 and C78) within Building 1 were sampled for dating. A sample of wood charcoal (*Salix* sp.) from the upper fill (C71) of pit (C70) was submitted for dating, yielding a radiocarbon measurement (SUERC-49672). Additionally, a sample of wood charcoal (*Alnus*) from the fill (C79) of a possible small pit (C78) was submitted for dating, yielding a radiocarbon measurement (SUERC-51335).

A thin charcoal-rich deposit (C56) lay under the Building 1 turf bank (C55). Samples of wood charcoal (*Betula* sp.) and roundwood charcoal (*Corylus*) were submitted for dating from this deposit (C56), yielding two radiocarbon measurements (SUERC-49666 and SUERC-51333). Both measurements from this deposit are interpreted as *TPQ* for the construction and use of Building 1, because it is unclear exactly how the deposit C56 relates to the construction, use, and collapse of the building. It is possible that C56 is related to the end of the burnt linear feature C14 which became spread and mixed with the bank material during construction of Building 1 (see above). Additionally, it is not feasible that these two radiocarbon samples are the same age, as the measurements do not pass a chi-square test (T=94.1; df=1; T'(0.05)=3.8), which could indicate this context either formed over a period of some longevity or that the earlier of the dated samples (SUERC-51333) may be residual.

Building 2

Building 2 is located between Building 1 and the ring-cairn, being adjacent to both. Beneath a possible stone foundation for Building 2 at the north-west end is a linear gully (C83). Two samples of wood charcoal (*Betula* sp. and *Alnus*) were submitted for dating from this feature C83, yielding two radiocarbon measurements (SUERC-49674 and SUERC-51337). The linear gully C83 was up to 0.5 m in width and 0.1 m to 0.15 m in depth. The purpose of the gully is unknown; however, being located beneath the possible stone foundation suggests it is related to the building, and most likely is indicative of activity that predates Building 2. Both measurements from this feature C83 are interpreted as *TPQ* for the construction and use of Building 2, because it is unclear if the feature predates the use of Building 2 or if it is functionally related to its use. It is feasible that these two samples are the same age, as the measurements pass a chi-square test (T=0.1; df=1; T'(0.05)=3.8), suggesting that the samples were deposited over an extremely short period of time.

A sample of roundwood charcoal (*Corylus*) and two samples of hazel (*Corylus*) nutshell were submitted for dating from the fill (C128) of a hearth (C148) within Building 2, yielding three radiocarbon measurements (SUERC-57549, SUERC-57550, and SUERC-57551). It is feasible that these three samples are the same age, as the measurements pass a chi-square test (T=1.9; df=2; T'(0.05)=6.0), suggesting that the samples were deposited over an extremely short period of time. The youngest of the three radiocarbon measurements

OxCal v4.3.2 Bronk Ramsey (2017); r:5 intr whole IntCal13 atmospheric curve (Reimer et al 2013)

SUERC-57552: Small Cairn (Tr 19)	
SUERC-49676: Burnt material C39 in structure 4	
SUERC-57553: Building 7 bank of material C125	
SUERC-79014: Upper fill C279 of pit C278	
SUERC-74162: Roundwood charcoal with bark (Salix sp)	
SUERC-74161: Roundwood charcoal with bark (Corylus)	
Phase Hearth C248	
SUERC-65406: Burned layer C164	
SUERC-65410: Cobble filling C166	
SUERC-65411: Fill C168 of likely post-hole C169	
Phase Building 3	
SUERC-57551: Nutshell (Corylus)	
SUERC-57550: Roundwood charcoal (Corylus)	
SUERC-57549: Nutshell (Corylus)	
Phase Fill C128 of hearth C148	
SUERC-49675: Wood charcoal (Prunoideae) - Not Displayed	
SUERC-51339: Wood charcoal (Salix)	
Phase Fill C86 of post-hole C85	
SUERC-49674: Wood charcoal (Betula)	
SUERC-51337: Wood charcoal (Alnus)	
Phase Fill C84 of linear gully C83 below stone foundation	
SUERC-49673: Wood charcoal (Prunoideae)	
SUERC-51336: Wood charcoal (Betula)	
Phase Fill C82 of post-hole C81	
SUERC-51343: : Fill C90 of post-hole C89	
SUERC-51338: Fill C92 of post-holes C91 & C93	
Phase Building 2	
SUERC-51335: Fill C79 of a possible pit	
SUERC-49672: Fill C71 of pit C70	
SUERC-49667: Fill C63 of post-hole C64	
SUERC-49671: Wood charcoal (Alnus)	
SUERC-51334: Charred grain (Hordeum)	
Phase Fill C68 of post-hole C67	
SUERC-49666: Wood charcoal (Betula)	
SUERC-51333: Roundwood charcoal (Corylus)	
Phase Deposit C56 beneath turf bank C55	
SUERC-51329: Wood charcoal (Alnus)	
SUERC-42424: Wood charcoal (Betula)	
Phase Fill C20 of pit C19	
SUERC-42420: Turf wall, Slot 3 C21	
SUERC-51328: Wood charcoal (Betula)	
SUERC-42419: Wood charcoal (Betula)	
Phase Base C14 of linear feature	
Phase Building 1	

3500 3000 2500 2000 1500 1000 500 1calBC/1calAD 500 1000

Calibrated date (calBC/calAD)

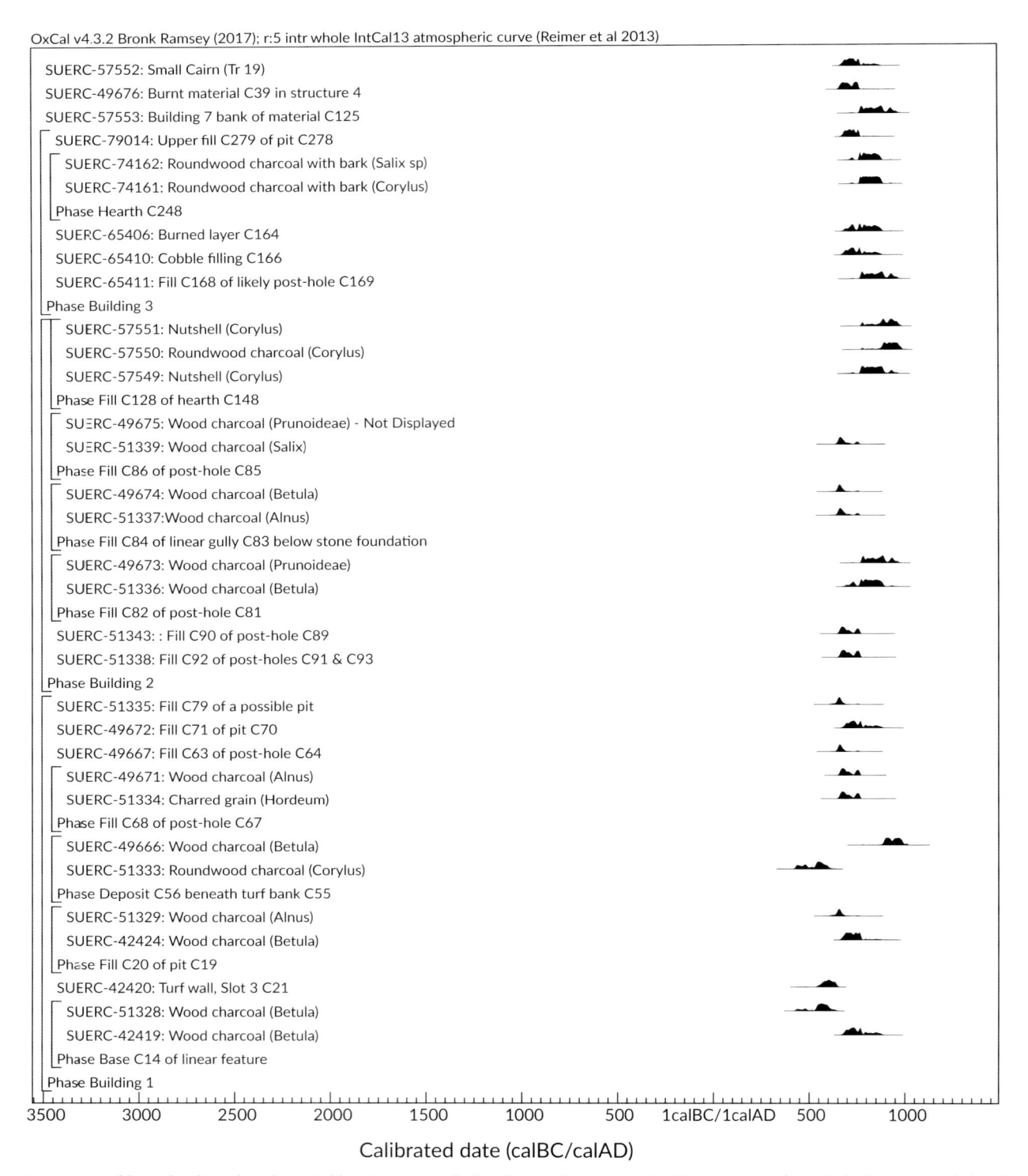

Figure 2.27 Calibrated radiocarbon dates. Calibrations were calculated using the terrestrial calibration curve (IntCal13) of Reimer et al. (2013) and the probability method of Stuiver and Reimer (1993) with OxCal v4.3 (Bronk Ramsey 2017). Radiocarbon dates are grouped into their corresponding contexts.

(SUERC-57549) provides the best estimate for the date of the hearth (cal AD 760–950, 95% confidence), because this measurement is likely the closest in time to the actual date of context formation.

Four post-hole contexts associated with Building 2 were also sampled for dating. Although it is not clear whether post-holes C85, C89, C91 and C93 relate to Building 1 or 2 (see above), for the purposes of this analysis, they have been associated with Building 2, though as mentioned previously it is possible that they are remnants of earlier activity that predates the upstanding Building 2. A sample of wood charcoal (*Salix* sp.) from the fill C92 of two adjacent post-holes (C91 and

2. Results of Archaeological Fieldwork, Radiocarbon Dating, Peat-Stratigraphic and Pollen Analyses

C93) was submitted for dating, yielding a radiocarbon measurement (SUERC-51338). A sample of roundwood charcoal (*Salix* sp.) from the fill (C90) of post-hole C89 was submitted for dating, yielding a radiocarbon measurement (SUERC-51343).

Two samples of wood charcoal (Prunoideae and *Betula* sp.) were submitted for dating from fill C82 of another possible post-hole (C81) within Building 2, yielding two radiocarbon measurements (SUERC-49673 and SUERC-51336). It is feasible that these two samples are the same age, as the measurements pass a chi-square test (T=1.2; df=1; T'(0.05)=3.8), suggesting that the samples were deposited over an extremely short-period of time. The younger of the two radiocarbon measurements (SUERC-49673) provides the best estimate for the date for the post-hole (cal AD 770–970, 95% confidence), because this measurement is likely the closest in time to the actual date of context formation.

Two samples of wood charcoal (Prunoideae and *Salix* sp.) were submitted for dating from fill C86 of another post-hole (C85) within Building 2, yielding two radiocarbon measurements (SUERC-49675 and SUERC-51339). It is not feasible that these two radiocarbon samples are the same age, as the measurements do not pass a chi-square test (T=3084.7; df=1; T'(0.05)=3.8), suggesting that SUERC-49675 may be residual. Therefore, the younger of the two radiocarbon measurements (SUERC-51339) provides the best estimate for the date (cal AD 640–770, 95% confidence) of this post-hole C85, because this measurement is probably the closest in time to the actual date of context formation.

Building 3

Like Buildings 1 and 2, Building 3 was located in close proximity to the ring-cairn. This building exhibited many of the characteristics of the classic Pitcarmick type with rounded ends, an external oval enclosure attached to one external wall and signs of a sunken internal area (Section 2.3 above). A pit (C278) within Building 3 is tentatively interpreted as a foundation deposit for the building. Material comprising the adjacent slumped turf wall (C212) sealed the pit (C278). A sample of an articulated cattle bone (*Bos* sp.) from the upper fill (C279) of this pit C278 was submitted for dating, yielding a radiocarbon measurement (SUERC-79014).

A sample of roundwood charcoal (*Corylus* sp.) from a burned layer (C164) associated with Building 3 was submitted for dating, yielding a radiocarbon measurement (SUERC-65406). This burned deposit C164 lay atop the natural substrate across the northern internal area of the building. The deposit C164 represents a distinct episode of burning within the building.

A sample of wood charcoal (*Betula* sp.) from the fill (C168) of a possible post-hole (C169) within Building 3 was submitted for dating, yielding a radiocarbon measurement (SUERC-65411).

A sample of roundwood charcoal (*Corylus*) from the filling (C166) of a wide central sunken area of Building 3 was submitted for dating, yielding a radiocarbon measurement (SUERC-65410). Although the true extent of the feature was not uncovered within the excavation trench it appeared to represent the purposeful infilling of a sunken interior of the building to create a more level floor whilst also acting as a drain/sump.

The fill (C248) of a central hearth (C235) within Building 3 is tentatively interpreted as one of the last archaeological contexts created during the Building 3 occupation. Two samples of roundwood charcoal with bark (*Salix* sp. and *Corylus*) were submitted for dating from the primary fill (C248) of this hearth, yielding two radiocarbon measurements (SUERC-74161 and SUERC-74162). It is feasible that these two samples are the same age, as the measurements pass a chi-square test (T=0.2; df=1; T'(0.05)=3.8), suggesting that the samples were deposited over an extremely short period of time. The younger of the two radiocarbon measurements (SUERC-74161) provides the best estimate for the date for the hearth (cal AD 760–900, 95% confidence), because this measurement is likely the closest in time to the actual date of context formation.

Other dated contexts

Other archaeological structures sampled for dating include Building 7, a circular structure (C43), and a small cairn (C137). Building 7 is a turf and stone building with no internal occupation features or deposits, suggesting that it may have been a store or barn instead of a dwelling. A sample of wood charcoal (*Betula* sp.) from an earthen bank (C125) part of Building 7 was submitted for dating, yielding a radiocarbon measurement (SUERC-57553). It is possible that this bank represents a foundation of earth on top of which the stone wall was constructed; however, it could equally represent the remains of an earlier structure on top of which the low stone wall was placed. The radiocarbon measurement from this feature (C125) provides a *TPQ* for the construction and use of Building 7.

A stone defined circular structure was identified near the central portion of the settlement (Structure 4; Figure 2.1). A sample of wood charcoal (*Alnus*) from a small patch of burnt material (C39) within this structure was submitted for dating, yielding a radiocarbon measurement (SUERC-49676). This patch of burnt material C39 could have formed a portion of the floor surface but has no secure context and the radiocarbon measurement obtained from this sample (cal AD 660–

780, 95% confidence) merely reflects the general period of early medieval activity in the vicinity.

A small cairn was also identified (C137) beneath a thin layer of turf, heather, and topsoil (C1) near the central portion of the settlement. A sample of roundwood charcoal (*Corylus*) from the base of the cairn was submitted for dating, yielding a radiocarbon measurement (SUERC-57552). The radiocarbon measurement from this fill C137 is interpreted as a *TPQ* for the creation of this context, because it is feasible that the dated roundwood is a residual sample.

Bayesian models and results

The radiocarbon dates have been placed into unordered phases corresponding to their archaeological context. The dates are grouped by building and feature, while the First and Last commands were used to produce estimates for those groups within the overall chronological framework. Boundaries were used in OxCal to estimate the start and end date of the overall unordered group. One measurement (SUERC-49675) was excluded from modelling because it calibrates (2290–2050 cal BC, 95% confidence) to the Late Bronze Age and is not reflective of the timing of early medieval activity.

There is good agreement between the model assumptions and the radiocarbon dates (A_{model}=82.5). The model estimates that early medieval activity at Lair began in *cal AD 550-650* (*95% probability*; Figure 2.28; *Primary Model: Start Glenshee*) and probably in *cal AD 590-640* (*68% probability*).

The primary dated activity related to Building 1 is estimated to have begun in *cal AD 575-655* (*95% probability*; Figure 2.28; *Primary Model: Start Building 1*) and probably in *cal AD 605-650* (*68% probability*). The model estimates that activity related to Building 1 ended in *cal AD 725-885* (*95% probability*; Figure 2.28; *Primary Model: End Building 1*), probably *cal AD 740-870* (*68% probability*), lasting for *90-275 years* (*95% probability*; Figure 2.30; *Primary Model: Building 1 Span*), probably *110-235 years* (*68% probability*). Depending upon the specific archaeological interpretation of these deposits, these date estimates relate to either the upstanding building or the previous activity, which was potentially another structure, at this location. If interpretation favours the upstanding structure being a later construction using turves that subsequently formed over the earlier structure, then the modelled date for SUERC-49666 (*Betula* sp. charcoal), which is the latest date sealed under the turf wall in C56, provides a *TPQ* for the construction of *cal AD 775-975* (*95% probability*), and probably *cal AD 880-930* (*68% probability*).

Activity related to Building 2 is estimated to have begun in *cal AD 640-715* (*95% probability*; Figure 2.28; *Primary Model: Start Building 2*) and probably in *cal AD 650-680* (*68% probability*). The model estimates that activity related to Building 2 ended in *cal AD 835-970* (*95% probability*; Figure 2.28; *Primary Model: End Building 2*), probably *cal AD 880-940* (*68% probability*), lasting for *160-310 years* (*95% probability*; Figure 2.30; *Primary Model: Building 2 Span*), probably *205-275 years* (*68% probability*). However, if the cut features associated with Building 2 are evidence of earlier activity on the site, then the only reliable dates for the building come from the three results from Hearth 148, which date to somewhere between the late 8th to late 10th centuries AD.

Activity related to Building 3 is estimated to have begun in *cal AD 675-770* (*95% probability*; Figure 2.28; *Primary Model: Start Building 3*) and probably in *cal AD 685-735* (*68% probability*). The model estimates that activity related to Building 3 ended in *cal AD 805-945* (*95% probability*; Figure 2.28; *Primary Model: End Building 3*), probably *cal AD 840-895* (*68% probability*), lasting for *75-235 years* (*95% probability*; Figure 2.30; *Primary Model: Building 3 Span*), probably *115-190 years* (*68% probability*).

The model estimates that activity related to these structures ended in *cal AD 860-1005* (*95% probability*; Figure 2.28; *Primary Model: End Glenshee*) and probably in *cal AD 895-960* (*68% probability*), spanning *230-430 years* (*95% probability*; Figure 2.30; *Primary Model: Glenshee span*), probably *270-365 years* (*68% probability*).

Sensitivity analysis: an alternative Bayesian model

An alternative Bayesian model was created as a form of sensitivity analysis. This model is identical to the primary model, except in its treatment of radiocarbon measurements from potential heartwood. Specifically, a charcoal outlier model (Bronk Ramsey 2009b) was adopted as a strategy for accounting for the unknown in-built age offset in wood charcoal samples to create a more accurate and robust model (Hamilton and Kenney 2015). The model assumes an exponential distribution, with an exponential constant τ of 1 taken over the range −10 to 0, of the charcoal dates (Bronk Ramsey 2009b). These shifts are scaled by a common scaling factor that can lie anywhere between 10^0 and 10^3 years.

There is good agreement between the alternative model assumptions and the radiocarbon dates (A_{model}=92.5). The alternative model estimates that early medieval activity at Lair began in *cal AD 565-720* (*95% probability*; Figure 2.29 *Alternative Model: Start Glenshee*) and probably in *cal AD 620-690* (*68% probability*).

Activity related to Building 1 is estimated to have begun in *cal AD 585-735* (*95% probability*; Figure 2.29; *Alternative Model: Start Building 1*) and probably in *cal AD 630-700* (*68% probability*). The alternative model estimates that activity related to Building 1 ended in *cal AD 740-945* (*95%*

2. Results of Archaeological Fieldwork, Radiocarbon Dating, Peat-Stratigraphic and Pollen Analyses

probability; Figure 2.29; *Alternative Model: End Building 1*), probably *cal AD 760–890 (68% probability)*, lasting for *80–275 years (95% probability*; Figure 2.30; *Alternative Model: Building 1 Span*), probably *115–225 years (68% probability)*. As with the primary model for Building 1, the alternatively modelled date for SUERC-49666 provides

a potential *TPQ* of *cal AD 785–985 (95% probability)*, and probably *cal AD 890–955 (68% probability)*, for the construction of the upstanding building.

Activity related to Building 2 is estimated to have begun in *cal AD 650–760 (95% probability*; Figure 2.29;

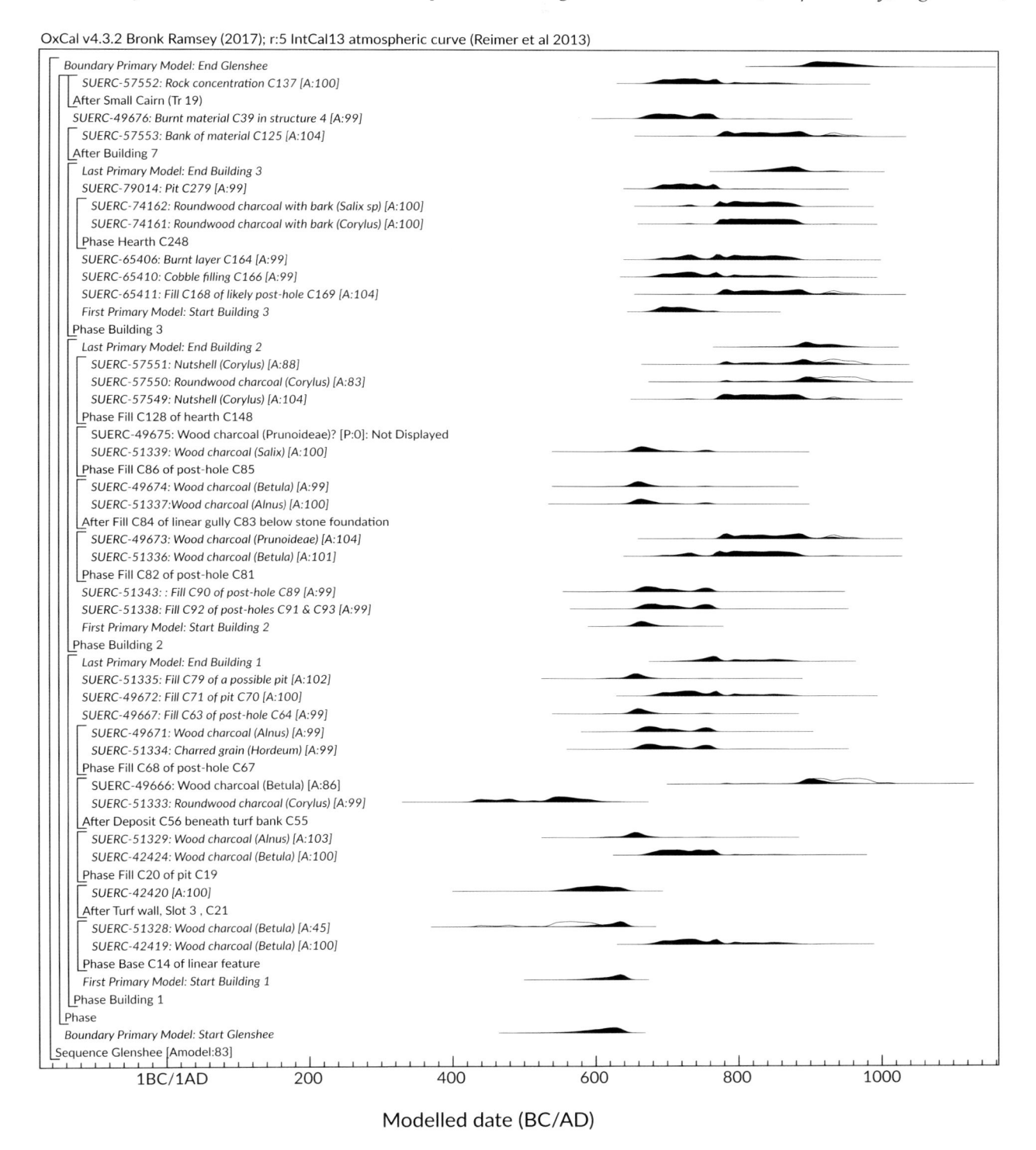

Figure 2.28 Results and structure of the primary Bayesian model. For each of the radiocarbon measurements two distributions have been plotted, one in outline, which is the result of simple radiocarbon calibration, and a solid one, which is based on the chronological model use. The other distributions correspond to aspects of the model. The large square 'brackets' along with the OxCal keywords define the overall model exactly.

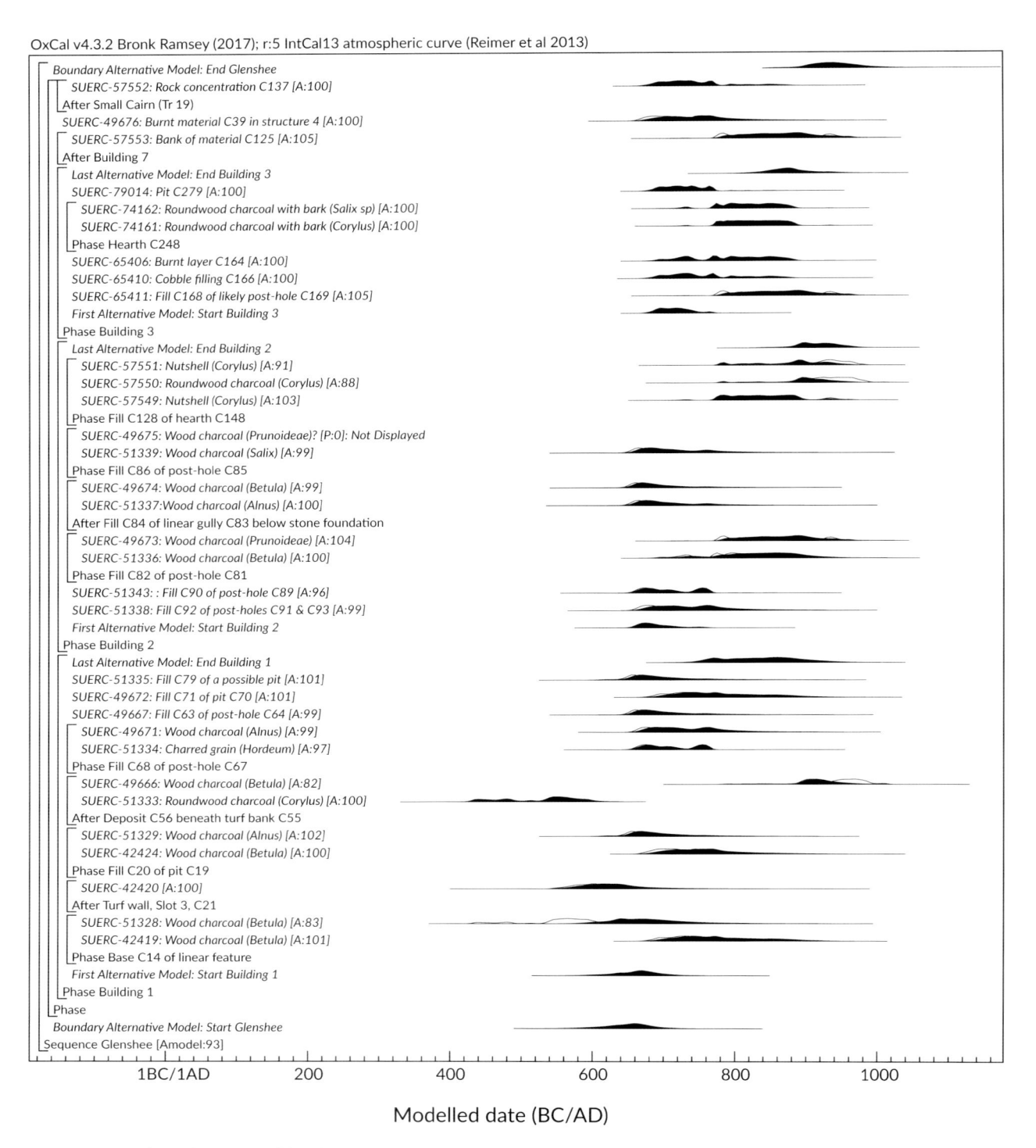

Figure 2.29 Results and structure of the alternative Bayesian model. The brackets and keywords define the model structure. The format is as described in Figure 2.28.

Alternative Model: Start Building 2) and probably in *cal AD 655–705* (*68% probability*). The alternative model estimates that activity related to Building 2 ended in *cal AD 850–980* (*95% probability*; Figure 2.29; *Alternative Model: End Building 2*), probably *cal AD 885–945* (*68% probability*), lasting for *140–305 years* (*95% probability*; Figure 2.30; *Alternative Model: Building 2 Span*), probably *190–275 years* (*68% probability*).

Activity related to Building 3 is estimated to have begun in *cal AD 675–770* (*95% probability*; Figure 2.29; *Alternative Model: Start Building 3*) and probably in *cal AD 685–735* (*68% probability*). The alternative model estimates that activity related to Building 3 ended in *cal AD 815–960* (*95% probability*; Figure 2.29; *Alternative Model: End Building 3*), probably *cal AD 840–905* (*68% probability*), lasting for *85–250 years* (*95% probability*;

Figure 2.30; *Alternative Model: Building 3 Span*), probably *115–200 years (68% probability)*.

The alternative model estimates that activity related to these structures ended in *cal AD 865–1015 (95% probability*; Figure 2.29; *Alternative Model: End Glenshee*) and probably in *cal AD 905–970 (68% probability)*, spanning *185–405 years (95% probability*; Figure 2.30; *Alternative Model: Glenshee span*), probably *235–340 years (68% probability)*.

As there is very little difference between the two models, the primary model appears to provide robust estimates of the timing and duration of activities related to the excavated Pitcarmick-type buildings at Lair.

Conclusions

The calibrated dates from Lair, Glen Shee, are primarily in the early medieval period (Figure 2.27; Table 2.1). Bayesian chronological models of this data provide some insight into the timing of the activity at Glen Shee and of the individual Pitcarmick-type buildings. Specifically, both the primary and alternative Bayesian chronological models suggest that activity associated with the dated structures began in the 7th century AD and ended in the 10th century AD.

Twenty-nine radiocarbon dates are from contexts associated with Buildings 1–3. Both the primary and alternative Bayesian chronological models suggest that activity associated with Buildings 1 and 2 started in the 7th century AD and that activity associated with Building 3 started in the late 7th or early 8th century AD. Likewise, both the primary and alternative Bayesian chronological models suggest that activity associated with Building 1 ended in the 8th or 9th century AD, while activity associated with Building 3 continued until the 9th century AD, and activity associated with Building 2 continued until the late 9th or early 10th century AD.

A relative order for the activity associated with these buildings can be suggested based on the probabilistic ordering of the modelled data (Tables 2.2 and 2.3). Specifically using the primary model there is a *99% probability* (primary model) that activity at Building 1 began *(Start Building 1)* before activity at Building 2 *(Start Building 2)* and a *96% probability* that activity at Building

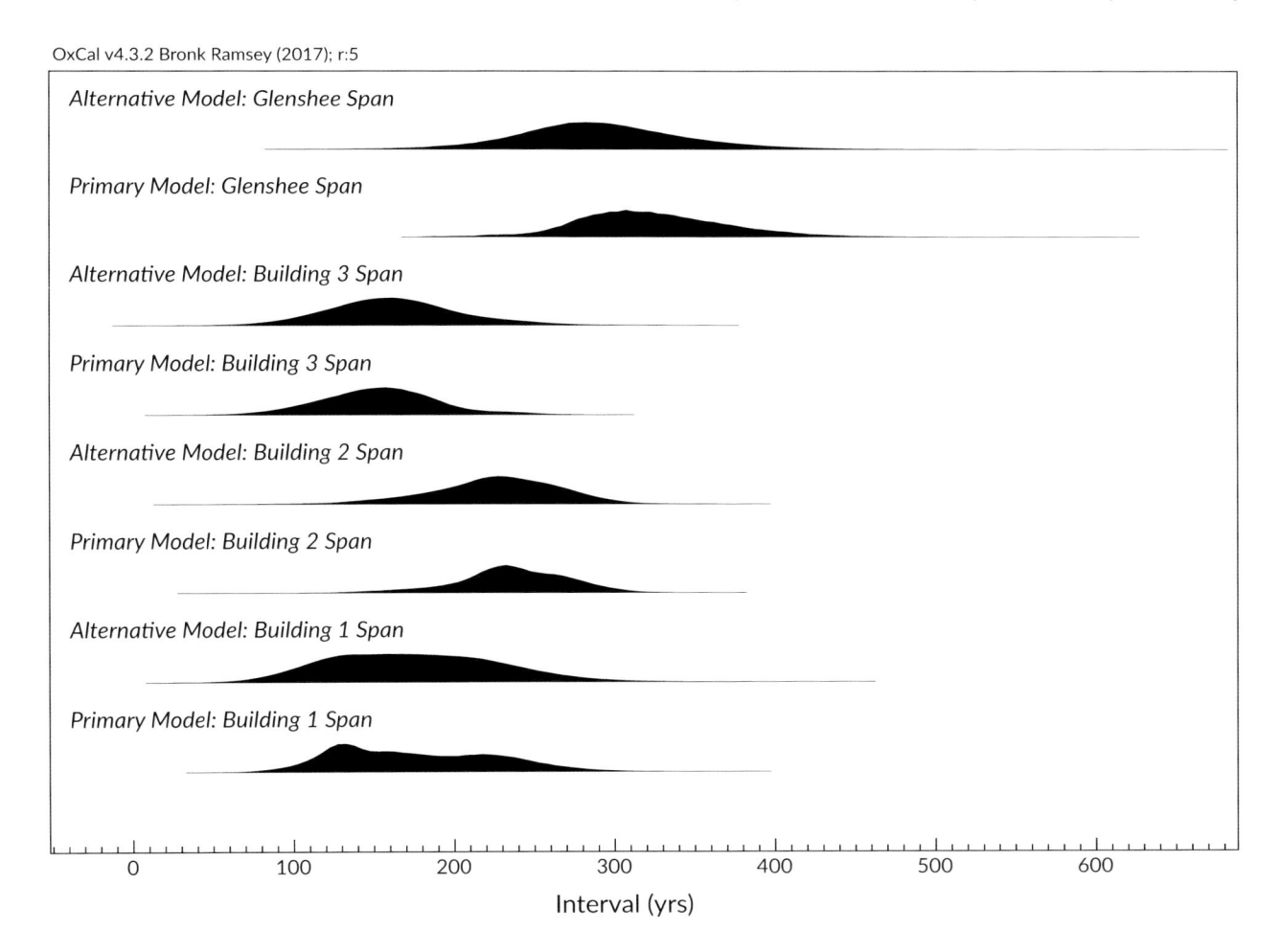

Figure 2.30 Estimated spans of activity from the primary and alternative models.

2 began before activity at Building 3 (*Start Building 3*); indicating that the construction sequence is very likely to have been Building 1 followed by Building 2 followed by Building 3. Building 1 is the first of these buildings to fall into disuse and there is a *96% probability* in the primary model that activity at Building 3 began before activity at Building 1 ended (*End Building 1*); suggesting a degree of contemporaneity between these three buildings after the construction of Building 3. Finally, there is a *91% probability* in the primary model that activity at Building 1 ended (*End Building 1*) before activity ended at Building 3 (*End Building 3*) and an *83% probability* that activity at Building 3 ended before activity at Building 2 (*End Building 2*); indicating that the abandonment sequence is very likely to have been Building 1 followed by Building 3 followed by Building 2.

2.6 Peat-stratigraphic and pollen-analytical evidence for environmental and land-use change

Danny Paterson and Richard Tipping

Introduction

The moorland immediately around the archaeological monuments at Lair includes extensive areas of peat. One of these, Basin 2 (below), is within tens of metres of the Pitcarmick buildings and later cultivation traces (cf. Figure 2.1). Because the economic foundation for these buildings is unclear, a programme was constructed to understand the form, age and evolution of the peats and to record through detailed pollen analyses the natural and anthropogenic changes to plant communities in later prehistory and the early medieval period. This section describes this programme and the results. Discussion of the implications from this work for the economy of the Pitcarmick buildings at Lair and the wider landscape is presented in Chapter 4.

Holocene peatland evolution on the lower slopes of Allt Corra-lairige

Substantial areas of the valley floor comprise large basin peat deposits (Figure 2.31), not blanket peats as mapped by the Soil Survey of Scotland (Sheet 56). To understand peat development a programme was developed of (a) recording peat stratigraphies along transects with a 2.5 cm diameter Eijelkamp peat gouge, with ground surfaces surveyed to arbitrary data, and (b) AMS ^{14}C dating of peat at key sediment-stratigraphic depths sampled by a 1.0 m by 6.0 cm diameter closed-chambered Russian corer.

Straddling the northern watershed is Basin 1, c. 0.1 km^2 in area and nearly circular with a heavily peat-cut surface dominated by *Sphagnum*, with narrow baulks of drier *Calluna*, and surrounded by well-defined cultivation traces. The peat drains north via sub-surface peat pipes, and also south over the surface to Basin 2. The floor of the basin is flat and peat depth

Table 2.2 Probability matrix that event τ_1 occurred before event τ_2 in the primary model.

$\tau_1 < \tau_2$ τ_2 τ_1	Start Building 1	Start Building 2	Start Building 3	End Building 1	End Building 3	End Building 2
Start Building 1		99%	100%	100%	100%	100%
Start Building 2	1%		96%	100%	100%	100%
Start Building 3	0%	4%		96%	100%	100%
End Building 1	0%	0%	4%		91%	98%
End Building 3	0%	0%	0%	9%		83%
End Building 2	0%	0%	0%	2%	17%	

Table 2.3 Probability matrix that event τ_1 occurred before event τ_2 in the alternative model.

$\tau_1 < \tau_2$ τ_2 τ_1	Start Building 1	Start Building 2	Start Building 3	End Building 1	End Building 3	End Building 2
Start Building 1		74%	92%	100%	100%	100%
Start Building 2	26%		79%	100%	100%	100%
Start Building 3	8%	21%		99%	100%	100%
End Building 1	0%	0%	1%		74%	90%
End Building 3	0%	0%	0%	26%		80%
End Building 2	0%	0%	0%	10%	20%	

2. Results of Archaeological Fieldwork, Radiocarbon Dating, Peat-Stratigraphic and Pollen Analyses

Figure 2.31 Oblique aerial photograph looking south over the peats (dark brown) of Basin 1 in the foreground and the northern edge of Basin 2 in the background, separated by improved pasture displaying cultivation traces. Both basin peats have been heavily cut which has created fen peat around them. The position of the pollen site in the fen of Basin 2 is marked by the cross (© Crown Copyright: HES DP226321).

a consistent 280-320 cm. Basal peat was not dated but linear extrapolation from two AMS ^{14}C assays at borehole E1 (NO 13596 64126: Table 2.4) suggests that peat began to form at *c.* 8500 BC. Peat at 55.0-56.0 cm depth has an age of 3537-3710 BC, indicating severe truncation of the peat above this, such that upstanding baulks have themselves been truncated: the present peat surface has an extrapolated age of *c.* 2500 BC. Peat-cutting has wrecked the peat stratigraphy at Basin 1 but without a very detailed ^{14}C dating and pollen-analytical programme (e.g. Tipping 2010, 63-81) the periods when peat was cut cannot be defined.

To the south, Basin 2 has an area of *c.* 0.015 km^2, the very dry surface covered by *Calluna* and little else, dry because the edge is fringed by recent scallop-shaped peat-cuttings (Figure 2.31). Encircling the peat and cutting into it is a more poorly delineated spread of wet Cyperaceae-*Sphagnum* peat. Figure 2.32 is the key 50 m long sediment-stratigraphic transect of 12 boreholes across the valley-side mire (boreholes A1-A7) and basin peat (A9-A6): also shown are inferred phases of peatland development. Table 2.5 is the sediment description of borehole A1 (NO 13721 63879), which was sampled for pollen analysis. Table 2.6 gives the four AMS ^{14}C assays obtained on borehole A1.

From a *c.* 2.5 m high cliff cut in till on the north-east, a 20 m wide, 2.5 m deep valley underlies boreholes A1-5. A buried ridge separates this from a deeper valley or basin to the south-west, poorly defined by coring but more than 4.5 m below the surface of Basin 2 in boreholes A8 and A6. Over this, and in both valleys is a wood peat with abundant and large wood fragments (Phase 1: Figure 2.32). Basal peat was not ^{14}C dated but linear extrapolation from assays -51235 and -47003 (Table 2.6) indicates peat formation at *c.* 6500 BC. Herb peat with no wood then accumulated in both valleys. This is very thick south-west of borehole A11 but much thinner in the shallower valley. The base of this peat

Table 2.4 AMS ^{14}C assays on peat in Basin 1.

Site	Borehole	Depth (cm)	Sample	Fraction	Laboratory Code	^{14}C BP ±1σ	‰	Cal BC/AD (95.4%)
Basin 1	E1	55.0-56.0	herb peat	humic acid	SUERC-48323	4864 ± 34	-27.6	3537-3710 BC
Basin 1	E1	180.0-180.5	herb peat	humic acid	SUERC-47649	7317 ± 29	-28.4	6086-6233 BC

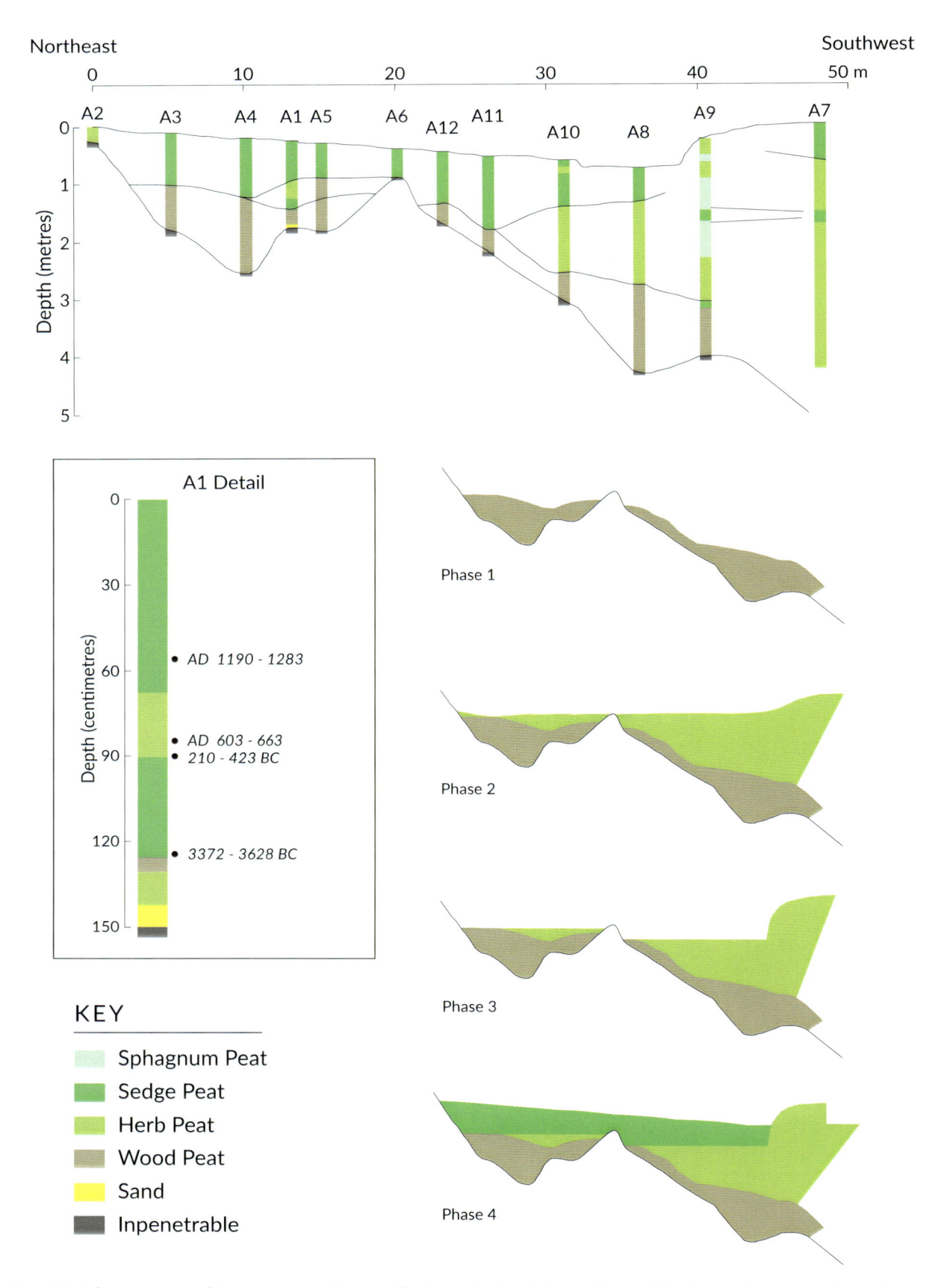

Figure 2.32 Sediment-stratigraphic transect across the peats of Basin 2 with inferred phases of peatland development from AMS ^{14}C dating: (Phase 1) a blanket of wood peat shortly before 3372-3628 BC; (Phase 2) herb peat accumulates over wood peat until c. 1000 AD; (Phase 3) conjectured surface of the basins shortly before AD 1190-1283 with peat-cutting in the south-westerly basin; (Phase 4) formation of Cyperaceae (sedge) peat after abandonment of peat-cutting shortly before AD 1190-1283, save for a new bank cut in the surface of herb peat at the south-west.

2. Results of Archaeological Fieldwork, Radiocarbon Dating, Peat-Stratigraphic and Pollen Analyses

Table 2.5 Sediment description of borehole A1 in Basin 2.

Depth (cm)	Description
50-68	Very dark brown herb-Cyperaceae peat with abundant horizontally bedded fine fibrous stems, and rare disseminated sand; sharp to
68-89	Dark brown amorphous peat with common-many Cyperaceae stems and few fine fibrous stems, and rare disseminated sand; gradual to
89-125	Dark brown herb peat with occasional Cyperaceae stems and rare disseminated sand; sharp to
125-131	Dark brown wood-rich amorphous peat with abundant fragmented large wood fragments and few roundwood pieces, few herb stems and rare disseminated sand; sharp to
130-142	Very dark brown amorphous peat with rare to few fibrous stems; sharp to
140-147	Reddish-brown amorphous peat with rare fibrous stems; sharp to
147-149	Pale brown-fawn structureless poorly sorted silt with sand and rare fine black fleshy herb stems; gradual to
149-152	Fawn structureless silt with sand onto bedrock or till.

is dated at borehole A1 to 3372-3628 BC. The herb peat in the shallower valley has a variable proportion of Cyperaceae stems that may have grown only in the deepest, wettest pockets, probably as water still moved through the fen. In the shallower valley, herb peat accumulated to 89 cm depth, dated at 90.5 cm depth to 210-428 BC. It grew here at a very slow rate of $c.$ 0.01 cm/yr ($c.$ 93.5 yrs/cm) but in the deeper valley would have grown much faster (Phase 1: Figure 2.32).

Herb peat at 84 cm depth in borehole A1 is dated to AD 603-663 (SUERC-54110: Table 2.6). Continuous peat growth from 90 to 84 cm depth at 0.006 cm/yr ($c.$ 160 yrs/cm) is probably untenably slow and the strong likelihood is that there is a hiatus between these depths despite the only gradual change in sediment type at around 89 cm depth (Table 2.6). Pollen data (below) suggest the break in sedimentation occurred at 85 cm depth. This interpretation determined the ^{14}C dating of peat immediately above this, at 84.5 cm depth, dated to AD 603-663. The inferred hiatus lasted between $c.$ 300 and $c.$ 550 years.

Above the hiatus a similar peat grew, though plant remains were less well preserved. Peat grew much faster. A significant sedimentological change at 68 cm depth at borehole A1 was the accumulation of loose, unconsolidated Cyperaceae (sedge) peat. The lower boundary to this is not directly dated. Peat at 55.5 cm depth has an age of AD 1190-1283. Assuming a linear growth rate between 84.5 and 55.5 cm depth, which is necessary but unlikely, peat at 68 cm depth has an interpolated age of $c.$ 1000 AD. The rate of peat growth between these depths was $c.$ 0.02 cm/yr ($c.$ 45 yrs/cm).

Loose Cyperaceae peat is traced along the transect to borehole A8 where it fills a peat-cutting made into the herb peat: Borehole A9 is directly above a cliff of cut peat (Figure 2.32). The abandonment of peat-cutting may have encouraged peat dominated by wetland sedges to rapidly infill peat banks that had been cut to below the water table. Abandonment is dated to before, probably only just before, $c.$ 1000 AD. Pollen data from borehole A1 record another change in pollen proportions at 66.5 cm depth (below) but there is no indication in these data of a hiatus at this depth (Figure 2.33). Cyperaceae peat probably quickly spread laterally to the shallower valley. Cyperaceae peat is still growing, at a rate since $c.$ 1240 AD of around 14 yrs/cm. To explain the uppermost Cyperaceae peat at borehole A7, the reconstruction in Figure 2.32 suggests (Phases 3 and 4) that people at some time in the recent past turned once more to cutting this drier, more compact herb peat.

In summary, peat has occupied basins in the lower slopes of the catchment from very early in the Holocene, at around 8800 BC at Basin 1 and around 6500 BC at Basin 2. The peat at Basin 2 initially supported trees on its surface but the peat at Basin 1 may always have been too wet for this. Trees were probably driven

Table 2.6 AMS ^{14}C assays on peat in Basin 2.

Site	Borehole	Depth (cm)	Sample	Fraction	Laboratory Code	^{14}C BP ±1σ	‰	Cal BC/AD (95.4%)
Basin 2	A1	55.0-56.0	sedge peat	humic acid	SUERC-51234	782 ± 35	-29.0	AD 1190 - 1283
Basin 2	A1	84.0-85.0	sedge peat	humic acid	SUERC-54110	1405 ± 25	-29.1	AD 603 - 663
Basin 2	A1	90.0-91.0	amorphous peat	humic acid	SUERC-51235	2309 ± 35	-29.0	210 - 428 BC
Basin 2	A1	124.0-125.0	herb peat	humic acid	SUERC-47003	4692 ± 29	-28.7	3372 - 3628 BC

from the peat surface at Basin 2 at *c.* 3500 BC, most likely by hydrological change to increased wetness. As peat filled Basin 2 it may have reversed the drainage, creating a watershed on its northern side which made water draining slopes to flow east and south around the peat (Figure 2.31). On this watershed, the shallower valley at Basin 2 probably stopped growing, perhaps for several hundred years from *c.* 110 AD until *c.* 660 AD. This hiatus was not through peat-cutting because only a negligible thickness of peat could have been removed and because the sedimentological signal of peat-cutting, the accumulation of loose Cyperaceae peat, is not seen then, only later in the 11th century AD.

Pollen analyses from borehole A1, Basin 2

Methods

Sediment cores collected at borehole A1 with a closed-chambered Russian corer were stored in a cold store in the dark at 4 °C. Samples for pollen analysis of *c.* 1 cm^3 were no more than 2.5 mm thick. Residues passed through a 150 µm metal sieve and retained on 10 µm nylon sieves were treated by acetolysis and stored in silicone oil. Pollen analyses were made using an Olympus BX40 binocular microscope. Counts were made at magnification x400 with critical examinations made at magnification x1000 under oil immersion, sometimes using phase contrast. Pollen was identified by reference to Moore, Webb and Collinson (1991), other sources and the University of Stirling pollen reference collection. Counts were based on a minimum of 300 grains total land pollen (tlp). Pollen nomenclature follows Bennett (1994) and plant nomenclature follows Stace (1991). Separation of *Corylus avellana* and *Myrica gale* remains controversial: three categories were used in this study: (a) *Corylus*, (b) *Myrica* and (c) *Corylus avellana* type to include grains not positively identified as either *Corylus* or *Myrica* (cf. Blackmore *et al.* 2003; Edwards 1981; Moore *et al.* 1991; Punt, Marks and Hoen 2002). Separation of Poaceae to cereal groups follows Andersen (1979) with additions by Beug (2004) and Tweddle, Edwards and Fieller (2005). *Hordeum* group pollen *sensu* Andersen (1979) includes several wild grass taxa but Tweddle, Edwards and Fieller (2005: Table 7) cautiously suggest refinements based on the form of the boundary of the annulus to the exine and the thickness of the annulus in relation to that of the exine. Measurements of Poaceae pollen grains with a-axes >35 µm are given in Table 2.7: *Hordeum* group grains that may represent cereals are indicated. During counting, pollen was also assessed for deterioration and assigned to one of five categories: normal, crumpled or folded, split or torn, corroded, and degraded (Lowe 1982; Tipping 1987). Indeterminable pollen was assigned to one of five categories: hidden, crumpled, split, corroded and degraded. Microscopic charcoal was counted in five size classes on a-axis length (10-25 µm, 25-50 µm, 50-75 µm, 75-100 µm and >100 µm: cf. Tipping 1995a). Data are presented in Figure 2.33. The chronology is that discussed above for Basin 2. Depths in Figure 2.33 are given in millimetres (mm) because sampling intervals above 80.0 cm depth (800.0 mm) are very close. The record is divided into three local pollen assemblage zones (lpaz): Lair 1-3, with lpa zones 2 and 3 further divided into two sub-zones (a and b), marking major and minor changes in the pollen stratigraphy, interpreted from stratigraphically constrained cluster analysis implemented via CONISS (Grimm 1987).

The pollen source area and its relation to the archaeological structures

The peat in the shallow valley at the north-eastern edge of Basin 2 (Chapter 4: Section 4.1) was selected for analysis because the coring site is only some 70 m from the nearest Pitcarmick building: Building 20 (Figure 1.16). The shallow, *c.* 20 m diameter basin (Figure 2.32) will probably receive pollen from several hundred metres around. Much of the pollen source area up-wind to the west and south is dominated by peat-forming plant communities on peaty podsols (Figure 1.12), so that indicators of anthropogenic activities in the pollen record will very likely have originated on the dry mineral soils north-west to south-east of the pollen site (Figure 2.31). The ring-cairn (Section 1.8) is some 230 m south-east of the pollen core; two roundhouses (Figure 2.1) and the excavated complex of Pitcarmick buildings are the same distance. Building 21 is 150 m north.

Interpretations

Lpaz Lair 1 (1200-1125 mm) 3200-2950 BC to 2500-2250 BC

Sediment accumulated at *c.* 9 mm/yr, the four samples a uniform *c.* 20 mm apart, around 180 years, and each sample averages the pollen import of around 20-24 years.

Arboreal taxa comprise more than 50 % tlp throughout this zone. Woodland grew in the pollen source area. *Betula* (birch) dominates the assemblage with up to 45 % tlp at 1175 mm (2970-2700 BC): proportions decline to around 25 % tlp by the top of the zone. *Betula* was the most numerous tree around the pollen site. *Quercus* is represented at values very likely to indicate local presence (Broström *et al.* 2008; Huntley and Birks 1983), probably confirmed by the presence of *Polypodium vulgare* (polypody), an epiphyte growing on tree trunks and commonly associated with *Quercus. Betula* trees replace those of *Quercus* at altitudes higher than *c.* 275 m OD (McVean 1964: 151). *Quercus* will have grown on dry ground. *Corylus* was also probably locally present and will have formed part of the woodland canopy.

2. Results of Archaeological Fieldwork, Radiocarbon Dating, Peat-Stratigraphic and Pollen Analyses

Table 2.7 Size measurements and possible identification of Poaceae pollen grains with a-axes >35 µm: Key to columns: (a) depth of sample (mm); (b) length (a-axis: µm); (c) width (b-axis: µm); (d) annulus diameter (µm); (e) annulus boundary; (f) annulus: exine thickness ratio; (g) Andersen (1979) Group.

(a)	(b)	(c)	(d)	(e)	(f)	(g)
597.5	35	35	9	diffuse	1.5	Hordeum group
597.5	37	35	9	diffuse	1.5	Hordeum group
637.5	33	33	9	sharp	3	Hordeum group (cereal?)
657.5	37	37	10	sharp	3	Avena-Triticum
667.5	35	35	9	diffuse	2	Hordeum group
667.5	35	35	10	sharp	?	Hordeum group
667.5	37	37	10	sharp	?	Hordeum group
677.5	37	35	8	diffuse	1.5	Hordeum group
677.5	35	34	8	diffuse	1.5	Hordeum group
677.5	35	35	8	diffuse	1.5	Hordeum group
687.5	37	35	9	sharp	2	Hordeum group
697.5	35	20?	9	sharp	?	Hordeum group
707.5	47	45	10	sharp	4	Avena-Triticum
717.5	38	35	10	diffuse	1.5	Hordeum group
727.5	42	40	10	sharp	?	Avena-Triticum
727.5	37	35	9	sharp	?	Hordeum group
737.5	36	35	8	diffuse	1.5	Hordeum group
747.5	39	37.5	9	sharp	3	Hordeum group (cereal?)
757.5	38	30	9	diffuse	1.5	Hordeum group
757.5	37	35	8	diffuse	1.5	Hordeum group
767.5	40	38	9	sharp	3	Hordeum group (cereal?)
777.5	42	39	11	sharp	2.5	Avena-Triticum
787.5	45	37	10	sharp	4?	Hordeum group
817.5	35	35	8	sharp	3	Hordeum group (cereal?)
837.5	42	40	10	sharp	3	Avena-Triticum
837.5	50	42	11	sharp	4	Secale cereale
837.5	39	38	8	diffuse	?	Hordeum group
837.5	42	40	10	diffuse	?	Avena-Triticum
837.5	41	40	10	?	?	Avena-Triticum
877.5	42	40	9	sharp	4	cf. Avena-Triticum
917.5	37	35	9	sharp	2.5	Hordeum group
957.5	40	30+	8	sharp	3	Hordeum group (cereal?)
1117.5	40	40	10	sharp	3	Avena-Triticum

Lonicera peryclymenum (honeysuckle) is today associated in Scotland only with *Betula* woodland (McVean 1964: 151), and within this community, in *Vaccinium*-rich *Betula* woodland. *Vaccinium* (bilberry) pollen is present in this zone though it is not abundant. It probably grew locally within *Betula-Quercus-Corylus* woodland or at the edge of the fen in open conditions. *Calluna* and other dwarf shrubs are very minor components of the pollen assemblage in this zone. They may have grown on the peat surface but not in any abundance.

Pinus sylvestris (Scots pine) values oscillate from 2-5 % tlp. *Ulmus* (elm), initially around 5 % tlp, declines to 1 % tlp above 1175 mm depth (2970-2700 BC). Neither are likely to have been present in any abundance at Lair, though isolated individuals may have been. The sharp fall in *Ulmus* values at c. 2600 BC is probably not the earliest *Ulmus* decline in the region (Edwards and Whittington 1998; Tipping 1995a). *Sorbus* (rowan) need not have grown locally given its rare representation, though it is insect-pollinated, with very limited pollen dispersal. The consistent presence and comparative abundance of *Salix* (willow), an insect pollinated plant typically under-represented in the pollen stratigraphy (Broström *et al.* 2008; Bunting, Schofield and Edwards 2013) suggest a fen-carr grew, perhaps with *Betula*. *Ribes rubrum* (red currant) may have grown in this carr. If locally present, *Alnus* was not abundant: it is possible

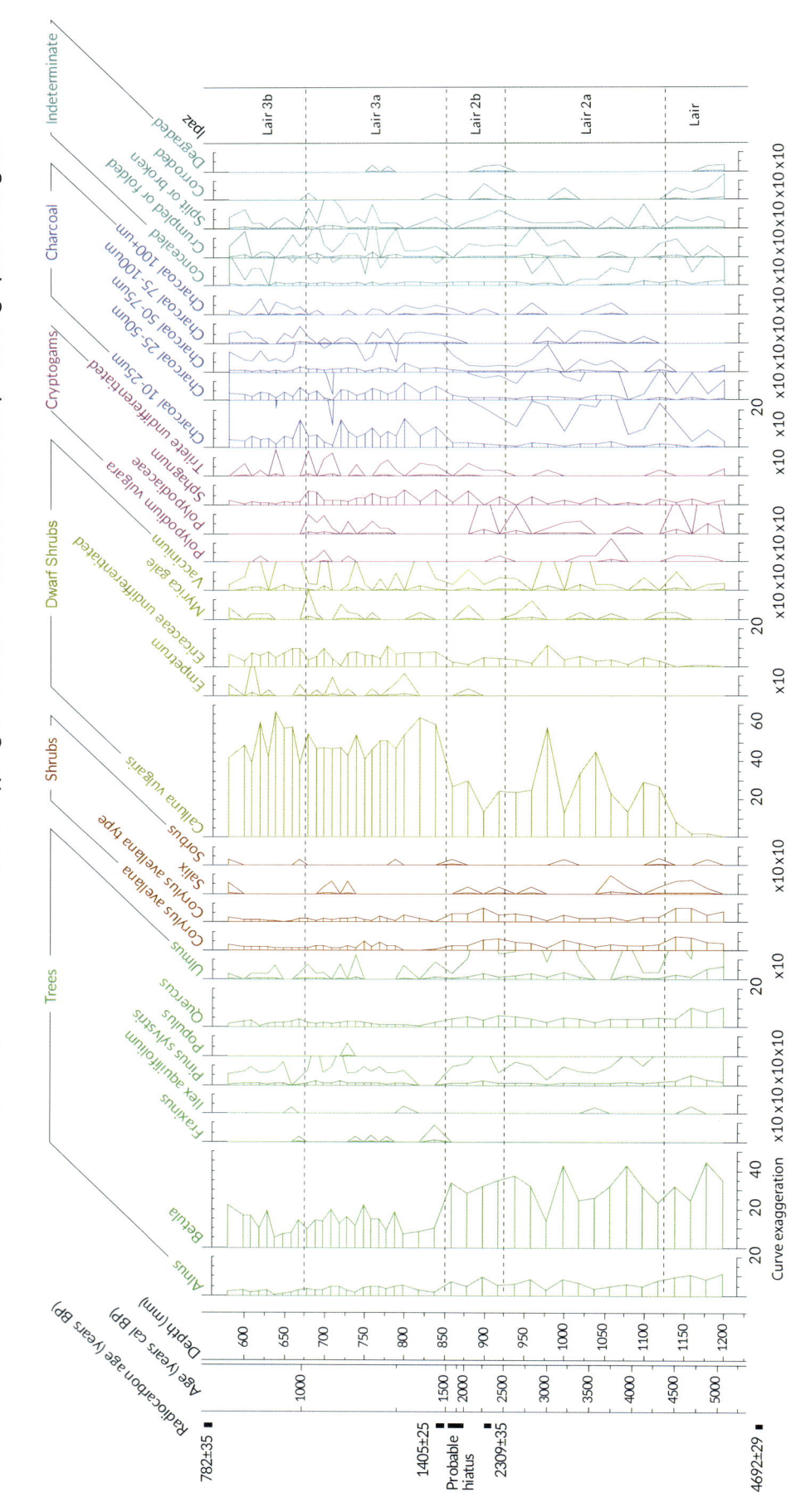

Figure 2.33 Complete percentage-based pollen diagram at borehole A1, Basin 2 with depth (mm) and with age (cal BP).

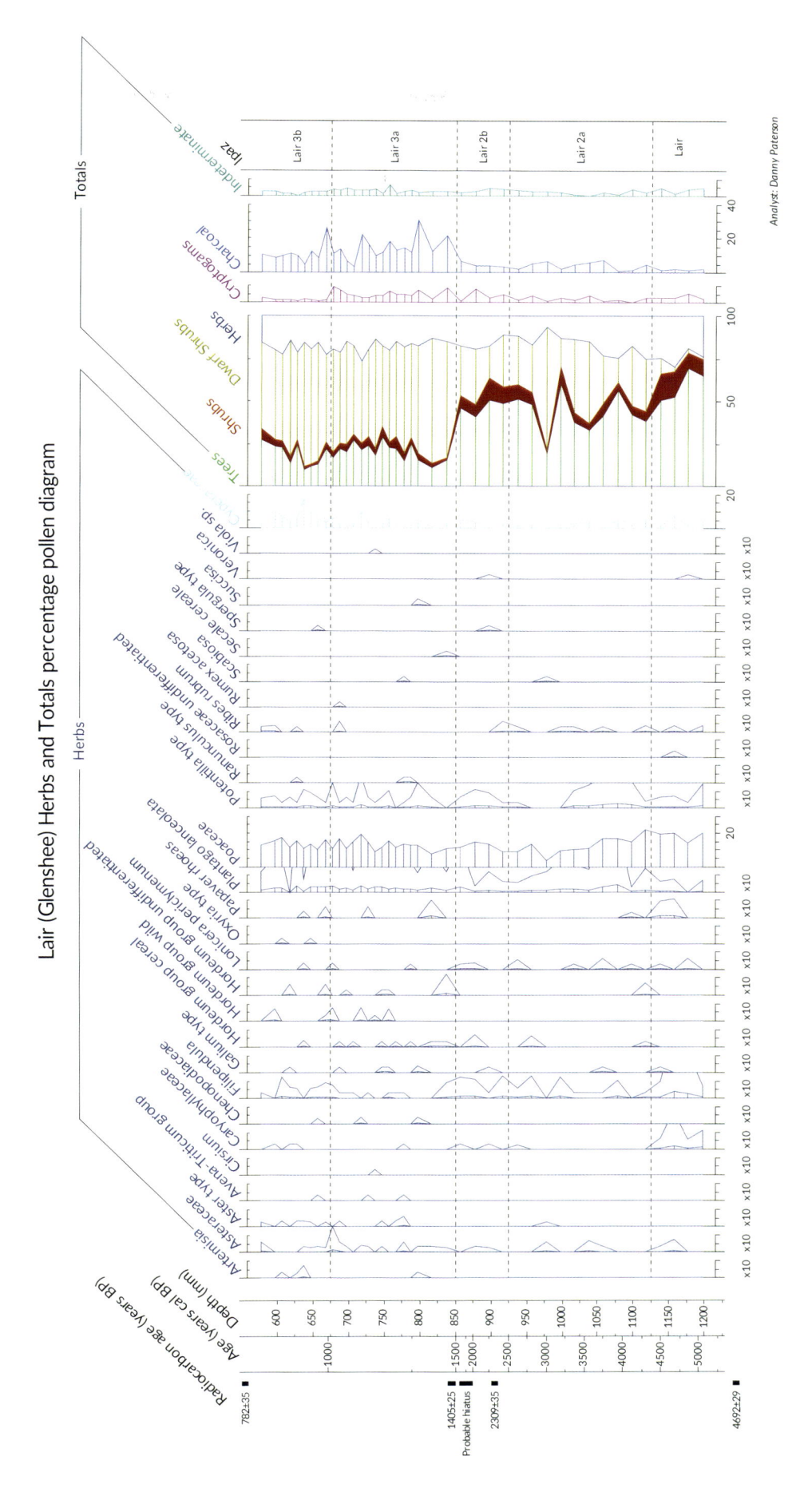

2. Results of Archaeological Fieldwork, Radiocarbon Dating, Peat-Stratigraphic and Pollen Analyses

Figure 2.33 continued, Complete percentage-based pollen diagram at borehole A1, Basin 2 with depth (mm) and with age (cal BP).

that the valley-floor of the Shee Water around 1 km to the east was the source of pollen.

The field layer of the woodland was principally composed of wild grasses (Poaceae with annulus diameters <8 um). It is likely that the tree canopy was open or patchy, with wild grass communities growing in open ground. Pollen grains of the genera within the wild Poacaeae cannot be separated under the microscope and so ecological reconstruction is poor. There are sporadic appearances of several grassland herbs, including *Filipendula* (meadowsweet), *Potentilla* type (tormentil, cinquefoils) and species of Asteraceae (daisy family), *Papaver rhoeas* type (poppies) and Caryophyllaceae (pinks). *Filipendula* is a tall grassland herb; so are several species of the Asteraceae. Their appearance might imply no or only slight grazing pressure. Some Asteraceae are associated with disturbed ground, as are *Plantago lanceolata* (ribwort plantain) and poppies (*Papaver rhoeas* type), both recorded at this time. *P. lanceolata* is associated with grazing, and though its high pollen productivity and ease of dispersal (Favre *et al.* 2008; Mazier *et al.* 2006; Mazier *et al.* 2009) mean it need not have grown locally the presence of other herbs makes its local presence likely. Caryophyllaceae pollen is comparatively abundant but the very large number of species in this pollen taxon precludes detailed analysis. If the current core distributions of species in this family (Fitter 1978) are taken to represent those in the past, and those confined to upland habitats (King and Nicholson 1964; McVean 1964), then species growing at Lair were, perhaps, *Stellaria* (chickweed, stitchworts), *Cerastium* (mouse-ears), *Sagina* (pearlworts), *Lychnis* (ragged robin) and *Silene* (campions) growing in some form of probably ungrazed, comparatively species-rich free-draining acid grassland (King and Nicholson 1964). The low proportions of charcoal are probably from the general region and not necessarily from the hillside at Lair.

Lpaz Lair 2a (1125-965 mm) 2500-2250 to 1000-750 BC

Sediment in lpaz 2 still accumulated at 9-10 mm/yr, the samples still a uniform *c.* 20 mm apart, around 180 years, and each sample again averages the pollen import of around 20-24 years.

Betula and *Calluna* are the main components. *Betula* persisted as the most important tree at Lair. *Quercus* values fell sharply at 2500-2250 BC though the occurrence of *Lonicera periclymenum*, *Vaccinium* and to a lesser extent, *Polypodium vulgare* suggest that *Quercus* still grew locally. *Corylus avellana* and *Corylus avellana* type also fell sharply at this time. *Alnus*, *Ulmus* and *Pinus* pollen became reduced, a probable reflection of human activities in the region rather than at Lair.

Calluna became significantly more important, as did species of Ericaceae indeterminable to higher taxonomic levels. *Calluna* undoubtedly grew locally after 2500-2250 BC. It may have colonised or expanded across both the herb peat surface of Basin 2 and the wetter fen surface around borehole A1, and by this spread will have reduced the representation of other pollen types. *Calluna* is unlikely to have colonised mineral soils above the fen because local woodland loss was insignificant and *Calluna* is shade-intolerant. Reasons for its establishment are hard to identify from the pollen record but the better representation of *Myrica gale* suggests the development of drier peat surfaces. The decline to probable local absence of *Salix* above 1050 mm depth (1800-1560 BC) might suggest increasing soil acidity, although soils would always have been nutrient-poor. There is no major change in the peat stratigraphy (Table 2.5).

The proportions of wild Poaceae (annulus diameters <8 um) decline gradually from 20 to 5 % tlp. This may be due to *Calluna* reducing the representation of wild grasses rather than being related to competition between the two plants. *Plantago lanceolata* was markedly more abundant, probably though not certainly locally. *Filipendula* was far less abundant, and species of Caryophyllaceae and *Papaver* are not recorded. Together the changes in these taxa indicate local grazing, though disturbance was limited. The single grain of *Avena-Triticum* pollen at 1115-1120 mm depth (2400-2150 BC: Table 2.7) may indicate local cultivation.

Charcoal values increase slightly, in all size categories, from 1800-1650 BC. Increases in charcoal abundance are often associated, with considerable caveats, with human activity (Edwards 1998; Tipping 1996) and larger charcoal particles are associated with closer proximity of fire source (Peters and Higuera 2007). Increases in both, in combination with evidence of extra-local to regional disturbance and with the possibility of cultivation, agrees with other evidence for increased human activity at Lair, and with activity becoming more proximal to the fen. It does not necessarily indicate activity close to the peat.

Lpaz Lair 2b (965-850 mm) 1000-750 BC to AD 80-320

Sediment still accumulated at *c.* 9mm/yr, the samples still a uniform *c.* 20 mm apart, around 180 years, and each sample again averages the pollen import of around 20-24 years.

This sub-zone probably reflects a period of slightly reduced disturbance to, and consequently slight recovery of woodland plant communities. *Betula-Quercus* woodland appears to have been undisturbed. It is unclear, however, whether *Quercus* grew in the pollen source area because the frequency with which *Lonicera*, *Polypodium vulgare* and *Vaccinium* are recorded is markedly less. *Corylus avellana* and *C. avellana* type pollen is more common, suggesting re-growth and this is also the interpretation for *Salix*. *Ulmus* pollen values are more constant and *Pinus* slightly increased, though whether either tree grew at Lair is very uncertain.

Percentages of *Calluna* and wild Poaceae (annulus diameters <8 μm) show little variation. The herb assemblages have some similarities with lpaz Lair 1, with Caryophyllaceae, *Filipendula* and *Potentilla* type consistently present, suggesting limited grazing pressure. *Plantago lanceolata* is consistently present but at reduced values. One grain of *Hordeum* group pollen is recorded at 957.5 mm depth, one at 917.5 mm depth and one grain of *Avena-Triticum* at 877.5 mm depth (Table 2.7), at 900-800 BC, 600-300 BC and 160 BC-AD 80. Between these times evidence for human activities around Lair 1 is slight.

Lpaz Lair 3a (845-665 mm) AD 660-600 to AD 975-1025

Sediment accumulated much faster in lpaz 3, at *c.* 2 mm/yr. Samples above 800 mm depth 10 mm apart, around 20 years between samples, with each sample averaging the pollen import of around 5 years.

In the probable hiatus in peat growth, *Calluna* values increased to 60 % tlp and they remain at 40-60 % tlp. *Betula* is <10 % tlp at the bottom of the zone, and despite recovering slightly above 800 mm depth (AD 690-750) remains between 10 and 20 % tlp. Values of wild Poaceae (annulus diameters <8 μm) oscillate around 10-15 % tlp but there are three peaks between 15 and 20 % tlp above 725 mm depth (after AD 850-900).

Betula-Quercus-Corylus woodland had declined. *Betula* probably persisted but at much lower abundances. *Quercus*, *Ulmus* and *Corylus* probably ceased to grow in the pollen source area and *Salix* was also lost. The light-demanding *Fraxinus* (ash) may have grown in low numbers. Woodland was replaced by an open dry heath growing now on mineral soils, characterised by *Calluna*, together with other Ericaceae, *Empetrum* and *Vaccinium*. *Vaccinium* may have benefitted from woodland loss only by increased pollen productivity and greater ease of dispersal, but *Calluna* must also have greatly expanded its range from comparative rarity on bog surfaces onto mineral soils, *Empetrum* growing with *Calluna* on free-draining acid soils on open ground formerly covered by woodland (Bell and Tallis 1973). The rapidity of this substantial change cannot be defined save that it was less than the duration of the hiatus, perhaps *c.* 400 years.

Grassland should have benefitted most from woodland loss because it is thought that wild grasses (Poaceae annulus diameters <8 μm) formerly formed the field layer of the woodland. Though values remain significant, proportions do not increase. It is possible that the landscape at Lair after AD 600-660 was not as dominated by heaths as the pollen record suggests, as grasses may have been cut for hay (Segerström and Emanuelsson 2002) or directly consumed by herbivores, limiting pollen production. It is also probably simplistic to think that grassland and *Calluna* heath were separate plant communities. A *Calluna-Empetrum-Vaccinium* dry heath would have included grass species and herbs like *Potentilla* (cf. tormentil), *Galium* (bedstraws) and *Succisa* (scabious). *Plantago lanceolata* pollen is present at 2-3 % tlp throughout the zone but is not significantly better represented. The erratic representation of *Filipendula* may indicate slightly heightened grazing pressure.

There is a suite of herb taxa associated with cultivation. These include *Cirsium*, Chenopodiaceae (goosefoot family) and *Papaver rhoeas* type. The occurrences of *Hordeum* group pollen and *Avena-Triticum* (oat or wheat) are of importance (Table 2.7). The very poor dispersal of grains of cultivated grasses (Vuorela 1973) means that these grains are likely to have originated from within a few tens of metres of the pollen site. Below 740 mm depth (before AD 810-875) charcoal particles <50 um long become more important, above this, larger particles, particularly >75 μm long. An increase in all size categories of microscopic charcoal fragments strongly suggests that fires were more common in this agrarian context originating from human activities, though what these were cannot be defined. Few taxa relating to the environment of the fen itself are abundant. *Sphagnum* spores become more abundant, though this may have no great significance.

Lpaz Lair 3b (665-580 mm) AD 975-1025 to AD 1140-1200

Calluna is still the dominant taxon but with a declining trend from >60 % tlp to around 50 % tlp. *Betula* has a rising trend from around 10 % to around 25 % tlp. Poaceae grains with annulus diameters <8 um remain at similar levels to the previous zone, oscillating around 10-15 % tlp. *Alnus*, *Quercus* and *C. avellana* remain present in every level, each with less than 5 % tlp. *P. lanceolata* is present at similar values to previous zones. *Filipendula* is also present in nearly every level, together with *Potentilla* type but there is a slightly sparser assemblage of other herb taxa. *Avena-Triticum* pollen is found at 655-660 mm depth (AD 990-1050) and *Hordeum* group at 635-640 mm depth (AD 1030-1090) (Table 2.7).

The open dry grass heath of the previous zone remained. At the base of the zone *Betula* pollen is at proportions when local presence is uncertain. Above 652 mm depth (after AD 1000-1050), however, small increases in *Betula* might mean that this tree re-appeared on the hillside, perhaps impinging on *Calluna* heath, though woodland did not re-form. The re-appearance of species of Caryophyllaceae and *Filipendula* may again imply reduced grazing pressure or their protection from herbivores.

It is likely that there was continued cultivation of cereals until AD 1110-1175. After this time no pollen from these groups is identified. This is an absence of evidence, of course, and so problematic, but probably meaningful for *Hordeum* group. Some taxa associated with cultivation in lpaz Lair 3a (Chenopodiaceae, *Papaver rhoeas* type, *Spergula* type) are also no longer recorded but their limited representation in that zone means little can probably be made of their absence in the subsequent zone. *Artemisia* (wormwood) re-appears with increased frequency, associated with bare or disturbed ground, but what disturbance is impossible to define. Little can be made also of *Oxyria* type pollen because the pollen taxon includes many common docks and sorrels.

The occurrence of van Geel's (1978) Type 62 non-pollen (algal) palynomorph (NPP) indicates open water, presumably on the fen surface, but no pollen of aquatics is recorded and spores of *Sphagnum* are reduced in numbers. Type 62 could reflect the flooding of peat banks abandoned after cutting (Section 4.1). Charcoal values are slightly decreased but insufficient to indicate much change to the locations, frequency or intensity of fire.

In summary, the pollen record commences at 3200-2950 BC. An open canopy *Betula-Quercus-Corylus* woodland grew around the pollen site on slightly acid, comparatively free-draining soils on till above the acid fen. *Vaccinium* heath was a minor component of the woodland field layer. *Betula* may also have grown with *Salix* on the edge of the fen. The fen surface was probably of Cyperaceae and *Sphagnum*, probably with rare *Calluna*. Grassland within the wood and possibly in open ground was only lightly grazed. If grazed by domestic livestock, this is the only indication of local human activities until 2500-2250 BC when *Quercus* and *Corylus* populations were reduced, though not significantly. Though the proportion of wild grasses declined, the grassland was undoubtedly grazed more intensively. Fire was a more common feature of the pollen source area, though not necessarily at Lair. There is a single grain of barley type at 2400-2150 BC. There was a slight recovery of woodland plant communities after 1000-750 BC as grazing pressures were probably lessened. Barley type pollen, not necessarily a cereal, is recorded at *c.* 850, *c.* 450 and *c.* 40 BC.

Within the hiatus in peat growth after AD 80-320 the *Betula-Quercus-Corylus* woodland declined and *Quercus*, *Ulmus* and *Corylus* probably disappeared around the pollen site, as did *Salix* in the fen. *Betula* may well also have been lost before peat growth resumed around AD 600-660. A dry *Calluna* heath with other Ericaceae, *Empetrum* and *Vaccinium* rapidly colonised acid mineral soils. The local abundance of *Calluna* pollen may mask the abundance of grassland in the wider area. The grassland was once more grazed but the major change was the appearance of cereal type pollen. Fires became more common and probably close to the pollen site. Cultivation of cereals possibly persisted around the pollen site until AD 1110-1175, after which there is an absence of evidence for crop growing. At AD 1000-1050 *Betula* trees began to re-colonise the hillside, though in small numbers only. The extent of grassland probably remained the same but may have been grazed less.

2.7 Charcoal analysis

Susan Ramsay

Introduction and methodology

Charcoal analysis of material recovered from two specific contexts was undertaken to aid interpretation of the archaeology, in addition to the identifications in Table 2.1. These contexts comprised the area of linear burning uncovered beneath the south-eastern end of Building 1 (C14) and the lower fill of the stone-lined hearth of Building 3 (C248).

Samples were processed by flotation for the recovery of carbonised remains, using standard methods. Dried flots and retents were examined using a binocular microscope at variable magnifications of x 4 – x 45. For each sample, estimation of the total volume of carbonised material >4 mm was made. For each sample, all charcoal fragments > 4 mm were identified, together with any carbonised seeds, cereals or other plant macrofossils present within the samples. The internal anatomical features of problematic charcoal fragments were further identified at x 200 magnification using the reflected light of a metallurgical microscope. Reference was made to Schweingruber (1990) and Cappers, Bekker and Jans (2006) to aid identifications. Vascular plant nomenclature follows Stace (1997).

Results

The results are presented in Tables 2.8 and 2.9 below: interpretation is incorporated into the results of the excavation (Section 2.4 above).

2. Results of Archaeological Fieldwork, Radiocarbon Dating, Peat-Stratigraphic and Pollen Analyses

Table 2.8 Charcoal identification from sample of linear burning (C14).

	Context	014
	Sample	017
Vol charcoal >4mm		500ml
Charcoal	**Common name**	
Betula sp.	birch	531 (157.24g)
Corylus	hazel	24 (1.31g)
Salix sp.	willow	2 (0.08g)
Carbonised cereals		
cf *Hordeum vulgare* sl	cf barley	1
Cereal indet	indet cereal	1

Table 2.9 Charcoal identification from sample of lower hearth fill (C248).

	Context	248	248
	Sample	113	115
Vol charcoal >4mm		15ml	100ml
Charcoal	**Common name**		
Betula sp.	Birch	57 (2.80g)	316 (21.24g)
Corylus	Hazel	7 (0.20g)	11 (0.71g)
Pinus sylvestris type	Scots pine type	-	4 (0.27g)
Salix sp.	willow	3 (0.10g)	1 (0.05g)
Carbonised cereals			
Avena sp.	Oats	-	7
Hordeum vulgare sl	cf barley	1	6
Cereal indet	indet cereal	1	9

3. The Small Finds

Strachan and Sneddon

with contributions from Wright, Clarke, Johnson, McLaren, Hall, Campbell and Smith

3.1 Introduction

The following reports present and discuss the small finds recovered during excavation. They are arranged by material and vary from artefacts of recognisable material culture to animal and plant remains, although it should be noted that sampling and analysis was not exhaustive in relation to carbonised botanical remains. Consideration must be given to the nature of the material recovered and what we can reasonably assume to have been lost through the acidic nature of the soils (Section 2.3). Later cultivation and the process of bioturbation within the collapsed turf of the buildings have also disturbed the upper levels of stratigraphy across much of the site. Given this, the survival of the iron work assemblage is notable, as is the preservation of bone within pit C278 of Building 3's annexe (Section 2.3), though bone preservation was otherwise poor, and the charred unidentified bark fragments within the turf wall of Building 1 (C3). However, the site is free-draining and no water-logged deposits were found. While the distribution of artefacts is considered further in Chapter 4, individual artefacts are discussed below within each specialist report and can be cross-referenced with ^{14}C dates (Table 2.1). Note: Artefacts recovered from sample processing have only catalogue (Cat) numbers as their unique identifier.

3.2 Lithics

Dene Wright

The assemblage comprises 38 pieces, of which 21 are of quartz and 17 of flint. Whilst the quartz could be from local sources, there are no known flint sources near Lair, and Lossiemouth, Moray and a number of other locations in Aberdeenshire are the nearest recorded sources (Wickham-Jones and Collins 1977: 9-12). The pitted cortex of the flint suggests that it was derived from glacio-fluvial sediment or glacial till. References to specific artefacts cite the catalogue number followed by the small finds number, where available.

The lithics are fresh apart from a burnt flint core fragment (Cat 34), a flint flake (Cat 2, SF2), and a quartz flake (Cat 5). The frequency of burnt pieces is probably underestimated. Experimental work on flint indicates that some burnt pieces need not retain evidence of burning (Finlayson 1990: 53). Table 3.1 shows the character of the assemblage.

Table 3.1 Characteristics of the lithic assemblage.

	Total	Flint	Quartz
Tested Split Pebbles	2		2
Chunks	1		1
Core	1	1	
Core fragment	1	1	
Flakes	24	8	16
Primary	4	1	3
Secondary	11	3	8
Tertiary	9	4	5
Primary regular			
Primary irregular	4	1	3
Secondary regular			
Secondary irregular	11	3	8
Tertiary regular			
Tertiary irregular	9	4	5
Blades	2	1	1
Primary			
Secondary	1	1	
Tertiary	1		1
Primary regular			
Primary irregular			
Secondary regular	1	1	
Secondary irregular			
Tertiary regular			
Tertiary irregular	1		1
Small Fraction	3	2	1
Modified	4	4	
Awl	1	1	
Barbed-and-tanged arrowhead	1	1	
Scraper	2	2	
Total	38	17	21

3. THE SMALL FINDS

Table 3.2 Analysis of recovery locations by context and sub-analysed between primary and secondary technologies.

	Context(s)	Total	Primary	Secondary
Unstratified	001	5	5	
Linear hollow	016	1		1
Pit/post-hole: Building 1	020	1	1	
Collapsed walls: Buildings 1, 2 & 4	002, 003, 005, 119, 120, 195	19	19	
Collapsed wall: Building 1	005	1		1
Hearth deposit: Building 2	128	1	1	
Interior floor: Building 3	162	7	5	2
Interior sunken area: Building 3	166	2	2	
Burnt material within interior floor: Building 3	289 (within 162)	1	1	
		38	34	4

Contexts

Table 3.2 shows the contexts from which lithics were recovered. All the lithics are likely to have undergone secondary re-deposition to some extent, meaning the contexts that they were recovered from may not reflect where the artefacts were initially deposited.

Primary technology

The flint core (Cat 25, SF37) and core fragment (Cat 34) have simple platforms for flake production. A platform reduction strategy produced eight of the nine flint and five of the quartz blanks, i.e. flakes and blades. A flint core rejuvenation flake (Cat 6) and four of the quartz blanks have evidence for anvil support. This refers to the placing of the platform core on an anvil for support in facilitating the removal of blanks. The other quartz blanks, two tested split pebbles, one chunk and a flint flake are bipolar. Generally, bipolar blanks will be under-represented because not all debitage products will present attributes associated with a bipolar reduction strategy (after Kuijt *et al.* 1995: 117). Anvil support suggests that platform and bipolar reduction strategies may have been coeval (cf. Wright 2012).

Secondary technology

Flint awl (Cat 1, SF1), Figure 3.1:

Recovered from a disturbed deposit (C5) post-dating the slumped turf bank of Building 1. There is inverse scalar retouch to the distal end and to both sides of the flake fragment. The lateral retouch combines to create the awl/borer point.

Flint barbed-and-tanged arrowhead (Cat 10, SF7), Figure 3.1:

A barbed-and-tanged arrowhead was recovered within an accumulation of material (C16) above the linear burnt feature which ran beneath Building 1. The

CAT 36, SF 74

CAT 10, SF 7

CAT 1, SF1

CAT 28, SF 42

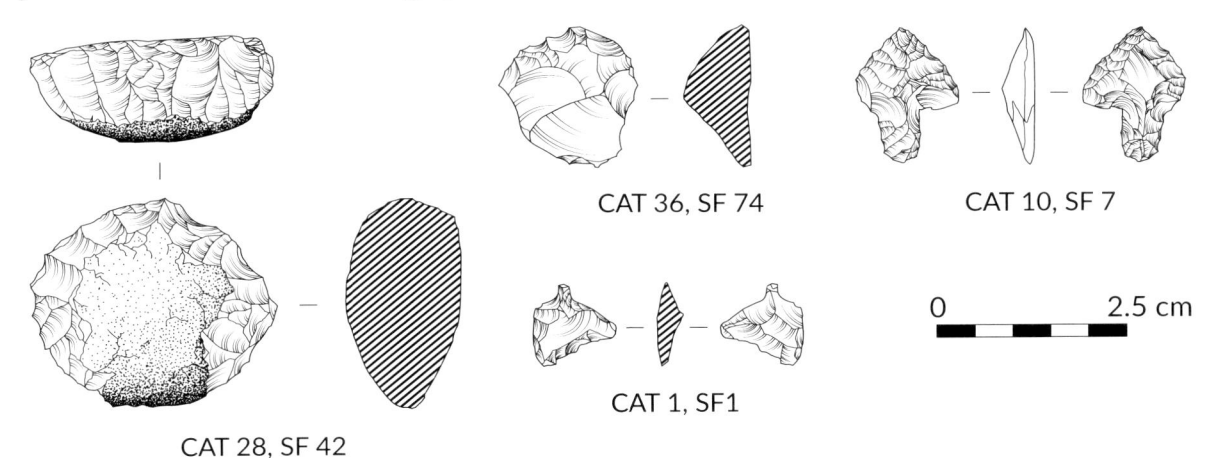

0   2.5 cm

Figure 3.1 Flint artefacts: Cat 1, 10, 28 and 36.

left hand side barb was broken during manufacture leading to abandonment and discard of the artefact. The retouch to the dorsal covers the whole surface. The ventral retouch is only semi-invasive, suggesting that the artefact was incomplete. The arrowhead is a Kilmarnock type [sub-type O] (Green 1980).

Flint sub-angled scrapers (Cat 28, SF42 and Cat 36, SF74), Figure 3.1:

Recovered from the floor/working surface (C162) of Building 3. Both artefacts have scalar retouch to two edges meeting to create the sub-angled scraper attribute. Other artefacts from C162 include a flint core (Cat 25, SF37), flint and quartz flakes, pottery, burnt bone, miscellaneous ferrous objects, slag and a spindle whorl.

Discussion

The limited evidence of the cores, tested split pebbles and primary flakes suggest that primary knapping of flint and quartz was undertaken near the structures at Lair. A Bronze Age provenance may be ascribed to the awl and the barbed-and-tanged arrowhead (Edmonds 1995: 205; Green 1980). Other lithics are non-diagnostic and cannot be ascribed to a specific archaeological period.

3.3 Stone tools

Ann Clarke

A diverse range of stone tools and objects were found, most of which (19 in total) are from Building 3 and its annexe, and two stone objects from Building 2 (Table 3.3). The assemblage is discussed with reference to the types of artefacts, their distribution and a comparison with other excavated sites.

Cobble tools and ground stones

The finest tool is a faceted smoother (SF39, Figure 3.2) made from a small, flat and circular waterworn cobble of banded quartzite. A finely ground flat narrow facet has been worn on one end from use on a harder surface and there is incidental light pecking around the perimeter of both faces. Both faces have been worn to a smooth polished surface from use on a soft pliable surface. A tiny quartz pebble (SF41) also has a polished face and may have been used in the same manner as the smoother (SF39). A rectangular schist cobble (SF21) has areas of smoothing and patches of coarse pecking around the surface of the stone. There were two plain hammerstones with pecking on the end (SF49 and un-stratified) and these were clearly not used to any great extent.

A large spall was removed from an oval cobble to create a concave face (SF29, Figure 3.2) and this surface was

Table 3.3 Stone artefacts.

	Building 2	Building 3
Whetstones		3
Cobble tools	1	5
Ground stones		2
Ground/structural slab		1
Anvil/whetstone		1
Anvil		1
Spindle whorl		1
Lamp/mortar		1
?Hollowed stone	1	
Rotary grinder		2
Rotary quern?		1
Quartz flake		1
Total	**2**	**19**

subsequently used as a grinder/smoother leaving small patches of grinding around the edge. Spalling damage has removed a significant amount of the original surface of an irregular cobble (un-stratified) but slight traces of smoothing indicate that this may have been used lightly as a grinding stone.

An irregular-shaped jasper pebble (SF70) does not appear to have been worn through use and it was most likely collected for its distinctive orange/red colour, perhaps as a gaming piece or for personal use.

Whetstones, anvil/whetstone and anvil

The finest whetstone (SF54, Figure 3.2) is a fragment of a small, rectangular-sectioned piece of micaceous siltstone. The surviving face and both sides are worn flat and smooth and there are striations from the edge of a fine blade running diagonally across one side.

Three other whetstones were formed on larger cobbles of schist or other metamorphosed rock. An irregular oval cobble of metamorphosed siltstone (SF78) is cracked and fragmented along fault lines. The surface has taken a high polish with some multi-directional striae from use. Two parallel V-shaped grooves made by a metal blade run along the length of one face and there are patches of lighter striations in the concave centre of another face.

A large sub-rectangular bar of schist (SF76, Figure 3.3) has broken across the width. Parts of the surfaces have been worn flat and smooth from use. The surviving face has been deeply worn, with a wide shallow channel running the length of the tool and accompanying narrow V-shaped grooves down one side.

3. THE SMALL FINDS

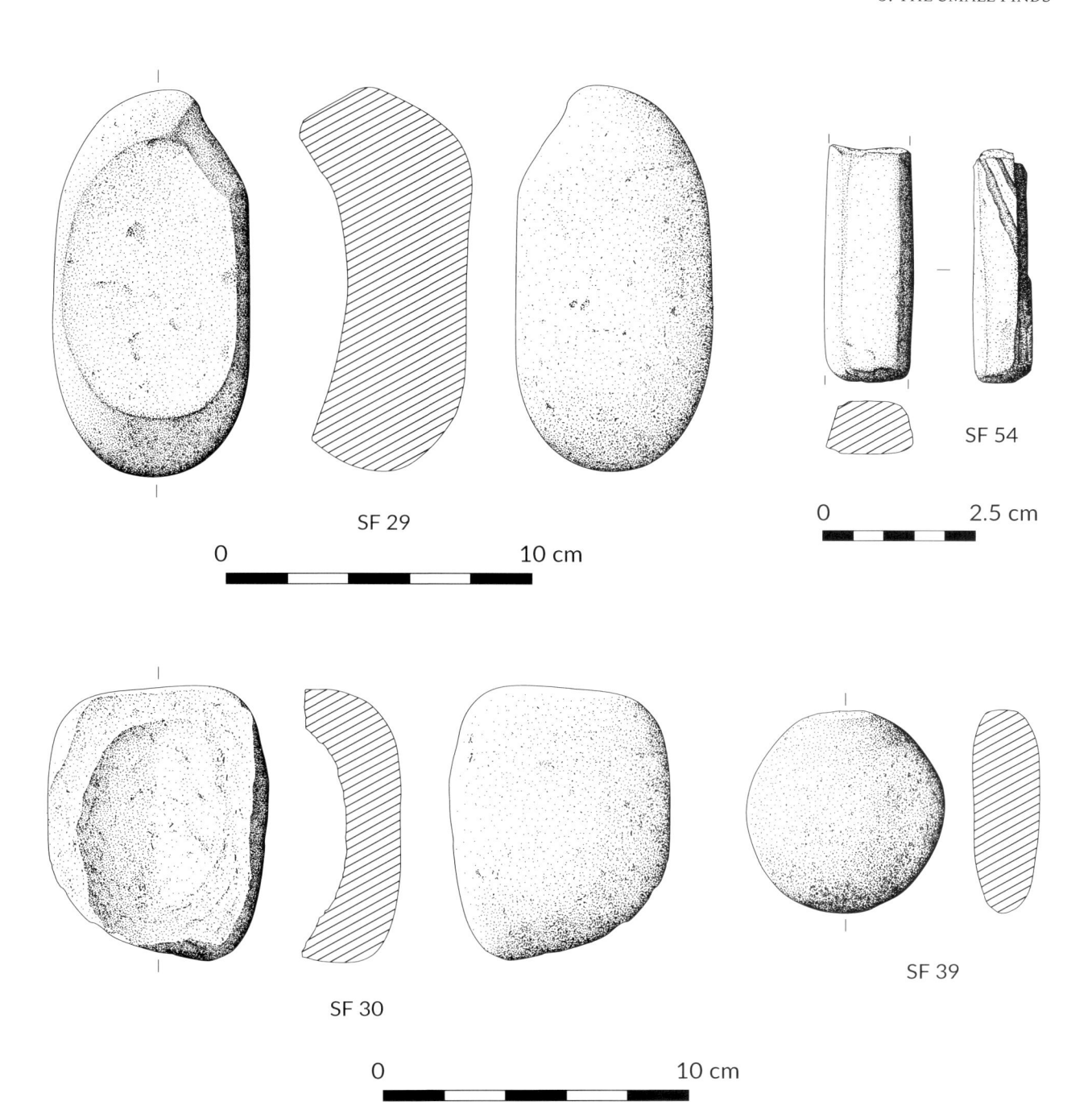

Figure 3.2 The faceted smoother (SF39), grinder/smoother (SF29), lamp/mortar (SF30), and whetstone (SF54).

A large sub-rectangular waterworn cobble of metamorphosed sandstone (SF58, Figure 3.3) was used as a whetstone leaving smooth areas on the faces and sides with patches of polish. Single shallow V-shaped grooves also run along the length of both faces from the maintenance of a metal blade. The whetstone was then used as an anvil, leaving a circular patch of coarse pecking which truncated the sharpening groove on the upper face, and there is also a lighter spread of pecking on the opposite face.

Another anvil (SF81) has been made on a tabular cobble of metamorphosed sandstone. One face has been used as an anvil leaving a deep patch of pecking in the centre of the face. On the opposite face there is a shallow U-shaped groove ground around the slightly curved face.

Rotary grinders

A segment survives of a thin rotary grinder (SF55, Figure 3.4) made from medium-grained red sandstone that has been imported to the area since it is not a local rock. The grinder has been worn heavily around the perimeter to a smooth skewed surface. Both sides are also worn smooth and there are deep V-shaped grooves from blade edge maintenance on one side. The radii of the faces from the edge of the central perforation vary

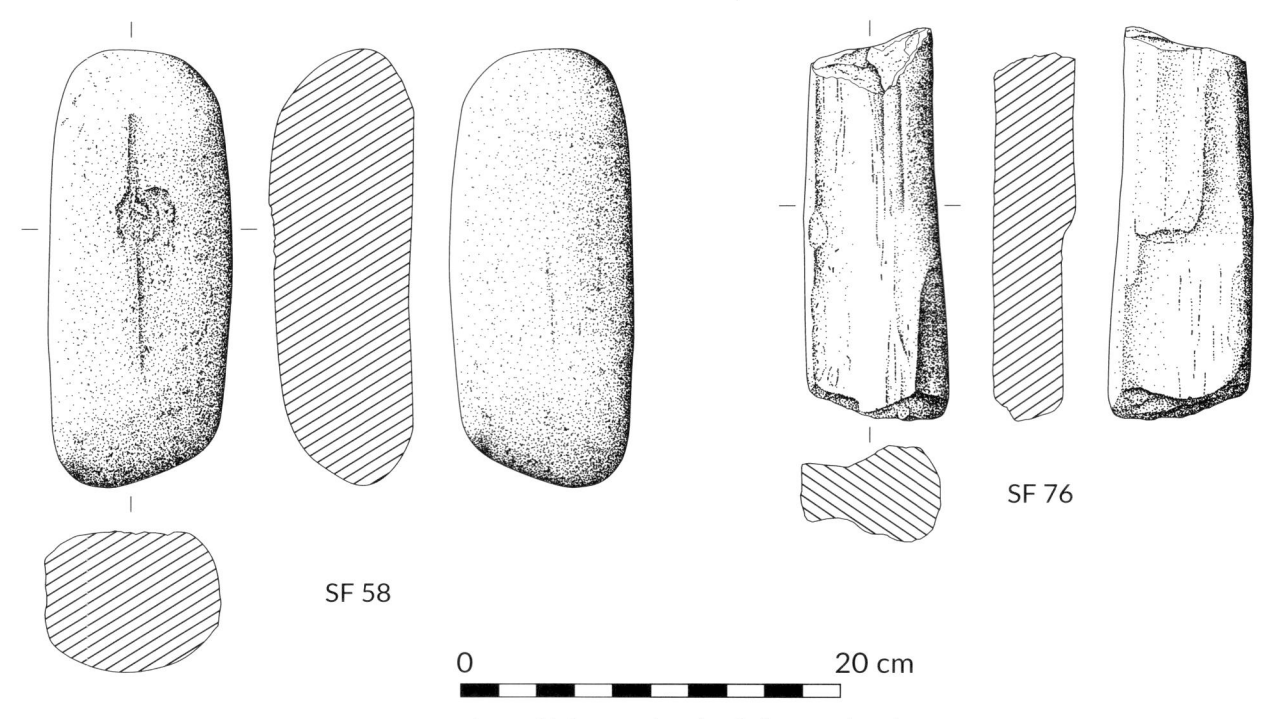

Figure 3.3 The anvil/whetstone (SF58) and whetstone (SF76).

from 145 mm to 165 mm, suggesting the grinder had been worn to a sub-circular outline prior to breakage. It has a maximum thickness of 51 mm.

The other grinder (SF86, Figure 3.4) is very different in form. It is a complete stone of medium-grained red sandstone similar to SF55. It is thick (95 mm) and has a large, eccentric perforation. The outline of the grinder is distinctly oval in plan (265 mm long and 240 mm wide) and accords with the stone having rotated around an off-centre perforation. The perimeter is heavily worn to a smooth, skewed surface. One side is dressed by chisel and has not been worn - this was face-up when found. The opposite side has been worn to a smooth, skewed surface and there are additional V-shaped grooves from blade edge maintenance. The perforation is wide at 95 mm, and parallel-sided, and must have been made to accommodate something larger than a rotating spindle – possibly a thick wooden axle.

This is an unusual form of grindstone – its thickness, eccentric hole and oval outline have few, if any parallels in the literature. The closest published comparison is from Baliscate, Mull, Argyll and Bute (Ellis 2017: illus 42), which is similar in shape and manufacture to the Lair example and with a similar thickness, though it is smaller in diameter and the perforation is consequently smaller in diameter too. Though the Baliscate piece is broken the illustration suggests the perforation to be slightly eccentric, yet another similarity to that from Lair. This came from blocking of the original entrance to a 14th century turf and stone structure, but the occupation of the site began in the 6th century AD (Ellis 2017) so it may have derived from the earlier activity at the site.

A survey of the Scottish medieval archaeology literature suggests that thin rotary grinders are found at sites with a similar date to Lair (Table 3.4). One from Inchmarnock, Argyll and Bute (Lowe 2008), is made from red sandstone and likely to have been imported. It has a similar radius *c.* 145 mm to that from Lair and is a bit thinner at 36 mm. Other rotary grinders have been found at Clatchard Craig, Fife (Close-Brookes 1986) and Dunadd, Argyll and Bute (Lane and Campbell 2000) whilst those with a larger diameter tend to be found in later medieval contexts, such as St Paul St, Aberdeen (Murray 1982).

Rotary quern

A fragment of coarse-grained quartz schist (SF56) is probably a segment from a rotary disc quern. It is abraded over the whole surface destroying the original surface, and therefore no wear or tooling marks survive. The base is flat with a possible radius >210 mm and a surviving maximum thickness of 75 mm.

Ground/structural slab

This sandstone slab fragment from C162 bears wear marks that might have been caused by it being part of a floor surface. One face has been worn to a slightly smooth skewed surface with multi-directional striae and there is a shallow irregular curved groove towards one end. There are also two distinct U-shaped grooves on the opposite face: one is at right angles to the break

3. The Small Finds

Figure 3.4 Rotary grinders SF55 (top) and SF86 (bottom).

Table 3.4 Rotary grinders from selected Scottish medieval sites.

Site	Diameter mm	Thickness mm
Lair, Glen Shee	>300	51
Lair, Glen Shee	265	95
Baliscate, Mull	220	110
Clatchard Craig, Fife	322	43
Inchmarnock, Bute	>290	36
Dunnad	210	55
St Paul St, Aberdeen	380	Not given
St Paul St, Aberdeen	366	Not given

and the other runs diagonally across the opposite end. These grooves may have been worn by an action such as 'furniture' movement and the worn surface may be a result of foot traffic.

Lamp/mortar

This is formed from an oval cobble which has been split lengthwise and then worked to a hollow on the fractured face (SF30, Figure 3.2). The hollow is rough inside and round-based, and it has an irregular rim. It is probably an unfinished lamp or mortar.

Slab with hollow

This is a sub-angular slab of sandstone (SF24) with what is most likely to be a naturally formed hollow located on one face. The interior of the hollow has a natural rough surface and it is *c.* 180 mm in diameter and 25 mm deep.

Distribution

The distribution of the stone tools points to different areas of deposition within and around Building 3 (Table 3.5). The spindle whorl and all the cobble tools as well as the large bar whetstone (SF76) and a possible ground stone (No SF number) were all found on the west floor. In contrast the stone tools from the east floor, entrance blocking and annexe comprised, anvils, whetstones and rotary grinders. The whetstone (SF78) and lamp/mortar (SF30) were found amongst bank material.

The complete rotary grinder (SF86) was found in paving at the entrance of Building 3 and its deposition bears a close resemblance to the similar rotary grinder from Baliscate, Mull which was also placed in the blocking of an original entrance, albeit dated to the early 14th century (Ellis 2017). Given the span of c. 500 years between the deposition of grinders at Lair and Baliscate it might be unwise to compare the two actions too closely. It is worth noting, however, that rotary querns were often redeposited in significant positions within structures as opening or closing deposits (see discussion in Strachan 2013) and it is not unreasonable to think that the rotary grinders from Lair and Baliscate were also placed as some form of closing deposit to mark the end of a previous use of the structure, or the beginning of another.

Presuming the majority of stone tools relate to the use of Building 3 and the annexe, rather than earlier occupation, there is a divide between the deposition of artefacts in the west of Building 3, which appear to relate to spinning and processing of materials with small cobble tools, and which might be interpreted as 'light' or 'domestic' work, to the heavier 'industrial' activities that needed blade maintenance using rotary grinders and whetstones in the annexe and east floor. The presence of anvil surfaces on portable tools also suggests manufacturing or maintenance activity. Given the large size of all but one of the whetstones and the use of rotary grinders, the annexe could have served to keep large metal blades in condition, perhaps for agricultural implements such as ploughs, hoes and spades, or possibly weapon edges. The small rectangular whetstone was clearly a personal item kept to sharpen small knife blades.

Stone tools from Building 2 comprised just one cobble tool (SF21) from the turf and a slab with a natural hollow (SF24) from wall collapse. The lack of tools here suggests that the building had not been occupied in the same manner as Building 3, or that it had been cleared out during or after abandonment.

Comparison with other sites

Despite the similarities between the turf buildings at Pitcarmick and Lair, the range of stone tools recovered from the excavations at Pitcarmick (Carver *et al.* 2012: Online archive 7.3) are different to those found at Lair. At Pitcarmick the assemblage includes: a spindle whorl, a stone polisher, a hammerstone, a stone disc and a group of six possible digging tools made from large stone flakes. Tools such as whetstones, anvils and rotary grinders, however appear to be absent. This might

Table 3.5 Stone artefacts from stratified Building 3 contexts.

	West Floor 162	East floor 166/157	Entrance blocking	Annexe	Bank material	External
Spindle whorl	1					
Cobble tools:						
Faceted smoother	1					
Pebble polisher	1					
Plain hammerstone	1					
Unused jasper pebble	1					
Ground stone	1					1 (C159)
Ground/structural slab	1					
Whetstone	1			1	1	
Anvil/whetstone				1		
Anvil		1				
Rotary grinder			1	1		
Lamp/mortar					1	
Rotary quern?		1 (C157)				
Total	8	2	1	3	2	1

suggest that the maintenance of large metal blades was not carried out at Pitcarmick and by extension the activities that they imply were not practised there.

A craft area in the early monastic enclosure at Inchmarnock and dating to the 9th century AD had a similar range of stone tools to that found in the enclosure and east floor in Building 3 at Lair, including a rotary grinder (see above), whetstones, anvils, hollowed stones and cobble tools (Lowe 2008). It is unlikely that the manufacturing activities of the monastery and the Lair buildings were the same but it does indicate that stone was used for a suite of tools that were in daily use at this period.

3.4 A decorated stone spindle whorl

Catherine Johnson

A stone spindle whorl (SF33) was found in 2015 in the western end of Building 3, Trench 23, within an artefact-rich occupation layer (C162). The circular sandstone whorl is complete and has relatively flat sides, giving it a rectangular cross-section. It measures 36 mm in diameter, ranges from to 4 to 8 mm in thickness and weighs 16.2 g. There is a single central hole measuring approximately 11 mm in diameter. The whorl is made of a beige, fine-grained sandstone not native to Glen Shee (Ewan Campbell *pers comm*) and may have come from a region some 25 km or so south of the site.

The decoration and markings

One face of the spindle whorl is heavily marked (Figure 3.5) and while some markings appear to be accidental gouges and scratches, a number are deliberate carvings. Some of these are deep and highly visible, whilst others are light and faint. This lack of consistency suggests episodes of carving, perhaps by more than one hand.

The carvings are often overlapping, making it unclear where one carving ends and another begins. The incisions do not indicate any predominant orientation. The spindle whorl has been loosely divided into three areas: Area 1, Area 2, and Area 3 as indicated in Figure 3.5.

The carvings in Area 1 are deep and stand out as the most coherent group of lines. They appear to be intentional and consist of an ovoid or sub-rectangular outline, with the lower side flat and the upper somewhat concave. Four slightly curving lines of similar length project out from the underside, roughly parallel with one another. If this is the correct orientation, these lines could plausibly be interpreted as the body and limbs of a quadruped, such as a horse or deer, but this is highly uncertain. Just above the ovoid 'body' are additional lines that may be associated, perhaps intended to represent the horns or antlers of the supposed animal. Further deeply incised lines of similar type are within Area 2, which are particularly tangled and perplexing. On the outer edge of the whorl is a set of lines of similar length and depth. It is not clear if these are intended to be read together as a series of figures, in which case they could be read as the Latin letters K, I, and K or H. The resemblance is slight, however, and especially given the extreme rarity of 'K' in this period, likely to be merely coincidental. The possibility that these markings could be runes is also highly unlikely given that their resemblance to these is so slight.

Area 2 also has additional incisions near the inner edge of the spindle whorl, underneath the three characters previously described. These lines create geometric and convoluted figures that cannot be easily described nor understood. It is possible that they are merely formed by natural weathering of the stone: however, one particular component is a rectangular-like feature with a cross-like motif in the centre, which is perhaps

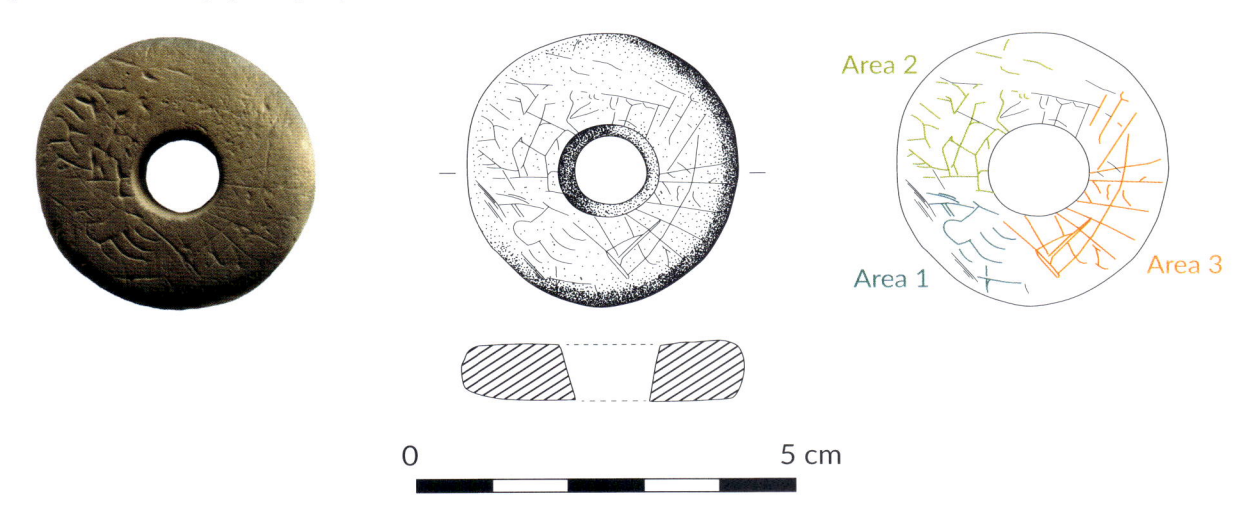

Figure 3.5 Spindle whorl (SF33): image extracted from RTI and incisions described in the text (RTI courtesy of H. Christie and S. Jeffrey of Glasgow School of Art).

deliberate. There are additional slight scratches and gouges, which could be attributed to natural abrasion, but the rest of Area 2 is relatively clear of markings. Area 3 contains a series of lightly, but deliberately carved vertical and horizontal lines that create a radial design. A long line runs at a slight curve for about 38 mm, approximately mid-way between the inner and outer edges of the whorl. Roughly bisecting this main line is a series of eight lines, five of which radiate from the central hole to the outer rim. Beyond this are two, possibly three, lines parallel to one another and lying at a sharper angle. These may or may not be associated with the previous five lines. It has been suggested that this carving may be an inscription in the ogham script but, for the reasons set out below, this is rather uncertain. At the other end of the mid-line is a deeper and longer line connecting the mid-line to the ovoid figure in Area 1. It is unclear whether this was deliberate and to what this line is associated. Furthermore, there is an additional shorter incision running above and parallel to the mid-line that crosses through three of the bisecting radial lines.

Discussion

Spindle whorls are evidence of domestic textile production traditionally associated with feminine gender roles. Used to add weight and momentum at the end of a spindle for hand-spun textiles, they are found widely throughout the archaeological record. They are believed to have been highly personal items, enough to be frequently included as grave goods. At the Anglo-Saxon cemetery of Castledyke South, Barton-on-Humber, North Lincolnshire, spindle whorls were found at the hip of female skeletons, suggesting that they were held in a belt or girdle (Foreman 1998: 294), further indicating that they were important enough to be kept close to their owners. In the British Isles they are found throughout the Neolithic to later medieval periods within burial and household contexts, as well as stray finds, a trend that is evident in other periods and locations, including within Roman, Merovingian, Scandinavian, Germanic and Gaulish cultures (Green 2012: 98-100; Jesch 1991: 14). The decoration on these whorls is incredibly varied, from detailed and patterned paintings, carvings and moulds to minimal markings. Bronze Age clay spindle whorls from Troy depict a multitude of highly individualised geometric and stylistic designs, many of which resemble the casual doodles on the Glen Shee example (Schliemann 1875: PL XXIII-PL XXXI).

The radial decoration on the Glen Shee spindle whorl was brought to attention due to its visual similarity to ogham script. Spindle whorls with similar carvings that have been described as 'ogham-like' include one from the Broch of Burrian, North Ronaldsay, Orkney (National Museums Scotland X.GB 58), which is dated to *c*. 400-800 AD and has seven radial lines arranged along a circular stem line, a resemblance to ogham that MacGregor states is purely coincidental (1974: 92). Another example is a whalebone disc, 99 mm in diameter, from Foshigarry, North Uist, Eilean Siar, decorated with interlace designs as well as a circumferential line along its outer edge with 74 short radial lines at varying angles (Hallén 1994: 217). Hallén's suggestion that the incisions were intended to imitate ogham is refuted by Forsyth (1996: 512-13) who states that the resemblance is too slight to be certain. A lead spindle whorl from Colchester, Essex displays similar linear markings that have been described as 'early writing', but are also a mere resemblance rather than genuine ogham (Colchester Treasure Hunting and Metal Detecting 2017).

An apparently unpublished stone spindle whorl found in Fintray, Aberdeenshire (British Museum 1906: 0421.202), has similar radial lines expanding out from the central perforation but without a central stem line. This spindle whorl is dated from the Neolithic to Bronze Age, illustrating that this type of linear decoration may be widespread. There are a high number of spindle whorls from Scandinavia of varying shapes with renditions of this type of decoration. These include a cylinder-shaped one from Jæren, Rogaland county, Norway (Arkeologisk Museum, Stavanger: S1531), a dome-shaped whorl from Voss, Hordaland, Norway (Universitetsmuseet i Bergen: B6288r), and a disc-shaped wooden spindle whorl from Oslo that also displays a runic inscription (Kulturhistorisk Museum, Oslo: C31266h; MacLeod and Mees 2006: 51). A conical spindle whorl from Kvam, Hordaland, Norway (Universitetsmuseet I Bergen: B14979_1), has three horizontal lines circling around its sides and is nearly identical to a steatite whorl from Jarlshof, Shetland (National Museums Scotland: X.HSA 422; Treasure Trove: TT 8/07), which is decorated with a horizontal groove running through linear incisions (Heald 2007: 175). From Jarlshof and Dunrossness, Shetland are a number of Pictish stone discs with intricate designs and ambiguous carvings resembling the markings on the Glen Shee example (Scott and Ritchie 2009: 16-17; National Museum of Scotland: GA.425).

There exists a wide corpus of inscribed spindle whorls, including a large number from the continent with Gaulish, Gallo-Latin and Latin inscriptions, most of which contain erotic messages to women (Meid 1994: 52-56). There is a suggestion that these were not actual spindle whorls but 'spinning-room amusements' given as gifts to women from their admirers (Meid 1994: 53). More relevant to this discussion is the 8th century spindle whorl from Buckquoy, Birsay, Orkney which is incised with an ogham inscription circling around its face reading (B)ENDDACTANIM(L), 'a blessing on the soul of L' (Forsyth 1995: 688). Runic inscriptions on spindle whorls are more numerous and include a whorl from Lincolnshire with a particularly long prayer to Nordic gods in Norse runes (Daubney 2010), a steatite whorl from Stromness, Orkney, stating that 'Gautr carved the runes' (National Museums Scotland: BE360; Holman 1996: 258-59), and a number of whorls from Norway containing personal-names and often more personal messages. An example is the previously mentioned wooden spindle whorl from Oslo that states in runes, 'Nikulás loves well the woman called Gýriðr, step-daughter of Pétrs(?)-Ragna' (Kulturhistorisk Museum, Oslo: C31266h; MacLeod and Mees 2006: 51). An Anglo-Saxon jet spindle whorl from Whitby Abbey, North Yorkshire is inscribed with a runic inscription transliterated as Wer, possibly a male personal-name or the West Saxon wœr, meaning 'token of friendship' (Page 1973: 171; Peers and Radford 1943: 74). These inscriptions illustrate that the whorls were highly personal possessions, ones that were continually handled, used and valued in societies in which textile manufacture was present.

The Glen Shee spindle whorl fits in with other decorated whorls, but stands out due to its informal and casual quality. The doodles have a spontaneous graffiti-like element to them and suggest a complex biography of the object in which the decorations were done at different episodes of its life. Certainly some of the markings were deliberate incisions, in particular the possible quadruped animal. The radial carving also appears to be deliberate, possibly inspired by spindle whorls such as the Broch of Burrian. The possibility of an intended inscription cannot be ruled out but it is likely to be coincidental. If so, it may represent the two ogham letters I or R, followed by G or O (Katherine Forsyth *pers comm*), but it is highly ambiguous. Pictish ogham stones from the Perth and Kinross sites of Dupplin, Abernethy, and Inchyra House, St Madoes (Forsyth 1996: 241 and 333-59; Southesk 1895), illustrate that the ogham script was certainly known within the surrounding region. It would, therefore, not be too much of a stretch to suggest that the spindle whorl's incisions could be ogham or ogham-influenced. Whether the carvings on the Glen Shee spindle whorl were meant to represent anything recognisable or not, they can still be described as deliberate additions to the object either as intentional 'decorations' or casual 'doodles'. The whorl remains a fascinating representation of early medieval material culture in Scotland and provides archaeologists with a direct connection to human agency of the past.

Additional note on decorated spindle whorl SF33

Ann Clarke

There are traces of a dark 'residue' around the outer edge of the whorl which could be lanolin from sheep wool transferred from the fingers. There are also wear traces on the whorl which would suggest that it had been worn as a pendant. There is a slight dint in the circumference of the perforation marked by an irregularity inside the perforation. The decoration at this point on the face is much fainter, and the edges of the circumference are more rounded at this point than elsewhere. These wear marks may reflect the rubbing wear from a cord that had been laced through the perforation for suspension, in which case the dark 'residue' around the edge may have come from fingering the pendant whilst it was being worn.

3.5 The iron objects

Dawn McLaren

Introduction and methodology

A minimum of 35 iron objects were recovered during the Lair excavations. The iron items survive in a range of conditions from poor and fragmentary, to substantially complete. The number of identifiable artefacts amongst the assemblage is not large but a variety of tools, household fittings and dress accessories are present, each of which provides glimpses into the activities, crafts and day-to-day life at the settlement during early medieval times. Several of the pieces were too corroded or fragmentary to identify with confidence but substantially complete knife blades, buckles and pins were easily recognisable and where possible have been classified in accordance to established typologies.

Few of the items present are categorically diagnostic of early medieval date, finding both earlier Iron Age and Roman parallels as well as later medieval equivalents. Exceptions to this are the dress accessories recognised amongst the assemblage which are distinctive of an early medieval date. Yet the assemblage fits comfortably with the type and range of metal-work found in association with a variety of early medieval sites across Scotland and beyond.

The identification of the ironwork has relied heavily on x-radiography of the corroded objects to aid macroscopic examination. The corroded and fragmentary condition of many of the objects places certain limitations on identification where aspects of surface treatment or form are obscured with heavy corrosion or damage. Precise identification in some instances is not straightforward and a range of possible interpretations of function and date have been considered below.

A running sequence of catalogue numbers has been applied post-excavation to the iron objects to allow those collected as 'General Finds' to be easily referenced. A full archive catalogue with a numerical concordance between the Catalogue Number and Small Find Number is presented in the archive.

Knives

The knife is a classic multi-functional tool and is amongst the most common and recognisable tool types from early medieval sites in Scotland. Three substantially complete but broken whittle-tanged knives (Catalogue numbers 1-3) were recovered in association with Building 1, deriving from the collapsed turf-built walls (C8, C21 and C55), whilst a fourth, incomplete blade (Cat 4), came from an occupation or floor surface within Building 3 (C162). Several of the blade types familiar in the early medieval period are long lived types with Roman antecedents (Manning 1985: 116, types 17-20; Ottaway 1992: 563) that continue in use with little modification into the medieval period (Duncan and Spearman 1984: 354, illus 25.1; Ford 1987: 132, ills 65, no 80-81; Goodall 1990: 835-860). Standard typologies (e.g. Blakelock and McDonnell 2007; Cowgill *et al.* 1987; Goodall 2011: 105-111; Laing 1975: 288, fig 99; Ottaway 1992; Ottaway *et al.* 2009a) rely on analysis and sequencing of the form and composition of intact examples. Despite the incomplete and corroded condition of the Lair examples, analysis of form has been attempted here by examining the shape of the back of the blade, a feature which is unlikely to have seen alteration as the result of use, as opposed to the cutting edge, which may have been significantly modified as the result of re-sharpening (Ottaway *et al.* 2009a: 203).

Three examples from Lair (Cat 1-3; Figure 3.6) conform to Ottaway's Type A blade, defined as 'angle-backed' blades (1992: 561), which are broadly consistent with Laing's Type 2 blade (1975: 288, fig 99) and Blakelock and McDonnell's type A (2007: 41, fig 2). This knife form features an abrupt change in plane of the back of the blade at some point between the shoulder and the tip. This form of blade originates in the Roman period and is commonly encountered amongst metal-work assemblages of early medieval and medieval date across Britain (Rogers 1993: 1273), seeing a floruit of use during the 9-11th centuries AD (Ottaway 1992: 564). Subtle variations in the form of angle backed blades have been analysed in larger knife assemblages, such as those from Coppergate, York, which have allowed a series of sub-categories of these blades to be recognised (Ottaway 1992). These variations may reflect differences in personal preference, workshops and function (Alcock and Alcock 1987: 107; Heald and Hunter 2008: 43). All three of Ottaway's (1992) sub-groups of angle-backed blades (Types A1-A3) are present at Lair. A damaged knife (Cat 2) missing a substantial portion of its tang and tip is consistent with Ottaway's Type A1, defined as having a back horizontal and parallel to the cutting edge (1992: 562-4). In this instance, the cutting edge is badly corroded, making it difficult to differentiate between modification as the result of wear or re-sharpening and post-depositional damage. It was recovered from (C21) in Building 1. Catalogue number 3 is of the more typical type of angle backed blade form with an upward sloping, abruptly angled back, conforming to Type A2. This type of blade does not appear to occur until the late 8th or 9th centuries AD at Coppergate and Fishergate, York (Ottaway 1992: 564; Rogers 1993: 1273). This early medieval date is consistent with the context of discovery at Lair. Catalogue 1 from C8 has been extensively used, causing modification to its form, but its back slopes slightly downwards towards the tip from the shoulder, suggesting it is more closely attributed to Ottaway's Type A3 blade than the previous two types discussed (Ottaway 1992: 565).

The fourth knife fragment (Cat 4) is incomplete, making precise classification of form impossible. The blade has broken squarely across the width, resulting in the tip of the blade being lost, and the extreme tip of the tang is also missing. The surviving fragment is of a straight-backed blade with parallel cutting edge and a tapering rectangular tang set centrally. Strong right-angled shoulders are present at the junction between the blade and the tang.

Despite the substantially complete condition of most of the knives within the assemblage, none of the blades from Lair were intact; three were broken at the junction between the blade and the tang resulting in the loss of the handle, whist a fourth example was broken cleanly across the width of the blade causing the loss of the tip. This type of damage suggests breakage during use. Three blades show some evidence of re-sharpening in the form of concave wear on the cutting edge, particularly the example from C8, whilst Cat 4 displays some thinning of the blade that is consistent with wear and whetting, but not to the extent demonstrated on the other examples. Traces of mineralised wood were noted on the stub of the tang of the blade (Cat 1) from C8.

Metallurgical analysis of early medieval knives has demonstrated the high level of craftsmanship employed in the production of blades during this period, including composite blades of iron and steel and some with applied steel cutting edges (Blakelock and McDonnell 2007). No evidence for such treatment can be detected on the x-radiographs of the Lair examples but no metallurgical analysis has been carried out to confirm this.

Catalogue

(Abbreviations: L length; W width; T thickness; D diameter; Cat catalogue number; SF small find number). *Terminology used follows Ottaway 1992: 559, fig 226.*

Cat 1 Knife, tang broken, Figure 3.6:

Small whittle-tanged knife blade surviving in three joining fragments; the tang is broken beyond the junction with the blade and the original length of the knife is unknown. Central broken tang, rectangular sectioned; the junction between blade and tang is weakly defined, with the tang expanding gradually to the blade but with a distinct upwards stepped shoulder 32 mm from broken end of tang. From this step, the back of the blade angles downwards gently towards the tip, then at *c.* 7 mm the gradient steepens sharply to the tip. The cutting edge of the blade has a similar step beyond which the blade curves gently upwards and then straightens towards the tip. This curvature is likely to be a product of whetting the blade. The form of the blade is consistent with Ottaway's (1992) Type A3. Surviving L 73 mm; tang: surviving L 15 W 4 T 3.5 mm; blade: L 58 W 7-13 T 5 mm. No SF number (C8).

Cat 2 Knife, tang and tip broken, Figure 3.6:

Small whittle-tanged knife blade, tip and tang are lost and cutting edge is badly damaged. The back of the blade rises steeply upwards from the vestigial stump of the central tang, flattening out to form a straight back which then angles down steeply towards the tip. The cutting edge is badly corroded so its shape is not possible to define, but the level of corrosion suggests damage and wear prior to deposition, probably the result of whetting. The form of the blade is consistent with Ottaway's (1992) Type A1. Surviving L 84.5 mm; tang: L 16 W 5.5 mm; blade: L 68.5 W 17 T 5.5 mm. SF10 (C21).

Cat 3 Knife, tang broken, Figure 3.6:

Substantially intact whittle-tanged knife blade with distinct rising angled back extending from vestiges of central rectangular tapering tang, broken at the junction with the blade. No distinct shoulder between back and tang, but a downwards curving choil is present between the tang and the cutting edge, which appears to be straight, curving gently upwards towards the tip. The form of the blade is consistent with Ottaway's (1992) Type A2. Surviving L 74.5 mm; tang: surviving L 4 W 7 mm; blade: 70.5 W 16.5 T 8 mm. SF15 (C55 - same as C3).

Cat 4 Knife, blade fragment:

Incomplete straight-backed blade, with parallel single cutting edge broken squarely across width, resulting in the loss of the tip. The cutting edge is thinned and marginally concave, suggesting limited wear and whetting. The tapering, rectangular, narrow tang is centrally positioned with strong, right-angled shoulders; the extreme tip is lost. A large corrosion blister (17 x 16 x 17.5 mm) protrudes from one face of the blade beyond the shoulder junction. Surviving L 69 mm; blade: surviving L 32 W 15 T 3-4.5 mm; tang: L 37 W 6 T 3.75 mm. SF40 (C162).

Other tools

A very limited number of tools has been recognised amongst the assemblage, consisting of a possible tanged awl (Cat 5; Figure 3.6), the hooked tip of a tool of uncertain form (Cat 6) and an elongated, conical iron ferrule (Cat 7; Figure 3.6), which probably functioned as a poker tip.

The tanged awl (Cat 5) is difficult to classify with certainty due to its fragmentary condition. In form it has a rectangular bar-shaped handle or tang, tapering into a broken sub-circular or triangular sectioned shank, the tip of which has been lost. It is not possible to determine the form of this now lost tool tip, but it is possible that it was a fine awl, punch or spoon bit. The latter is a tool typically associated with woodworking whilst tanged awls and punches could have seen a wider range of functions, including use as leather or woodworking tools. It is also unclear whether the rectangular bar-shaped 'handle' is a tang which would have been encased in a fine wood or bone handle. No organic traces now survive.

The clenched tip of the Lair tool is similar to a tanged awl from Whithorn, Dumfries and Galloway, and a tanged punch from Coppergate which are bent over to secure the iron tool at the butt end of the handle (Nicholson 1997: 422, no. 50.8; Ottaway 1992: 519, no. 2239), but it also bears similarities to an iron object from the medieval friary at Perth interpreted as a spoon bit (Stones 1989: 161, illus 104:426). Tanged tools such as those just described are not chronologically distinctive types but are known *inter alia* from early medieval contexts at Whithorn (Nicholson 1997: 422), Kildonan Fort, Argyll and Bute (Fairhurst 1939: 211-2, pl 77, no.1) and Bruach an Druimein, Argyll and Bute (Heald and Hunter 2008: 45-6) as well as medieval levels at Perth (Franklin and Goodall 2012: 143, nos 171 and 173).

The possible hooked tool tip (Cat 6) is a little more difficult to classify; such a small fragment of this item survives that close identification is impossible. Tentative suggestions on its identification include the tip of a possible agricultural implement such as a pruning or reaping hook, or even the spike from the tip of the back of a billhook blade (Goodall 2011: 80, fig 7.5; Manning 1985: 58-59, fig 14: 2). The latter is the most likely of the three suggestions made here on the basis of the cross-section of the fragment, which is thicker on the innermost curving edge, a feature somewhat inconsistent with the profile of pruning or reaping hook blades. Billhooks saw use in coppicing, trimming stakes and rails of wattle, and for laying hedges from the Roman Iron Age to the present day (Goodall 2011: 80).

An elongated conical sheet metal ferrule (Cat 7) was recovered from the same building as the hooked tool tip just described. Similar conical ferrules are regular finds amongst metal assemblages of late Iron Age to early medieval date in Scotland, such as those from Brough of Birsay, Orkney (Curle 1982: 66, ill.41, 470 and

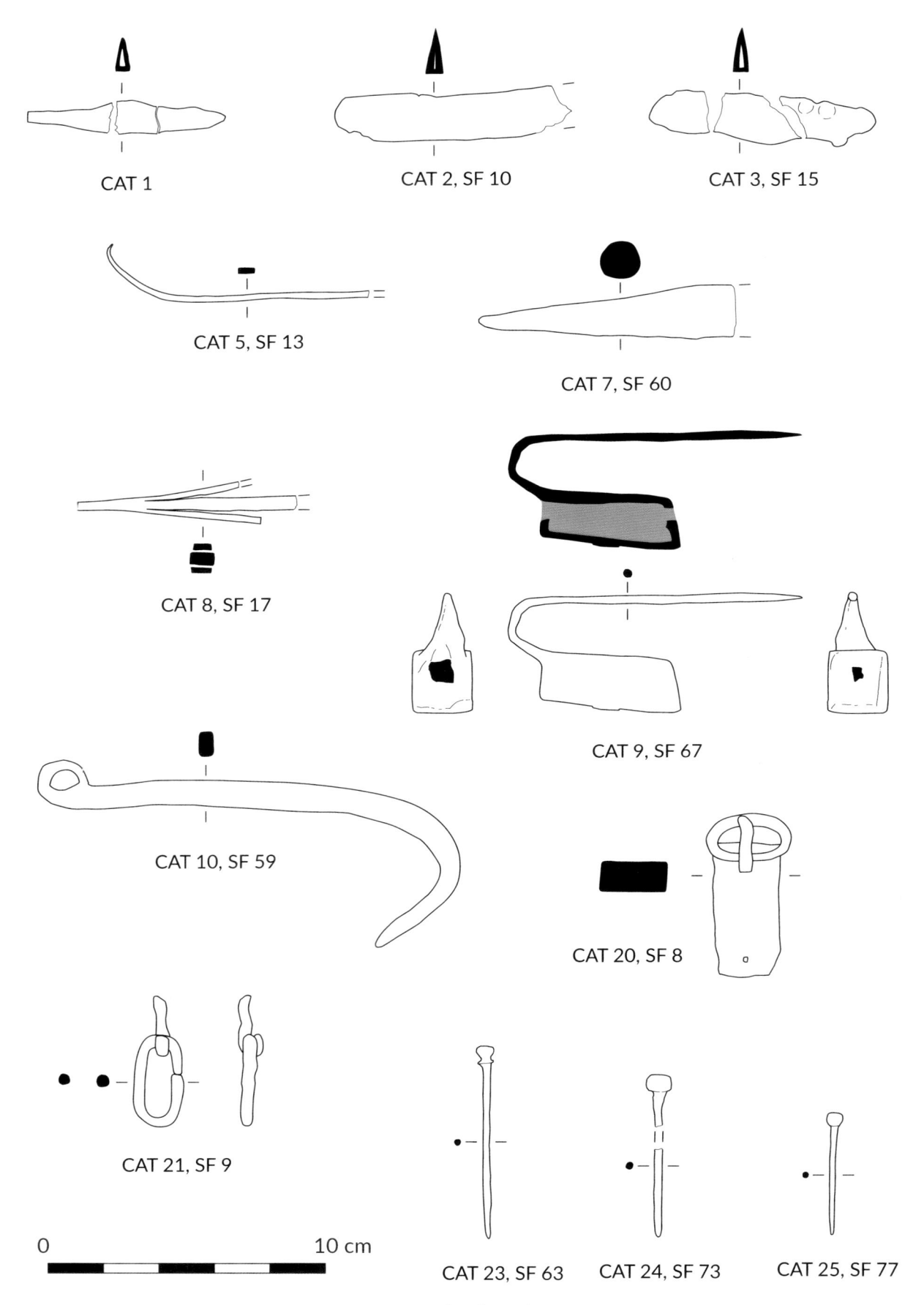

Early Medieval Settlement in Upland Perthshire: Excavations at Lair, Glen Shee 2012–17

CAT 1

CAT 2, SF 10

CAT 3, SF 15

CAT 5, SF 13

CAT 7, SF 60

CAT 8, SF 17

CAT 9, SF 67

CAT 10, SF 59

CAT 20, SF 8

CAT 21, SF 9

CAT 23, SF 63

CAT 24, SF 73

CAT 25, SF 77

0   10 cm

Figure 3.6 Selected iron objects.

472), Mote of Mark, Dumfries and Galloway (Laing and Longley 2006: 86, 88, Figure 41), and Scalloway, Shetland (Campbell 1998: 159, fig 102:7). Several simple conical ferrules were found during excavations at Dunadd, Argyll and Bute (Lane and Campbell 2000: 162, illus 4.71). It is perhaps not surprising considering their recovery from the early medieval stronghold at Dunadd that these ferrules were interpreted as spear or javelin tips, although it is clearly acknowledged that an association with weaponry is but one of many possible functions for such simply made and versatile objects (Lane and Campbell 2000: 162). Ferrules such as this example may simply have protected the bottom of wooden poles or staffs from wear (Manning 1985: 141; Ottaway 1992: 655). Several features of the Lair ferrule (Cat 7) suggest a different function, however: the shape is remarkably elongated, the tip is narrow but rounded, and it was recovered from the fill of a hearth (248) in Building 3. Rather than a projectile, or a staff-butt, it may be that this saw use (or re-use) as an iron poker tip affixed to a wooden shaft that was used to loosen the fire and stir the fuel (Goodall 2011: 11).

Catalogue

Cat 5 Possible tanged awl, Figure 3.6:

Long, fine rectangular-sectioned bar (W 7 T 3 mm), tapering asymmetrically at one end towards a narrow point which is bent at right angles at the tip. The opposite end is broken, but here the rod narrows in width and thickness into a triangular-sectioned or sub-oval tapering rod (W 5 T 4 mm). Surviving L 96 mm. SF13 (C39).

Cat 6 Hooked tool tip:

Thick, curving, rounded tip of a tool, possibly detached from the tip of a billhook or pruning hook. The surfaces of the fragment are severely damaged as the result of a detached corrosion blister. Surviving L 127.5 W 17.5 T 6-9 mm. SF43 (C162).

Cat 7 Probable poker tip, Figure 3.6:

Elongated conical sheet metal ferrule with rounded tip, closed seam and open squared wide end. The rounded narrower end (D 4.5 mm) is closed to protect the end of the wooden staff that this would have enclosed. Organic material survives in the interior of the squared open end (D 18.5 mm). The surface is badly cracked with fractures running along length of the ferrule. L 93 mm. SF60 (C248).

Security equipment

Amongst the assemblage are two items of security equipment in the form of a barbed padlock bolt (Cat 8; Figures 3.6-3.8) and a substantially complete padlock case (Cat 9; Figures 3.6-3.8). These are both components of the same form of lock.

Barb-spring padlocks, as represented by the padlock case (Cat 9), have a long currency of use. They first appeared in Britain in the Iron Age and continued in use throughout the medieval period until around the 16th century (Egan 2010: 91-2; Goodall 2011: 231, 246-250; Laing 1975: 294, fig 104, no.9; Manning 1985: 95-6). These simple cases were sub-rectangular or barrel-shaped in form, with either round or square cross-section, from one end of which projects the arm of a U-shaped bar, which forms the hasp (Manning 1985: 96). These padlock cases would be used in conjunction with loop-headed barbed bolts to secure, and a slide key to open. Barbed bolts, like Cat 8, are the spring mechanisms which would be inserted into a square or rectangular aperture at one end of the padlock case, its looped head slipping over the projecting U-shaped hasp of the case, securing the lock in place. These types of padlocks were opened by slide keys, which were inserted into a narrow slot at one end of the padlock case, positioned at the opposite end of the case to that which housed the barbed-bolt. Once inside the padlock case, the bit of the key would be passed over the springs or barbs of the bolt, compressing them to release the bolt, which could then be extracted to release the lock (Egan 2010: 91-2, fig 64; Goodall 2011: 231). Such padlocks are thought to have been used on doors and chests, although use to secure animals or people is also possible.

The padlock case from Lair is of sub-rectangular form consistent with those of Roman Iron Age and later date (Manning 1985: 95-6). Most of the surface details are obscured by corrosion and minor surface damage, but the backwards curving tapering bar or spine, on to which the looped head of the barbed-bolt would have been secured, is intact. Deriving from the same form of padlock mechanism is a possible fragmentary and damaged barbed-spring padlock bolt (Cat 5). The identification of this item as a barbed bolt rather than a broken pricket candle stick remains tentative but rests on its robust manufacture, the rectangular-section of the barbs and their difference in length; all common traits of barbed-spring bolts (Goodall 2011: 231-2). The tips of both barbs are damaged so basing identification on their form alone is problematic; however, the robust, squared form of the tip of the bolt is consistent with identification as a padlock bolt but would be unusual for a pricket candlestick tang which tends to taper to a distinct point, allowing the tip to be inserted into a wooden fixture (Egan 2010: 140-1, fig 107; Goodall 2011: 299). Similar simple spring mechanisms are found in medieval contexts as single barbed bolts or double paired bolts (Egan 2010 93, fig 65. No 243); the example from Lair, although broken, appears to be a single bolt variety. It is unclear whether this bolt was originally

Figure 3.7 The barb-spring padlock (Cat 9) after conservation (© AOC Archaeology Ltd).

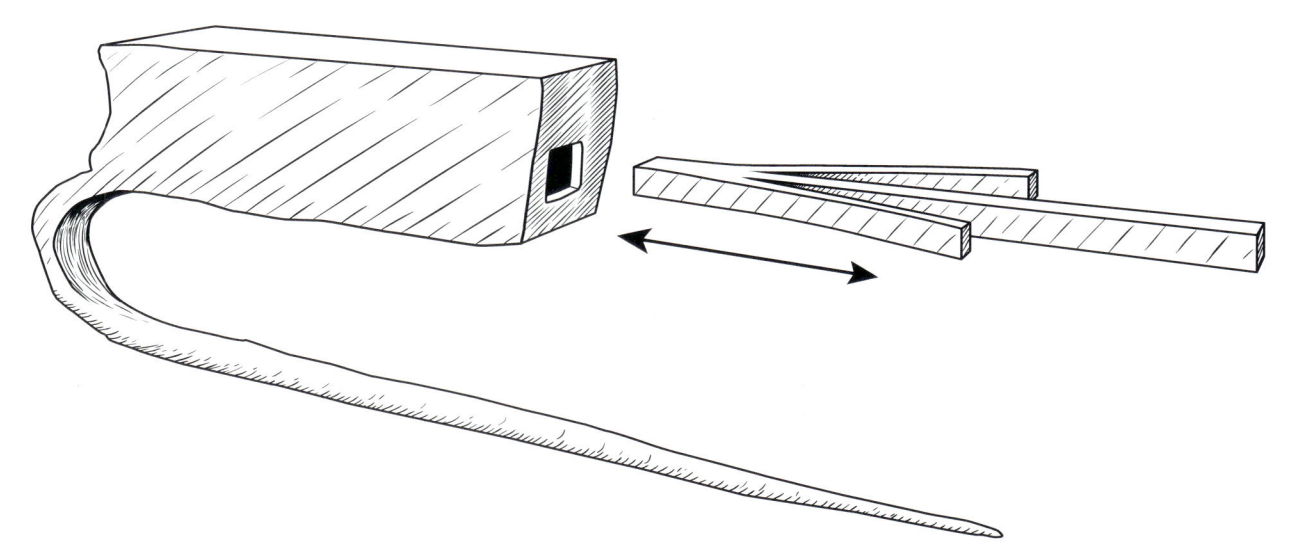

Figure 3.8 A schematic of the barb-spring padlock and bolt.

U-shaped in form such as that from 14th century contexts at Lochmaben Castle, Dumfries and Galloway (MacDonald and Laing 1975: 148, fig 11.21), or one with an integral circular closing plate such as that from the early medieval fort at Dundurn, Perth and Kinross (Alcock et al. 1989: 218, fig 15, no 7). The Lair bolt is quite substantial in size, surviving to 78 mm in length, and is comparable with that from Dundurn, where the surviving length suggested use as a door fixture rather than for a chest or casket (Alcock 2003: 99).

In addition to the Dundurn example, more complete examples of barbed padlock bolts of early medieval date come from Whithorn (Nicholson 1997: 416) and from early excavations of Buiston crannog, North Ayrshire (Munro 1882: 221; Wilson 2000: 139, fig 120, no 237). The stratigraphy of the last example is not well understood. On the basis of form it was considered to be consistent with a Roman Iron Age date, but it was found in the vicinity of a refuse-heap which is now thought to post-date AD 630 (Wilson 2000: 139). Both the Dundurn and

Buiston bolts have looped integral plates set at right-angles to the barbed bar. No padlock bolts or certain keys were found at Dunadd but two fragmentary iron objects were thought to be incomplete barrel padlock keys, indicating that similar items would once have been present at the fort (Lane and Campbell 2000: 167). The Lair padlock and barbed spring bolt certainly suggest a continuity of Romano-British technological traditions (Wilson 2000: 139).

The Lair bolt came from C56, a layer underlying the collapsed turf wall of Building 1. Samples from this charcoal-rich deposit produced two radiocarbon dates (late 9th-early 11th century AD and early 5th-early 7th century AD, see Chapter 2, Section 2.5) suggesting it either formed over a period of time or that at least one of the dated samples was residual. Although C56 may not be stratigraphically secure, comprising the spread remains of burnt linear feature (C14/24) that had partially mixed with the collapsed turf wall of Building 1 above (see Chapter 2, Section 2.4), a pre-11th century AD date for use and deposition of this object is possible. The padlock case came from Building 3; it was recovered from the possible occupation/floor surface (162).

Catalogue

Cat 8 Possible barbed-spring bolt, Figures 3.6-3.8:

Square-sectioned fine central bar splits mid-length, with two fine rectangular-sectioned damaged prongs (W 4 mm T 2 mm) radiating from central broken bar (D 3.5 mm). The opposite end of the central bar tapers to a narrow squared point, the extreme tip of which is damaged through use but not broken. L 78.5 mm. SF17 (C56).

Cat 9 Barb-spring padlock, Figures 3.6-3.8:

Substantially intact, rectangular padlock case, square in cross section but with a hollow interior. A long circular sectioned bar with tapered rounded tip, curves out and forms the top of the case, recurving to sit parallel with the long axis of the case, projecting *c.* 42 mm beyond its squared end. Overall, the iron surfaces are degraded, and spalls have detached in places, now stabilised by conservation. A large square or rectangular recess is present at the squared end to accommodate the insertion of the barbed-bolt, partially obscured by corrosion and possible mineralised wood traces. X-radiography confirms the case to be hollow. A narrow, horizontal, rectangular slide-key slot (16.5 x 5 mm) is faintly visible at the opposite end of the case, directly below the curving bar. Consistent with Manning's Type 1 barb-spring padlock (1985: 95-96, fig 25:10). SF67 (C162).

Household equipment

While only Building 3 has been confirmed as a domestic dwelling (Section 2.3), the scarcity of household equipment across the site is notable. A looped, curving hook (Cat 10) recovered from C162 may have seen use as a pot or cauldron hanger. Whether this hooked arm is part of a composite hanger, a type of suspension chain which saw widespread use across Europe from the Iron Age to medieval period, as illustrated by Manning (1985: 100-2; fig 27; Piggott 1953), is open to question. These hangers typically consist of a pair of arms, each formed of two rods, usually with decorative twisting, the lower one of which ends in a strong hook (Manning 1985: 100). The tops of these arms are linked by a ring attached to a chain, sometimes interspersed with linked short rods. The Lair hook lacks the decorative spiral twisting that is a common component of Iron Age and Roman hangers.

At Flixborough, North Lincolnshire 13 probable iron pot hooks and a composite cauldron suspension chain were recovered from contexts dating from the 7th to 11th centuries (Ottoway *et al.* 2009b: 173-4). Each of the pair of hooks from the Flixborough cauldron chain share certain similarities to the Lair example, namely a robust looped head and distinctly upwards curving hook, yet both display far more wear as the result of carrying the weight of a full cauldron, a feature absent from the Lair example. The Flixborough cauldron hanger hooks are also substantially more robust in thickness than that under discussion here and comparison to a smaller hook with postulated similar function from Urquhart Castle, Highland (Samson 1982: 469, fig 4. No. 58) may be more appropriate.

Catalogue

Cat 10 Possible pot hanger, Figure 3.6:

Curving rectangular bar with looped head (D 15 mm; interior D 7 mm), curving strongly at the opposite end into a tapering, robust, circular-sectioned hook (D 7 mm) with narrow tip (D 3 mm). Patches of damage are visible to the edge of the bar on x-ray. L 154 W 8-9 T 6-8 mm. SF59 (162).

Fittings

A variety of small nails, tacks, mounts and fittings were recovered from Buildings 1 and 3, all of which are likely to derive from internal household fixtures and fittings, including items of portable timber furniture such as chests and caskets. These comprise three possible tacks, which are difficult to distinguish here from damaged horseshoe nails because of their corroded forms (Cat 11, 13 and 15), two nail fragments (Cat 16 and 18), a z-shaped staple or fine brace (Cat 12), a possible rove fragment (Cat 14), and two further incomplete mounts or fittings, both broken across perforations (Cat 17 and 19). These last objects are difficult to classify with certainty due to their incomplete and heavily corroded condition. The expanded sub-circular head of a perforated fitting (Cat 17) may be the head of a hinged strap (e.g. Goodall 2011: 210, fig 9.23, H508-510) of the sort that may have seen use on a timber door or casket, whilst the curving perforated strip (Cat 19) is almost certainly a fine binding strap, but for what form of timber fixture or object is uncertain.

Cat 11 Tack or horse-shoe nail:

Flattened oval head (W 7 T 1.5 mm) expanding from short circular-sectioned shank which tapers to a slightly bent tip. L 24.5 D 5 mm. Sample number 5. No SF number (C3).

Cat 12 Z-shaped staple or fine brace:

Surviving L 11 D 4 mm. Sample number 5. No SF number (C3).

Cat 13 Tack or horseshoe nail head:

Robust, squat, triangular head expanding from a narrow, tapering square-sectioned shank, broken mid-length. The shape of the head suggests that the nail saw only light use prior to breakage. A further two small square-sectioned bar fragments, probably shanks from fine nails, are associated but no longer join and are likely to be from separate objects. Surviving L 13.5 mm; head: H 14.5 W 14.5 mm; shank: D 5 mm. SF19 (C57 - same as C49).

Cat 14 Rove or fitting:

Squared end fragment of a small, thin, quadrilateral sheet with irregular damaged edges, broken across a circular perforation, positioned at the centre of the sheet. Surviving L 27.5 W 25.5 T 4.5 mm. Context 'burrow' in vicinity of Building 3.

Cat 15 Tack or possible horseshoe nail:

Short rectangular-sectioned iron nail, head heavily corroded, obscuring details of its form. Short shank tapers slightly towards curved, almost clenched, tip. Macroscopically no surface details are discernible due to heavy corrosion; identification relies on x-ray. L 20.5 mm; Head D 6 x 7 mm; shank D 4 mm. SF28 (C163 – same as C178).

Cat 16 Probable nail head:

Small, flattened ovoid fragment of iron, surfaces spalled and heavily corroded with a protruding, rounded, corrosion blister (10.5 x 9 x 7.5 mm) on one face. Identification is not certain but it is likely to be a small nail head, detached from its shank. L 16.5 W 13 T 4 mm. SF48 (C162).

Cat 17 Fitting or mount:

Fragmentary and heavily degraded fragment of a rectangular fitting, slightly curving along its length, with an expanded, sub-circular head (D 33.5 mm), of which only a portion survives having broken across a squared perforation (D 16.5 mm). The opposite end is also broken and the original form of the object is unknown. An irregular void is visible mid-length by x-radiography, unclear if this is a damaged perforation or corrosion damage. Surviving L 67 W 22 T 8.5 mm. SF64 (C162).

Cat 18 Nail head:

Flat, sub-oval nail head, broken across the shank, below the head. Surviving L 17.5 mm; head: W 15.5 T 4.5 mm; shank: D 4.5 mm. SF64 (C162).

Cat 19 Fitting:

Narrow, thin, rectangular strip, slightly curving along its length, broken at both ends. A series of three or four fine sub-square holes perforate the strip at regular intervals, two of which have sub-rectangular tack or nail heads (22 x 17 mm; 18.5 x 18 mm) *in situ*. Surviving L 84 W 13.5 T 3-5 mm. SF68 (C286).

Dress accessories

A small but significant group of dress accessories was recovered from Buildings 1 and 3. These comprise two iron buckles (Cat 20 and 21; Figure 3.6) and three substantially complete iron pins (Cat 23-25; Figure 3.6). A further pin tip (Cat 22), representing a fourth example, also came from Building 1.

The two buckles comprise one intact oval frame and pin with a damaged folded rectangular plate (Cat 20) and another oval frame with pin, probably deriving from a similar plate buckle (Cat 21). Both came from the collapsed turf walls of Building 1 (C3 and C21). The buckle plate would have provided a means of attaching the frame to the leather or textile strap in a more secure way than sewing the strap together to hold it in place (Egan and Prichard 1991: 55). The damage to the rivetted end of one face of the plate of Cat 20 suggests that it was broken during removal from the end of the belt that it had been attached to.

Belt buckles are common personal items within graves of early medieval date, particularly in Anglo-Saxon burials (Alcock 2003: 95). They are less well represented in settlement contexts but parallels do exist, such as that from Fishergate, York, seeing a floruit of use in the 7th century (Rogers 1993: 1346, fig 650: 5045 and 5046). Two almost identical iron buckles come from both settlement and funerary contexts at Yeavering, Northumberland: one was found at the waist of an extended inhumation (grave group BZ; Hope Taylor 1977: 183, fig 87, no 1) and another from building A3 (Hope Taylor 1977: 187, Figure 88, no 2). The example from building A3 was associated with ceramics that indicate a 6th to 7th century AD date.

The three simple iron pins (Cat 23-25) and the tip from a fourth (Cat 22) are an intriguing discovery from the Lair buildings. Typically iron stick pins form only a small component of larger pin assemblages dominated by examples in bronze or bone, such as those from Dunadd (Lane and Campbell 2000). A variety of different types of pin were used as dress fasteners in the late Iron Age and early medieval period. The most basic types are stick pins with simple slender shanks and shaped heads, which come in a range of forms, and the metal examples are closely related in size and form to versions made in bone (Laing 1993: 34-5; Foster 1989, 1990). Despite the tip of the shank being lost in two instances (Cat 24 and 25), each of the substantially intact pins from Lair can be classified as short stick pins, defined on the basis that they measure *c.* 70 mm or less in length (Foster 1990: 150).

The examples here consist of fine circular-sectioned shanks which lack any swelling and are not 'hipped'; the latter shank forms are understood to be indicative of a 7th century AD date or later (Foster 1990: 145, 150-1). The simplest of the three pins from Lair is Cat 25 from C288/158, which has a simple spherical head and is consistent with Foster's Group 6A form, commonly seen in Scottish contexts in both bone and bronze (1989: 149, fig 12: 6A). The second example, Cat 24 (C162), is a little harder to assign and lacks exact parallels. In form it has a simple flattened sub-rectangular head, but this is obscured by traces of mineralised organic remains revealed during conservation, meaning that identification rests heavily on the details demonstrated by x-radiography. This pin is most similar to Foster's Group 9:E pin with a rectangular-shaped transversely flattened head (Foster 1989: 149, fig 12: 9E). A similar pin, made from bone rather than iron, is known from Jarlshof (Foster 1989: 333, no. 1027; Hamilton 1956). The third example from Lair consists of an intact stick pin (Cat 23) which was recovered from the fill of the hearth (C282) in Building 3 and is directly associated with two radiocarbon dates from roundwood samples, to the early-8th to late-9th century AD (SUERC-74161 and 74162). This pin has a fine circular-sectioned shank and its head consists of an ovoid knob below which is a ring-shaped collar of the same diameter as the knob. It is a particularly elegant form of pin to be executed in iron. No exact parallels are known but the recovery from a directly dated context means we can be confident of its early medieval date. It bears similarities to a knob-headed bronze pin from Lismore, Argyll and Bute (Type 27: Foster 1989: Fig 13:27), a fine mushroom headed bronze pin from Luce Sands, Dumfries and Galloway (Foster 1989: Figure 13, no. 868) and a bronze example recovered from a medieval context at Kildrummy Castle, Aberdeenshire (Apted 1963: 232, fig 14, no 53). Further afield the head form of this pin can be paralleled by a copper alloy example from Fishergate, York (Rogers 1993: 1362, 1476, Figure 662: 5342) which was recovered from a Period 4 deposit, dating from the 10th to 12th centuries.

Catalogue

Cat 20 Intact plate buckle, Figure 3.6:

Flat rectangular iron strip with rounded corners, bent over on itself mid length (L 54 W 23 mm), with an asymmetric rectangular recess (L 11 W 4.5 mm) cut slightly off-centre at the folded over end. A leather or textile belt would have been held between the folded over plate, secured at the 'open' end with a small rivet. The end of one face of the plate has been broken across the small square rivet hole (D 3 mm), which still holds the stub of the rivet shank (D 2 mm). At the opposite end, held within the fold of the plate, are the tapering terminals of an oval iron buckle hoop (W 29 H 20.5 mm) produced by bending a circular-sectioned rod (D 2.5 mm) over on itself so that the terminals abut but do not join. Looped over this junction, sitting within the rectangular recess in the buckle plate, is a short pin. The pin has been formed from a short tapering circular-sectioned rod (L 20.5 D 3.5 mm), hammered flat at one end to form a rectangular strip which has been looped over the terminals of the buckle hoop. The pin tip curves gently to allow it to rest on the curving edge of the buckle hoop. L 61 mm. SF8 (C3).

Cat 21 Buckle hoop and pin, Figure 3.6:

Forged oval buckle hoop from a plate buckle with a short tapering pin *in situ* at one edge. The hoop is oval in plan (W 34 H 18 mm) and has been formed by bending a gently tapering rod (D 3 mm) around on itself so that the ends almost abut. A gap of *c.* 3 mm is present between the squared head of one end of the rod (D 4 mm) and the narrow tapering tip (D 2 mm). The pin, which remains attached to the buckle loop, consists of a short tapering circular-sectioned rod (*c.* L 20 D 3 mm) which has been hammered flat at one end to create a strip; the strip has then been looped over the buckle hoop to secure. The pin would originally have sat over the abutting terminals of the buckle hoop, held in place by the now lost buckle plate; the pin has become dislodged and is now corroded into position protruding out horizontally from one edge of the buckle hoop. SF9 (C21).

Cat 22 Tip of pin shank:

Fine, circular-sectioned tapering rod; one end is broken, the other tapers to a fine point. Surviving L 33 D 3 mm. SF18 (C56).

Cat 23 Pin, Figure 3.6:

Intact iron pin in two joining fragments. Small sub-globular head (D 5 mm), with a rounded top and the sides tapering to a ring collar (D 5.5 mm) on a fine circular-sectioned shank; not hipped. Head form can be paralleled by a copper alloy pin at Fishergate, York (Rogers 1993: 1362, 1476, Figure 662, 5342). L 75 D 2.5 mm. SF63 (C282).

Cat 24 Pin, Figure 3.6:

Survives in two joining fragments, extreme tip of shank lost. The head is obscured by corrosion but by x-ray appears to be a flattened globular form. Shank is fine and circular in section, and not hipped. Surviving L 46 mm; head: H 17 W 9; shank: D 3.5 mm. SF73 (C162).

Cat 25 Pin, Figure 3.6:

A substantially intact iron pin with a spherical, 'ball'-shaped head, no collar, and a fine circular-sectioned shank, not hipped, the extreme tip of which has been lost. It can be paralleled with an intact example from Dunadd in both form and dimensions (Lane and Campbell 2000: 167, illus 4.77, no.1312). Surviving L 47 mm; Head: D 6.5 mm; Shank: D 2.5 mm. SF77 (C158/288).

Miscellaneous

A further ten fragmentary sheet, bar and rod fragments were recovered across the excavated areas (Cat 26-35). Due to the small, fractured and fragmentary condition of this material, closer identification of original form and function is not possible.

Catalogue

Cat 26 Unidentified:

Fragment of an iron object with a fine copper alloy riveted band at one broken end. It comprises a small flat sheet fragment of iron with one straight original edge surviving, wedge-shaped in cross-section with a fine narrow copper alloy strip (W 3.5 mm) at one broken end encircling the width of the object; the squared-ends of the strip abut towards the middle of one face and are held in place by a small copper/bronze rivet (D 2 mm), visible only on x-ray. Surviving L 24.5 max W 13.5 T 5 mm. (C1).

Cat 27 Bar fragment:

Short robust rounded bar fragment; surviving end is rounded, opposite end is broken but appears to be gently expanding in width. Surviving L 51.5 W 18 T 6 mm. SF14 (C55 - same as C3).

Cat 28 Unidentified:

Heavily fractured, degraded fragment; lentoid in cross-section. Surviving L 33 W 23 T 4 mm. SF16 (C56).

Cat 29 Bar fragment:

Damaged squared end of an iron bar or bar-like object with rounded corners. Surviving L 17.5 W 9 T 7 mm. (C21).

Cat 30 Sheet fragment:

Small, flat, sub-square sheet fragment, curving and slightly distorted on both planes; no original edges survive. L 18 W 17.5 T 2.5 mm. (C84).

Cat 31 Sheet fragment:

Small angular fragment of iron sheet, all edges broken except for one curving edge. The sheet is gently curved in profile. Surviving L 23.5 W 16.5 T 2 mm. (C128).

Cat 32 Sheet fragment:

Two joining flat, angular but amorphous spalls detached from the surface of an unidentified object. Surfaces are heavily corroded obscuring any details. X-radiography confirms that no original edges survive. Surviving L 23.5 W 19 T 3.5 mm. SF34 (C167).

Cat 33 Unidentified:

Thirteen small, flat, angular fragments (and multiple flecks) detached from the surface of a completely degraded iron object. No original edges or surfaces survive. Largest fragment: L 11.5 W 8.5 T 2.5 mm. SF36 (C162).

Cat 34 Robust rod fragment:

Three joining degraded angular fragments and a detached corrosion blister (19 x 12.5 mm; T 4.5 mm) from the shank of a robust circular-sectioned rod, broken at both ends. The original form is unknown. Surviving L 32.5 W 18 T 14.5 mm. SF45 (C162).

Cat 35 Unidentified sheet fragment:

Two joining irregular fragments of iron sheet; possible organic material is noted on reverse face but this is not identifiable. Surviving L 47.5 W 27.5 T 4.5 mm. SF57 (C162).

Distribution

The majority of the iron objects (18) came from Building 3 and its sub-circular annexe or enclosure. Twelve of these items were recovered from an occupation/floor surface in the interior of the structure including a fragmentary knife (Cat 4), a hooked tool tip (Cat 6), a padlock case (Cat 9), a pot or cauldron hanger (Cat 10), nail fragments (Cat 16 and 19), fittings (Cat 17 and 19) and a stick pin (Cat 24), as well as several unidentified fragments (Cat 33-35). Most of these items are damaged or incomplete. Were these broken items incorporated into a floor surface as the detritus of day-to-day living and left behind on the abandonment of the structure? Or, with the evidence of blacksmithing activities within the structure (Section 3.6), could these be broken and fragmentary items, scrap, collected together for recycling? In addition, the conical ferrule, postulated as a poker tip (Cat 7), was recovered from the lower fill (C248) of the stone hearth (C282), while an intact stick pin (Cat 23) also came from the hearth (C282). A further pin came from the slumped turf wall (C288) and an incomplete perforated strip fitting (Cat 19) was found in pit (C286).

A total of 13 items were recovered from Building 1. Unlike those from Buildings 2 and 3, the majority of the iron objects from Building 1 came from contexts representing collapsed turf walls (C3, C8, C21 and C55: Cat 1, 2, 3, 11, 12, 20, 21, 27 and 29). Although it is possible the objects were accidentally incorporated into the collapsed walls after the building had gone out of use it is more likely they were present in the soil attached to the turves, in a similar fashion to that noted at Little Dunagoil, Argyll and Bute (Marshall 1964: 52). The latter would suggest that they do not relate to activities undertaken within Building 1 itself, but are residual finds from an area of the site stripped of turf to construct the walls of the structure. Three objects, comprising a fragmentary padlock bolt (Cat 8), a pin shank (Cat 22) and an unidentified fragment (Cat 28), came from a layer of soil in Building 1 which underlies the collapse of the upper turf walls (C56), and thus may be more securely associated with the use of the building. Three objects came from Building 2. Two were sheet fragments detached from unidentified objects (Cat 30 and 31), one of which was recovered from the fill of a linear gully (C84) below the stone foundation at the western end. The other came from the hearth deposits (C128) below the collapsed turf wall of the building. A tack or horseshoe nail (Cat 13) was recovered from the collapsed turf walls of Building 2. Another tack or possible horseshoe nail (Cat 15) was recovered from the fill of a gully at the end of Building 5, while a tanged awl (Cat 5) came from a possible floor surface in the circular Structure 4 excavated in trench 4 (C39).

Discussion

Amongst the more diagnostic of the iron artefacts from the site are the four knife blades; ubiquitous tools from sites of early medieval date (Alcock 2003: 95). Angle-backed blades such as those already discussed have a long history of use which spans several centuries, but the forms present are amongst the most common blade types found on early medieval sites in Scotland. Similar knife blades come from a range of different site-types including early medieval forts and duns, including Dunadd, Dunollie and Kildonan Bay in Argyll and Bute (Lane and Campbell 2000: 162-3; Alcock *et al.* 1989: 217, illus 15; Fairhurst 1939: 210), Dundurn in Perth and Kinross (Alcock and Alcock 1987: 141, illus 8, no.14 and 16), and Mote of Mark in Dumfries and Galloway (Laing and Longley 2006: 86), open settlements (e.g. Bruach an Druimein, Argyll and Bute; Heald and Hunter 2008), ecclesiastical sites (e.g. Whithorn; Nicholson 1997: 426-9), and crannogs (e.g. Loch Glashan; Crone and Campbell 2005) emphasising their widespread and general purpose use. Although the group from Lair is small, it conforms to the mid-range of blade sizes from Bruach an Druimein and Dunadd (Heald and Hunter 2008: 45, illus 28).

The general paucity of other tools and household fittings from the buildings at Lair is surprising. While possibly a few more fragmentary and heavily corroded items were not recognised in the course of the excavation, it perhaps indicates the routine recycling of scrap. A possible handle (Cat 27) was noted and a curving sheet fragment (Cat 30) may have come from the collar of a socketed tool, but neither can be classified more closely. A single broken tanged implement, possibly a fine awl, punch or drill bit (Cat 5), came from an unsecure context comprising burnt material within Structure 4. Although a sample from this deposit has been dated to between the mid-7th to late 8th centuries AD this could merely reflect the general early medieval activity in the area. The association of this item with two fragments of ferrous metal-working waste could suggest a connection with metal-working but it could equally be an item of scrap awaiting recycling. In Building 3, a conical ferrule (Cat 7) may have been used as the tip of a poker for stirring the hearth (C284), whilst a robust hooked fitting, a possible pot or cauldron hanger (Cat 10) was found amongst the floor deposits next to the hearth (C162). Dated charcoal samples from the hearth demonstrate that it was in use between the late-8th and 9th centuries AD.

The broken barbed bolt (Cat 8) and padlock case (Cat 9) from at least one barb-spring padlock is also unexpected but not unparalleled in an early medieval context. Similar items have been found at Buiston, North Ayrshire, Dundurn, and Whithorn (Alcock *et al.* 1989; Munro 1882: 221; Nicholson 1997: 416). The use of barb-spring padlocks is known from the Roman Iron Age (Manning 1985: 95-7) and padlock slide keys have been noted amongst ironwork assemblages of early medieval date such as that from Dunadd, attesting to the use of security equipment to safeguard property (Lane and Campbell 2000: 167). The bolt was recovered from a layer underlying the upper turf collapse of one of the walls in Building 1 (C56) and the case was found amongst the occupation or floor surface within Building 3 (C162), making it unlikely that they derive from the same padlock set. Although it is impossible to say what the padlocks were used to secure - it may have been a chest, box or even a door - these pieces of security equipment indicate that the owner had items considered valuable enough to lock away, and that theft was an issue in society at this time.

The ornaments, in the form of the pins and probably also the buckles, are not simple clothes fasteners; they were a medium by which aspects of personal identity and wider affiliations could be demonstrated and maintained (Heald 2011: 230). Although this concept is more commonly emphasised in studies of decorative bronze accessories of late Iron Age and early medieval date, the same can be said for similar items made of iron. Iron was rarely used for pins, and then mainly in the middle Iron Age (Foster 1989: 58-9; 1990: 150), but examples from a wide range of late Iron Age and early medieval sites such as Clatchard Craig, Dunadd, Dundurn, Keil Cave in Argyll and Bute, Easter Kinnear in Fife and Whithorn, attest to their extended duration of use (Alcock *et al.* 1989: 217; Close-Brooks 1986: 171, illus 28, no 30; Driscoll 1997: 104; Lane and Campbell 2000: 166; Nicholson 1997; Ritchie 1967: 109, fig 2: 16). Perhaps the most instructive is the quantity of stick pins, including some in iron, that were recovered during excavations at Dunadd. Here, the pin types were mainly simple ball-headed, drum-headed and dome-headed forms, similar in size and style to those at Lair. Like those from Lair, none of the Dunadd pins were obviously hipped or very long in length (Lane and Campbell 2000: 166). Both are indicators of a date not earlier than the 7th century AD (Foster 1990: 150-3).

Despite recent work on early medieval material culture in Scotland, emphasis has often been placed on the exotic end of the metal artefact spectrum focusing on imported materials, high-status metal-working and personal ornaments which incorporate precious metals (Campbell 1996, 2007; Clarke *et al.* 2012; Huggett 1988), rather than on the more prosaic aspects of material culture such as household fittings, tools and everyday dress accessories. With a few notable exceptions (e.g. Alcock 2003; Foster 1989, 1990; Laing 1975), little detailed consideration has been given to this material, in contrast to that attempted for the medieval period (Hinton 2005). It has been observed elsewhere that except for the products of fine metal-working, evidence for crafts and industry in mainland northern Britain is both scarce and scattered during the early medieval period (Alcock 2003: 93). These factors together create difficulties in attempting to understand the wider significance of small ironwork assemblages such as that from Lair, which appear to be principally domestic in character.

3.6 The vitrified material

Dawn McLaren

A modest assemblage of vitrified material was recovered from the site, representing a relatively small quantity (4.6 kg) of limited range. The material was visually examined allowing the residues to be sorted into broad categories based on morphology, colour, density, texture and response to a magnet. This has enabled two distinct groups of vitrified material to be identified: those indicative of ferrous metal-working, and other pieces which have undoubtedly been the result of a high-temperature pyrotechnic process but are not necessarily linked to metal-working. The material from Lair is dominated by ferrous metal-working waste

Table 3.6 The range of vitrified material recovered during excavation.

Range of vitrified material	Weight (g)
Indicative of ferrous metal-working (Fe)	
Plano-convex cakes and fragments (PCC)	722.7
Unclassified Iron Slag (UIS)	540.9
Tapped slag (TS)	412.4
Magnetic vitrified residues including hammerscale (MVR-HS)	1976.5
Slag-attacked stones	781.6
Not diagnostic of metal-working	
Iron spall	9
Heat-affected stone	70.3
Magnetic vitrified residue (MVR)	72.73
Non-magnetic vitrified material (NMVR)	5.3
Ore	18.3
Total	**4609.75**

including fragments diagnostic of smithing blooms or blacksmithing. A single fragment of tapped slag, indicative of iron smelting, is also present. The vitrified material will be summarised by process where possible, and has been described using common terminology (e.g. McDonnell 1994; Spearman 1997; Starley 2000). A full catalogue of vitrified material is presented in the archive.

Ferrous metal-working waste

A total of 4.4 kg of waste indicative of ferrous metal-working activities was identified amongst the assemblage, comprising fragments of plano-convex slag cakes, likely to be hearth bottoms from smithing blooms or blacksmithing, unclassified iron slags, magnetic vitrified residues which include small quantities of hammerscale flakes, and a single fractured fragment of tapped slag. In addition, 0.78 kg of slag-attacked, heat-affected schist, probably representing the lining of a metal-working hearth or furnace, was also present.

Plano-convex slag cakes

Two complete sub-rectangular and oval plano-convex slag cakes (PCC) and three fractured pieces were identified (722.7 g). It is often difficult to distinguish between cakes produced during smelting or smithing. The criteria are traditionally based on the size, weight, texture and visible inclusions, as well as the slag's response to a magnet (McDonnell 1994: 230, 200, 219; Starley 2000: 338). Where possible, chemical analysis can aid in refining these identifications. The plano-convex cakes from Lair are of small diameter and thickness with infrequent charcoal inclusions, consistent with hearth bottoms produced during smithing.

Smithing hearth bottoms are accumulations of iron, iron-scale and silica which have fused together at the rounded base of a blacksmith's hearth. They are recognisable by their characteristic plano-convex form, having a rough convex base and a smoother, vitrified, upper surface, which is typically flat or even slightly hollowed as the result of the downward pressure of the air blast from the bellows. One example, recovered from backfill associated with Building 3, appears to be an amalgam of at least two small superimposed cakes. The upper layer (T 25 mm) is an amalgam of ferrous slag, hearth/fuel debris and vitrified hearth lining (magnetic); under magnification this is a black vitrified matrix with frequent heat-affected quartz inclusions. The lower two layers (T 15 and 19 mm) are red-brown/dark grey dense but vesicular ferrous slag. The cake is quadrilateral with rounded corners and steeply-angled but rounded edges which taper towards a short, straight, fractured end. It is likely that this point is where the cake was detached from the hearth. The lower surface is convex and uneven, with frequent small charcoal impressions and voids. The two intact cakes (SF75 from C162, and the general find from Building 3, just described) and a fragment representing approximately 45 % of a small circular cake (SF35), also from C162, correspond closely in dimensions, ranging from 90.5 to 93 mm in length and 40.5 to 51.5 mm in thickness. The size of these pieces is suggestive of episodic, small-scale smithing, consistent with the occasional maintenance or repair of iron tools or blades, rather than regular production.

Tapped slag

A single substantial fragment of a silver-grey coloured, dense, molten-looking slag (412.4 g), which has detached from a much larger piece, is probably waste from iron smelting. Substantial flows of fully molten slags are indicative of waste that has been allowed to run from a furnace and are often called 'tapped slags' (TS). This is the only fragment of slag amongst the assemblage that confidently points towards iron smelting at Lair. This fragment was recovered from the occupation or floor surface (C162) in Building 3, alongside fragments of iron smithing waste.

Unclassified iron slag

Also present are small quantities of unclassified iron slag (540.9 g), which consist of fractured or amorphous pieces of red-brown to grey coloured, vesicular, vitrified material. Although it is possible to identify such slags as the debris from ironworking, this group of material has insufficient characteristics to allow the stage of production (e.g. smelting or smithing) to be determined through visual examination alone. These slags are often referred to as undiagnostic or unclassified iron slags that are best described as rake-out material from either a smelting furnace or smithing hearth (McLaren and Heald 2006: 156).

Hearth lining

Fragments of severely heat-affected schist with attached fragments of iron slag (781.6 g) were recovered alongside pieces of unclassified iron slag and plano-convex slag cake in pit C313 within Building 3. These are probably dismantled fragments from the lining of a metal-working hearth or furnace.

Diagnostic micro-debris: hammerscale

Over 1.9 kg of small magnetic vitrified residues incorporating small magnetic flakes and possible filings came from the interior of Building 3, with concentrations in pits C228, C314 and C316. This material comprises mixtures of magnetic stone grits, low-density cinder-like prills and occasional ferrous-rich flecks, including diagnostic hammerscale flakes. This form of slag is expelled from the surface of a bloom or iron object during smithing and when found in concentrated quantities they can indicate the focus for blacksmithing activities (Bayley et al. 2001; Dungworth and Wilkes 2009). In general, the quantity of diagnostic flakes per sample was very low.

Other vitrified material

In addition to the hammerscale-rich residues just described, there are small quantities (72.73 g) of undiagnostic magnetic residues. These consist of mixtures of both heat-affected, magnetised stone grits and globules of low-density, porous and vesicular waste, similar in texture and consistency to fuel ash slag. Fuel ash slags tend to be brittle, glassy, porous amorphous nodules of heavily vitrified material which have formed through silica, earth or clay, stone, fuel ash from the fire, and organic material fusing together in a domestic hearth (Bayley et al. 2001: 21). Both these, and the non-magnetic glassy residues are not indicative of metal-working but are likely to be an unintentional by-product of a high temperature pyrotechnic process. A similar scattering of low-density slags was observed at Carn Dubh, Perth and Kinross, and was also thought to have been formed by domestic rather than industrial processes (Rideout 1995: 174).

Although not vitrified, a single fragment of bog ore (18.3 g) came from C162 within Building 3, as did fragments of heat-affected schist, undoubtedly spalled from the face of the slag-attacked stone within pit C313.

Table 3.7 Distribution of vitrified and heat-affected materials across the excavated area by type and weight. The key to the abbreviations used in the table above can be found in Table 3.6.

Year	Context	Trench	St.	Context interp.	PCC	UIS	Tap	MVR-HS	Slag-attacked stones	Heat affected stones	MVR	NMVR	Fe	Ore	Total Weight g
2012	2	1	1	Collapsed and slumped S turf wall of structure							2.7				2.7
2012	3	1	1	Collapsed and slumped N turf wall of structure							4.1				4.1
2012	14	1	1	Burnt linear feature beneath Building 1							8.5				8.5
2012	16	3	n/a	Charcoal flecked sandy silt, burrow							11.2				11.2
2012	18	1	1	Possibly turf bank core							8.6		9		17.6
2012	21	1	1	Burnt linear feature beneath Building 1							4.7				4.7
2014	39	4	?	Possible floor surface of circular structure		32.6									32.6
2013	50	9	2	Compacted sandy silt								4.1			4.1
2013	56	10	1	Charcoal flecked sand, lies beneath turf bank 055 and above 061							6.1	0.1			6.2
2013	68	10	1	Fill of post-hole 067							0.2	1.1			1.3
2013	79	10	1	Fill of small pit 078							1.8				1.8
2013	138	18	n/a	Natural deposit below cairn		51.7									51.7
2015	161	22	5	Compacted deposit within 175		17.5									17.5
2016/17	162	23	3	Probable floor surface	423.12		412.4				15.3			18.3	869.12
2017	168	22	3	Fill of post-hole				1.4							1.4
2016	220	23	3	Turf layer in large pit/ditch 202							1.54				1.54
2016	229	27	3	Lower fill pit 228				4.62							4.62
2016	230	27	3	Upper fill pit 228				3.5							3.5

3. The Small Finds

2016	232	27	3	Lower fill pit 231					2.3		2.3
2016	233	27	3	Upper fill pit 231					1.49		1.49
2016	248	27	3	Lower fill of hearth 235		9.48					9.48
2017	279	30	3	Upper fill of pit 279					1.3		1.3
2017	286	30	3	Primary fill of pit 278					2.7		2.7
2017	296	31	3	Fill of post-hole 295		0.3					0.3
2017	314	31	3	Fill of pit 313	39.3	1482.7	781.6				2813
2017	316	31	3	Fill of pit 315		465.6					465.6
2017	318	31	3	Fill of post-hole 317		8.9					8.9
2017	320	31	3	Fill of post-hole 319					0.2		0.2
2017		27		Un-stratified	42.7						42.7
2016				Un-stratified	217.6						217.6
Total					722.72	540.9	412.4	1976.5	781.6	70.3	72.73	5.3	18.3	4609.75

Distribution

The majority of the vitrified material from Lair was recovered from deposits associated with Building 3 (Table 3.7). This includes 4.3 kg of ironworking slags, particularly those indicative of blacksmithing. Concentrations of ferrous metal-working waste (2.8 kg) consisting of a fragment of plano-convex slag cake, unclassified iron slag, magnetic residue, including hammerscale flakes, and probable slag-attacked hearth lining came from C314, the fill of pit C313 which may represent a deliberate dump of waste or a disturbed hearth. Further collections of ironworking waste came from the adjacent pit C315 and the floor surface (C162), whilst a lower-density scatter of ferrous-rich micro-debris came from a suite of pits, post-holes and a hearth (C168, C229, C230, C248, C296 and C318). High precision radiocarbon dating from the hearth in Building 3 returned dates of AD 760-900 (SUERC-74161) and AD 720-890 (SUERC-74162).

The single fragment of tapped slag, indicative of iron smelting, seems out of place amongst the assemblage from Building 3 as no further distinctive smelting waste was recognised across the site. The fragment from C612, however, suggests that iron smelting was practised at Lair and was perhaps an activity undertaken outside the structures in an area not investigated by excavation.

The remaining 148.3 g of vitrified and heat-affected materials represent a widespread but low-density residual scatter of undiagnostic magnetic vitrified residues found across the excavated areas. It is associated with Buildings 1, 2, 3 and 5, the circular Structure 4 investigated in Trench 4, and the cairn in Trench 18. These residues are often associated with evidence of burning in the form of heat-affected soils (e.g. C14) or charcoal inclusions (e.g. C56), indicating that the vitrified fragments are probably the result of a non-industrial high-temperature process.

Ironworking at Lair and beyond

Despite the limited quantity of ferrous metal-working waste recovered at Lair, the direct dating of the associated deposits is significant as well-dated early medieval evidence of ironworking is rare in Scotland. This may simply be a problem with recognition; there is nothing morphologically distinctive about the slags from Lair that would easily differentiate them from earlier, Iron Age slags or later, medieval waste.

A similar picture was encountered during analysis of a collection of smithing and smelting waste deposited in a pit at Culduthel, near Inverness, Highland (Cruickshanks and McLaren forthcoming). The ferrous metal-working debris there was recovered from a pit situated adjacent to an extensive Iron Age settlement and metal-working site (Hatherley and Murray forthcoming). Based on visual examination alone, the morphological appearance, composition and range of types present was consistent with the ironworking slags found in association with the suite of well-dated Iron Age smelting furnaces at an adjacent site (McLaren and Dungworth forthcoming) but the radiocarbon assay returned from a sample of associated carbonised material indicated a firm early medieval date for deposition (Hatherley and Murray forthcoming).

The small quantity of smelting and smithing debris from Lair necessarily places limitations on discussions of technological processes and consideration of comparable material but we can be confident from the quantities of micro-debris and hammerscale that small-scale blacksmithing took place inside Building 3 during the mid-7th to late-9th century AD. The recovery of a well-used rotary grinding stone attests to this also and implies the maintenance or manufacture of blades, amongst other items. The quantity of metal-working found in association with this building is insufficient to indicate large-scale working and may instead relate to the day-to-day maintenance and repair of iron tools. Whether this building was a purpose-built smiddy or a structure which fulfilled a range of functions is open to debate.

More comprehensive evidence of early medieval ironworking associated with metal-working hearths and structures are known from Burland and Scatness in Shetland, Portmahomack, on the Nigg peninsula in Highland (Carver and Spall 2004; Heald and McLaren 2013; McDonnell 1998: 158) and pre-Norse deposits at Birsay, Orkney (McDonnell 1986a: 202-3). More scattered residual debris indicative of early medieval ironworking was found at Easter Kinnear and Clatchard Craig in Fife (Driscoll 1997: 105; McDonnell 1986b), Dunadd, Bruach an Druimein and Iona in Argyll and Bute (Barber 1981: 349; Heald and Hunter 2008: 47; McDonnell 2000: 220), and Mote of Mark in Dumfries and Galloway (Crew 2006). Despite there being no evidence for iron production at the fort at Dundurn, Perth and Kinross, the excavators suggest many of the iron objects found during excavation may have been made on site (Alcock *et al.* 1989: 217).

Interestingly, despite the similarities in building type, size and layout, no evidence of metal-working was identified at the broadly contemporary settlement at Pitcarmick (Carver *et al.* 2012). As the evidence of metal-working activities at Lair appears to concentrate in a single building within the settlement, and hints towards further activities outside the buildings themselves, it is not difficult to see how such evidence could be undetectable on a site where excavation was more restricted in scope and scale.

3.7 The pottery

Derek Hall

The excavations produced six sherds of pottery ranging in date from prehistoric to the medieval period. This material has been examined by eye and x 10 lens and where possible assigned to a recognised fabric name. No petrological analysis has been carried out.

Catalogue

Cat 1: SF6 (C4). Building 1 or earlier:

Rim-sherd in very micaceous fabric with light grey brown external surface and grey black core (prehistoric).

Cat 2: (C4 - recovered from Sample 16). Building 1 or earlier:

Joining body-sherds in fine unglazed Whiteware fabric.

Cat 3: SF11 (C20). Building 1 or earlier:

Body-sherd in very micaceous fabric with light grey brown external surface and grey black core (prehistoric).

Cat 4: SF22 (C122). Building 6:

Body-sherd from splash glazed jug in Scottish Redware fabric with external purple heat skin.

Cat 5: SF32 (C156/158). Building 3:

Body-sherd in very micaceous fabric with light brown external surface and grey black core (prehistoric).

Cat 6: SF27 (C162). Building 3:

Fired clay or daub, orange brown in colour with blue grey core.

Prehistoric sherds

Three of the sherds, from C4, C20 and C156, are in a similar very micaceous light brown fabric with a grey core and would appear to be hand-made. They are all undecorated and would seem to fit the parameters assigned to pottery of prehistoric date. The lack of any diagnostic features makes them difficult to assign to a specific period, although a middle to late Bronze Age date would seem likely (Ann McSween *pers comm*).

3. THE SMALL FINDS

Medieval sherds

A body-sherd from C122 (SF22) is in a Scottish Redware fabric with a distinctive external purple heat skin and comes from a splash glazed jug. This is likely to date to between the 13th and 15th centuries and is a product of one of the assumed production centres in the Tay Valley (Haggarty *et al.* 2011). Two small joining sherds from C4 are in a very hard unglazed Scottish White Gritty ware fabric (Jones *et al.* 2006), which dates to between the 12th and 15th centuries.

Daub

There is a single piece of possible daub (building material) from C162, which is associated with Building 3.

Discussion

The three potentially prehistoric sherds are likely to originate from the relict prehistoric landscape around the excavated structures. A similar 'background' of earlier material was also encountered in excavations at Pitcarmick (Sheridan 2012: 173-176). The medieval sherds are un-abraded and suggest the presence of medieval activity in the area: again similar fabrics were recovered at Pitcarmick (Hall 2012: 179-180).

3.8 The glass bead

Ewan Campbell

Description

A tiny segmented green bead of bubbly, semi-translucent glass. The bead has three segments and the colour is light apple green (two segments) and dark green (one segment). Each segment is a flattened globular shape, 2 mm high, 3 mm in diameter. The segments are fused together, the darker green one at an angle to the other two, suggesting the darker one has been added to an existing double bead. The hole has a funnel shape at the top, narrowing to a very fine diameter. Size 3 x 3 x 6 mm. From sieving C20, fill of Pit C19, Trench 1 (Figures 3.9 and 3.10).

This very small segmented bead is an extremely rare find in a Scottish context, as a recent survey of Scottish beads shows that there is only one other known example of a segmented bead of this colour (Christie 2014). Green is in general uncommon in beads in Scotland, forming approximately 7 % of the Scottish bead assemblage (Christie 2014: fig 3.6). The bead is also exceptionally small and irregular in shape, this and its colour immediately distinguishing it from the well-known Norse period segmented beads, as exemplified by the burial necklace of yellow and blue segmented

Figure 3.9 The segmented bead showing colour variation (M. Bell: 2018).

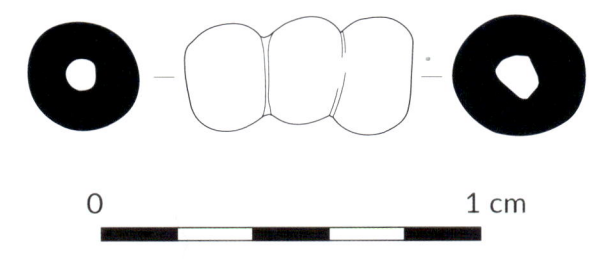

Figure 3.10 The bead indicating scale.

beads from Cnip, Lewis, Eilean Siar (Welander *et al.* 1987). That class of bead was manufactured in the Near East. Somewhat similar beads are known from the Roman period in Britain (Guido 1978: 91-93), though these are made differently, and the Lair bead falls into a type better known from Anglo-Saxon pagan burials. These latter beads, classed by Guido as type 5vi (Guido 1999: 44-45) and Brugman as 'Segmented Globular' (Brugman 2004: 75) are common in late 5th to 7th-century burials, and are believed by Guido to have been made in Frisia. Examples showing that the type continued in use well into the 7th century have been recorded from the mid-7th century cemetery at Street House, West Yorkshire (Sherlock 2012: 55, Pl 3.13). Single and double segmented examples are common in green glass in England, but triple and quadruple ones do exist (Guido 1999: 245-7). The Lair bead seems to have a double segment (both are the same colour), then an extra segment of darker colour has been added. In Germanic areas these very small beads, sometimes referred to as spacer beads, were often strung with other beads in necklaces, though they do occur in many other contexts, singly or with other artefacts.

The method of manufacture of the bead is interesting. There is no indication that the segments were made by crimping or rolling a drawn glass tube, the normal method for Norse period and metal-in-glass segmented beads. Nor is the bead formed by winding around a rod as in some Roman examples, or by being blown. Instead, the irregular, slightly flattened shape of each segment, and the tapered hole, suggest each globular segment was pierced, then fused together. If this is the case, there is a possibility that this was a locally made, or compiled bead, imitating a Germanic type. Another Scottish example of a bead being formed by fusing two beads comes from Luce Sands, Dumfries and Galloway (Christie 2014: 52-3, fig 3.34; NMS X.BHB 17), and there are numerous examples of locally made beads in the Scottish corpus (Christie 2014: 67). However, on balance, it is more likely that this is an import, either directly from the continent, or via Anglo-Saxon England, where there are many similar examples which seem to have been made in the same way.

The closest parallel in Scotland is a green segmented bead from Hound Point, Dalmeny, City of Edinburgh (NMS X.EQ 340), which was part of a necklace from a long-cist grave (Baldwin Brown 1915). Other beads on this necklace are of 7th century or later date. The dates for parallels do not conflict with the radiocarbon date from the pit which produced the Lair bead. In Scotland, other segmented beads, in a variety of different colours but probably of similar date, are known from Dunadd (Lane and Campbell 2000: 177, no. 155), Mote of Mark (Laing and Longley 2006: 101, no 3057), Dundurn (Alcock et al. 1989: 216, no. 29) and Yeavering (RCAHMS 2007: 20, nos 82.2, 82.3), all high status fortified sites; another is recorded from the Culbin Sands, Moray (unpublished finds in National Museum of Scotland), a possible manufacturing site.

Other Anglo-Saxon or Germanic-derived beads are known from Scotland. Two 6th-century types were found on the industrial site at Lavacroon, Orkney (Batey and Freeman 1986: 298, illus 9). Recently another 6th-century type has been recorded from the early monastery at Fortingall, Perth and Kinross (ID24995). Others are known from Earlston, Scottish Borders, and Mouswald and Loch Ronald, Dumfries and Galloway. In addition, glass of Germanic origin is becoming increasingly recognised on Scottish sites (Campbell 2007: Group B; 2009, illus 11.1). All these bead sites differ from Lair in being of high status, and situated on the coast or major routeways. Beads are one of the most mobile and widely traded of artefacts, often occurring far from their production source, so this bead does not necessarily imply the presence of a person of Germanic origin at Lair. Beads in Germanic society are usually, though not invariably, associated with women, but we know almost nothing about how they were worn in Celtic-speaking societies due to the lack of furnished burials. How this bead came to Lair is an interesting question, perhaps suggesting that the site was connected to a higher status lowland site.

3.9 Animal bone

Catherine Smith

Introduction and methodology

The buildings at Lair produced a small but intriguing animal bone assemblage. As is often the case on acidic upland soils, bone preservation was poor and with only two exceptions the surviving bone consisted of small calcined, abraded fragments. Those exceptions, particularly a deposit of cattle bones (SF83) from a pit C279 within the annexe of Building 3, are therefore of some interest.

Mammal bones were identified by direct comparison with modern comparative material and allocated to particular bone and species where possible. Where it was not possible to identify species, the terms *large ungulate*, *small ungulate* and *indeterminate mammal* were used. On this basis, all large vertebrae other than the atlas and axis are described as large ungulate, while small vertebrae are described as small ungulate. Ribs were similarly allocated depending on their size. Large ungulate bones were most likely to originate from cattle (on the basis of frequency), but could also derive from horse or red deer. Similarly, small ungulate bones were most likely to come from sheep, but could be from goat or pig. It should be noted that no definite evidence of goat was found and all the bones thus described were thought to be from sheep. All other mammalian fragments for which neither species nor bone could be ascertained are described as indeterminate mammal.

The use of the term *medium mammal* has been avoided as far as possible due to the shrinkage associated with burning of bones, but where necessary has been used to describe fragments from animals of the size of a lamb or small sheep.

Measurements were made on intact adult long bones where these occurred and made in accordance with the scheme of von den Driesch (1976), expressed in millimetres. Diagnostic zones are used where applicable and follow Dobney and Rielly's scheme (1988). Mandibular tooth wear and eruption patterns were assessed using Grant's (1982) scheme for cattle, sheep/goats and pigs, and Payne's (1973) scheme for sheep/goats.

Condition: in order to compare the condition of bones across the site, a method of attribution scoring has been used. The following attributes are scored for selected samples:

General: provides a general short-hand description of the overall condition of the bone, and scored (in brackets): very poor (1), poor (2), fair (3), good (4). 'Good' would be applicable to fresh bone and is not typical in an archaeological context.

Surface abrasion: describes the degree of erosion of the surface caused by taphonomic factors such as weathering, soil conditions, etc. Scored as heavy (1), moderate (2) or slight (3).

Density: describes the 'heaviness' of the bone. In general, the better preserved bone is, the heavier and denser it is, whether through retention of organic material or re-mineralisation from the soil. Scored from 1 to 5, where 1 is the least dense.

Friability: describes the degree of crumbliness. Scored from 1 to 5, where 1 is the most crumbly and 5 is the least crumbly.

Total score therefore reflects preservation, with most poorly preserved material scoring only 4 while the best could potentially score 17.

Condition scores as well as species, bone element, side, part, state of epiphyseal fusion, diagnostic zones (whether gnawed or butchered), pathology and anatomical measurements are presented in the animal bone catalogue, which is available in the site archive.

Results

The condition of the bone was in some cases very poor. Condition scores ranged from as low as 4 for burnt fragments to a maximum score of 12 for only two bones from the entire site. Bone density was also poor as a result of mineral leaching, and the material was, in the worst-preserved examples, light and friable with a tendency to disintegrate on handling. Teeth, which are usually more resistant to challenging conditions, were also affected and in some cases where the dentine had been attacked they had disintegrated into their component parts, leaving only the more durable outer enamel shell and the central enamel 'islands' or infundibula.

Species found were domestic cattle, sheep/goat (most likely sheep) and pigs. Wild mammals and birds were not identified in the assemblage.

The distribution of species was notably biased in the different features in which bones were found: a large deposit of cattle bones, representing at least three immature/adult individuals and one neonatal calf (SF83), was recovered from a pit within the annexe of Building 3 (C279), but no sheep remains were recovered from it. The only evidence of pigs, consisting of three incisor teeth, also came from this pit. By contrast, although what may have been part of a very poorly preserved sheep skeleton was retrieved from C166, no cattle remains were found there. Further associated sheep remains were found in C1, although as this context was fairly close to the surface they may have been of no great age. Neither the cattle remains in C279 nor the sheep in C1 and C166 were burnt, but several stray calcined unidentifiable fragments were retrieved from C2, C3, C6, C16, C21, C128, C130, C162, C291 and C320. Two burnt cattle bones were also found mixed amongst the unburnt cattle bone in pit fill C279.

Several of the adult/immature cattle bones in pit fill C279 were in association, indicating the remains of complete limbs may have been deposited together while still connected by soft tissue. Several articulations between bones were noted, in particular a group of five left carpals, two left tarsals, and a distal tibia articulating with the small os malleolare. The neonatal calf bones probably represented a right hind leg deposited as the remains of a single joint of meat.

Evidence of butchery was present on several of the cattle bones in C279, including knife cuts visible on the shaft of a humerus of one of the immature/adult individuals, as well as on a large ungulate rib shaft and on the femur of the neonate, above. Notably a cattle skull has a deep hack at the sagittal suture, in the midline of the frontal bone, implying the skull has been split in two to extract maximum nutrition from it. An axis vertebra (second cervical of the neck) has been chopped both in the sagittal (median) plane and also medio-laterally. Other long bones have been chopped across the shaft medio-laterally but there is no real indication of heavy marrow splitting in which it is expected that the shafts would be split lengthwise in the sagittal plane.

The impression gained was that the butchered cattle bones in the pit represented 'associated bone groups' (ABGs) or partial skeletons, implying consumption and disposal in the same locus. Although the bones were dry and friable, surface abrasion was not excessive, implying they had been buried rapidly after disposal, rather than having been left lying on an open surface exposed to the elements for a long period. Although all parts of the post-axial skeleton were deposited within the pit, the incidence of ribs and vertebrae was low, perhaps indicating disposal of those joints of meat containing the spine elsewhere on the site.

The sheep remains in C166 and C1/162 were in much poorer condition than the cattle bone in pit C279, but these too probably came from ABGs. Neither of these two sheep was fully adult. Mandibular tooth wear and epiphyseal fusion evidence from the individual in C1, SF53, indicated the animal was juvenile/immature at the time of death, possibly between 1 and 2 years old. The other individual, in C166, SF65 and 66, was also immature. The bones in this context (C166), the fill of a sunken floor within Building 3, was radiocarbon dated to AD 670–880 (SUERC-65410). Unsurprisingly, given the extremely poor condition of the bone, no evidence of butchery remained, but it would seem that the bones were not chopped.

Other items besides bone were recovered from the submitted samples. A tiny fragment of abraded nacreous shell was recovered from C131. It has the appearance of having been polished by wear, possibly by natural water-rolling, although use-wear is also possible. The fragment is too small to allow for further identification, but whether it is of marine or freshwater origin it must have been brought some distance to the site. In C162 a fragment of fractured calcined tooth (SF69) was recovered although its species could not be determined.

Discussion

The bone assemblage is notable for the presence of parts of a calf and at least three older cattle in a pit within the annexe of Building 3. Sheep were surprisingly absent from the pit, but two younger individuals had been buried elsewhere on site in the secondary fill of a sunken floor (C166) and in C1/162, a deposit of burnt material.

Carver *et al.* (2012) interpreted the type site for Pitcarmick buildings in Strathardle, radiocarbon dated to the 7th-9th centuries AD, as having been based around a dwelling with an attached byre for overwintering livestock, presumed to be cattle. The animal bone from Pitcarmick appears to have been in even poorer condition than that from the present site, however large mammal fragments were recovered (Holmes 2012: 180–1). The present site is therefore important in confirming the presence of cattle in the economy of the Pitcarmick buildings.

It is also perhaps significant that several shieling huts, admittedly of unknown but probably later date, are located within the immediate vicinity of the site (ID29445 and ID29453; Black, Strachan and Sneddon 2017: 7). An alternative use of the structures at Pitcarmick has been postulated by Carver *et al.* (2012: 194) as shielings. The practice of shieling or transhumance involves the temporary removal of people to the hills with their cattle in search of good grazing and dairying. 'Going to the shieling', was an early summer custom which survived into the 19th century in some parts of Britain and is remembered in many place-names of upland Perthshire (Bil 1992; McNiven this volume: Section 1.6). Possibly the buildings at Lair may have been used in connection with shieling. Certainly the presence of the bones of a very young calf at Lair may imply seasonality if nothing else, as calves were (and are) liable to be born in the spring and early summer months.

The presence of unburnt cattle bones within a pit is interesting since Holmes (2012: 161, 163, 181) suggest throughout that since most of the bone from Pitcarmick was burnt, the implication is that bones were used as fuel. Most upland sites in Scotland, if they preserve any bone at all, retain only burnt bone, but this may simply be differential preservation. Burning to the point where all the organic material has been removed results in a change to the crystalline structure of the bone, which in turn allows it to survive better than unburnt bone (Mays 1998: 207–9). This does not rule out the use of bone as fuel, but may explain why often only calcined bones survive at such sites.

The burial of a collection of cattle bones within the pit inside the annexe of Building 3 may also be significant. Radiocarbon dated to AD 670–780 (SUERC-79014), these were older than material dated from the hearth inside the building. As more sites of the Iron Age and early medieval period are discovered, a pattern of deliberate deposition of animal bodies, or parts of bodies, is beginning to emerge. Most of the comparanda are from the Western Isles (Eilean Siar) where preservation is better than on the mainland; the best examples of ritual deposits of sheep are probably those from Iron Age sites in the Uists, particularly the wheelhouse at Sollas on North Uist (Campbell 1991). Here, and at the eroding wheelhouse site at Sloc Sabaidh, Baile Sear, numerous pits were dug within the wheelhouse floor and quickly filled with the remains of individual sheep and lambs. These were both burnt and unburnt, the burnt remains having been raked out of the fire and combined with unburnt bones (Smith in prep). It is possible that the pit deposit at Lair, containing what appears to be parts of several individual cattle, both older and newborn, may be of a similar 'ritual' nature, be that merely a celebratory meal for a group of people, perhaps eaten at a particular time of the year and deposited in a particular way. Such a feast is likely to have marked a significant event and given the early date of the deposit, it may mark the foundation of the building. The 'lost' parts of the adult cattle skeleton in pit C278, the vertebrae and ribs, which are assumed to have been disposed of in a location other than the pit, may in fact have been disposed of by throwing into a fire, in a similar manner to the sheep from Sollas. The fact that two burnt bones survived in the pit may add fuel to this particular fire.

4. Discussion

Strachan, Tipping and Sneddon
With contributions from Halliday, Postma, Banaszek and Cowley

4.1 Introduction

Having presented the background and results of the fieldwork at Lair, this chapter considers this evidence in a regional, national and international context. Section 4.2 considers the archaeological and pollen-analytical evidence for later prehistoric settlement and use of the uplands at Lair and more widely across north-east Perth and Kinross. We then explore evidence in the region for Iron Age to early medieval settlement continuity (Section 4.3), and for the landscape at Lair immediately prior to occupation in the 7th century AD (Section 4.4) when the pollen record (Paterson and Tipping: Section 2.6) is mute because peat had stopped growing: reasons for the re-establishment of peat growth at *c.* 600 AD are found in both anthropogenic activities and climate change. The chronology of the excavated buildings at Lair (Krus and Hamilton: Section 2.5) is summarised in Section 4.5 while Sections 4.6 to 4.8 consider their form, evolving functions, phasing and spatial organisation, before our understanding of their architecture is used to re-evaluate what characterises Pitcarmick buildings (Section 4.9).

Section 4.10 considers the origins of the Pitcarmick-type 'longhouse' while Section 4.11 reviews the biases in preservation of Pitcarmick buildings in the region, before using their known distribution to explore the environmental determinants on their spatial patterning. The economy of the communities at Lair is considered in Section 4.12, recognising the importance of crop-growing, made possible by rapid climatic amelioration in the early 7th century AD. Section 4.13 takes similar evidence from across Scotland to suggest that agrarian revival was widespread in the 7th century AD. The functions of Pitcarmick buildings are discussed in Section 4.14, and the established assumption that they were early medieval shielings is challenged. Section 4.15 draws on archaeological and place-name evidence to argue that these farming communities, far from living in a marginal setting, were probably ambitious pioneers, with sufficient resources to establish successful, prosperous and permanent farms. The archaeological and palynological evidence both strongly suggest that settlement and its characteristic economy at Lair ended in the late 10th century AD. Why this was the case is explored in Section 4.16, as well as what came after.

4.2 Archaeological and pollen-analytical evidence for later prehistoric settlement and use of the uplands

Although there are no pollen data that describe the primary or original woodland at Lair there is nothing to doubt that it was deciduous and comprised a mix of birch, oak and hazel. Birch dominated the local woodland when it is first recorded, in later prehistory (Section 1.4), a product of altitudinal controls (McVean 1964) and a reminder that Lair is close to 400 m OD. Hazel was part of the woodland canopy. Rowan, elm and ash probably grew as scattered individuals. Alder was rare, in contrast to Coire Fee and Caenlochan (Huntley 1981) and Carn Dubh (Tipping 1995a; Figure 1.3). Scots pine is unlikely to have grown locally despite the proximity of upper Glen Shee to its fastnesses in the Cairngorm (Bennett 1996; Paterson 2011), probably because it was out-competed by deciduous trees on warmer east- and west-facing slopes.

A large area of the lower part of the hydrological catchment at Lair (Figure 1.12) was covered in peat before the first palynological indication of human activities (Section 2.6), the fullest lateral extent of Basin 2 occurring close to its formation at *c.* 6500 BC. These areas of peat were confined to basins and shallow valleys carved during deglaciation. This is similar to what is known of peat development at Carn Dubh to the west, where blanket peat in confined basins formed before *c.* 9000 BC and spread from these after *c.* 7850 BC (Tipping 1995a), and at other locations throughout the Scottish uplands where peat spread is also of early Holocene age (Tipping 2008). Trees and bushes like birch and willow would have grown on both peat basins at Lair.

Human activities in the pollen source area at Lair are first recorded from pollen analyses at 2500-2250 BC when there were grazing-driven changes to plant communities (Section 2.6). Oak trees were probably lost from the pollen source area. Late Neolithic and Early Bronze Age activity seems to have been common in these uplands (Section 1.4: Caseldine 1979; Tipping 1995a). At Dalnaglar on the valley floor below Lair (Durno 1962) the first significant anthropogenic vegetation change is estimated at *c.* 2400 BC and its cessation around 200 years later. At the southern end of Glen Shee, the large deforestation event at Rae Loch (Edwards and Whittington 1998) at 1681-2131 BC is very unusual for this time in its large spatial scale (Tipping 1994). These rather disparate data might suggest that people in prehistory colonised the lowland and the floors of valleys at the same time they colonised the valley sides. Evidence for upland crop growing at Carn Dubh (Tipping 1995a) was questioned by re-interpretation of the pollen record (Tipping 2013), and that around Loch Mharaich (Caseldine 1979) from *c.* 2000 BC needs to be confirmed by modern pollen-analytical identification. The one pollen grain of the right dimensions to be of cereal type at Lair (lpaz Lair 2a) at 2400-2150 BC need not be a cultivated grass. Rideout (1995) nevertheless found ard-marks beneath Mid-Late Bronze Age roundhouses at Carn Dubh.

The uplands of north-east Perth and Kinross contain some of the most exceptionally well-preserved later prehistoric cultural landscapes in Scotland (Cowley 1997; Halliday 1993; RCAHMS 1990). The earliest monument at Lair is the ring-cairn (Sections 1.8 and 1.9: *passim*), probably of Early Bronze Age date. It is the largest known example in the area and may in some way reference the largest hill in the area, Mount Blair, across the valley, and also perhaps the two distinctive glacial mounds just downslope at Lair (Figure 1.13). There are no known pre-Bronze Age settlements in the area (RCAHMS 1990).

Later roundhouses, often clustered, are found between 210 m and 420 m OD, being particularly abundant between 350-390 m OD and occasionally found as high as 490 m OD (Harris 1985; Hooper 2002). Of the five prehistoric roundhouses ^{14}C dated at Carn Dubh, Buildings 1, 5 and 6 have calibrated age ranges spanning *c.* 1260-795 BC, within the Late Bronze Age (Rideout 1995). At Pitcarmick (North), charcoal from birch twigs in a hearth belonging to a stone and turf built roundhouse was ^{14}C dated to 1398-920 BC (Carver *et al.* 2012). Many unenclosed roundhouse settlements date from this period, but the single date of 745-385 BC (GU-2429) from the burnt threshold timber of Building 2 at Carn Dubh warns that this was also a long-lived form, particularly in eastern Scotland. The three roundhouses at Lair (Figure 2.1) more probably date from the Middle to Late Bronze Age. Roundhouses are often associated with field-systems, comprising scatters of 'clearance' cairns, and occasionally lynchets and stony banks, covering areas from *c.* 2-20 ha, but on average between 8-14 ha (Harris 1985). Barrett and Downes excavated elements of these at Pitcarmick but found no dating evidence (Carver *et al.* 2012). A number of clearance cairns at Lair were excavated (Section 2.3) and roundwood charcoal from the base of one produced a date of AD 680-800 (SUERC-57552). Others may equally relate to Bronze Age land use however. Their spatial distribution at Lair was restricted to areas free of heather and in areas less affected by later cultivation (Banaszek and Cowley: Section 1.8).

There is pollen-analytical evidence at Lair from *c.* 1000-750 BC for the slight recovery of birch, hazel and, perhaps of oak, sustained to the period AD 80-320 when peat stopped growing at Basin 2 (Section 2.6). It is probable that there was a reduction, perhaps a pause, in land use: grazing pressures were reduced, but there is no clear evidence that the hillside ceased to have an agrarian purpose. These changes do not represent pell-mell 'retreat' from or abandonment of the agricultural margin (Barber 1998; Tipping 2002). They began before the climatic deterioration at *c.* 650 BC, which is suggested to have driven 'retreat' and continued beyond it (cf. Brooks 1996; Charman *et al.* 2006; Tipping *et al.* 2012; van Geel and Berglund 2000).

Huntley (1981), however, interpreted slightly increased grazing pressures after *c.* 900 BC in the hills at Coire Fee and Caenlochan and woodland loss may have commenced around Dalnaglar, across the valley from Lair at, very roughly, *c.* 700 BC (Durno 1962). Pastoral activity was also sustained at Carn Dubh, and the pollen record suggests a discontinuous presence of people and livestock as herders drifted in and out of the pollen source area. Activity intensified after *c.* 400 BC and led to soil erosion after *c.* 300 BC (Tipping 1995a; 2013). This last pressure may represent a shift in the regional economy similar, though more muted, to the later Iron Age agricultural expansion in southern and central Scotland (Dumayne 1993a, 1993b; Tipping 1997, 2010). This is best seen in the lowlands at Rae Loch, near Blairgowrie (Edwards and Whittington 1998) at *c.* 160 BC-AD 300, which bears close comparison to the scale of land-use change seen in pollen records from pre-Roman central Scotland.

4.3. A Late Iron Age–early medieval settlement continuum?

Whether there was continuity of settlement between the later Iron Age and the early medieval period in Scotland is a subject of continued debate (e.g. Dodgshon 2015: 178; Harding 2009; Parker Pearson 2012). The spatial coincidence of Pitcarmick buildings with earlier roundhouses, rather than later townships (RCAHMS 1990: 12), may primarily be a product of monument survival resulting from the impact of subsequent land use (Banaszek and Cowley: Section 1.8), and does not imply continuity. However, the question remains as to whether the Pitcarmick builders deliberately chose to occupy the sites of much earlier roundhouse settlements. The re-use of field-systems has been suggested by Carver *et al.* (2012: 185) while Cowley (1997: 166) in Strathbraan, proposed that early medieval builders were 'drawn to ground that had already been at least partially cleared and improved'. Pollen-analytical evidence at Lair, however, suggests that there was no direct agrarian continuum (Section 2.6), and the longer the interval between different phases of farming, and at Lair this may have spanned many hundreds of years, the more difficult it is to accept that old field-systems were either recognisable or useful. Simpler agrarian needs, common to all times, may have determined site selection more: the availability of water; aspect and exposure; good soils and availability of building materials. We should not underestimate, however, the capacity of early medieval farmers to have recognised the traces of earlier stone clearance, but it may only have been additional to a suite of more compelling factors.

At Pitcarmick, one of two hearths (Context 014: Carver *et al.* 2012: 152) was ¹⁴C dated by two fragments of *Alnus* to AD 263-550 (GU4256) and AD 404-535 (GU4527). If the fire represented by this charcoal was used at one period only, then a 6th century AD date is most likely. These hearths are not associated with buildings, however, and are inferred to have been in the open air and as such offer no indication of permanent settlement. Carver *et al.* (2012: 190) also argue that in the uplands west of the Tay, some monumental roundhouses (or 'fortified roundhouses') were in use well into the 1st millennium AD. Of these, however, Site 1 at Aldclune, near Blair Atholl, was shown to be occupied 'at some time in the second half of the first century AD or first half of the third century AD' (Hingley *et al.* 1997: 436), and the example at Black Spout, Pitlochry, is earlier, dated to the later centuries BC (Strachan 2013). As outlined in Section 1.3, while early medieval activity at these massively-walled sites is a recurring theme, domestic occupation is less certain, and limited re-use for specialist activities such as metal-working appears more likely. While the unusually high magnetometry readings within the ring-cairn at Lair (Section 2.2) may indicate prehistoric burning events, it is possible they may result from metal-working, possibly in the early medieval, although only excavation can confirm this.

Nevertheless, the alignment of early medieval Buildings 1 and 2 on the ring-cairn at Lair (Figure 4.1), and the inclusion of the kerb-stones from the latter within Building 2, clearly indicate that the monuments of both the immediate and more ancient past were being referenced during the early medieval period (Section 2.3). While this could be interpreted as an entirely utilitarian re-use of convenient material, the alignment of the buildings and recycling of the kerb-stones might also suggest that the cairn was repurposed at this date, perhaps for metal-working as suggested above. A substantial structure such as the ring-cairn would have offered a similar resource to the monumental roundhouses elsewhere: an open circular space protected by a massive stone wall with limited access. The re-use at Lair can also be read as a deliberate, reverential acknowledgement of the past, perhaps in a similar way that the Pictish royal elite appropriated monuments of the prehistoric 'ritual landscape' at Forteviot to add weight to their status and ownership (Driscoll *et al.* 2010) or as contemporary genealogists usurped king-lists (Woolf 2007). The re-use of stone from such a dominating and ancient structure may have had significance to the Pitcarmick-type builders, signifying connection with 'ancestors' and legitimising their occupation.

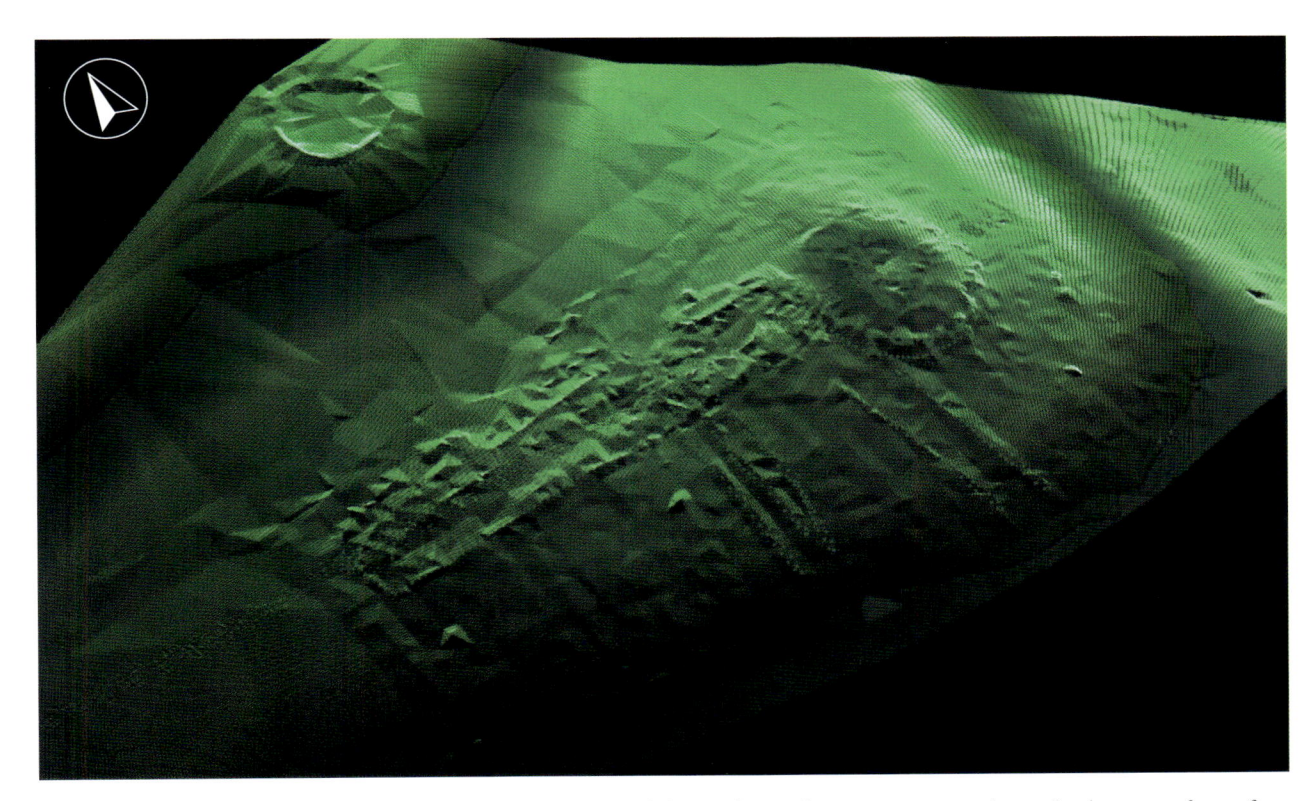

Figure 4.1 The alignment of Buildings 1 and 2 with the ring-cairn and showing later cultivation remains to the south. The re-use of stone from the cairn in Building 2 may suggest re-use of the cairn or a reverential act of acknowledgement of the structure.

4.4 Lair immediately prior to the construction of the Pitcarmick buildings

There is no evidence that Lair was occupied in the centuries immediately preceding the 6th century AD. This period saw a significant shift in vegetation from open deciduous woodland to *Calluna* heath in the pollen record, between local pollen assemblage zones 2b and 3a, but the shift cannot be dated because of the hiatus in peat formation in Basin 2 (Section 2.6): it happened between AD 80-320 and AD 600-660. Peat stopped growing at the pollen site rather than it being cut or burnt. A lower water-table in the peat will have caused this. Drainage of the fen to improve the quality of peat vegetation for grazing (Segerström and Emanuelsson 2002) is possible though human activity was low immediately before peat stopped forming. A shift to a drier climate c. 150-350 AD (Charman et al. 2006) would have had a similar effect.

Palaeo-climatic records provide one reason why peat began to grow again, in a shift to higher water-tables between c. 300-770 AD (Blackford and Chambers 1991; Charman et al. 2006; Hall and Mauquoy 2005; Kerr et al. 2009; Proctor et al. 2002), closely dated to c. 600 AD by Baker et al. (2015).

There is also evidence drawing on the single-entity samples selected from early archaeological contexts for AMS ^{14}C dating (Krus and Hamilton: Section 2.5; Ramsay: Section 2.7) for disturbance, possibly clearance, of locally growing deciduous scrub species (hazel, birch, alder, willow and species of Prunoideae (Amygdaloideae), which includes rowan and hawthorn) immediately prior to building construction. A key feature here is C14 beneath Building 1 (Section 2.3), a line of charcoal, including large fragments, on top of scorched subsoil where 95 % of the charcoal identified from a bulk sample comprised birch (Ramsay: Section 2.7; Table 2.8). Two pieces of young roundwood were ^{14}C dated (Krus and Hamilton: Section 2.5), to AD 430-640 (SUERC-51328) and AD 670-880 (SUERC-42419), most likely trees of different ages growing together. During excavation this feature was tentatively interpreted as a fence or wood from felled trees raked together in a ragged line for burning. However, an alternative, and perhaps more likely interpretation is that C14 represents the truncated sunken element of an earlier building containing structural remains and domestic debris (Section 2.3), in which case we have no evidence for land clearance. These possibilities are summarised in the next section.

4.5 Chronology and sequence of the buildings at Lair

The Bayesian-generated ^{14}C chronology of Buildings 1-3 at Lair has been considered in detail by Krus and Hamilton (Section 2.5) but is summarised below. This stratigraphy-based chronology assumes that all negative features within each building are contemporary and do not relate to earlier structures.

- activity at Building 1, using the primary model, is estimated to have begun in *AD 575-655*, lasting for *90-275 years* and ended in *AD 725-885*. The alternative model has activity at Building 1 beginning at *AD 585-735*, lasting for *80-275 years* and ending at *AD 740-945*.
- activity at Building 2, using the primary model, began at *AD 640-715*, lasting *160-310 years*, and ended *AD 835-970*, and from the alternative model, began in *AD 650-760*, lasted *140-305 years* and ended *AD 850-980*.
- activity at Building 3, from the primary model, began in *AD 675-770*, lasted *75-235 years* and ended *AD 805-945*, whilst from the alternative model, activity began in *AD 675-770*, lasted *85-250 years* and ended in *AD 815-960*.

Activity measured by ^{14}C assays at these large buildings persisted at each for, minimally, more than 75 years, around three human generations, although activities could have been sustained for much longer. These minimal durations, if continuous, suggest that these buildings stood for much longer than those estimated for buildings on crannogs (Barber and Crone 2001; Cavers and Crone 2017) and for prehistoric roundhouses by Halliday (2007), of around 5-15 years. There is no archaeological evidence for repair to these buildings (Section 2.3; below); however, recognition of this in turf constructions is challenging and would require better preservation than existed. Urbańczyk (1999: 129) notes that, depending on location and climate, well-designed turf buildings in Iceland might be used for c. 100 years, with regular roof conservation every 10-20 years. At Building 3, however, there is evidence of at least two phases of construction, including major remodelling with the relocation of the entrance.

Krus and Hamilton (Section 2.5) suggest that Building 1 preceded Building 2, which was followed by Building 3, but that it is very likely that there was a 'degree of contemporaneity' between all three. Radiocarbon dated activity need not be the same as human occupation, but this is assumed here. Bayesian modelling suggests that the order in which these buildings were constructed was not the order in which activity ended. What is termed by Krus and Hamilton (Section 2.5) as 'the abandonment sequence' is very likely to have been: Building 1 followed by Building 3 followed by Building 2. Building 7 is the only other building at Lair to produce a ^{14}C date, with a single assay of AD 770-970 providing a *Terminus Post Quem (TPQ)* for the structure.

However, as outlined in Sections 2.3 and 2.5, an alternative interpretation of the archaeological features

4. DISCUSSION

and deposits has been proposed and indeed, considered more probable. This would suggest:

- Some or all of the negative features at Buildings 1 and 2 in fact pre-date them and relate to an earlier structure(s): they have all been truncated in the construction of Buildings 1 and 2. Samples retrieved from these features yielded relatively uniform radiocarbon date ranges of the 7-8th century AD (Table 2.1); all being earlier than the *AD 775-975 (95% probability)*, and probably *AD 880-930 (68% probability)* modelled *TPQ* date obtained from C56 for the construction of Building 1 (Section 2.5; below).
- Building 1, the visible earthwork, is a later construction using turves that subsequently formed over the earlier structure(s). The modelled date for SUERC-49666 (*Betula* sp. charcoal), which is the latest date sealed under the turf wall in C56, provides a *TPQ* for the construction of Building 1, as defined by the collapsed turf walls visible on ground surface, of *AD 775-975 (95% probability)*, and probably *AD 880-930 (68% probability)*.
- The cut features associated with Building 2 are evidence of earlier activity, meaning the only reliable dates for Building 2 come from the three samples recovered from Hearth C148, which date to between the late 8th to late 10th centuries AD: *AD 760-950, AD 770-990* and *AD 770-990* (SUERC-57549-57551 respectively; *95% probability*).

Although, on balance, this scenario is perhaps the more probable, it precludes more detailed modelling of the dates, as it is not possible to clearly assign each cut feature to a particular phase of occupation. However, the dates from Hearth C148 indicate Building 2 was in use at some point between the late 8th to late 10th centuries AD and the modelled *TPQ* date for the construction of Building 1, would show it was built sometime after the late 8th to late 10th centuries AD. These would represent the last buildings at this location. The earlier cut features, including the linear feature C14, gully C83 and at least some of the other cut features beneath both buildings, indicate structures were here prior to the late 8th to late 10th centuries AD and most likely in the centuries immediately prior to this.

4.6 The buildings at Lair: form and function

Buildings 1 and 2

This pair of aligned buildings (ID29510; Section 2.3) were classed as Pitcarmick 'related' buildings by RCAHMS (1990: 149-150). Building 1 was constructed entirely of turf, timber and thatch, with walls of *c.* 1 m thickness containing almost no stone. It was very long (*c.* 25 m internally) with rounded ends and relatively straight sides. The west end was built over a notable downward slope and it had at least one south-west facing entrance, *c.* 5m from the south-east end, although others may have existed (Figures 2.4, 2.5 and 4.2). A large post-hole at the south-east (C19) end is similar in position to those found at buildings C1 and E1 at Pitcarmick (Carver *et al.* 2012). This recurring feature may suggest structural upright timbers to support the roof structure, perhaps in a similar way to the 'end crucks' of Scottish post-medieval cruck-built longhouses (Walker 2008: 91, Figure 22). No hearth or other structural features were found in Building 1 and relatively few finds were recovered, although excavation was of limited extent. While finds were recovered from negative features and the turf banks, notably including buckles and knives from the east end, they probably represent residual material from an earlier occupation incorporated into the wall within cut turves. While its shape and scale may suggest a byre-house, with a domestic east end and a byre at its sloping west end, no floor levels or hearth were identified and the byre never developed the sunken character of the Pitcarmick buildings. The primary Bayesian model would place Building 1 early in the sequence of structures, perhaps with a second phase of use as an outbuilding, once Building 3 was established as a byre-house (below). In the alternative interpretation, whereby Building 1 is late in the sequence, it may have been constructed as an outbuilding to serve Building 3 and used as a barn, sheep shed, and perhaps in part for storage and/or a workshop. The south-east end appears slightly wider than the north-west end which may indicate different functions at either end, possibly a domestic/animal division of space, although no evidence of internal partitioning was found. The north-west end is also constructed over a significant downward slope suggesting the need for drainage, probably as a result of housing animals or potentially storing manure.

In contrast, Building 2 included considerably more stone in its turf construction and was much shorter (internally *c.* 13 m in length), with slightly more bowed sides giving a more oval appearance in plan (Figures 2.4, 2.8 and 4.2). The use of stone in the turf walls at ground level was noticeable at both ends and more occasionally along the side walls. It had an entrance approximately half way along the south-west facing façade and contained the remains of a large if informal hearth set in the middle of the south-eastern end. There were very few finds and the hearth's informal nature suggests it was both short-lived and occurred late in the life of the building and probably as part of a workshop or shelter rather than domestic living quarters. The relative absence of material culture could also suggest that it housed animals or was used as a store.

Figure 4.2 Reconstruction of Buildings 1 and 2 and the ring-cairn (A. Braby and G. McSwan: 2014).

As with Building 1, there are alternative interpretations. Building 2 may have been constructed as an outbuilding to Building 1 as a byre-house. Alternatively, it could equally have served as the house for a non-domestic Building 1, or perhaps as an outbuilding, along with Building 1, to Building 3.

Buildings 3-5

The initial interpretation of Buildings 3-5, all oriented west-south-west to east-north-east, was as a sequence of three buildings (RCAHMS 1990: 149-150). Buildings 3 and 4 are broadly aligned, with Building 5 being constructed in parallel beside Building 3, which had a circular annexe attached to its west end and, because of this and its more pronounced surviving earthworks, appears to have been the most prominent structure of the three, at least in its final development.

Building 3

Building 3 was large (*c.* 20 m in length and up to *c.* 5.5 m wide internally) with slightly bowed side walls and rounded ends. Its walls were at least 1 m thick, possibly as much as 1.5 m, and were constructed primarily of turf and earth (Figure 2.15), although also incorporating significantly more stone internally than Buildings 1 and 2. It was wider at the west end, where it was built over a noticeable slope to the east (Figures 4.3 and 4.5) and had a partially sunken eastern interior which also sloped to the east but much more gradually.

Building 3 appeared to have at least two phases but due to the lack of intact stratigraphy it was not possible to comprehensively map the detail of this phasing or even ascribe individual features to either phase. Remodelling is illustrated by two south-south-east facing entrances, only 0.5 m apart, in the southern side just under halfway from the west end. One of these was defined by two large post-holes on the inside edge of the wall line, the other having stone paving leading from the exterior to internal steps to a partially paved interior. One appears to have replaced the other. Further, a concentration of shallow stake-holes was present at the western end of the sunken and stone filled area of Building 3 (Figure 2.13). The westernmost of the stake-holes form a distinct edge running across the interior and are likely to represent some form of wattle division between the living quarters and the byre (Figures 4.3 and 4.6). Although the stake-holes were found beneath the raised stone floor and could be interpreted as an earlier phase of activity, it is equally conceivable that the stakes and stone floor were contemporary and that the stakes protruded through the floor layer. In either case, when fixed to the roof structure for support they would have been wattled and daubed to create a partition wall.

The eastern half of the building is interpreted as a byre, with a sloping floor draining out of its south-east corner (Figures 4.3 and 4.5). The area exposed in the excavation contained three post-holes, along the axis of the building. These may indicate a two-aisled building with occasional central supports, perhaps in support of the roof structure (Figures 4.3 and 4.5), relating to internal divisions and doors, or to provide localised weight-bearing support for a raised platform in the roof space, effectively a loft space utilising a cross beam (Figures 4.4 and 4.5). A combination of these functions is equally likely. The west end of the building, measuring 8 m in length from the interior face of the west wall to the wattle internal division, contained a large central hearth which was probably in use throughout both phases (Figures 2.13, 4.5 and 4.6). The internal partition, separating it from the byre, the presence of the hearth, and a clear concentration of small finds (Figure 4.3) further confirms this as the dwelling end of what can then be classified as a byre-house.

Building 3 had a circular annexe adjoined to its south-west corner, measuring *c.* 5 m in diameter within turf walls around 0.5 m thick. It contained a number of pits, not all of which are likely to have been in use at the same time. At least one of these had been capped by turf

4. Discussion

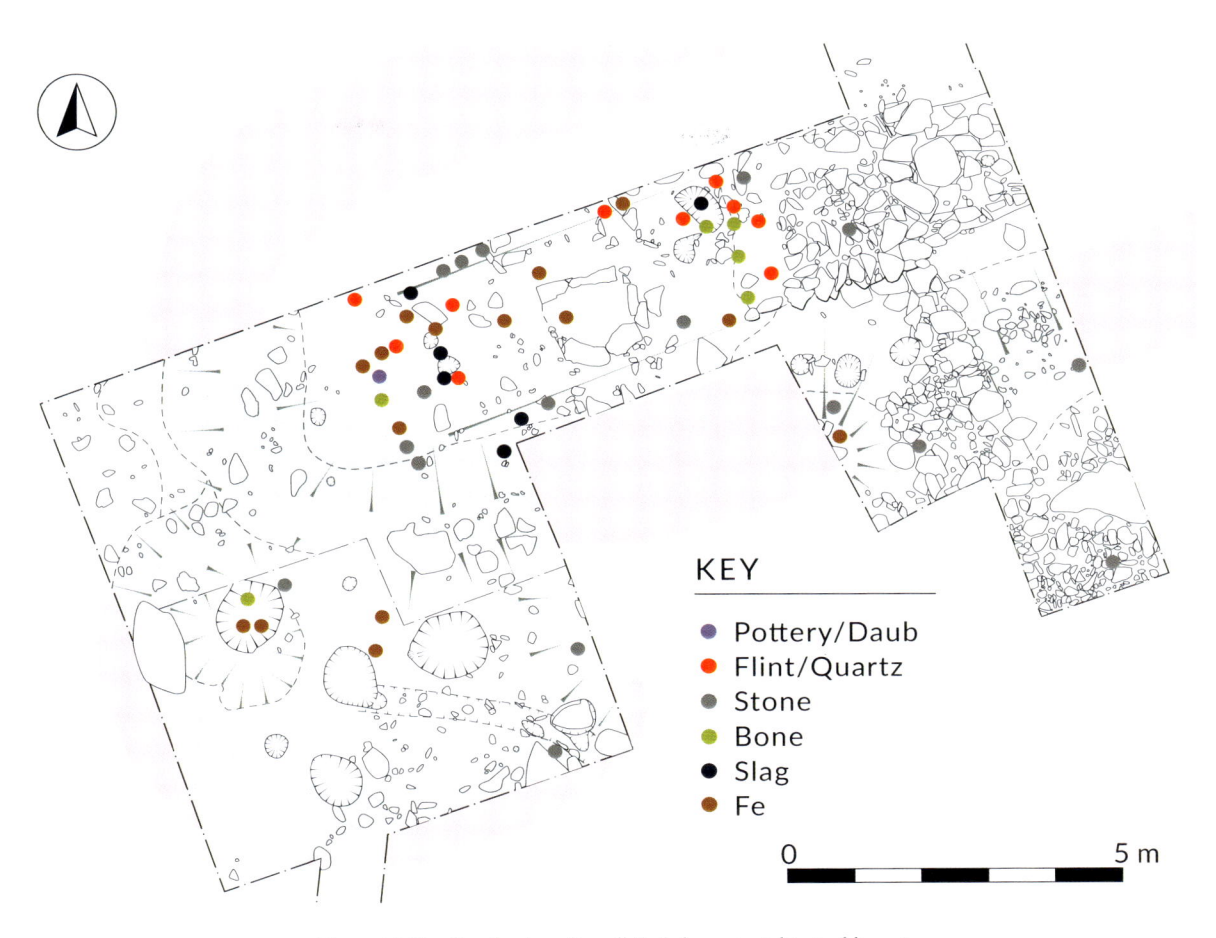

Figure 4.3 The distribution of small finds by material in Buildings 3.

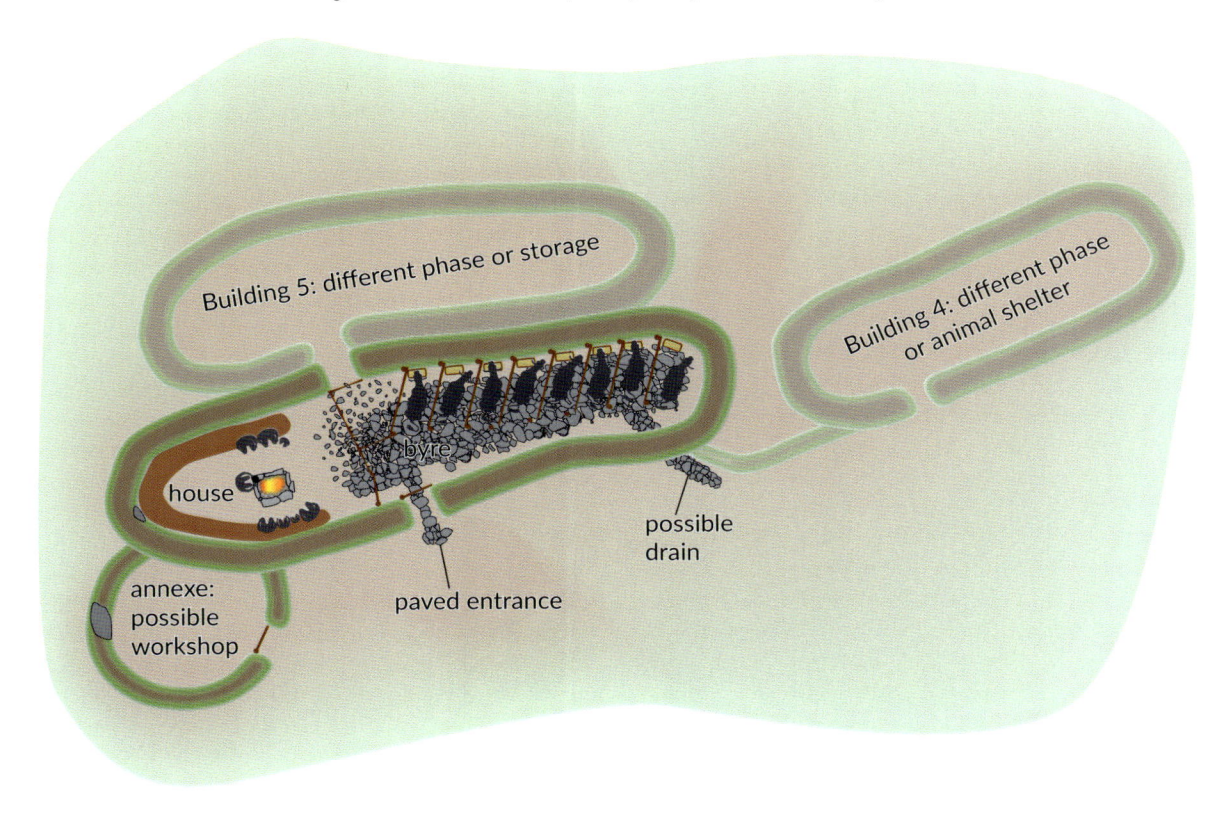

Figure 4.4 Reconstruction plan of Building 3.

113

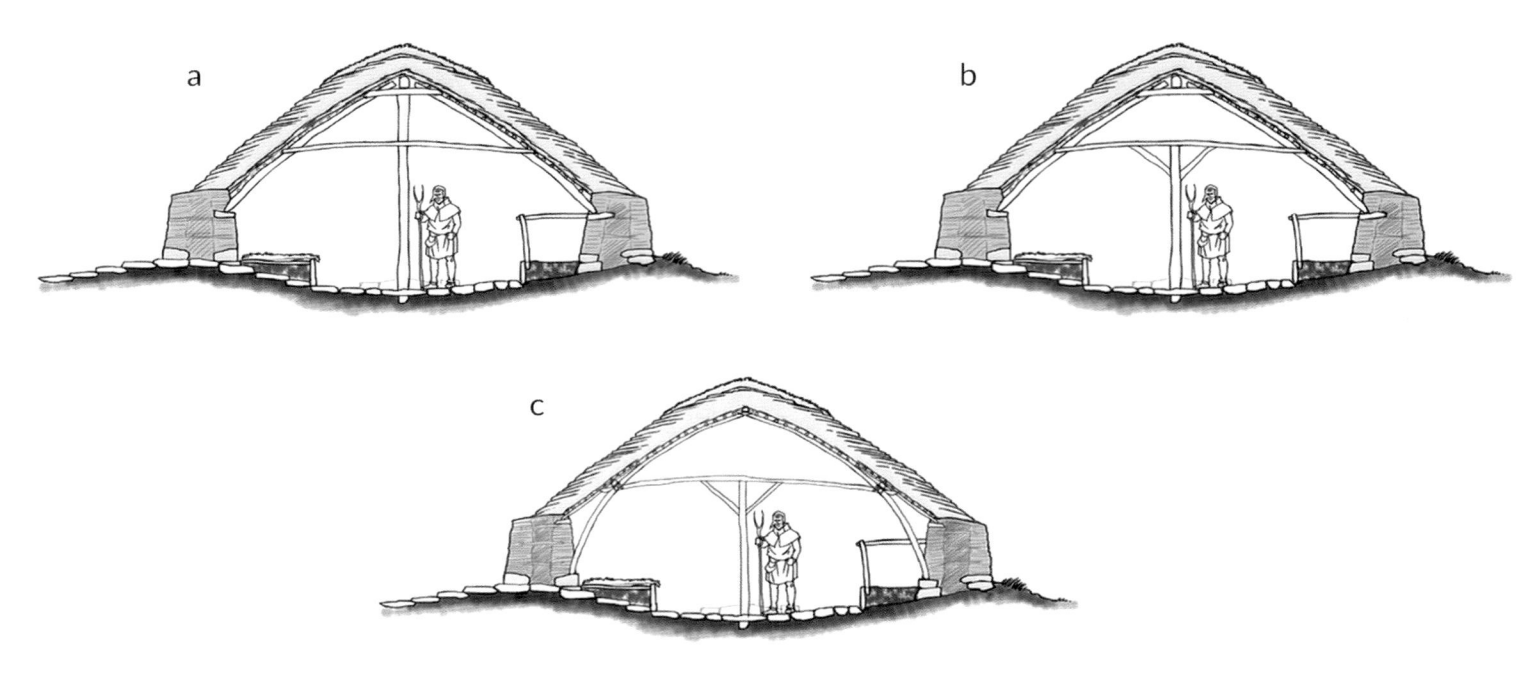

Figure 4.5 Schematic sections across Building 3 showing a) rigid A-frame 'caber' roof option, b) the same with loft space, and c) a roof supported by lighter-weight round wood poles under tension and with loft space (C. Mitchell: 2018).

at least once, suggesting the burial of waste material, while another contained the remains of a 'feast' of cattle and calves, the remains of a spring-time meal (Section 3.9). The annexe floor deposits contained charcoal flecks and burnt bone, while internal pits produced small iron sheet fragments, a small broken whetstone, an anvil/whetstone and hammerscale (Section 3.5), all suggestive of iron tool maintenance. Significantly, part of a rotary grinder was found in a depression at the entranceway to the annexe (Section 3.3) which may have been a symbolic deposit similar to the very worn rotary grinder placed at the main entrance to Building 3 (Section 3.3; below).

Accepting Building 3 as a byre-house, the limited space afforded to the house is notable, tempting the interpretation that the annexe was roofed to provide additional floor space. Its mixed collection of features and finds assemblage are suggestive of this outbuilding being used for storage and working, perhaps changing use over its lifespan. The ^{14}C date from bone within pit C278 in the annexe was earlier (AD 675-775: SUERC 79014: Table 2.1) than those from the hearth (AD 772-887 and AD 729-885: SUERC 74161 and SUERC 74162: Table 2.1) and may well represent a foundation deposit, while the hearth material provides a likely end-date for occupation of the byre-house.

Buildings 4 and 5

Limited excavation could only confirm the extents of these structures and, while it is possible that the group represents a sequence of byre-houses as suggested by the RCAHMS (1990: 12, 150), it is equally possible that they are outbuildings added sequentially with Buildings 3 and 5 connected by an entrance (Figure 2.12). This is how we have chosen to represent this cluster in our reconstruction (Figure 4.7), while also exercising some artistic licence in the depiction of the western ends of both Buildings 4 and 5.

Building 6

Buildings 6 and 7 are noticeably different from Buildings 1-5 in that they are smaller, have associated enclosures and are further downslope, set on a gently sloping terrace overlooking the Allt Corra-lairige (Figure 2.1).

Building 6 was the smallest building identified at Lair, being internally only *c.* 7 m in length by *c.* 3 m wide, with walls of *c.* 1m thickness constructed from turf, earth and stone, surrounded by a shallow gully. With very limited internal floor-space, it is suggestive of a shieling or an outbuilding to a settlement elsewhere. Both the walls and interior of the building contained a significant amount of stone, suggesting a composite turf and stone construction, possibly including stone internal fittings. The entrance appears to be south-facing. Building 6 was within a larger enclosure with a south-west facing aspect and also appeared to overlie an earlier, longer building which was partially visible as an earthwork. Building 6 and its predecessor sat within a sub-circular enclosure, the perimeter of which, excavation showed to be built entirely of turf and earth (Section 2.3). This shadowy predecessor is reminiscent of Buildings E1 and E2 at Pitcarmick (Carver *et al.*

4. Discussion

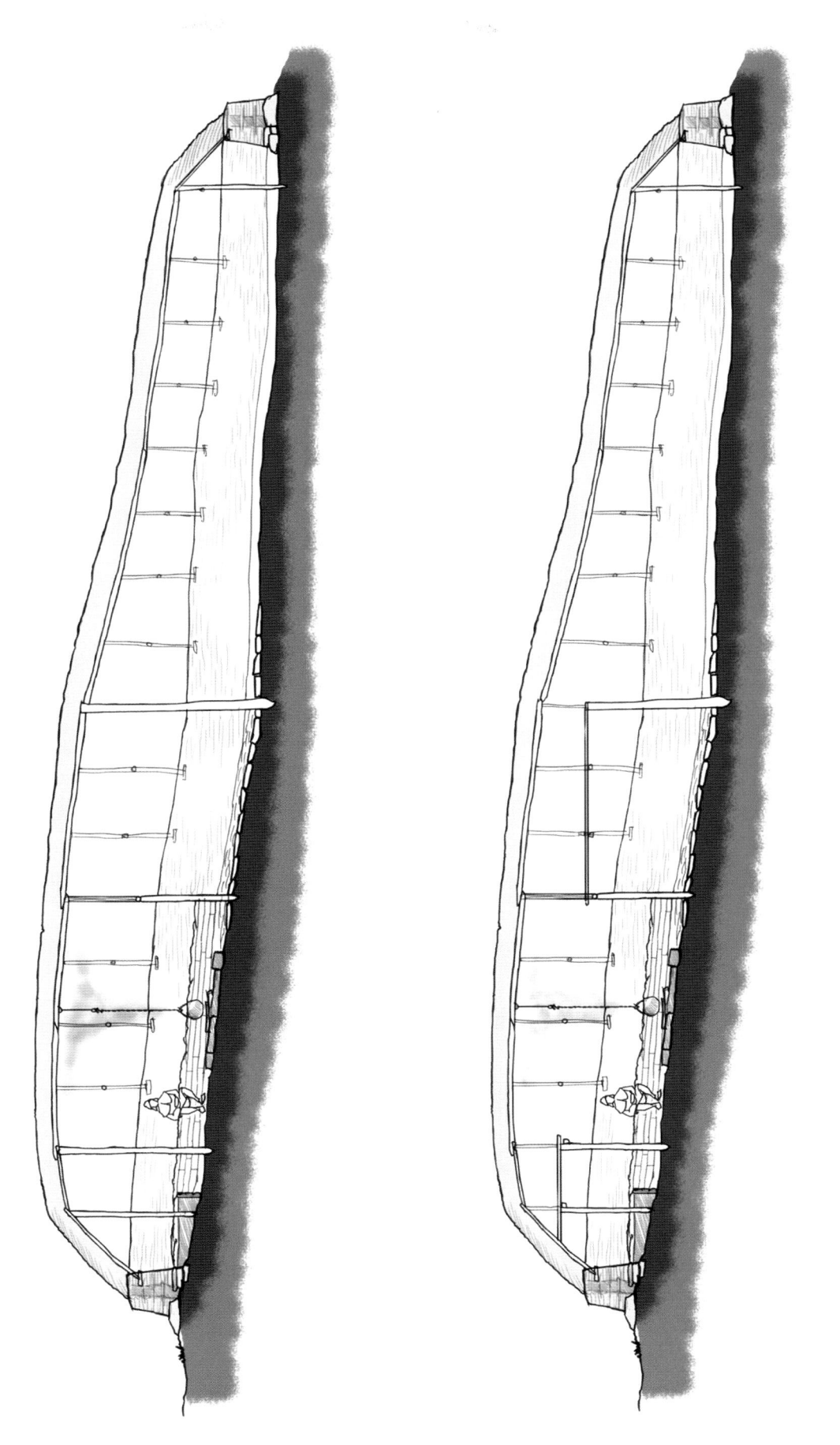

Figure 4.6 Schematic longitudinal sections through Building 3 illustrating the noticeable slope of the domestic area (left) compared with the byre on the right hand side, below shows the loft space option (C. Mitchell: 2018).

Figure 4.7 Artists' reconstruction of Building 3 as a byre-house over-wintering cattle (C. Mitchell: 2018).

2012). Indeed, Building 6 produced a sherd of medieval pottery from the 13-15th centuries (Section 3.7), later than the suggested 11-12th century date for occupation of Buildings C1 and E2 at Pitcarmick (Section 4.16). Building 6 may well represent a high medieval shieling, or outbuilding, set within a small enclosure to control stock, which may have operated in combination with the larger enclosure to the south-east (Figures 2.1 and 4.8). The southern line of the latter is curvilinear, with a sharp right-angled turn at its eastern end and, like the other enclosure, its boundary was built of turf and earth. The enclosures could have retained animals or excluded them. It is possible that it was constructed on the footprint of an early medieval building.

Buildings 7 and 8

The RCAHMS noted that the best-preserved building of this group (Building 7) 'superficially resembles a Pitcarmick type building' (1990: 151) but while this is the case, it is noticeably smaller, being internally *c.* 14.5 m in length by *c.* 3.5 m wide. The reason for its prominence as an earthwork is its low coursed-stone and earth footing, *c.* 1 m in thickness, which appeared to have supported a turf wall. Building 7 was the only one investigated at Lair to have this feature. The wall was surrounded, like Building 6, with a shallow gully. With rounded ends and south-facing entrance, this already narrow building had a very restricted internal floor-space, no indication of a hearth and no significant small finds, collectively indicating that use as an outbuilding is more likely than use for human occupation. A *Terminus Post Quem (TPQ)* of AD 770–970 was secured from charcoal found beneath the stone footing, however, this may have been constructed on the footprint of an earlier structure.

Along with Building 8, measuring internally *c.* 13 m in length by *c.* 4 m, the pair are broadly oriented east-west with their layout and associated enclosure taking advantage of the local topography, Building 7 being constructed on a slightly raised ridge while Building 8 is terraced into the south-east facing slope of the hill within a small natural depression. The turf and earth boundary wall of the sub-rectangular enclosure incorporates a small outbuilding identified on the ground by the RCAHMS (1990) and from remote sensing data (Section 1.8), but now difficult to distinguish in the field. While it is possible that the unexcavated Building 8 was a small dwelling the terraced, relatively low level

Figure 4.8 The Weaver's house at the Highland Folk Museum shows how the wall footings of Building 7 may have looked; the roofs at Lair were probably lower due to their exposed location and high altitude (D. Strachan: 2013).

of its floor suggests it may have been prone to dampness and so was more suitable to house animals. On balance it is suggested that Buildings 6-8 together represent a group of medieval or post-medieval outbuildings relating to nearby settlement, probably downslope in the main glen (Figures 2.1 and 4.9).

In conclusion, there are alternative possibilities for how the group of Buildings 1-5 developed at Lair. In the first model Buildings 1 and 2, classified as Pitcarmick-related by RCAHMS, were the earliest in the sequence and were precursors to Buildings 3-5, the Pitcarmick-type proper; however, they may have remained in use once Buildings 3-5 were established. Although Building 1 has the morphology that would suggest an early byre-house there was little evidence found internally to confirm this, albeit excavation here was limited. The alternative, more likely model, suggests Buildings 1 and 2 were late in the sequence (though still of early medieval date), and may have replaced a previous structure represented by the truncated remains of linear feature C14 and at least some, if not most, of the pits and post-holes and gully found beneath the collapsed turf and earth walls of Buildings 1 and 2. In this scenario, Buildings 1 and 2 may represent outbuildings to the multi-phased Building 3, which clearly required additional floor space, as indicated by the construction of the circular annexe. It is possible that Buildings 1 and 2 represent a later development to separate the house from the byre, after Building 3 had gone out of use. A parallel for this may be found in high medieval Iceland where houses and byres are separate, unlike the byre-houses commonly found in Iron/Viking age Scandinavia, and Berson (2002: 60-61) suggests a trend of distancing cattle from people from the Viking Age into the Middle Ages, and notes that most sites where the byre is separated by a greater distance from the dwelling are dated from the 11th century AD onwards. The other significant implication is that Pitcarmick buildings had associated outbuildings, as they have to date been largely viewed as solitary byre-houses.

While not proven through excavation the scale, morphology and orientation of Buildings 12 and 13 suggest a similar scale of early medieval settlement existed across the burn. The much disturbed Building 14, crossed by the track to the east of Buildings 1-5, seems to be another, with its circular annexe apparently replicating the form of Building 3 (Figures 2.1 and 4.9). Whether these close but separate settlements represent the farms of contemporary communities, dynamic movement by a single pioneer community, or second and third generation expansion of the initial occupation of the Allt Corra-lairige is unknown, though the first of these three options is preferred here. As such, the overall interpretation of the early medieval

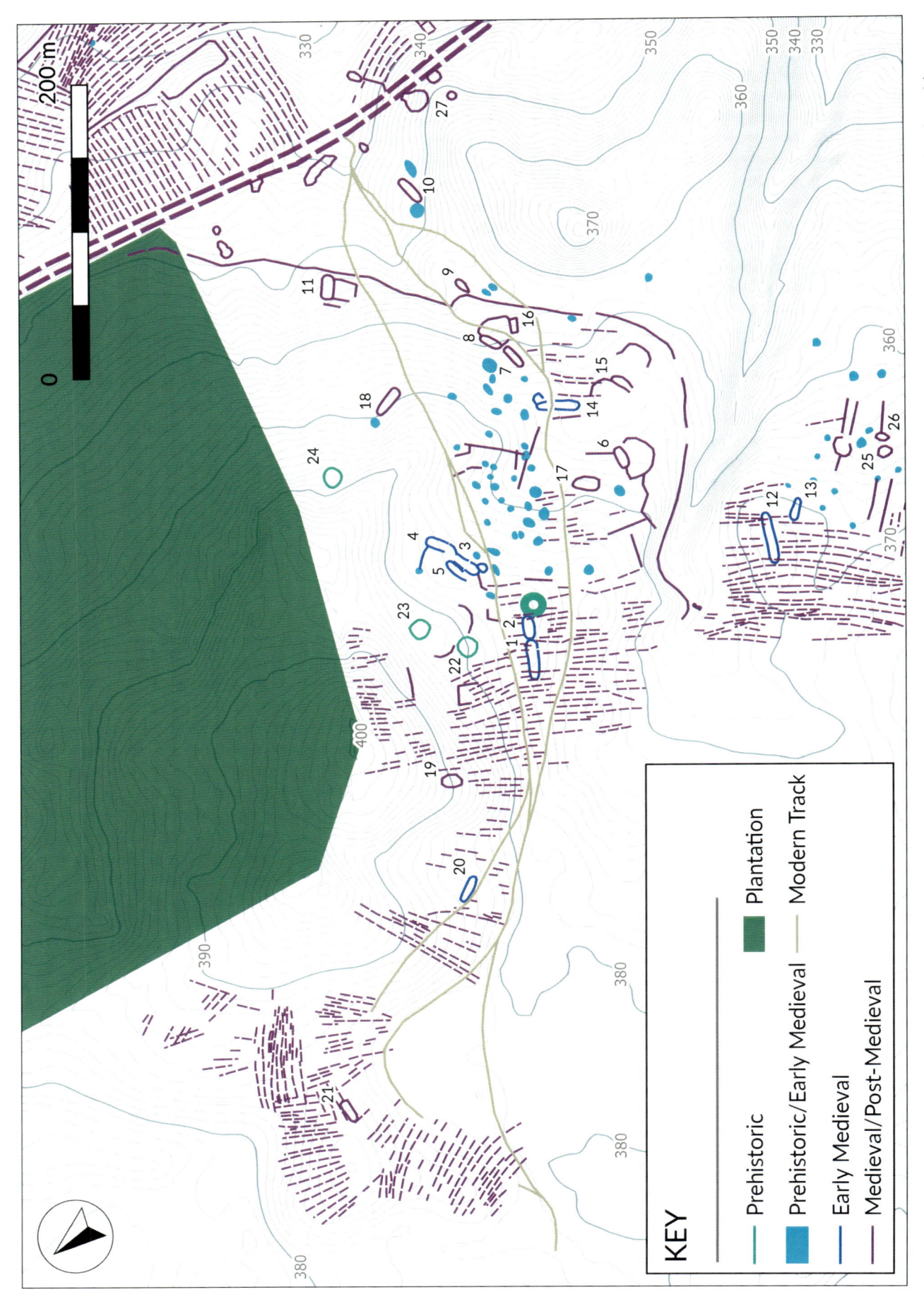

Early Medieval Settlement in Upland Perthshire: Excavations at Lair, Glen Shee 2012-17

Figure 4.9 The probable broad phasing of the visible remains at Lair: early medieval Buildings 1-2, 3-5; probably 12-13, and possibly 14 (© Historic Environment Scotland (Source: contour data derived from DTM (2018) © Bluesky International Limited & Getmapping Plc.)).

118

buildings at Lair is as a series of dispersed farms rather than a village (Figure 4.9).

Buildings 6 and 7 are later, possibly late medieval, as suggested by the well-preserved stone foundation in Building 7, medieval pottery from Building 6 and the fact that both buildings included gullies, a feature absent from the early medieval buildings excavated. The significance of later medieval buildings having these improved foundation and drainage features is explained below.

4.7 The buildings at Lair: turf, stone, timber and thatch

While the origins of turf construction in Scotland have been suggested to lie in the Neolithic (Loveday 2006), it is a well-known material in later prehistoric roundhouses (Romankiewicz 2011). The later 1st millennium AD date of the buildings at Lair, together with their elongated shape, place them at a key phase of transition from circular to rectangular forms, the origins of a long tradition in Scotland of vernacular turf construction continuing to at least the 18th century AD (Allen 1979; Fenton 1968; Noble 2000; Walker and McGregor 1996), with parallels to building techniques used throughout other parts of the British Isles and Ireland (Evans 1969; Gailey 1984; Blair 2018). Both the results of experimental archaeology and experience in maintaining Icelandic buildings, however, confirm that turf structures require regular maintenance and repair. The more readily degradable nature of the organic building material, which can also be recycled on the fields, makes old turf buildings both difficult to locate and excavate (Section 2.3) and which may also begin to explain why excavated townships in Scotland cannot so far be dated prior to c. 1750 AD (Wilkinson 2009: 16-17). Research into the skills and crafts of Scottish turf construction (Walker 2006a) has done much to promote and inform this aspect of rural architecture, as have international comparisons (Section 4.10). Equally important have been the experimental reconstructions at the Highland Folk Museum in Newtonmore, based on excavations at nearby Easter Raitts (Noble 2003), and Icelandic turf construction (given the reservation in Section 4.10 that Icelandic traditions are not easily compared to the North Sea littoral) where an active skills base still exists (Sigurðarddottir 2008). In 2013-2014, while the Lair excavations were ongoing, the co-directors (Strachan and Sneddon) trained in turf construction in the Skagafjörður district of north-west Iceland and this practical insight has proved an invaluable aid both in the interpretation of the remains and the more general appreciation of turf as a building material. This section discusses these different building materials, their sources and the diverse construction techniques likely to have been employed.

Sources of turf

The nature and selection of turf for construction is an important factor. In Iceland, good quality turf is often cut some distance from the building site. A strong root system is an important attribute, holding together the soil. Suitable turves can be cut wet from boggy areas and partially dried prior to construction, or can come from dry sources such as heath. Both these potential sources of turf were available at Lair and soil micromorphological analyses may, in time, reveal these (Sections 1.9 and 2.4).

At some time in the first half of the 1st millennium AD the dry, silt-rich sandy soils around the peat basins ceased to support a cover of open, secondary deciduous woodland and grass, and a form of dry grassy heath developed. This was not through natural pedological change, the substrates in the catchment probably having supported podsolic soils since the early Holocene, but probably from anthropogenic changes to the vegetation. With the loss of trees, the turf would have become more tightly bound with shallower but much denser grass and heather roots. Any grazing, particularly by sheep, would have helped to further compact and increase root density in the turf. We can therefore assume relatively thin, densely rooted turves of c. 10 cm soil depth could be cut from a relatively stone-free soil composed of sand and silt mineral sediments. This would suggest strip, or 'divot' construction, rather than thick turf blocks (see below), which is consistent with the, albeit slight, archaeological evidence from the site (Section 2.3, Building 5, Figure 2.15). However, from borehole records across the marsh of Basin 2 (Section 2.6) there is no evidence of soil washed or blown in from de-turfed soil onto the peat, so it is unlikely that turves were cut from around the buildings themselves.

The use of stone

Stone is used in turf wall construction in several ways: as occasional or alternate courses; as formal 'dwarf' walls or footings; and as an occasional inclusion at foundation level. The use of alternate courses of stone is known in both Scottish (Fenton 1968; Fenton and Walker 1981: 73–7; Walker et al. 1996: 17) and Icelandic (Sigurðardóttir 2008: 20-21; Urbańczyk 1999: 126-7) building, and as a composite construction would have improved both stability and wear (Walker 2006a: 29). The use of stone in wall construction would also offer an opportunity to clear boulders from around the building site. So efficient has this been over millennia that the ground surfaces around many sites are now largely free of loose stones. The technique is proposed for Buildings C1 and E1 at Pitcarmick (Carver et al. 2012: 184), although the limited evidence for stone in Building C1 suggests its wall may have been primarily of turf (Carver et al. 2012: 159). Of the early medieval buildings at Lair, only Building 2 used some stone in the turf walls at ground level. The later Building 6 contained significant stone in the walls, which was surrounded by a gully, and Building 7 included a complete stone wall footing, thought to have been earth mortared, again surrounded by a shallow gully.

The use of 'dwarf' walls or footings is also widely known in turf construction in Iceland (Sigurðardóttir 2008: 12-13) and Scotland (Walker 2006a: 35, 37; Walker et al. 1996: 8-9) and would have protected the lower courses of the turf superstructure from erosion by rain, snow and frost, frost heaving being a particular threat if the bottom of the turf work becomes saturated with water. The shallow gully found in occurrence with these stone footings is held to have fulfilled the same purpose of keeping the wall dry. The construction of the wall footings could consume local debris and may in part have had an aesthetic function. At Lair a formal full-circuit stone footing was found only at Building 7 (Section 2.3) which, while undated, is thought to be relatively late in the overall chronology, perhaps part of a later medieval trend towards greater longevity of buildings (Section 4.10).

While less evident in the literature, the incorporation of occasional stones at foundation level in the wall line is more common at Lair and involves either *in situ* boulders or the movement of stray stones, or stones from other structures being incorporated in the construction of new turf walls. The former is best represented in Building 3 where *in situ* large boulders on the line of the wall have been incorporated into its foundation, while others have been added by way of consumption. The clearest example of incorporation from other structures is at the south-east end of Building 2 where large stones from the kerb of the nearby ring-cairn have been robbed and appear to provide buttress-like support to the end (Section 2.3).

A third use at Building 2 is the incorporation of occasional stones at ground level along the length of the external facade of the building (Figures 2.8 and 2.9). Such occasional use would not offer the structural benefits afforded by the stones at the end of Building 2 (above) or the protection provided by a dwarf foundation wall, and it is proposed as relating to the marking out of the building prior to wall construction, effectively offering a guide to the builders. Finally, stone could also be used to repair and maintain turf walls, for example in filling holes with stonework rather than pre-shrunk turves.

Turf wall construction

Much has been written about turf wall construction in Scotland (Fenton and Walker 1981; Noble 2003; Walker 2006a) and Iceland (Sigurðarddottir 2008; Van Hoof and Van Dijken, 2008; Wilkinson 2009) and in both regions turves are cut as either strips (*divet* or *divot* in Scots and *torfur* or *strengir* in Icelandic) or blocks (*Faill*, *Fale* or *Feal* in Scots and *hnausar*, *klambra* or *kekkir* in Icelandic).

In both cases turf can provide stable walling with excellent thermal properties and can be used in conjunction with stone as outlined above. The evidence from Lair suggests predominantly turf walls of *c.* 1-1.5 m thickness. Excavation evidence for the method of turf construction at Lair was very limited due to subsequent ploughing, natural degradation and bioturbation of the soils: however, where turf lenses did survive in section they appeared relatively thin, even when considering the effects of degradation and compaction (Section 2.3). This suggests thinner turves (i.e. divot) had been used rather than thick blocks (*fale*). In one or two locations there is evidence that the walls comprised an outer and inner retaining façade of turf with an earthen core. In all cases, the earth core consisted of a homogenous mass of subsoil with only occasional turf lenses representing the scant remains of the outer and

Figure 4.10 Icelandic turf wall construction: herring-bone facades of klambra *or 'clamped block', and alternate courses of* strengur, *with an earthen/turf core on a dwarf foundation wall (D. Strachan: 2013).*

4. Discussion

Figure 4.11 A rounded corner from Tyrfingsstaoir, Iceland, with a herring bone pattern of klambra *blocks and a stone foundation, both interspersed with* strengur *strip turves (D. Strachan: 2013).*

inner facades (Section 2.3). Despite being subject to over a millennium of degradation, including in places cultivation, the relatively small amount of material within the banks of the buildings gives the general impression that the walls did not stand to any great height and are unlikely to have exceeded a maximum of 2 m.

Full-scale reconstructions of excavated post-medieval buildings at the Highland Folk Museum in Newtonmore (Noble 1984, 2003) illustrate turf construction well and have added much to our understanding of their performance over time. In Iceland, useful parallels can also be found. There, turf walls of 1-2 m in thickness can be built in stages with two retaining facades of one or two layers of blocks infilled with earth and turf cuttings, brought to a level. At several stages flat turf strips are applied to tie these retaining elements together. The result of this manually compacted earthen core is a very stable heavy construction (Figures 4.10 and 4.11).

Wood and thatch: the superstructure

While consideration of more recent vernacular architecture in Scotland and abroad can provide a useful appreciation of turf as a building material, together with issues relating to its procurement and use, a degree of caution must be employed in using these sources, particularly when considering the possible configuration of roofs. In most cases little archaeological evidence exists, meaning many interpretations are possible while very few are demonstrable.

Scottish vernacular building methods (Dixon 2002) offer useful parallels when considering options for a single span roof, either with or without central internal support. In Iceland too, Urbańczyk (1999) presents a variety of options for rafter and purlin roofing based on post-medieval examples, mainly for two- and three-aisled structures (Urbańczyk 1999: 127-129; Figures 6 and 7). One option at Lair is for the use of cuppills (other spellings include cupill, couple and cupple), from the Scottish vernacular, where the roof is supported by pairs of upright timbers forming trusses, ranging from A-shaped to fully rounded arch trusses, and connected through the addition of purlins along the length of the building. The cuppills are characteristically without diagonal bracing, and thus not a frame in the sense of a timber structure that is rigid in all directions. Purlin-only roofs, where support is provided by longitudinal, horizontal structural members resting on gables, are discounted here due to the extended length of the buildings at Lair.

Surviving cuppills are known to have been built earth-fast, on stone pads, resting on dwarf walls or placed at greater height in or onto the wall head. With the use of rafters (or brushwood or ropes used to the same effect) placed over the purlins, the weight of the roof structure and its cover is taken by the cuppills rather than the walls, which are often not load bearing (Walker 2008). Cuppills have historically been employed in a wide range of buildings, including byre-dwellings and barns and for buildings of higher social status, such as houses of tacksmen (Dixon 2002: 189). While Walker (2008) suggests an early origin in Scotland for the 'Celtic cuppill', from *c.* 1000 AD if not before, others consider them as a later medieval form (Piers Dixon *pers comm*). While medieval cruck-framed buildings in England often use large-scale timbers, there is no unsuitable tree-type for the 'Celtic cuppill' (Walker 2008: 75, 87-8) and Walker suggests their early medieval origin may be in boat building: he notes (Walker 2008: 102) the possibility that they may be represented in some hogback stones that appear to depict buildings with tegulated roofs (2008: 96). Cuppills could have been employed in the Lair buildings, perhaps partially raised within the substantial turf and earth walls, and resting on stone pads, which would leave no archaeological trace.

There are useful vernacular comparanda for rafter construction, including the blackhouses of the Western Isles, the thick-walled turf byre dwellings with a light hipped roof and with principal rafters resting on the inside lip of the wall (Walker and McGregor 1996). While a Viking origin has been suggested (e.g. Armit 2002: 213-214; Wilkinson 2009: 29) there are no intermediate examples from which to establish this developmental sequence, although they may simply have been lost to the plough (Postma 2010: 22) or await discovery. Another turf form, the Creel house (Cheape 2014; Fenton and Walker 1981), also known as 'stake and rice' construction, has an inner wall of stakes and wattle and an outer turf wall with a hip-ended thatched roof, supported on cuppills or with a lighter caber arrangement (Walker *et al.* 1996: 7).

If the timber for the Lair buildings came from trees like birch, hazel or alder, then a source close by can be sought: however, more substantial trees, such as oak, are unlikely to have been sourced in the immediate locality, or perhaps anywhere in the surrounding hills. It may have been that by the 7th century AD, such woodland was conserved, managed and traded (Tipping 2010: 80; Tipping *et al.* 2006). The lack of evidence for either post-holes for earth-fast roof supports, or indeed post-pads, within the Lair buildings suggests cuppills or self-supporting A-frames rested on the wall heads or were set into the fabric of the walls above ground level (Figures 4.4 and 4.5).

While full turf roofs are common in Iceland, and cannot be ruled out at Lair, the nature of the proposed roof (above) would suggest a thatch of heather as more probable, and there is abundant pollen evidence for ling (*Calluna*) heath in the vicinity (Section 2.6). Other potential thatch materials include *Pteridium* (bracken), and while bracken spores in a pollen record are very under-representative of the plant (Rymer 1976), bracken will have been common at Lair. The only archaeological evidence for thatch at Lair is for an overhanging eave suggested by the drip gullies around Buildings 6 and 7 which, along with the dwarf stone wall in Building 7, may indicate a later date. Whatever the thatch material employed, it may have been laid over a light 'divot' undercoat as found in the later vernacular tradition in Scotland (Holden 1998: 25; Walker and McGregor 1996: 48).

4.8 The buildings at Lair: spatial patterning

A total of 16 elongated buildings with rounded ends have been preserved on the south-facing slope of the hillside at Lair, on either side of the Allt Corra-lairige, at *c.* 350-380 m OD and around 50-60 m above the valley floor (Figure 4.9). Of these, three (Buildings 1-3) have been confirmed through excavation as being early medieval, while a further six (Buildings 4-5, 12-14 and 20) are suggested as being broadly contemporary (Section 4.5 above). The others (Buildings 6-11, 15-19 and 21) are assumed to be of medieval or post-medieval date (Figure 4.9). The orientation of buildings is likely to simply reflect the aspect of the hillslope and the availability of suitable locations on which to build, though some seem to reference the ring-cairn (above). In four instances buildings occur in pairs or larger groups (Buildings 1-2, 3-5, 7-8 and 12-13), three of which are confirmed or suggested as early medieval (Buildings 1-2, 3-5, and 12-13) and one suggested as being post-medieval (Buildings 7-8). The largest buildings occur in the three early medieval groups on either side of the burn at the highest altitudes: Buildings 12 and 3-5 at 375 m OD and Buildings 12-13 at 370 m OD. Buildings 1-5, all shown by ^{14}C dating or by structural relations (above) to be of early medieval date, can be divided into two smaller groups by their orientation: Buildings 1-2 are north-west to south-east; Buildings 3-5 are west-south-west to east-north-east. While orientations differ, these share similar topographic positions on either side of the ring-cairn, with south-facing aspects on the edge of a relatively flat terrace of glacial till.

Building 12, which may in fact be a pair of aligned buildings, and Building 13, are of comparable size to Buildings 1-5. They share a similar orientation to Buildings 1-2, albeit on the opposite side of the burn. Given their size and orientation, they too may be of early medieval date. Indeed, there may have been a crossing of the burn to connect these two groups where the later lade dam was built (Figure 4.9; Section 4.6).

4. Discussion

The RCAHMS interpreted Buildings 3-5 as three successive Pitcarmick buildings and Buildings 1-2 as 'buildings of a different kind', suggesting that these different building types represent 'a number of undocumented attempts at permanent settlement in the agricultural margins' (1990: 12). Buildings 1 and 2, in the first dating model, may have been the earliest buildings constructed and re-used once Building 3 was built. In the alternative chronology Buildings 1 and 2 were later additions on the site of an earlier building, indicated by continued building and rebuilding on the site over a period of over 300 years: albeit that its functions may have changed over time. This second, more likely scenario, could suggest the farm expanded, requiring new outbuildings to join the core byre-house Building 3-5, or that Buildings 1-2 represent a late development attempting to adopt a new fashion of separating the house and barn.

Downslope of Buildings 1-5, between 360-365 m OD, six smaller buildings are differentiated by their associated enclosures. Buildings 7-8 appear similar in construction and form a pair with a similar orientation to Buildings 3-5, though this may simply reflect available topography. Outside the enclosure, Building 7 has been shown to have a low stone footing: this contrasts with the Pitcarmick buildings and suggests a different, probably later, date. Building 8 faced into the sub-rectangular enclosure which may have incorporated the smaller rectangular Building 16 (Figure 4.9). The extant track running through this group (Figure 4.9) runs parallel to Building 7, directly passing its entrance, suggesting it was a recognised route at the time of construction. Building 6, the smallest at Lair, had at least one associated enclosure, although this was sub-circular. Together this group of buildings may relate to stock management (above). The poorly defined Building 14, with its circular annexe, may have been a Pitcarmick building although there is no trace of the typical sunken interior.

Further downslope, at 355 m OD, the orientation of Building 9 is dictated by the axis of the flat ridge that it occupies and Building 10, at 345 m OD, by the small flat terrace on which it is located. Neither has an associated enclosure (Figure 2.1).

As further discussed in Section 4.14, the number and range of outbuildings at Lair probably reflects complex permutations of function and date, embracing a range of activities that probably changed over time. They reflect a balanced regime of arable farming and animal husbandry rather than a simple, cattle dominated economy. Only comprehensive excavation of all structures would allow for a full understanding.

4.9 Re-visiting the morphology of Pitcarmick buildings

with Stratford Halliday

An early review (Ralston 1997) of the very small sample of Pictish houses then known from mainland Scotland demonstrated significant variation in form, albeit from very different locations. In addition to the cultural drivers discussed by Schmidt (1994: 156-158), Carver *et al.* (2012: 188) and Postma in Section 1.2 (evaluated further in Section 4.10 below), practical considerations may explain, at least in part, the adoption of the elongated form, loosely described as the 'longhouse' (Section 1.1) to replace the traditional, circular, arguably more stable form.

While RCAHMS (1990) noted some morphological variation in the Pitcarmick buildings, they share some or many of a range of general characteristics. These were identified as: being 10-30 m in length and 7-8.5 m in width; having rounded ends and slightly curved or bowed walls; being broader at one end than the other; having partially sunken interiors and being constructed on a slope; having a single entrance half way along one side, or slightly closer to the wider end; having an entrance porch, with paving; and often with a small annexe. Some sites were suggested as examples of successive buildings, including at Pitcarmick, Balnabroich, Welton of Creuchies and Buildings 3-5 at Lair (RCAHMS 1990: 12-13).

Further, RCAHMS noted that, occurring in broadly similar situations around the margins of the post-medieval landscape 'there are others that do not lend themselves so easily to classification', and while 'some may be close relatives of the Pitcarmick types...others are clearly buildings of a different kind' (RCAHMS 1990: 12). These occurred in isolation and were rarely accompanied by the enclosures that would identify them as 'farmsteads' in the field classification in use at that time. At some sites, such as Pitcarmick East, numbers of smaller buildings surrounding two Pitcarmick types were classed as possible shielings, while at others, such as Loch Benachally (ID27397), the buildings were adjacent to small areas of narrow strip-fields separated by low stony banks. RCAHMS concluded that these different building types reflect 'a number of undocumented attempts at permanent settlement in the margins.' Lair Buildings 1-2, 9-10, 18, 20 and 21 all fall into this category (Figure 4.9) and it is significant that Buildings 1 and 2 (i.e. 'buildings of a different kind') have been shown now to be of broadly early medieval date.

Close chronological comparison between the Pitcarmick buildings at Lair and those at Pitcarmick (Carver *et al.*

2012) cannot be made because those at Pitcarmick were not refined by Bayesian modelling but Building C1 at Pitcarmick has an age-range from AD 680 to 880 and Building E1 an age-range of AD 670 to 880. Both are contemporary with phases of occupation dated at Lair.

Since 1990 a number of buildings sharing many of the characteristics of Pitcarmick buildings have been identified west of the Tay both in Strathbraan (Cowley 1997) and at Bunrannoch at the east end of Loch Rannoch (MacGregor 2010). Examples from these latter areas are included amongst the comparative plans illustrated in Figures 4.11 and 4.12. Where once the distribution (Figure 1.10) of Pitcarmick buildings seemed to be restricted to north-east Perthshire, contrasting with the pattern of other architectural forms of later prehistoric and early historic date in the region (Section 1.2), now they appear much more widespread. In addition to those recorded in Strathbraan (Cowley 1997), good examples can be found at Balnaguard Burn (Figure 1.3: 26; ID26232) to the south of the Tay near Balnaguard, Balhomish (Figure 1.3: 25; ID92943) near Dunkeld, and Allt Cosach (Figure 1.3: 30; ID147855) near Blair Atholl. Further north-east of the Perthshire dataset (RCAHMS 1990), the national record lists some examples in the Angus Glens, particularly Glen Clova and Glen Prosen, and a possible outlier as far east as Bannock Hill, east of Glen Esk (Figure 1.10; ID36105) in what was formerly Kincardineshire, while Mitchell and Noble (2017) have recently reported 'hut ovals' at sites close to early medieval cemeteries along the Great Glen south-west of Inverness.

In the absence of excavation, the dating of these sites has yet to be confirmed, but the evaluation of one at Bunrannoch (ID24571; Figure 1.10) clearly reveals their potential. It is one of five 'longhouses' recorded by Stewart and Feachem (1961) on the valley floor of the east end of Loch Rannoch amidst later prehistoric roundhouses, including two monumental roundhouses comparable to that at Black Spout, Pitlochry (Strachan 2013). Stewart excavated a trial trench across one of these and subsequent further small-scale excavation was carried out in 2001 (Atkinson, Duffy and MacGregor 2003). This later excavation revealed two phases of construction, in which a building with stone footings had been superimposed on an earlier structure of wattle set in low banks, presumably representing the remains of a turf and earth wall. Several axial post-holes were found in the interior of the earlier structure, which was slightly sunken in the centre. Pits within the interior contained carbonised remains (including burnt bone and cereals), probably domestic rubbish, which returned a ^{14}C date of AD 680–940 (GU-11930). The earlier building had been burnt down and the destruction layer dated to AD 660–900 (GU-11929) (MacGregor 2010: 407). Apart from the monumental roundhouses, the assemblage of monuments is remarkably similar to those recorded in the margins of Strathardle and Glen Shee (Carver et al. 2012; RCAHMS 1990). Some of the 'longhouses' at Bunrannoch had one open end, which would have afforded easy access for the removal of manure or stalling animals, although it is not clear if this was a feature of the earlier buildings. In the vernacular tradition, one end of a stone building was sometimes built in turf so that it could be more easily dismantled for mucking out at the end of the winter (Walker and McGregor 1996: 16).

In addition to those discovered by fieldwork in the uplands, cropmarks recorded by aerial photography have revealed several structures that bear a striking, if superficial, resemblance to the plans of the Pitcarmick buildings. These include a small group of cropmarks named lobate enclosures (Barclay and Maxwell 1998: 5), comprising an elongated oval or oblong enclosure with at least one conjoined annexe or lobe. Several examples, such as one at Edenwood, Fife, apparently enclosed an elongated macula, implying that part of the interior was sunken. This recalled axial features also visible in some of a cluster of large rectangular buildings averaging about 25 m in length by 9 m in breadth at Lathrisk, Fife (Maxwell 1987: 33-4; Figs 1-2): comparable in scale with Pitcarmick buildings. Other examples have been recorded at Inchture, on the Carse of Gowrie, and at Inchtuthil (RCAHMS 1994: 69), though neither had clear evidence of a sunken interior.

In considering the cropmark evidence, however, it is important to remember that the only component of the Pitcarmick buildings that is likely to be revealed in this medium is the sunken end of the floor. The turf walls uncovered at Pitcarmick and Lair would leave no trace. It is in this sense that the resemblance of Maxwell's lobate enclosures to Pitcarmick buildings is superficial and possibly misleading. In short, we may struggle to identify Pitcarmick buildings in the lowlands. Nevertheless, the sunken floors excavated at Kintore (Cook and Dunbar 2008) have the same potential to form a cropmark as the internal ring-ditch of a timber roundhouse. Pursuing this logic back into the cropmark record, a host of possible rectangular sunken-floored structures emerges, for example at Inchcoonans, Blairhall and Balgarvie in Perth and Kinross, or Leuchars in Fife. A review of the whole collection of oblique aerial photographs held by RCAHMS in 2012 (Halliday unpublished) revealed no fewer than 200 examples in eastern Scotland between the southern shore of the Moray Firth and the Firth of Forth. The definition is variable and they are found in all sorts of shapes and sizes, some strictly rectangular, others elongated ovals, ranging in size from little more than 3 m across at Locheye to the order of 15m in length at Kercock on the south bank of the River Tay opposite Inchtuthil.

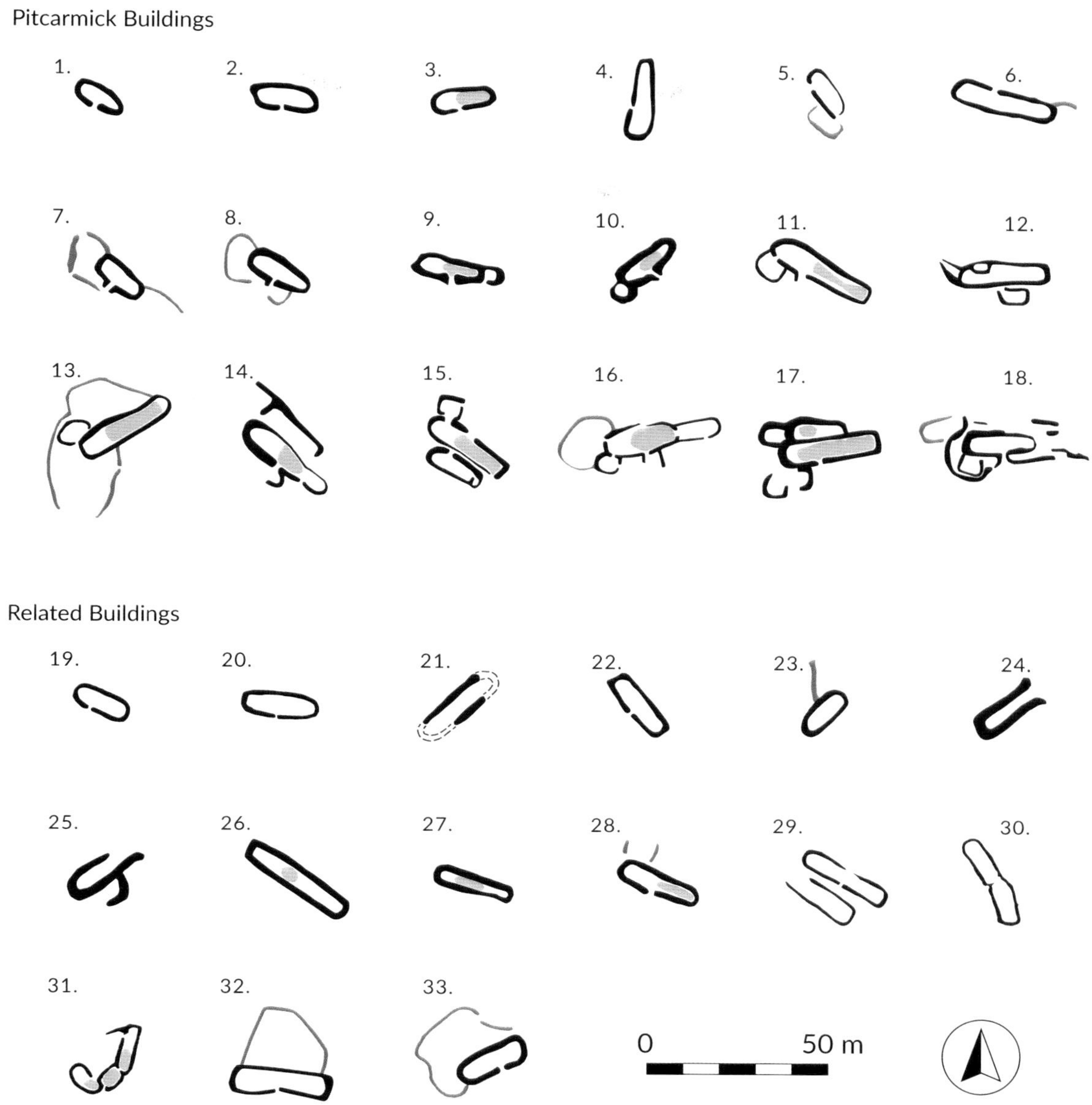

4. Discussion

Pitcarmick Buildings

Related Buildings

1: Balnabroich (227.2a)	12: Ashintully (222)	23: Bunrannoch F
2: Knockali (288.2)	13: Pitcarmick North (303.2)	24: Bunrannoch G
3: Pitcarmick West (302.1)	14: Balnabroich (227.1a)	25: Bunrannoch I
4: Knockali (288.5)	15: Pitcarmick West (302.8)	26: Glen Cochill C
5: Balnabroich (227.1b)	16: Knockali (288.4)	27: Ballinloan Burn D
6: Pitcarmick West (302.2)	17: Welton of Creuchies (326A)	28: Pitcarmick West (302.4)
7: Balnabroich (227.2b)	18: Pitcarmick West (302.6)	29: Glenkilrie (277.11a)
8: Balnabroich (227.2c)	19: Pitcarmick East (305.4)	30: Ranageig (310.16)
9: Pitcarmick West (302.1)	20: Glenkilrie (277.11b)	31: Broughdearg (232.11)
10: Knockali (288.3)	21: Bunrannoch L	32: Ballinloan Burn A
11: Dalnagar (253)	22: Heatherhaugh (280.1)	33: Balinreigh B

Figure 4.12 A selection of comparative plans of unexcavated Pitcarmick-type and related buildings showing variation in scale and morphology (based on RCAHMS: 1990; Cowley: 1997 and MacGregor 2010).

Pitcarmick Buildings

Related Buildings

1: Lair Buildings 3 - 5 (290.3A)   3: Lair Buildings 1 & 2 (291.13)   5: Bunrannoch K
2: Pitcarmick Area C & E   4: Lair Building 7 & 8 (291.9)

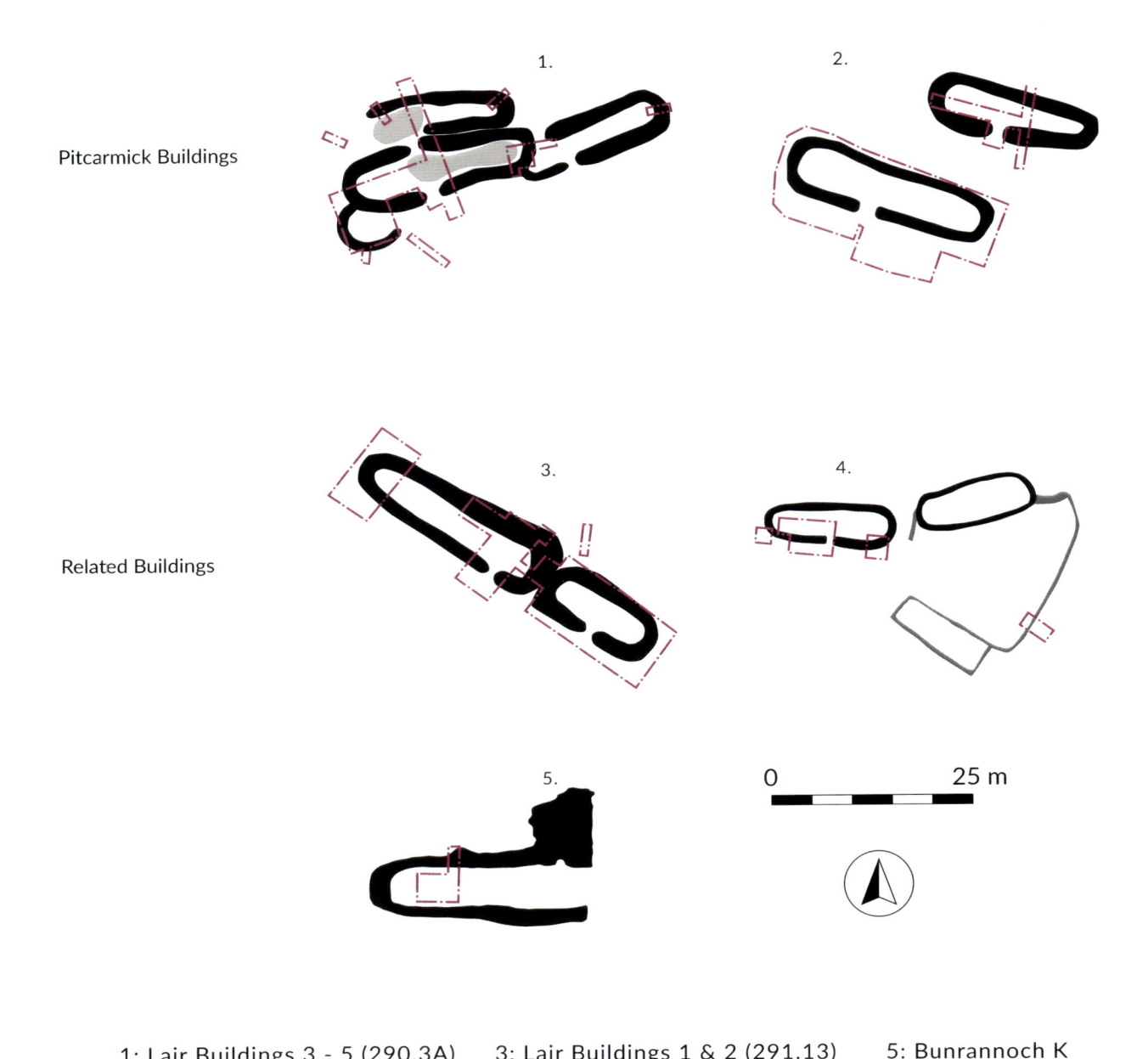

Figure 4.13 Comparative plans of the excavated Pitcarmick-type buildings from Lair (1) and Pitcarmick (2, based on Carver et al. 2012), and 'related' buildings at Lair (3 and 4) and Bunrannoch (5, based on MacGregor 2010).

It would be wrong to claim that these are all the remains of early medieval settlements scattered across the lowlands, let alone that they are Pitcarmick buildings, though a tapering mark some 12 m in length and 3 m in maximum breadth at Rossie Priory (ID73132) in the Carse of Gowrie must be a very good candidate. In the absence of excavation all we can be sure is that this represents a largely unexplored component of the archaeological record. Some of these structures identified in the lowlands are probably early medieval, but some will be later. To go from these diverse sets of cropmarks to pretending that we can present a complementary distribution of lowland early medieval settlements would stretch credibility (Section 4.13). Nevertheless, between Kintore and Rossie Priory there is sufficient evidence to suggest that turf-walled Pitcarmick buildings with partly sunken floors may not only be a monument of the uplands, but that they are probably also present the length of the lowlands of eastern Scotland.

4. Discussion

Elongation and scale

Most notable is the elongation of the building form and the considerable variation in scale (Figures 4.12 and 4.13). Contemporary comparanda from mainland Scotland are very rare and Ralston's review of Pictish houses showed significant variation in form in the very small sample of known sites, albeit from very different geographical locations (1997: Figure 1). Carver *et al.* (2012: 188) argued for Pitcarmick buildings as 'long houses' of continental sense; byre-houses with a residential (west) end separate from a longer byre to the east and with an entrance at the junction of these. They highlight two cases, one for the development of the Pitcarmick 'longhouse' from the local roundhouse tradition, and the other for similarities with continental forms which may suggest external influence (Carver *et al.* 2012: 191-2). Possible origins of the form are further discussed in Section 4.10: however, in addition to cultural drivers, practical considerations may also explain its adoption, and explain at least in part why the elongated form replaced the circular, arguably more stable and wind-resistant, traditional form. Assuming ground level occupation only, the 'longhouse' offers the opportunity to create larger internal areas with easier linear compartmentalisation, for example, to separate human and animal occupation.

The simplest explanation for the considerable variation in scale of the buildings would appear to be variation in function. While the range of 10-30 m in length for Pitcarmick buildings is matched by some of the 'related buildings' identified by RCAHMS, others are smaller, within the range of 5-10 m in length.

The choice to concentrate all the different functions required of buildings under one roof, or to disperse them into separate structures, evidently changes through time and space, ultimately leading to the rich variation of vernacular architecture to be found from northern Europe to Iceland. Some of these functions include houses, combined byre-houses, and a variety of 'outbuildings', such as animal byres, barns for the storage of tools and implements, fuel, manure, hay and other produce and seed stock. A study of the separate houses and outbuildings which are a feature of medieval Icelandic farms, however, found considerable variation in the length of byres, ranging between 8-14 m, barns from 4-14 m, and sheep sheds from 4-22 m (Berson 2002: *passim*). There may not, therefore, be any meaningful correlation between size and function, although clearly the smaller buildings would have more limited capacity for living space or storage.

Rounded ends

The most common shared characteristic of both Pitcarmick and their related buildings is the rounded end. While the origins of these remain debated a pragmatic case can be made that they limit turf erosion by weather and animal rubbing, and minimise deterioration through evaporation, whereas angular corners of turf would be a disadvantage. Postma (2015) however has noted that contemporary rural examples in the Netherlands in general employ angular rather than curved house ends and his experimental research suggests the use of rounded corners may have been to mitigate the negative effect of turf shrinkage that results in structural failure. Turf houses with fully rounded ends have very rarely been identified in the wider south-eastern part of the North Sea area, but timber parallels directly overlying short sections of earlier turf walls may hint at their previous existence in the northern Netherlands. Such a direct transition from turf to timber structures of similar design would suggest that their rounded house ends should be explained in terms of the buildings' function rather than the requirements of the applied construction materials, but more complete examples of relevant house plans is necessary to progress this discussion (Postma in prep.).

Bowed walls, width differentiation and sloping construction

Similarly, the morphological characteristics of the building plan may reflect as much practical concerns as cultural or aesthetic ones. Viking houses with curved or bowed long walls, for example, take advantage of the enhanced aerodynamic properties of the form and increased internal space around the central hearth (Milek 2007: 21). It is worth noting that this benefit does not directly apply in a byre-house, such as Lair Building 3, where the hearth is at one end of the building, although having the widest part of the building at the entrance does offer additional space for necessary infrastructure to control and separate human and animal access. The bowed walls of the classic Pitcarmick-type form certainly increases the internal area, though may also show cultural influence. What may be more significant is that one end is often wider than the other. The assumption, tested at Pitcarmick, is that the wider end is for human occupation, and the narrow elongated end for animals, with the residential area requiring more open space to accommodate a central hearth and furniture.

This division of broad and narrow spaces often corresponds to the position of a building on a slope, the broader end usually being set at a higher level. This is clearly seen in Building 3 at Lair and evidently would have facilitated drainage for animal waste away from the human quarters, while heat from the beasts may have transferred up the slope in the opposite direction. In many examples where one end is clearly wider than the other, this occurs at the west end, though why this should be the case is difficult to fathom; good examples are illustrated in Figure 4.12, for example those at Dalnaglar (11), Balnabroich (14), Knockali (10) and Pitcarmick (13 and 18). This division between broad and narrow spaces, however, may also give some insight into the origins of these structures, as a marriage of two separate and generally smaller components, the one a house, the other a byre. While we are yet unable to identify any independent byres before this date, the size of the broader domestic end perhaps finds some resonance in the building excavated at Easter Kinnear, Fife (Driscoll 1997).

Partially sunken interiors

From the sample of plans surveyed by RCAHMS (1990), partially sunken interiors feature in 50 % of Pitcarmick buildings and in all these cases the sunken area occurs in the eastern, narrower, end of the building (Figures 4.12 and 4.13). In the byre-house model there are several mechanisms which could result in this. Firstly, the simple process of poaching by cattle trampling in the byre, coupled with mucking out in the spring, a routine consequence of stalling beasts over winter, would lead to this. Secondly, the floor may have been deliberately lowered to improve the drainage, or indeed to insert a drain. A by-product of this might have been to reduce the height of the walls necessary to give headroom. Thirdly it might have been a deliberate choice to maintain the integrity of the walls from beasts jostling in their stalls. Another option floated by RCAHMS was that perhaps there was a suspended floor in the narrower end (1990: 12), reflecting what was then a current debate about the functions of ring-ditches in some prehistoric roundhouses; it may also have contained a nod to the interpretation of *grubenhauser* as cellars beneath a suspended floor, but seems the least likely explanation today. This feature of the Pitcarmick buildings is rarely found in any of the related buildings (Figure 4.12). Building 1 at Lair, for example, had no recoverable evidence of wear in its floor or at the entrance to indicate the passage of cattle. This contrast between structures may be an important indication of differing functions.

At Lair Building 3, however, there was some suggestion that the floor in the residential west end was also slightly sunken (Figure 4.5), though whether by accident or design could not be determined. It might have marginally increased the internal height available, a consideration if this end of the structure had contained a loft (above Section 4.6), but a more likely interpretation of this modest depression is that it reflects general wear, perhaps an indicator that this building was occupied for rather longer than Buildings 1 and 2.

Entrances

In all but one of the examples of Pitcarmick buildings (Figure 4.12) a single entrance was located around halfway along a south-facing side, usually slightly closer to the wider (west) end of the building. This would have provided access to both house and byre. Porches at entrances are identified by short stubs of wall to either side, best seen at Balnabroich (7 and 8) and Knockali (10). In other cases the flanking walls have been extended to create a larger enclosure, though whether this was covered is unknown. An example of the latter can be seen at another of the Knockali buildings (16), while at Pitcarmick West (18) the walls of the porch appear to be connected with adjacent enclosures. The positioning of an associated annexe immediately to one side of the entrance, as at Lair Building 3, may also have afforded some protection to the entrance. The records of the RCAHMS survey in north-eastern Perthshire should not be accepted as definitive for the presence or absence of these sorts of minor external features. While Dalnaglar (11) had been recorded previously (Stewart 1962: Figure 2) the significance of the group had not been recognised before, and there were no guides to the features that might be visible. The identification of porches came quite late in the survey and others may be hidden in the thickening of the collapsed walls sometimes observed at the entrances, such as at one of the Pitcarmick West buildings (9; RCAHMS 1990: 154, no.302.1). Nevertheless, there is clearly variation between examples, and potentially some complexity, as was demonstrated by Building 3 at Lair.

Annexes

The annexes are a feature of the site-type that has not been previously explored. While not found at all Pitcarmick buildings, they are relatively common, occurring at the majority of examples illustrated in Figure 4.12, at Pitcarmick West (9, 15 and 18), Knockali (10 and 16), Welton of Creuchies (17), Pitcarmick North (13) and Dalnagar (11). As outlined above (Section 4.6), the example at Lair Building 3 has been interpreted as a roofed workshop/storage area, although its use may have changed over time. Again, we should be wary of being too prescriptive on the basis of survey plans, and in several cases the assemblage of structures may reflect several periods of accretion, for example at Pitcarmick West (15; RCAHMS 1990:155; 302.6). In others, such as Balnabroich (7 and 8; RCAHMS 1990: 99, no. 227.2, fig 227B-C), it is less likely that they were roofed structures. Nevertheless, for the smaller examples like Lair Building 3 a parallel could be drawn with the Icelandic pit houses, suggested as women's workrooms, primarily for the production of woollen textiles (Milek 2012). Closer to home, at Ratho, City of Edinburgh, the lines of weights on the sunken floor of a small square building probably dating from the 7th century AD indicated the presence of three or four upright looms, finding parallels with other probable Anglian weaving sheds further south (Smith 1995: 104-11).

Pitcarmick-type group

Building 3 at Lair is a good example of many of the characteristics described above. Perhaps the most significant result of the Lair excavations, however, is that the simpler forms (Buildings 1 and 2), identified as 'different' to the 'Pitcarmick-types' by RCAHMS, have been shown to be contemporary with them. As a result the morphological characteristics of the Pitcarmick-type group has been shown to be more diverse than was originally thought, highlighting the increased variety of building forms of early medieval date that should now be considered 'Pitcarmick buildings'. The adoption of this elongated form with rounded ends may have been influenced by an architectural trend occurring across northern Europe at this time, but may also have developed from a number of pragmatic local factors such as those outlined above.

4.10 Early medieval buildings in the North Sea area

Daniël Postma

Previous research on turf-walled buildings

Academic research on turf as a building material initially focused on documenting folk customs (Sacher 1938; Peate 1946), while the remains of older turf houses were occasionally recorded during archaeological excavations (e.g. Leens, Netherlands: Van Giffen 1940; Tofting, Germany: Bantelmann 1955; Nødskovhede, Denmark: Steensberg 1952; Jarlshof, Shetland: Hamilton 1956; Lofoten, Norway: Johansen and Søbstad 1978). In the 1960s and 1970s, ethnological and archaeological studies on occasion informed each other (Evans 1969; Saeftel 1967), but no systematic research programme on turf houses developed from these early efforts.

The number of excavated (and published) turf houses increased more rapidly in the final decades of the 20th century, and in addition to these, efforts were made to gain better insight in the techniques of turf construction through building conservation (case studies in Walker 2006a; test walls in Morton and Little 2015) and archaeological experimentation (Noble 1984, 2003), later added to through experimental reconstructions in the Netherlands (Postma 2015). Today, many archaeologists and historians acknowledge the past ubiquity of turf-walled buildings (for Scotland particularly Parkin 2014; Parkin and Adderley 2017), although the investigation of these structures remains highly under-represented in current research agendas (c.f. ScARF 2012; for the Netherlands see Rijksdienst voor het Cultureel Erfgoed 2016).

Since the turn of the century, numerous studies have laid the foundations for systematic research on turf buildings (e.g. North Atlantic: Forbes and Milek 2014; Milek 2007; Mímisson 2016; Urbańczyk 1999; Scotland: Logan 2017, 2018; Loveday 2006; Walker 2006a; Wilkinson 2009; Netherlands: Postma 2010, 2015; Denmark: Andersen and Olsen 2014; Haue 2012). In addition to this, efforts have been made to retain surviving and re-learn lost turf building skills (Dijkstra 1996; Postma 2015; Sigurðardóttir 2008;), re-learn skills through experimental archaeology (Noble 1984, 2003; Postma 2015), deepen our scientific understanding of the material (Huisman and Milek 2017) and seek opportunities for its renewed application (Ferreiro *et al.* 2014; Little 2016; Little and Morton 2001; Postma 2015; Romankiewicz 2016; Stampfer 2018). This section attempts to bring much of this previous work together, though evidently many issues regarding turf construction remain largely unknown and in need of more structured, in-depth research.

Typological comparison

The remains of turf buildings throughout the North Sea and North Atlantic area demonstrate comparable variations in design and construction to contemporary timber buildings. With regard to length, for example, very short turf-walled buildings such as sunken feature buildings (SFBs, or *grubenhäuser*) have been excavated, as well as longer outbuildings, full-size longhouses and even examples of remarkable length: 60 m in the Netherlands (Den Burg; Woltering 1975: 28), 50 m in Germany (Archsum-Melenknop; Harck *et al.* 1992: 33) and 80 m in Norway (Borg; Herschend and Mikkelsen 2003, 51). Interior widths of turf houses, too, share the same range as timber buildings: from 2 m or less, to *c*. 6 m in single-aisled buildings and up to 8-9 m in three-aisled buildings. Similar to the shape of timber buildings, turf houses were circular, oval, square, rectangular or boat-shaped in plan. And finally, house ends of turf buildings are found to have been angular (i.e. straight with sharp corners), straight with rounded corners, or fully rounded, as again mirrored in the plans of timber buildings. In view of the above, the only single feature that distinguishes a turf from a timber house on a general typological level is the former's walling material: turf.

Despite this shared range of shapes and sizes, some specific patterns in the chronological and geographical distribution of turf houses may be provisionally outlined. For Iron Age Jutland, turf houses may be divided into two groups on the basis of their length (Haue 2012, 317-318). Similarly, for the early medieval northern Netherlands, ground plans have been identified from relatively narrow but long (Leens A type) and standard width but short buildings (Leens B type), as well as apparently average-sized longhouses, combining features of both other house types (provisional Leens AB type; Postma 2015). Plans of boat-shaped turf houses, on the other hand, are noticeably scarce in continental Europe but seem to have been the norm for medieval longhouse construction in Iceland and the Faroe Islands (e.g. Edvardsson and McGovern 2005; Mahler 1993; Milek 2007).

Rather more complex is the distribution of buildings with fully rounded house ends, a key characteristic of Pitcarmick buildings. While a round-ended turf house, superseded by a more rectangular timber building, is known from Oldorf in Germany (Schmid 1994), turf houses in the neighbouring Netherlands nearly all have straight house ends with angular corners (Postma 2015; Nicolay and Postma 2018). Moreover, several early medieval timber longhouses in the Netherlands have rounded ends (cf. Odoorn C type in Waterbolk 2009: 91; Postma in prep.), confirming that the feature is not a requirement of the use of turf walls. Indeed, rectilinear, timber-built structures with rounded ends have also been found in Scotland: at Newbarns, Inverkeilor; and at Green Castle, Portknockie (McGill 2004: 105-6; 115), however there is currently insufficient evidence to recognise and explain any pattern in the presence or absence of rounded house ends.

Use of space

Continental longhouses were generally divided in three main parts: dwelling area, working area and byre (Waterbolk 1979; Zimmermann 1988). It would appear, however, that 6-8th century AD turf houses in the northern coastal area of the Netherlands did not fully comply with the custom of having all three parts under the same roof. Instead, the farms' dwelling and 'business' functions appear to have been divided between the two sub-types mentioned above: Leens A type (byre and optional work area) and Leens B type (dwelling house; Postma 2015, in prep.). This functional division is partly based on the indicators for a byre function (e.g. byre drain or cattle stalls) only occurring in buildings with interior widths of 4.7 m or less, whereas partition walls, thought to be indicative of dwelling areas, have only been recognised in buildings with more 'normal' widths of 5-6 m.

It seems that from the late 8th century AD onwards, the average farmstead in the northern Netherlands once again revolved around a single main longhouse: the provisional Leens AB type (probable three-part longhouse) and a partially timber-built 'hybrid' version of this (see below). The initial difference in width between the separate dwelling and byre buildings remained intact in these subsequent 'proper' longhouses. The development described here raises the question whether the narrower byre ends in some of the Pitcarmick buildings may also be seen as a rudimentary feature of adjoining two originally detached byres and dwelling houses.

The typology-based use of space analysis of early medieval turf buildings in the Netherlands furthermore suggests that byres were only built with fixed layouts from the late 7th or early 8th century AD onwards, earlier examples apparently being open plan (Postma 2015: 166). The same changes were previously noted for timber longhouses elsewhere in the region. It has been suggested that the alterations were meant to accommodate the build-up of an *in situ* dung heap (Huijts 1992). The periodic removal of this heap gradually eroded the floors, causing a deepening of the byres over time. Possibly, the deepened byres in Pitcarmick buildings owe their formation to a similar process.

Building technology

Recent turf house analyses and experimental reconstructions in the Netherlands have shown that the use of rounded corners was meant to accommodate longitudinal shrinkage in the buildings' long walls, preventing these from tearing at the corners (Nicolay and Postma 2018; Postma 2015). By extension, fully rounded house ends and herringbone pattern bonding systems may be thought to have also developed in response to shrinkage issues in turf construction. Turf building techniques in continental Europe differed widely from those documented in Iceland, and the applied technology may be specific to certain regions and (soil) conditions. It cannot be assumed, therefore, that traditional turf building techniques in Scotland were similar to what one may find in existing buildings in Iceland.

Of greater importance here is the recognition, again in the plans of early medieval turf houses from the Netherlands, of the past use of lofts. Indicative of the presence of lofts in three-part turf longhouses is the occurrence of interior posts (i.e. a three-aisled configuration) exclusively in the byre end of otherwise single-aisled ground plans (Postma 2015). The localised addition of such (loft supporting) interior posts is also characteristic of contemporary timber buildings along the Dutch west coast (Dijkstra 2011; Woltering 1974: 1975). Timber buildings on the higher ground of the northern Netherlands lack this partial three-aisled setup but their plans do show other adjustments to accommodate lofts. There, any additional load-bearing capacity was created by decreasing the bay size in the byre area (i.e. placing trusses closer together). Future research may help to clarify whether the reduced spans of those narrower byre ends in some of the Pitcarmick buildings also relate to the presence of lofts.

Finally, attention must again be drawn to the close similarities between turf and timber buildings. Just how closely related some of these turf and timber house types may have been is very aptly illustrated by the 'hybrid' longhouse type (provisional Den Burg variety) briefly mentioned above. In such buildings, turf-walled byres (Leens A type) were directly attached to timber-built dwelling houses (short Katwijk or Odoorn types). Evidently, the short turf buildings and timber buildings in the early medieval northern Netherlands were of very similar structural design, irrespective of whether thick turf walls or thin timber walls with outside posts characterise their archaeological remains. This structural similarity with traditional longhouses in Scotland has been explored through a reconstruction model that considers the use of cuppills (Postma 2015; cf. Walker 2004, 2006b, 2008; cf. Dixon 2002). While an in-depth discussion of that model is beyond the scope of this contribution, it is clear that apparently prominent technical differences between building types can mask more significant structural similarities. The ground plans of Pitcarmick buildings may be clearly discernible from round, timber and/or stone-walled buildings from other areas and time-frames, but whether they reflect a significant structural distinction cannot be properly argued without a more detailed reconstruction model to aid comparison.

Concluding remarks on the international context of Pitcarmick buildings

As outlined in Section 1.2, a functional typology is the necessary basis to consider Pitcarmick buildings in their wider cultural context. This chapter contributes to that long-term objective by presenting the evidence in a structured manner, firstly for the Glen Shee area (Sections 4.6-4.9), then for the wider North Sea fringes in this section. In both instances form and function are outlined (i.e. typological and use of space analyses), and then structural considerations presented (i.e. technical analysis and reconstructions). After contextualising the Lair buildings at the settlement level on the basis of spatial patterning, a much wider reconsideration of the Pitcarmick type's morphological classification is made possible.

Carver *et al.* (2012: 191-2) highlighted both the case for the development of the Pitcarmick-type 'longhouse' from the local roundhouse tradition, and from external sources, for a continental origin from similarities with continental forms. A third point of origin, Anglo-Saxon England, they dismissed on the basis of byre-houses being absent in that area. Subsequently, however, an exception has been noted (Carver 2019: 213) in a group of possible byre-houses of the 8th century AD and later, found in Devon (Beresford 1979). The development of the Leens types in the northern Netherlands,

outlined above, helps to further nuance the apparently different morphology of Anglo-Saxon buildings south of the Clyde-Forth isthmus. Key is the conclusion that the earliest Leens types, introduced to the northern Netherlands by 5th century AD Anglo-Saxon immigrants from north-west Germany or Jutland, are thought to be have been separated dwellings and byres (Postma 2015). The contemporaneous appearance of similar short buildings in Anglo-Saxon England, sharing the same cultural origins as the Leens types, shows this continental connection was much stronger than previous, less detailed typologies seemed to suggest (cf. Hamerow 1999). More importantly, it appears that the traditional emphasis on differences between insular and continental typologies has obscured the observation that much longer buildings did become (part of) the norm in 8th century AD and later Anglo-Saxon England (Hamerow 1999: 122 and Figure 3; Hamerow 2012: 22-24 and Figure 2.3). This undervalued stage of early medieval building development is hardly a century apart from what has been described for the northern Netherlands (above) and provides an all-important background to the occurrence of similar turf byre-houses in Devon. The 7th century appearance of Pitcarmick buildings may well fit the same trend, making Anglo-Saxon byre-houses in England equally relevant to discussions on their origins as their continental counterparts.

We have argued (Section 4.3) that the roundhouse tradition in eastern Scotland ceased well before the 6th century AD. Carver's (2019: 188) overview argues that the transition from round to rectilinear architecture in northern and eastern Scotland, including Lair, is not recognised because current chronological resolution is too coarse. Hybrid buildings have monastic, not settlement, contexts (e.g. Portmahomack; Carver 2019: 152; also Carver 2008: 228-241 on bag-shaped buildings) or are too ambiguous (e.g. Easter Kinnear; Carver 2019: 185). It may be, however, that a transition from roundhouses to rectilinear buildings need not have involved a significant structural innovation or even a hybrid form despite the apparently sharp dichotomy of their ground plans. As outlined, this is what the most recent reconstruction of early medieval building in the northern Netherlands suggests, and a reconstruction model of similar depth is needed to clarify structural similarities, or differences, between round and rectilinear forms more precisely.

Blair (2018: 42) has argued for sustained contact between communities on the east coast of England and the Scandinavian region (Norway, Denmark, Jutland and southern Sweden) in the 5-6th centuries AD. Frisian influence is seen in eastern England between the 7th and 9th centuries (Blair 2018: 42) and one object at Lair, the Frisian glass bead (Section 3.8) hints at similar connections across the German Sea (Ayers

2016), though this could be simply a product of complex trade connections and is not by itself an indication of direct links.

In conclusion, the similarities between Pitcarmick buildings and other byre-houses, and indeed with other varieties of turf-walled and timber rectilinear buildings, implies a shared context with settlement around the rim of the North Sea, but the form of earlier roundhouse construction keeps open the possibility of a local Pictish development. On balance, it would appear likely that the idea of the elongated architectural form was influenced by, if not directly introduced, during the events of the migration period in line with the broader architectural trend across the North Sea area. The exact mechanism for this introduction, whether direct or via intermediary traditions established elsewhere on the continent, is not clear.

4.11 The socio-political context and geographic patterns of Pitcarmick buildings in north-east Perthshire

with Stratford Halliday

Sections 4.2 and 4.3 summarised the only limited archaeological and palaeo-economic evidence for Late Iron Age human activity in the Perthshire hills. This apparent lacuna may be a reflection on our sources and the general lack of excavation. The late date from a burnt timber from House 8 at Carn Dubh (Rideout 1995; Section 4.3) might suggest that settlement spanning the lacuna might lie unidentified because it is unexcavated. If the known densities and distributions of early medieval evidence, from symbol stones to *pett* place-names, do represent population densities in some way (Halliday 2006: 12-15; Fraser and Halliday 2007: 130-133 question this), most people lived and worked away from the hills, though few lowland houses are known to have been contemporary with Pitcarmick buildings (Sections 1.3, 4.3, 4.9; Driscoll 2011: 263). Nevertheless, the early medieval radiocarbon dates of AD 430-640 (SUERC-51328) and AD 420-610 (SUERC-51333) at Lair (Section 4.5), though not certainly associated with structural remains, are comparable with Late Iron Age-early medieval activity at Pitcarmick North (Section 4.3: Carver et al. 2012). People were not entirely absent from the hills immediately prior to the 7th century AD but they may have been simply herders tending livestock.

Forts, of central importance as power-centres in the 7th century AD (Alcock 1987: 203; Cook 2013a, 2013b; Noble et al. 2013: 1143; Ralston 1987) are almost absent, even as undated examples, in the hills above Glen Shee and Strathardle (Lock and Ralston 2017). The front cover of the RCAHMS (1990) monograph features the vitrified fort on Barry Hill (ID31061), the exception to this rule, though probably dating from the 3rd-4th centuries BC on current dating models for forts with massive timber-laced walls: its parallels are with Finavon (ID34813) and the White Caterthun (ID35007) further north in Angus. The closest fort now shown to be contemporary with Pitcarmick buildings is that at King's Seat, above Dunkeld, where ongoing work has demonstrated high status early medieval activity (Figure 1.3: 31; Strachan 2017). What this absence of power-centres implies for ownership and organisational structure of this upland landscape is unknown.

What property rights then existed on the hills is uncertain (Broun 2015; O'Brien 2002: 61), but if Gaelic law was comparable to Irish Law (Márkus 2017: 188) it is unlikely that the uplands were not owned or regulated in some way (Kelly 1998). Indeed, this is implicit in the evidence gathered by the late Alasdair Ross in Moray, where the organisation of the entire landscape into *dabhaicheans* from the mountains to the sea, was deeply rooted in the early medieval period (Ross 2011: 25-33, 52; 2015: 142-3). *Dabhaicheans* are by no means unique to Moray and the lands north of the Mounth, and are found widely to the south into Perthshire, though mixed with units labelled in the medieval period with other terms. They are certainly present in north-east Perthshire (see for example the parish of Blairgowrie at the mouth of Glen Shee: McNiven in Section 1.6; Rogers 1992: 125), representing individual holdings within larger estates. The establishment of the parochial structure in Perthshire from the 12th century AD (Rogers 1992) was based on this earlier pattern of secular estates, many of which appear to have been served ecclesiastically from the same sites occupied later by the parish churches (Rogers 1992: 405-7; cf. Ross 2015: 59-63). If the parallel with Moray is correct – and the situation in Perthshire is evidently much more complex (Ross 2019: 144) – the detached portions of the parishes in the lower reaches of Strathardle and Glen Shee (Stobie: 1783) reflect similar patterns of whole and dispersed holdings that made up these earlier estates.

The parish church of Kirkmichael was the *ecclesiam de Strathardolf*, the church of the royal manor of Strathardle (Rogers 1992: 409), one of four royal manors or thanages in Gowrie. Its lands and bounds were reconstructed in some detail by Rogers to show it was coterminous with the parish (1992:132-8). This reconstruction reveals an additional Pit- place-name in Glen Shee – Petgoram – while another in Strathardle – Petcarene (Tullachourene, now Tullochcurran) – is identified as a *dabhach* (Rogers 1992: 132). Although Lair does not figure as one of the lands of the manor as such, first appearing on Pont's map in the 1590s (McNiven 2014: 37), it is at least arguable that the bounds of this estate were established by the time the settlement in the Allt Corra-lairige glen at Lair was abandoned in the 11th century, if not long before. Further, the portion of the manor in Glen Shee appears considerably less densely settled than that in Strathardle itself (23 named places over a distance of about 15 km compared with 33 over 10 km: Rogers 1992: 133, Map 8). This may to some extent be a reflection of its more rugged character, but these different densities and the relatively higher altitudes of those in Glen Shee might suggest this was the upper end of that estate, the mountain pastures, beyond the margins of permanent settlement in conception, but providing niches that could be colonised in any expansion of the settlement pattern from the core of the estate. This possible relationship between different parts of Glen Shee and Strathardle is worth bearing in mind when considering the source of the colonisation represented by the Pitcarmick buildings (below).

The evidence from Lair itself strongly suggests that the Pitcarmick buildings represent a re-population of unoccupied parts of the uplands (cf Cowley 1997: 166; RCAHMS 1990: 12). It is in this context, laying a claim, that the appropriation of the later prehistoric ring-cairn (Section 4.3) should be seen. The timing of this re-population cannot be evaluated in detail on the dating evidence from only two archaeological locales, though there is exceptional agreement in age between the ^{14}C dated Pitcarmick buildings at Pitcarmick (Carver *et al.* 2012) and the much more precisely dated Pitcarmick buildings at Lair (Sections 2.5 and 4.5). There is nothing in the flimsy documentary record of this period to explain this movement (Section 1.5).

What can we say about the landscapes inhabited by Pitcarmick buildings in north-east Perth and Kinross? Here we use the records generated by the RCAHMS (1990) survey contained in Canmore in 2018 (Appendix A). This does not represent a complete corpus. As set out in the Introduction (Section 1.8), the visibility of archaeological monuments has been impacted by patterns of subsequent land-use change, and the distribution of the records is also constrained by patterns of archaeological survey and discovery. The original distribution of Pitcarmick buildings is unknown: they may once have occurred throughout zones 1 and 2 (Section 1.8) but have survived only in the margins of the post-medieval farming landscape of zone 2 and out into the rough pastures of zone 3. Even in zone 3 their complete recovery by survey cannot be assured, however, as it is possible some may remain to be found beneath later shielings, while later patterns of cultivation (Banaszek and Cowley: Section 1.8) may have destroyed others, despite sometimes representing no more than a season or two of outfield cultivation (Carter *et al.* 1997; Dodgshon 2015; Halliday 2006). Where cultivation has been light, earlier remains survive to varying degrees: while rig crosses Buildings 1-5 at Lair it has not obliterated the underlying structures (Figure 4.9). Nevertheless, it can be assumed for our purpose that the area was systematically and uniformly investigated by RCAHMS.

The distribution of known Pitcarmick buildings is dispersed, with most occurring singly, but there are several loose clusters: six at Balnabroich, though in two groups some 800 m apart (Figure 1.3: 10); possibly four at Glenkilrie (Figure 1.3: 4); five at Knockali spread over a distance of about 800 m (Figure 1.3: 7); at least six at Lair; and at least 14 at Pitcarmick itself (Figure 1.3: 9), the last disposed in several separate groups, including at least eight on the north side of Pitcarmick Loch, two south of Pitcarmick Burn, and three on a ridge to the north dropping down above Cultalonie; as at Lair, there are also other large buildings with rounded ends in attendance at Cultalonie and on the north side of the Pitcarmick Burn. Figures 1.10 and 4.17 depict the distribution of both individual and clustered extant Pitcarmick buildings. At the scale of Figure 4.17 the distribution appears more clustered than dispersed; though, as we have seen, the individual buildings within several of the groups are scattered over quite large areas. Elsewhere the larger intervals between buildings appear quite even: for example, south-west and west of Bridge of Cally, from Marleehill north to Pitcarmick (Figure 1.3) they show a marked regularity in their spacing (4.1 ± 0.4 km between sites) across this plateau. We conclude that the resource was also evenly distributed.

If this pattern was the result of a single phase of long-distance colonisation from an area of dense settlement in the lowlands of Strathmore, it might be anticipated that the incidence of Pitcarmick buildings would decline with distance. In Figure 4.14, distances to Pitcarmick buildings have been measured north-west from an axis drawn through Blairgowrie and Alyth. This clearly shows that, if anything, the incidence increases with distance from this line to around 20 km. Most (15 of 23: 65 %) are found between 10 and 20 km from this axis. The high numbers of extant hut-circle groups and cairn-fields in this band, as to the west of the River Ericht from the Muir of Gormack north-west to Loch Benachally and to the east around Tullymurdoch (RCAHMS 1990), would suggest that more recent destruction is not a key factor in this pattern. Simplistically, then, either people moved further from the lowlands than might be expected or this form of colonisation was not their origin.

Re-population from a single lowland core area may be too simplistic an assumption. The areas of alluvial floodplain (straths) along Glen Shee and Strathardle, assuming these to pre-date the 7th century, and the glaciofluvial terraces above them, which proved attractive locations for earlier and later settlement (Cottam and Small 1974), may have been locations

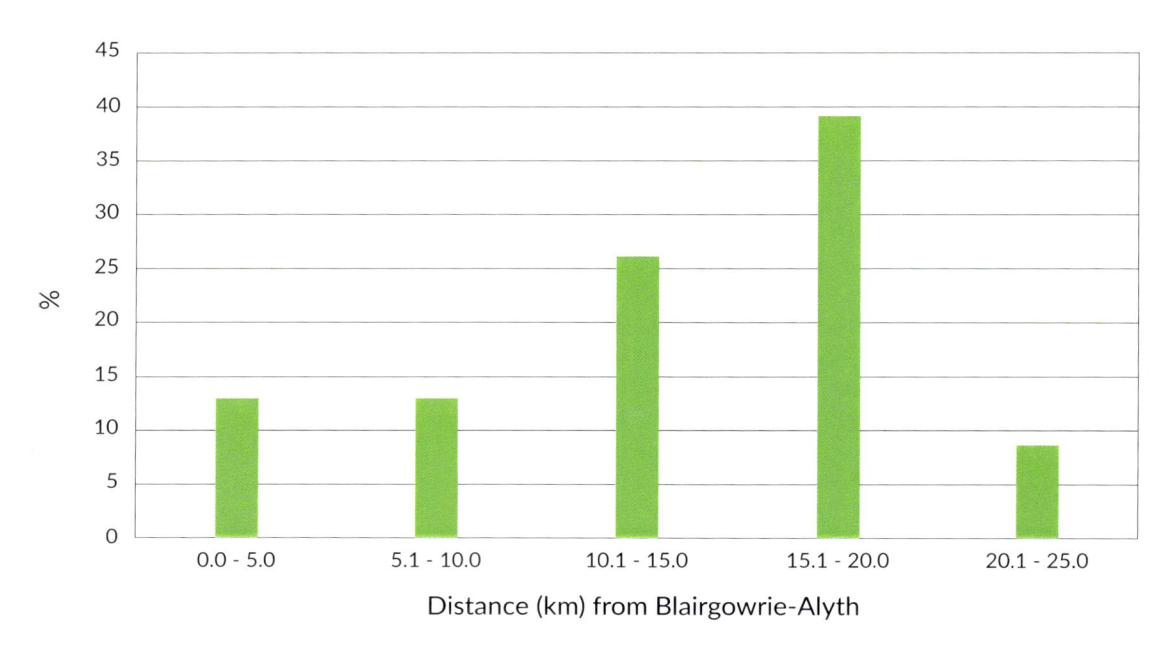

Figure 4.14 The numbers of Pitcarmick buildings at increasing distance (5 km units) along a straight line north-west of the Blairgowrie-Alyth axis.

for 'home' farms to have seeded expansion above the valley floor. Valley floor and riverine settings characterised by *aber*-names penetrate further inland along these valley floors (Barrow 1998: 57), places seen by Nicolaisen (1997: 114) to represent communities set apart from farmers (he called them "river people") with, perhaps, specialised skills. Figure 4.15 shows that 21 (70 %) Pitcarmick buildings/clusters are within 2 km uphill of the nearest strath. Migration a short distance uphill from these conjectural home farms would be an easy trek. The furthest Pitcarmick buildings from the nearest strath are those at Ranageig (Figure 1.3: 18) and Tullymurdoch (Figure 1.3: 13), lying more than 5 km distant, but these are also within the much more open and rolling moorland of the Forest of Clunie and Forest of Alyth at no more than 300 m OD, the same altitude as the valley floor at Lair.

Pitcarmick buildings are found at a wide range of altitudes, from 182 m OD at Marleehill to 416 m OD for one of the buildings at Pitcarmick: the mean is 341 ± 43 m OD. With the floors of the main glens rising northwards, it is unsurprising that the Pitcarmick buildings furthest from the Blaigowrie-Alyth axis tend to be nearer, altitudinally, to the strath (Figure 4.16a), with that at Dalnaglar, just across the glen from Lair, on

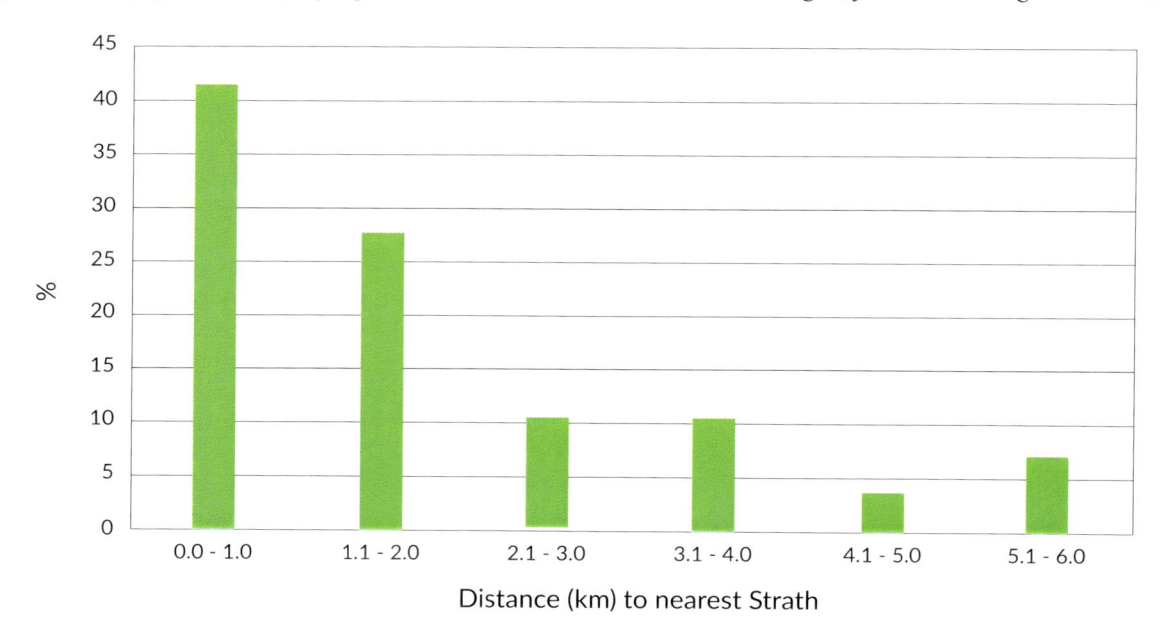

Figure 4.15 The distance from Pitcarmick buildings to the nearest well-drained strath terraces.

4. DISCUSSION

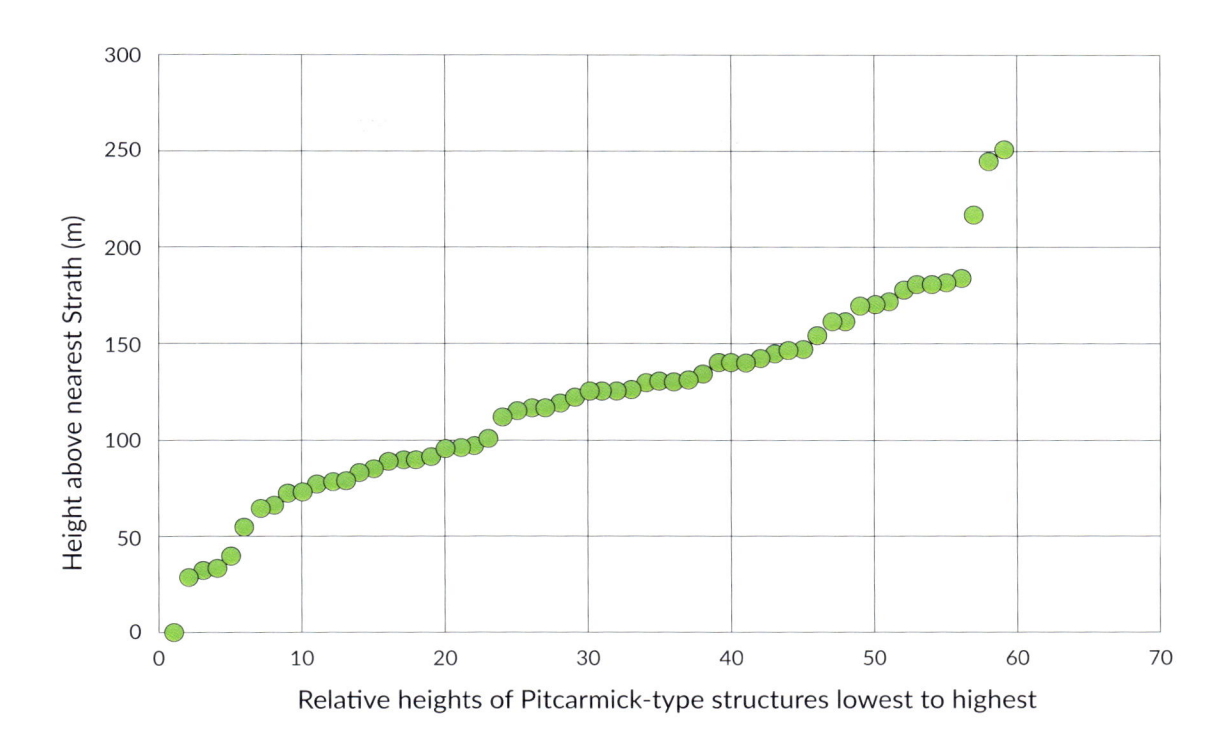

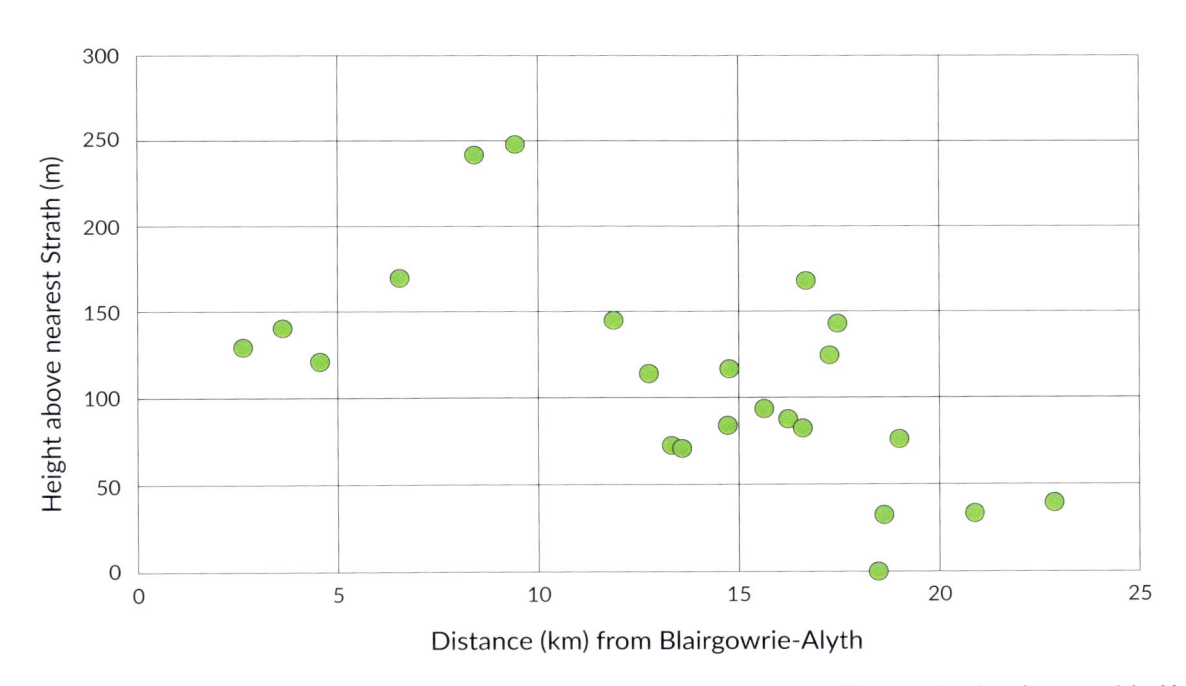

Figure 4.16 Graph showing (a) relative heights of Pitcarmick buildings above the nearest strath; (b) relative heights of Pitcarmick buildings ordered from lowest to highest.

a terrace no more than 30 m above the valley floor, but this pattern might suggest that straths furthest from Blaigowrie were themselves not occupied or farmed until the late 6th century or, at the very least, that there were still vacant lots in the pattern of permanent settlements there.

Because valley floors and plateau surfaces in Glen Shee and Strathardle rise north to the Cairngorm, absolute altitude is a less meaningful measure than their relative position above the valley floor. Figure 4.16b shows the Pitcarmick buildings ordered by relative relief. It shows no preferences in this respect by the people occupying these buildings, with the large spread around the mean (119 ± 50 m) suggesting that they did not colonise a particular altitudinal zone. The three outliers at the right of Figure 4.16b are at Pitcarmick, Ranageig and Hill of Ashmore (Sites 9, 18 and 12 respectively on Figure 1.3).

135

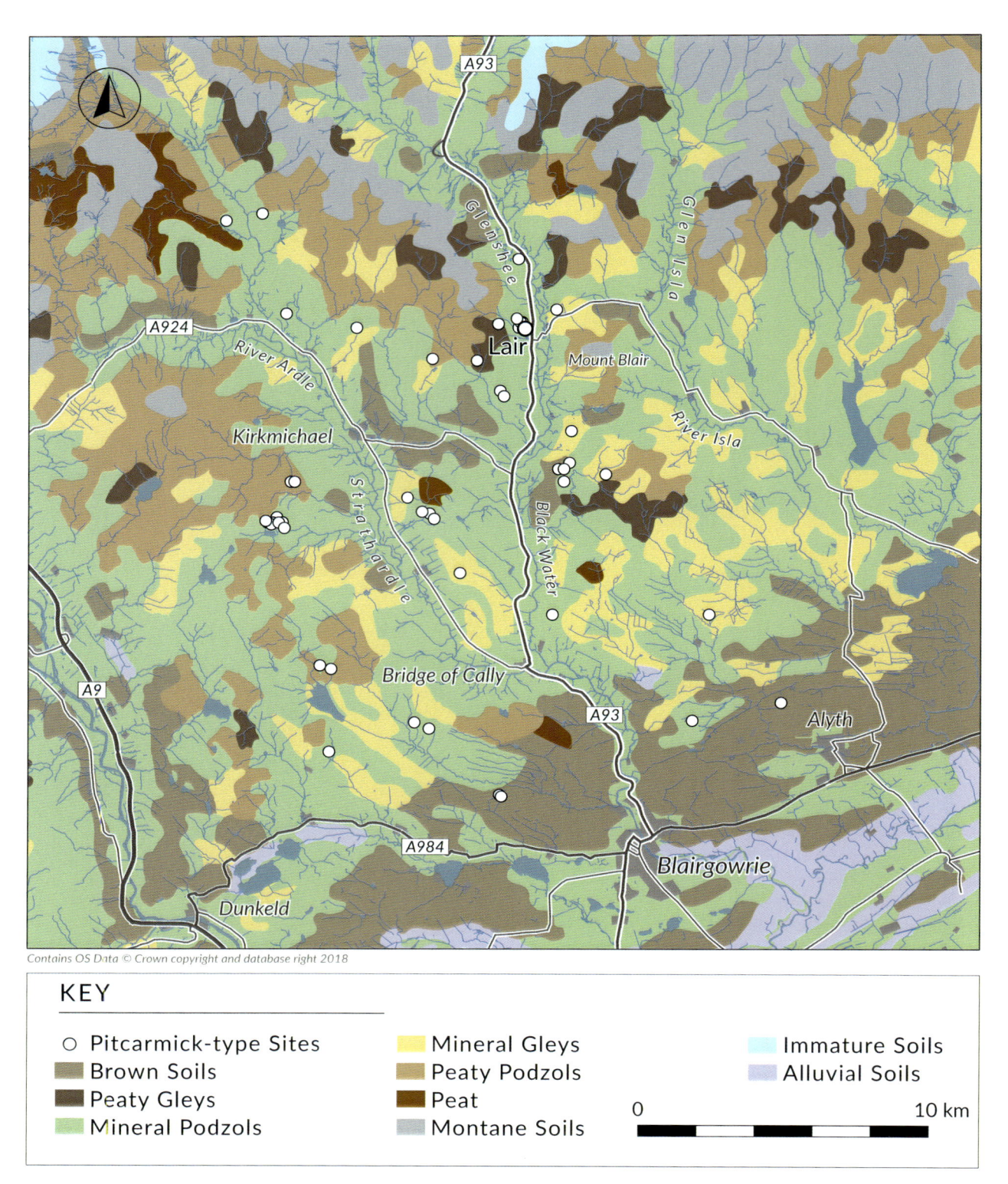

Figure 4.17 The distribution of known Pitcarmick buildings with soil types.

It is important to consider more specific factors in the sites that were chosen, such as soils, slope and aspect. Figure 4.17 shows the distribution of known Pitcarmick buildings with soil type. With the exception of the Hill of Ashmore (Figure 1.3: 12), it suggests that people shunned the wet and cold gley soils in the many waterlogged upland basins and valleys north and east of Bridge of Cally. Thus, the farmers seem to have been able to exercise some choice over the quality of land they settled. Possibly in opposition to this, however, no Pitcarmick buildings have been found on the good-quality brown forest soils which form a substantial sliver of base-rich limestone between Strathardle and Glen Shee, east of Kirkmichael. This anomaly may

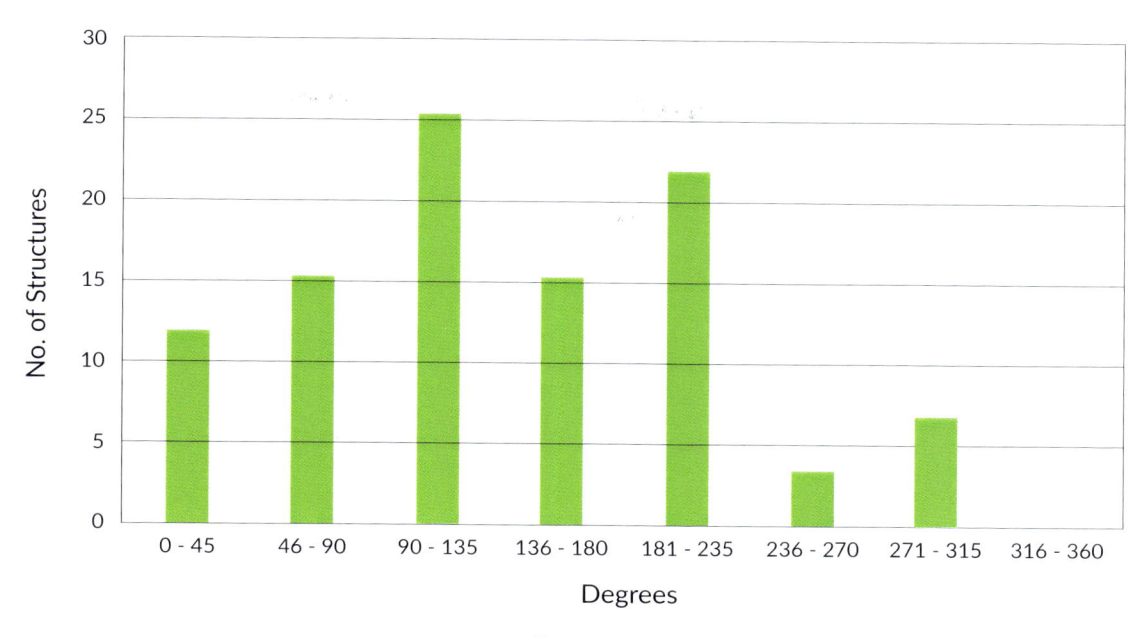

Figure 4.18 Aspects of known Pitcarmick buildings.

represent the destruction of buildings by later farming communities to judge from the concentration of farms mapped by James Stobie in 1783 (RCAHMS 1990: 5-7).

Almost all Pitcarmick buildings are on what is now moorland. This must be a measure of the survival of these monuments. Dalnaglar is not, and Marleehill in the south is now within post-enclosure farmland. Of the buildings/clusters, 62 % are on hillsides with average gradients (slopes) between 5 % and 23 %. In Strathardle where the valley sides are steeper and the bedrock geology forms extensive shelves, Pitcarmick buildings and clusters tend to lie on extensive upland plateaux. Some 77 % of buildings are on slopes that face between north-east and south-west, 10 % face between south-west and north-west, and none face north-west to north (Figure 4.18), indicating preferences for soils that are warmed by the sun.

Reflecting the same concerns of agricultural communities but more readily quantifiable is the relation of Pitcarmick buildings and clusters to solar irradiance: absolute values will vary historically but not relatively. The highest values (>1×10^6 KW/m^2/yr) in the area surveyed by RCAHMS (1990) are on steep south-facing slopes and the lowest (408,420 KW/m^2/yr) are on steep north-facing slopes. Mean solar irradiance for Pitcarmick buildings is 817,385 ± 38,141 KW/m^2/yr. Finegand (Figure 1.3: 2), facing east-north-east, receives the lowest irradiance (7376 KW/m^2/yr) and two buildings at Pitcarmick (Site 9: Figure 1.3) the most, almost twice as much. The Pitcarmick buildings on east- to south-east facing slopes at Lair are among the warmest (842,000 ± 18,000 KW/m^2/yr). Figure 4.19 presents the percentages of Pitcarmick buildings in ten arbitrary solar irradiance classes and compares them with the percentages of these classes in 50.0 m x 50.0 m cells across the area surveyed by the RCAHMS (1990). This shows a close match between percentages of both, which means that Pitcarmick buildings are not clustered in the warmest zones. We cannot, from this measure, demonstrate choice in the location of Pitcarmick buildings. There may have been choice, but without dating evidence from all Pitcarmick buildings, we cannot show that later farms were constructed in more marginal settings. The receipt of solar irradiance may, however, in part explain the high altitudes, commonly to and above 400m OD, of much past settlement of many periods in and around the north-east Perthshire hills (Harris 1985; RCAHMS 1990), in that valleys are oriented north-west to south-east, contrasting with the east-west structure of other valleys in Scotland, reducing contrasts in the receipt of sunshine and summer warmth.

4.12 The rural economy at Lair AD 600-660 to AD 975-1025: palynological evidence and implications

By AD 600-660, at the beginning of lpaz Lair 3a, woodland at Lair had been markedly reduced: most trees had been lost from the pollen source area. Woodland was replaced by dry *Calluna* heath and by grassland, or more likely a grass-heath where plants grew in a complex mosaic. This was probably heavily grazed, suppressing tree seedling establishment from any seed sources near at hand. Fires were common and probably originated from human activities, from domestic contexts, to continued manipulation of heath vegetation. The early historic upland landscape in north-east Perthshire was not wooded (Section 1.4) *contra* place-name evidence (Cottam and Small 1974; Fraser 1987; Laing and Laing 1993: 21).

Table 4.1 Pollen sites considered in Section 4.13.

Site and Location	Reference	Comments
Black Loch, Fife	Whittington et al. 1990; Whittington and Edwards 1993	the authors suggested that land abandonment characterised Roman occupation; full recovery occurred after c. 520 AD
Dogden Moss, Lammermuirs	Dumayne-Peaty 1999a	in recession after c. 200 AD; recovery dated to AD 419-602
Northern Cheviots	Tipping 2010	a fully productive agricultural landscape throughout the 1st millennium AD
The Dod, Southern Uplands	Innes and Shennan 1991	intensively grazed from c. 150-600 AD; large-scale woodland clearance only after c. 1100 AD
Burnfoothill Moss, Solway Plain	Tipping 1995b	recession after c. 300 AD when anthropogenic taxa are virtually absent; woodland clearance at AD 637-676 was followed by selective felling of oak at c. 900 AD
Carsegowan Moss, Kirkcudbright	Dumayne-Peaty 1999b	complete regeneration of woodland and cessation of farming after c. 200 AD until c. 500 AD
Brighouse Bay, Kirkcudbright	Wells et al. 1999	very intense grazing pressure from later prehistory to c. 200 AD: interpretation above this is problematic
Ellergower Moss, Galloway Hills	Dumayne-Peaty 1999b	recession after c. 600 AD and recovery after c. 900 AD
Bloak Moss, near Kilmarnock	Turner 1975	recession after AD 416-776 and emergence of an agricultural regime only after c. 1100 AD
Walls Hill, near Glasgow	Ramsay 1995	recession after 97 BC-AD 64 with no real recovery until AD 1237-1383
Lochend Loch, within Glasgow	Ramsay 1995	recession after AD 226-381 and recovery only after AD 810-980
Lenzie, near Kirkintilloch	Ramsay 1995	complete abandonment of farming after AD 447-607 and recovery after AD 816-985
Glasgow Bridge, near Kirkintilloch	Dunwell and Coles 1998	diverse agrarian economy in the 2nd century AD; recession perhaps with Roman withdrawal but recovery after AD 419-549
Fannyside Muir, near Cumbernauld	Dumayne-Peaty 1999b	partial woodland regeneration c. 350 AD to c. 940 AD
Cranley Moss, Carstairs	Dumayne-Peaty 1999b	absence of agricultural activity after c. 230 AD; recovery commenced c. 600 AD
Letham Moss, near Falkirk	Dumayne-Peaty 1999b	abandoned c. 375 AD to c. 650 AD, when grazing and crop-growing resumed
Blairbech Bog, north of Glasgow	Ramsay 1995	recession after c. 260 AD and recovery only in the high Middle Ages
Dunadd	Miller and Ramsay 2001; Housley et al. 2004; Housley et al. 2010	grassland common from the BC-AD boundary; dry woodland declined c. 650 AD. The agrarian signal is muted but the pollen site may have lain some distance from farmland (Tipping 2017)
Iona	Bohncke 1981 but see Tipping 2017	treeless by monastic colonisation but agricultural taxa are few
Gallanach Beg, Oban	Davies 1997	agrarian expansion from pre-Roman times and intensification after AD 719-1152
Lon Mor, Oban	Davies 1997	no 1st millennium AD recession
Arisaig	Carter et al. 2005	no agrarian recession in the last c. 2500 years

4. Discussion

Table 4.1 continued, Pollen sites considered in Section 4.13.

Site and Location	Reference	Comments
Achiltibuie	Bunting and Tipping 2004	no significant recession in the 1st millennium AD
Morvich, Kintail	Davies and Tipping 2004	Management of oak woodland after *c.* 200 AD within a thriving agrarian landscape until *c.* 650 AD; gradual decline over 600 years thereafter seen as consumption becoming more important than conservation
Glen Affric	Davies and Tipping 2004	expansion and/or intensification of agriculture after *c.* 300 AD, predominantly for livestock but with probable barley cultivation until after *c.* 1250 AD
Lairg	Smith 1998	woodland regeneration after *c.* 300 AD and recovery *c.* 1000 AD
Reidchalmai, near Golspie	Tipping *et al.* 2006	Oak management after *c.* 300 AD, trees then felled at *c.* 600 AD in a vigorous agrarian landscape
Loch Pityoulish, Spey Valley	O'Sullivan 1976	*Pinus* woodland dominated until clearance commenced *c.* 500 AD

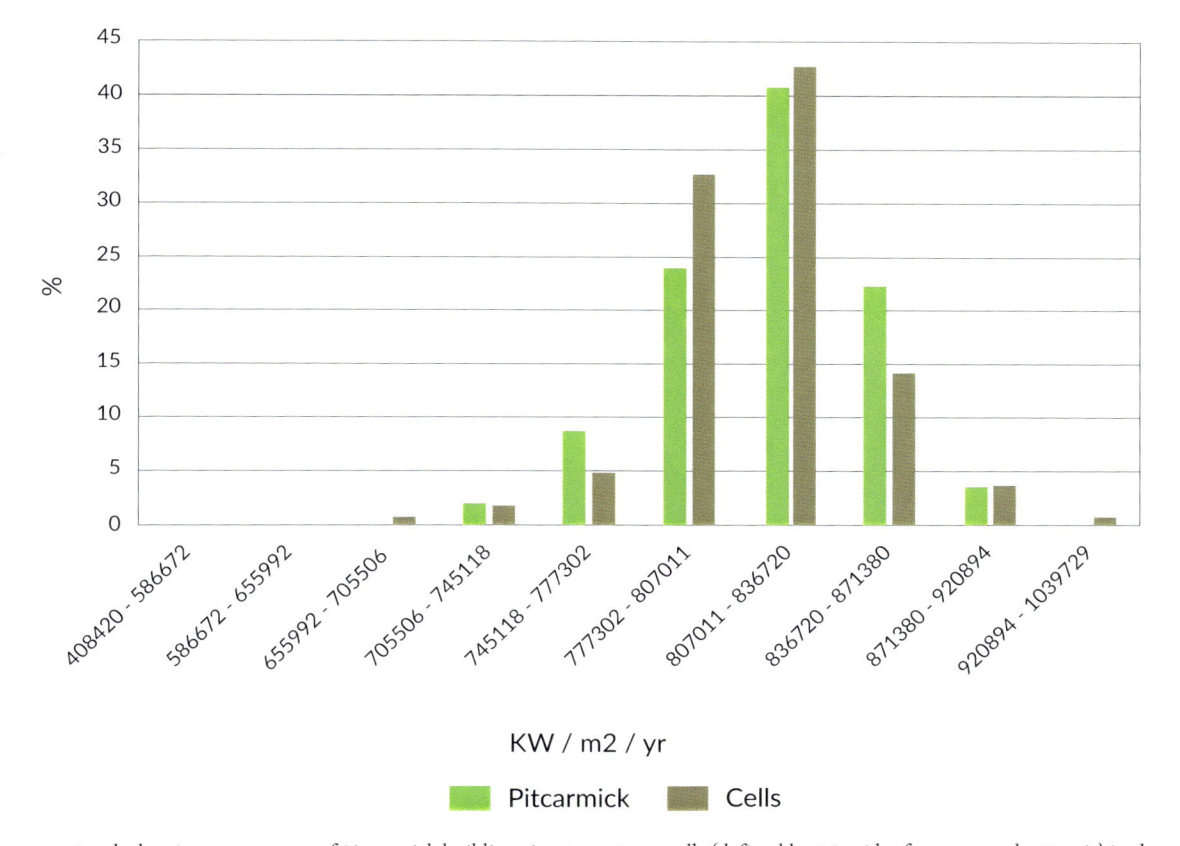

Figure 4.19 Graph showing percentages of Pitcarmick buildings in 50.0 x 50.0 m cells (defined by OS grid references on the X-axis) in the area surveyed by RCAHMS (1990) in ten arbitrarily defined equal-width bands of solar irradiance.

Important at Lair was the cultivation of cereal crops from the mid-7th century AD to *c.* 1000 AD (Section 2.6). The macro-fossil samples identified before ^{14}C dating (Ramsay: Section 2.7) include cf. *Hordeum* (possibly barley) in C14, dated to AD 670–880 and *Avena* (oat) in C248, dated to AD 760–900 (Krus and Hamilton: Section 2.5). This activity is very different to the pastoral activities around Carn Dubh at the same time (Tipping 1995a, 2013; Section 1.3). Crops at Lair were grown close to the pollen site, probably on the soils to the north-east and east of Basin 2, accompanied by a range of bare and disturbed ground herbs representing weeds in cultivated 'fields'. If the representation of cereals in the pollen record is that grown, barley was the most common crop, with oat (rather than wheat) and rye far less common: rye was a high medieval introduction to northern Europe (Myrdal 2012). Barley may have been grown for animal fodder but was also a staple of bread, porridge, gruel and beer (Banham and Faith 2014: 29; Hamerow 2012: 149). Both hulled and naked six-row barley were preserved as charred remains at Dundurn in upper Strathearn (Alcock 2003: 111). Contemporary field-systems around Pitcarmick buildings were not for the management of livestock alone (cf. Carver *et al.* 2012; Harris 1985; RCAHMS 1990). Arable was as central a concern at Lair as in the lowlands around Blairgowrie (Edwards and Whittington 1998; Whittington 1975).

Crops began to be grown at Lair, around 380-400 m OD, at some time before or, most probably, close to AD 600-660 (Section 4.4). Climatic reconstructions for north-west Europe suggest that colonisation of the Perthshire hills coincided with the end of a significant phase of cool climate, a major reconfiguration of northern hemisphere climatic regimes called the 'late antique little ice age'. Several high-precision analyses have shown this to have ended in the later 6th or early 7th centuries (Büntgen *et al.* 2016; Helama *et al.* 2017a, 2017b; Sigl *et al.* 2015; Steinhilber *et al.* 2009). Mean July temperatures before this had been *c.* 1-1.5 °C or up to 1.9 °C colder (Büntgen *et al.* 2016; Cheyette 2008; McCormick *et al.* 2012). Pitcarmick buildings were not associated with climatic deterioration as Carver *et al.* (2012) have suggested: quite the opposite. Climatic amelioration leading from the early 7th century AD through to the Medieval Climate Anomaly from *c.* 800 AD (Cheyette 2008; Hoffmann 2014: 69; Jones 1996; Mann and Jones 2003; McDermott *et al.* 2001) will have greatly facilitated upland cereal cultivation, particularly on warm east- and south-facing slopes as at Lair (Section 4.11). At Pitcarmick, ard points probably related to 7-9th century occupation and cultivation were found (Carver *et al.* 2012: 171: though see also Edmonds in Carver *et al.* 2012: 176), and one of Carver *et al.*'s interpretations (2012: 168, 172-3) was for ploughing of earlier structural remains in, broadly, the 9th to 11th centuries AD.

Woodland loss at Lair was for pasture as well as for arable fields. Early 7th century AD climatic amelioration and warmer and longer summers will have increased the biomass of hay and other fodder crops like, for example, sedges and grasses growing on peat. Climatic amelioration should also have reduced the need to shelter cattle over winter, as Bede understood of Ireland at the time (Sherley-Price 1968: 39), and as Banham and Faith (2014: 123) identified and as Dodgshon (1998: 209) indicated for coastal townships in post-medieval western Scotland. Nevertheless, increased seasonality, with warm summers but harsh winters, requiring the stalling of animals, has also been modelled for this period (McCormick 1998; Shabalova and van Engelen 2003).

At Lair the dominance of *Calluna* for hundreds of years, the unchanging ratio of *Calluna* to wild Poaceae (wild grasses), and the absence of tree regeneration are remarkable observations because such stable *Calluna* heath will not persist unless managed very carefully (Gimingham 1995): livestock grazing is a considerable skill. On mineral soils with no grazing pressures, *Betula* regenerates and with overgrazing, *Calluna* is replaced by grasses and sedges. On acid soils as at Lair (Section 1.7), low nutrient grasses like *Nardus* and *Molinia* will dominate and so *Calluna* heath can be the preferred feed for livestock. Management by fire can improve deteriorating heath (muirburn) but it is unclear whether the increased representation of microscopic charcoal in lpaz Lair 3a indicates this. Fires are interpreted to have been close to the pollen site but the values of microscopic charcoal are low and lack the intense peaks seen in settings where muirburn is applied (Rhodes 1995; Stevenson and Rhodes 2000).

Pollen data for crop-growing at Lair and archaeological evidence for cultivation at Pitcarmick suggest that the uplands were used in much the same ways to the lowlands, despite upland soils being more acidic than contemporary soils in the lowlands. Land use at Lair was, simplistically, extensive rather than intensive because both arable and pastoral elements of the rural economy are represented (Smith: Section 3.9), but there are biases in datasets that prevent us understanding entirely the balance of the two elements at Lair.

4.13 The wider context of 7th century AD agrarian expansion

with Stratford Halliday

How widespread was this agrarian expansion in Scotland? In a period that, in Scotland, is barely more than proto-historical, proxy economic data from pollen records are among the least ambiguous measures of economic success in the 1st millennium AD. Securely dated published pollen records that were analysed to high temporal precisions from mainland Scotland were inspected to understand the wider context of the agrarian change seen at Lair: where not calibrated in the original, ^{14}C age estimates have been calibrated using Intcal13 via OxCal 4.2. The farming economies depicted in pollen records were defined as either being in 'recession' or 'recovery' between *c.* 200 and *c.* 1000 AD from (a) changes in proportions of woodland on dry soils, (b) Poaceae (grasses), (c) grazing indicators and (d) cereal type pollen: interpretations offered below are not necessarily those of the original analyst. Some analyses provide more than these simple classifications. The data are summarised in Table 4.1 where they are ordered progressing clock-wise from Glen Shee, and in Figures 4.19 and 4.20.

In the area of present-day Scotland west, north-west and north of a line from Loch Lomond to Inverness the only evidence of agrarian recession in the 1st

4. Discussion

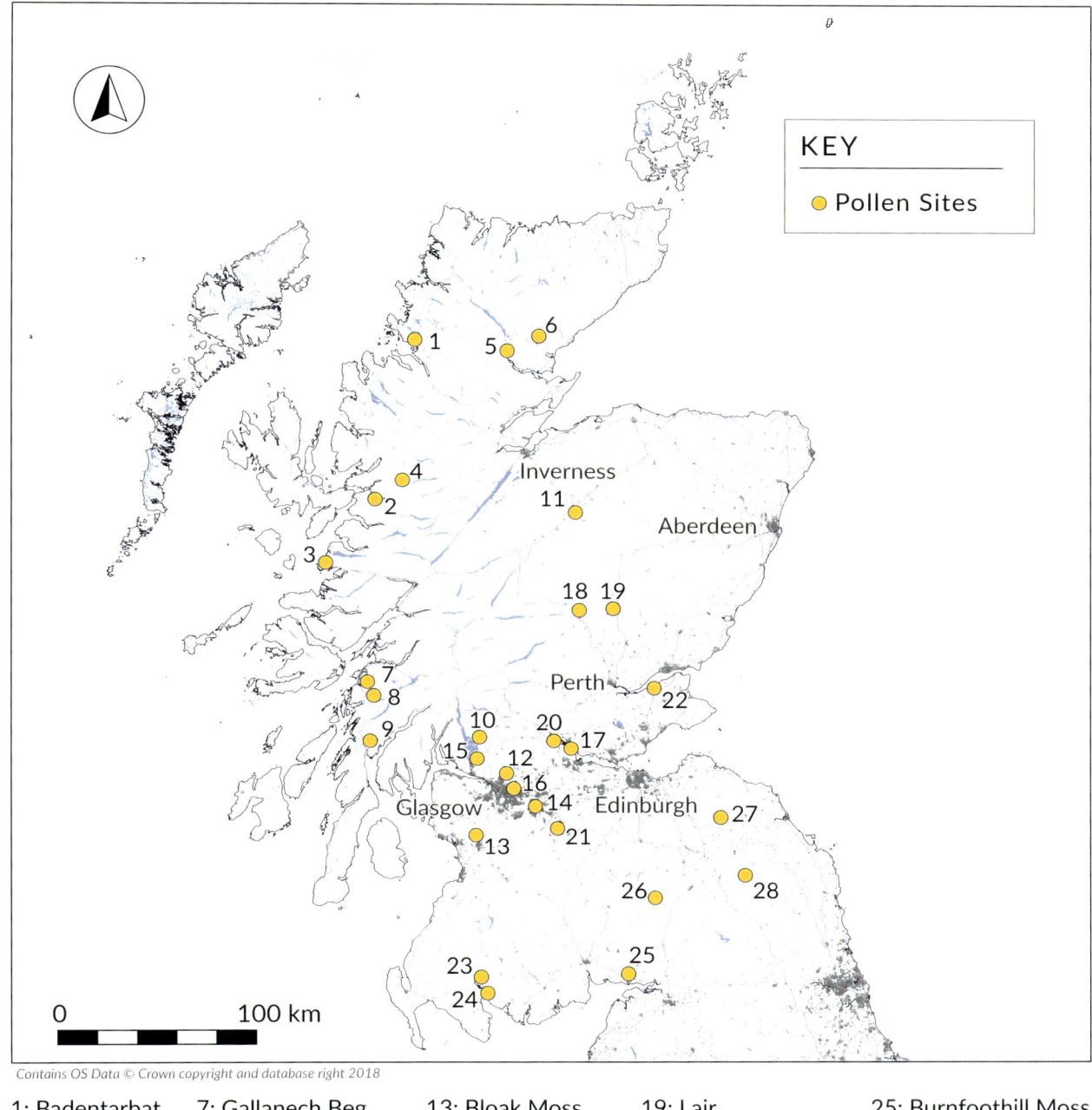

1: Badentarbat	7: Gallanech Beg	13: Bloak Moss	19: Lair	25: Burnfoothill Moss
2: Morvich	8: Lon Mor	14: Lochend Loch	20: Fannyside Muir	26: The Dod
3: Arisaig	9: Kilmartin Glen	15: Walls Hill	21: Cranley Moss	27: Dodgen Moss
4: Glen Affric	10: Blairbech Bog	16: Lenzie	22: Black Loch	28: Bowmont Valley
5: Lairg	11: Loch Pityoulish	17: Letham Moss	23: Ellergower Moss	
6: Reidchalmai	12: Glasgow Bridge	18: Carn Dubh	24: Carsegowan Moss	

Figure 4.20 The location of pollen sites in Table 4.1 and Figure 4.21.

millennium AD is at Lairg (Smith 1998), low in altitude but in pedological terms a cold, hard place, though not the only one. In what was once part of the Anglo-Saxon kingdom of Bernicia, in the northern Cheviot Hills, there was no recession either and on the Lammermuir Hills this was brief: Anglian advance was argued by Dumayne-Peaty (1999a) to have encouraged agricultural expansion.

Between these two regions the bulk of what would become Alba struggled with agrarian recession though only at Blairbech Bog at the foot of Loch Lomond and at Walls Hill near Glasgow did recession persist into the high medieval period. All the local and regional rural economies described in these pollen records underwent recovery, often stronger than before. When this happened cannot be precisely defined: calibrated

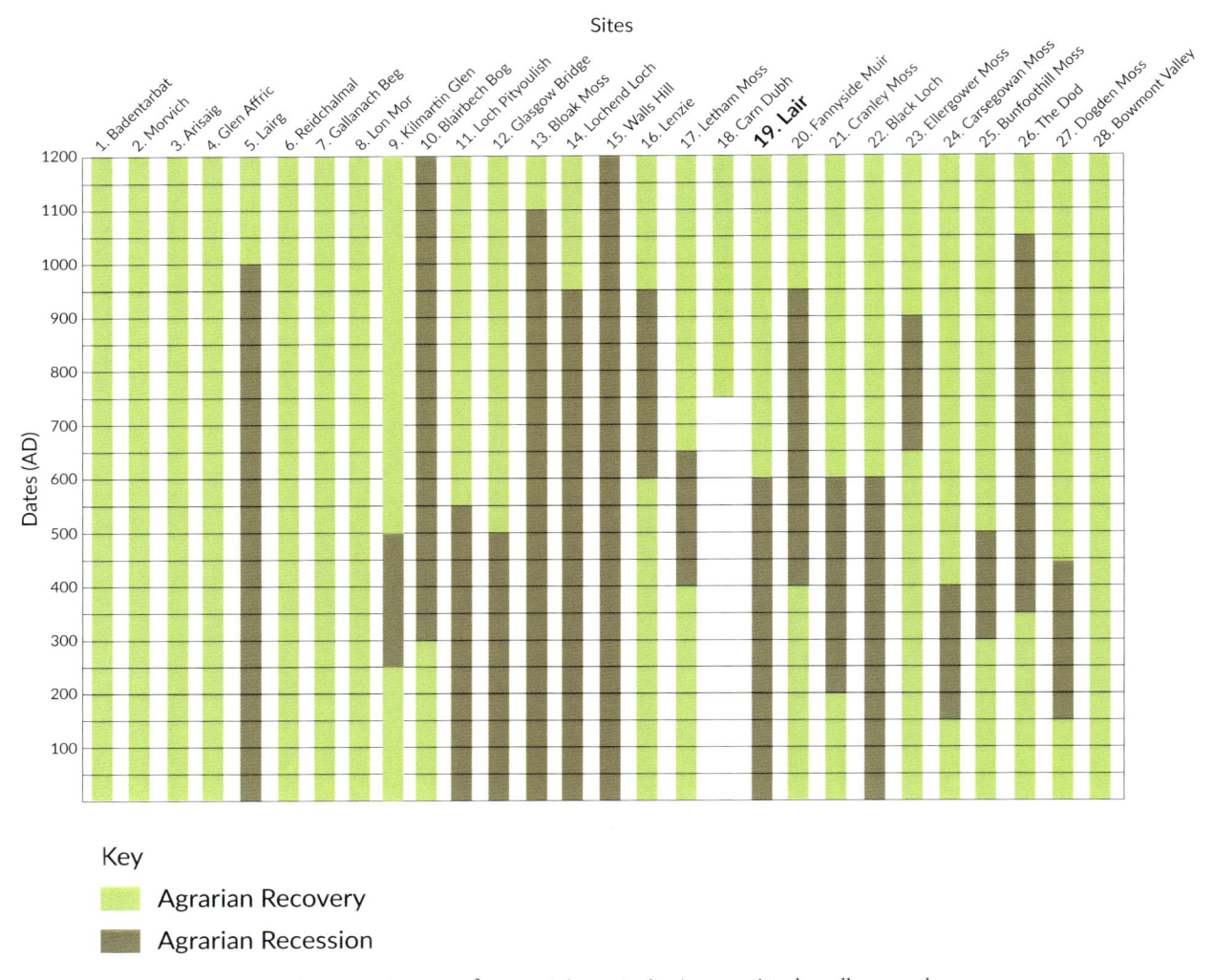

Figure 4.21 Patterns of economic 'recession' or 'recovery' in the pollen records.

age ranges are frequently large. However, the 6-7th centuries AD can be identified as the main period when recovery started in most landscapes, though for several pollen sites in Strathclyde recovery was not until the 10th and 11th centuries AD. There is a strong case for thinking that what happened at Lair in AD 600-660 was happening at the same time in a very large number of other places in Scotland.

In Ireland, the emergence of raths in the 7th century AD (Kerr *et al.* 2009; McCormick *et al.* 2014) is associated with permanent settlement, and arable rather than pastoral contexts. But further afield, the 6-7th century economic developments at Lair appear too early to be related to the 'long 8th century' agrarian expansions identified in lowland England by Hamerow (2012), Loveluck (2013) and McKerracher (2018) and in Scandinavia by Lagerås (2007) and Myrdal (2012). The landscapes of south-west England (Rippon 2007: 134-137) may accord most closely with those of upland Perthshire at this date. A few oval-shaped buildings in Scotland have been suggested as the 'final manifestation of the Iron Age roundhouse' with a tendency to 'elongation' (Harding 2009: 186), suggesting an evolution from roundhouse to Pitcarmick building. However, as argued in Sections 4.3 and 4.10, we see these as discrete and distinct in time, having early medieval radiocarbon dates. These include Building 8 at Carn Dubh where an early medieval house was constructed over two adjacent earlier roundhouses, resulting in a sub-rectangular plan rounded on the west and squared off on the east: a hearth was ^{14}C dated to AD 657-961 (Rideout 1995; GU-2428: calibrated by Oxcal in 2018), which broadly coincides in time, if not architecture, to Pitcarmick buildings. This floor plan is reminiscent of the 'bag-shaped' structure excavated at Portmahomack and associated with radiocarbon dates of AD 700-940 (SUERC-2621) and AD 670-870 (SUERC-33415; Carver *et al.* 2016: 215, D19) from a hearth in its earliest phase. Other buildings of this general date include the multi-phased Easter Kinnear example in the rich agricultural lowlands of north-east Fife, where a sub-square building had been reconstructed on at least four occasions over the 6th-7th centuries AD, with potential abandonment in the 8th century AD (Driscoll 1997), although in an alternative interpretation, this scoop is proposed as an earlier roundhouse on the same site (Halliday

2006). Excavation at Kintore, Aberdeenshire, has also revealed early medieval re-occupation at the site of an extensive roundhouse group, in this case, following a long history of settlement from the Middle Bronze Age to the Late Iron Age: the site does not seem to have been re-occupied until the 8th century AD (Cook and Dunbar 2008: 149-59). In all, four elongated sunken floors were located, ranging from 5-11 m in length by 1.6-5 m in breadth. Of two structures excavated at Forest Road, burnt structural remains on the floor of one produced radiocarbon dates of AD 660-890 (GU-10535) and AD 640-710 (SUERC-1335). The other two, yet to be published, are larger: c. 11 m by 4.5 m overall and have produced dates of AD 650-780 (SUERC-16351) and AD 680-900 (SUERC-16350) (Ann Crone *pers comm*). These larger examples fall within the lower end of the size range of the sunken portions of the Pitcarmick-type interiors. In addition, at Forest Road a comparable date was obtained from an axial post-hole in a linear gully at least 15 m long by 3.4 m wide that bears close comparison to the axial feature of Building E1 excavated at Pitcarmick (Carver *et al.* 2012).

Further, radiocarbon dates from pits at a wide range of sites in eastern Scotland reveal this same broad chronology. From the Moray Firth to the Forth, there are 45 radiocarbon assays from pits at 17 lowland sites where the 2σ spans of the assays fall somewhere in the range AD 400-1100. Six of these, from only four sites, fall before *c.* AD 600, whereas the chronology appears to pick up later, with no fewer than 32, from 12 sites, falling between *c.* 650-1000 AD. These include: fire-pits at Ardownie and Newmill, where there was evidently a long hiatus after the occupation of the adjacent souterrains (Anderson and Rees 2006: 56); at Alloa, Clackmannan, where paired dates from four pits fall AD 770-1020 (SUERC-19130; -19134-8; -19147-8), but where previous activity on the site was in the Late Bronze Age (Mitchell *et al.* 2010); at Hawkhill, Angus (Rees 2009) where following Roman Iron Age occupation, later activity spans the period AD 680-1040; and at Dyce, Aberdeenshire, where 1st millennium BC activity is followed by a hearth dated AD 418-555 (SUERC-69410), and with five other dates from pits, post-holes and hearths falling AD 711-1157 (SUERC-69401-2; -69407-9) (Woodley *et al.* 2018). In addition, the cropmarks of a long building partly excavated at Newbarns (McGill 2004), near the southern end of Lunan Bay, Angus, also belongs in this general period. With rounded ends and parallel walls, it measured *c.* 18 m in length by 6 m in breadth within a narrow ditch marking the line of the wall. The ditch does not seem to have been a construction trench as such: its primary fill contained in-washed sand with a few lenses of burnt material, while ash in the upper fill had apparently formed *in situ*. Charred grains from the lower fill returned dates of AD 780-1030 (AA-47747/GU-9751) and AD 870-1030 (AA-47748/GU-9752). Two of a series of outlying pits were sectioned, revealing complex fills that included deposits of burnt turfs and charred cereal grains; these produced eight comparable dates.

The most striking aspect of the chronologies of all these different sites is the long hiatus that separates early medieval activity from any earlier occupation. This is particularly so at several souterrains, where some measure of continuity is often claimed between Roman Iron Age and Pictish settlement (e.g. Harding 2004: 240; Watkins 1980). In the cases of Newmill and Ardownie (*supra*), however, the gaps in the radiocarbon chronologies are at least 500 years and over 340 years respectively. In the face of the growing body of radiocarbon dates accruing from commercially-led excavations, there is surely no case to argue continuity of settlement from the Roman Iron Age to the early medieval period from the handful of features of this date that have been excavated on souterrain settlements (Anderson and Rees 2006: 56; Armit 1999; Coleman and Hunter 2002; Maxwell 1987; RCAHMS 1994: 71-5; Watkins 1980). Their general abandonment by the beginning of the 3rd century AD fits into a much wider pattern of dislocation in the settlement record that can be detected from the shores of the Moray Firth southwards to the Northumberland coastal plain (Hodgson *et al.* 2012: 214-16; Hunter 2007: 43-4, 49), and most emphatically demonstrated by the detailed radiocarbon chronology from the fort at Broxmouth in East Lothian (Armit and McKenzie 2013). We have yet to identify where settlement moved to in the 3rd century AD, but it would appear that the expansion of settlement documented by the excavations at Lair was widespread throughout the lowlands and uplands of eastern Scotland whereby long abandoned sites were re-occupied.

Elsewhere, we might associate this phase with the emergence of raths in Ireland in the 7th century AD (Kerr *et al.* 2009; McCormick *et al.* 2014), associated with permanent settlement, and arable rather than pastoral contexts. But further afield, the 6-7th century economic developments at Lair appear too early to be related to the 'long 8th century' agrarian expansions identified in lowland England by Hamerow (2012), Loveluck (2013) and McKerracher (2018) and in Scandinavia by Lagerås (2007) and Myrdal (2012). The landscapes of south-west England (Rippon 2007: 134-137) may accord most closely with those of upland Perthshire at this date.

4.14 The function of Pitcarmick buildings

with Daniël Postma

It is probable that the use of turf as a building material was driven by particular environmental conditions or objectives, and appears most often to have been associated with one or more of the following factors:

ecological marginality and a shortage of other building materials (e.g. Beresford 1979; Munch, Johansen and Roesdahl 2003); economic marginality, and no means to acquire other building materials (e.g. Goslinga 2017; Logan 2017, 2018; Wilkinson 2009); transhumance and seasonal accommodation, such as shielings in a Scottish context (e.g. Kok 2005; Mahler 1993); pioneering of new territories (e.g. Cowley and Harrison 2001; Nicolay and Postma 2018; Welsch 1967); and cultural preferences, i.e. part of an established building tradition (e.g. Andersen and Olsen 2014; Postma 2015).

With regard to Pitcarmick buildings, their large size suggests that economic marginality was not a likely driver. Ecological marginality, in the absence of timber, would have made turf houses a preferred option for upland Perthshire. But pioneering may have provided the primary impetus (Sections 4.11 and 4.12). Indeed, several key indicators of agricultural change in early medieval farm settlements in the northern Netherlands were also present at Lair (Sections 4.8 and 4.9):

- farmsteads initially composed of multiple, relatively small buildings (i.e. 'simple type' dwellings, comparable to Leens A and B types with further outbuildings);
- farmsteads subsequently focused on single longhouses with outbuildings (i.e. main Pitcarmick type, or 'complex type' dwellings, comparable to provisional Leens AB and hybrid type);
- deepened byre ends, possibly relating to the collection of manure (i.e. for improving new agricultural land); and
- reduced span of byre ends, possibly to provide better support for lofts (i.e. for storing part of improved agricultural yields).

Marginality in the definitions above is specific to building materials, though, and not to landscape. The abundance of readily available turf at Lair, and very probably every Pitcarmick building, has been discussed in Section 4.7, and though circular in argument, the size of the principal buildings at Lair (Sections 2.3 and 4.6), Pitcarmick, and elsewhere in the central Highlands (Section 4.9), suggests turf was not in short supply. But marginality here relates also to the shortage of other materials. It is unlikely that stone was in short supply: though a few kerb stones of the ring-cairn were re-modelled, the cairn itself was not dismantled, as it could have been. Timber was limited, at least at Lair (Section 2.6), where perhaps the last woodland was consumed in site-preparation (Section 4.4), and very probably everywhere that is today moorland (Section 1.4). Large timbers may not have been needed for all uses of wood in the buildings (Sections 4.6 and 4.7) and timbers can be re-used but the means to acquire building materials other than turf (economic marginality) seems not to have been a limiting factor in decision-making. Whether these communities had the means to purchase wood, and whether there was the infrastructure to supply this, is unclear. Transport 'over land' in the 7th century AD is specified for oak and pine delivered to Iona for 'the great house' there (Crone and Watson 2003, 61-62).

Alcock (2003: 265) saw Pitcarmick buildings as early forms of shielings because their elevations, rarely below 300 m OD, were thought too high for crop-growing. Carver *et al.* (2012: 194-195) toyed with this idea, thinking them 'milk processing stations', although the importance of dairying in the early medieval period is so far a largely Irish trait (Kelly 1998; McCormick *et al.* 2014). McNiven (Section 1.6) shows how Gaelic place-names for shieling, post-*c.* AD 900, are most common in upper Glen Shee and Strathardle. Smith (Section 3.9) has also suggested that seasonality (spring occupation) is implied at Lair from the bones of a very young calf in the fill of the pit (C279) under the annexe of Building 3 (see also Section 4.8), but this does not preclude cattle being present all year. The possible foundation deposit beneath Building 3, the evidence for butchery (Smith: Section 3.9), and for smithing (McLaren: Section 3.6) does not fit well with the idea of Lair having been a seasonal focus for dairy products. Neither does the spatial separation of activities in Building 3 described by Clarke in Section 3.3, the size and scale of the principal buildings excavated, nor the suggested spatial organisation of buildings (Section 4.8).

The pollen record (Sections 2.6 and 4.12) indicates that climatic amelioration allowed cereal cultivation at these altitudes. This alone need not preclude Pitcarmick buildings as being shieling huts. Some shielings, Norse *heimseter* (Fellows-Jensen 1985: 74) or, in the early modern period in central Scotland, 'home shielings' (Dodgshon 2015: 135), were sufficiently close to the home farm that crops might have been planted at the shieling, and this was true also at some shielings in 18th-century Assynt (Adam 1960; Althea Davies *pers comm*). At Lair a home farm may have been but a short distance downslope on the valley floor, though such a farm is entirely conjectural. This cannot have been the case with other Pitcarmick buildings at considerable distances from straths (Section 4.11). Dodgshon (2015: 123, 175) also describes shielings at greater distances from home farms with arable attached, but these were in the later 18th century when population and economic pressures put a great strain on subsistence: such shielings became, after tathing, 'lived in all year round' (Dodgshon 2015: 123).

Despite the logic of transhumance in this context, there are no demonstrable archaeological examples of shielings in early medieval Britain (Banham and Faith 2014: 147-151; Dixon 2018). Gardiner (2018) records Wrathmell's proposal that very small sunken huts near Wharram Percy of 6-7th century AD date were seasonally occupied, and this appears to be the inference of Anderson and Suddaby (forthcoming) at Kersons Cleugh, near Longformacus in the Scottish Borders, but with no evidence: these are interpretations driven by models. The most recent intensive archaeological exploration of shieling landscapes close to north-east Perthshire, on the southern slopes of Ben Lawers, found their earliest archaeologically attested use in the late 14th-early 15th century AD (Atkinson 2016: 259). Winchester's (2000) historical survey of southern Scotland and northern England begins at AD 1400, though only by limitations of document survival, and he has recently suggested that shielings were 'an inherent part of the agrarian system of the twelfth century' (Winchester 2017: 293). Bil's (1990) analysis of Perthshire shielings commences even later, at AD 1600, but he suggests, though with little supporting evidence, that the transhumant tradition was strong in the 'Dark Ages' (Bil 1990: 2). Iron Age transhumance was suggested by the recovery of seeds at Oakbank Crannog, on Loch Tay, of a montane plant, cloudberry (*Rubus chamaemorus*) (Miller 2002) but this is tenuous evidence.

Barrow (1998) has argued most strongly for early medieval transhumance, on place-name evidence. He drew on ogel names (e.g. Ochils, Ochiltree, Ogilvie) to mean 'high settlement', equivalent to Welsh *hafod* (summer dwelling). Taylor (2011: 84), however, does not consider the root to imply settlement at all, and it is usually understood today to mean only a ridge or promontory (Rhys 2015: 319-321). Scottish equivalents to Welsh *pebyll* (e.g. Peebles, Cairnpapple, Pubil in Glenlyon), meaning tent, pavilion or temporary shelter, were seen by Barrow (1998: 62) to demonstrate 'conclusively' that Picts practised transhumance (see also Bil 1990: 2 and Bil 1992: 393), though tents were structures used by elites (Blair 2018: 65), not pastoralists, and whether such flimsy structures were ever intended for occupation over several summer months must be debateable. Scottish equivalents to Welsh *mynydd* (*monadh*: e.g. Monadhliath, Mounth, Kilmundy), 'hill ground' or 'rough pasture', were regarded by Barrow as evidence for transhumance, although the highest place named (Barrow 1998: 62; Figure 2.7) is less than 250 m OD. Barrow's proposal (1998: 67) that specifically named hills (e.g. Dunnichen Hill, Hayston Hill, both in Angus) related to their summer grazing by named communities, is challenged by Bil's suggestion (1992: 398) that such places were 'more akin to hill grazing than a genuinely transhumant situation'. The same might apply to *mynydd* names. Bil (1992) focused on the abundant Gaelic names in the Perthshire hills ('airigh', 'ruighe' and 'bothan') and Old Scots 'shiel', that may relate to transhumance, but at what date is problematic given the long currency of the Gaelic language here, from the 9th to the 19th centuries AD. One geographical relation, between 'airigh' and 'ruighe', was tentatively suggested to date to the 9th century AD eastward movement of Gaelic speakers into Pictland, but there are other, equally likely explanations which have no such chronological implications (Bil 1990: 392; McNiven: Section 1.6). Place-name evidence in montane Cumbria clearly indicates Norse transhumance (Whyte 1985), though from when in this period is unclear: Whaley (2006: xxii) suggested from the 9th until well into the 11th century. Ramm, McDowall and Mercer (1970: 3) thought such place-names to relate to the 10th and 11th centuries, and certainly many shielings at lower altitudes in Cumbria were permanently settled by the later 11th or early 12th centuries (Whyte 1985: 111).

Pitcarmick buildings were argued by Carver *et al.* (2012) to have functioned as byre-houses, suggesting that perhaps 20-24 small cattle could be accommodated in Structures C1 and E1 at Pitcarmick, comparable to nearly contemporary byre-houses along the eastern shore of the North Sea (Chapelot and Fossier 1985: 104-106). At Lair the evidence for Pitcarmick buildings having been byre-houses is less clear-cut. Building 1 may have been one, and Building 3 is more likely to have been one, with its sloping eastern end encouraging drainage, but no central drains or stalls were recovered as this area saw little excavation (Section 4.6). In any case, the settlement changed through time, with buildings changing function, and with this, early features are lost. Cattle dominate the percentages of domestic animal bones at nuclear forts (Alcock 2003: 113), and Smith (Section 3.9) finds the association of cattle with Building 3 at Lair compelling evidence for cattle to have been central to the economy, though cattle bones do not dominate the bone assemblages at either Pitcarmick (Holmes in Carver *et al.* 2012: 18), where sheep as well as cattle are suggested to have been kept (Carver *et al.* 2012: 185), or at Lair where bones of sheep (and possibly goat) and pigs were recovered (Smith: Section 3.9). The stalling of cattle over winter is described in the Old English *Gerefa* (Banham and Faith 2014: 123) and stalling cattle over winter was essential in parts of Scandinavia from the later Iron Age (Myrdal 2012: 216). Given the hostility of the winter climate in this region at the present day (Section 1.7; McClatchey 1996), and the modelling of heightened seasonality in the later 1st millennium AD, with cold winters (Shabalova and van Engelen 2003; Section 4.12), it is reasonable to assume that shelter for livestock would be required over the winter in the Perthshire hills.

A re-assessment of 13 medieval byres from farms in southern Iceland (Berson 2002) provides a useful basis for considering the potential complexity and fluidity in the spatial relationship between houses, byres and other outbuildings. High medieval byres in Iceland were separate from dwellings, in contrast to Iron/Viking Age byre-houses in Scandinavia, a distancing of cattle from humans from the 11th century onward (Berson 2002: 61) despite the advantages of heat transfer from byre to house when together. Icelandic byres were found only occasionally as part of the dwelling complex, close to houses, particularly at high altitudes snow-bound for many months. They were more usually at some distance, usually 20-40 m but as much as 70-80 m away. Berson (2002: 61) also identified low level human occupation in these separate byres, such as at Goðatættur and Hvítárholt. While Icelandic houses were commonly repaired and rebuilt, byres were seemingly not. Byres may have been fairly short-lived and semi-mobile, built on different parts of the farm to manure different parts of the infield. Byres and barns were commonly conjoined aligned pairs, built end to end, with the barn only accessed through the byre, giving the appearance of one long building: occasionally they were built side by side (Berson 2002: 60). Sheep sheds in 11th century Þórarinsstaðir ranged from 4-22 m in length (Berson 2002: 42).

Over-wintering is only one value of byre-houses: Chapelot and Fossier (1985) suggested that shelter for animals in all seasons was increasingly important as woodland was cleared. Carver *et al.* (2012: 194) suggested protection from theft or from predators as well as from cold winters. Dodgshon (2008) argued that byre-houses were critical not for animal products but for the concentration of manure that could be applied to arable fields: the reason for stalling livestock was the betterment of the arable crop. Oosthuizen (2013: 66) also emphasised how important middening became in central-southern England to increasing cereal production in the 'long 8th century' AD 670-830 (see also Hamerow 2012: 147). Nevertheless, byre-houses were absent in Anglo-Saxon England (Banham and Faith 2014; Hamerow 2012).

4.15 The social status of 'Pitcarmick' communities

Though there is a strong spatial association between prehistoric hut-circles and Pitcarmick buildings (RCAHMS 1990; Strachan 2013: illus 63) and though, on occasion, Pitcarmick buildings overlie hut-circles (RCAHMS 1990), these do not imply continuity of either settlement or land use from later prehistory (Sections 2.6 and 4.2). Land use at Lair after the mid-7th century AD was not a continuation of the later prehistoric economy, nor a replication of it (Section 4.12). Pitcarmick buildings were elements of new, pioneer economies (Cowley 1997; RCAHMS 1990; Section 4.11) like others of different architectures seen in the uplands throughout the British Isles (Dixon 2017: 266-7; Dodgshon 2015: 47; Fowler 2002: 150; Fox 2012: 166; Johnson 2014).

The complexity of their economy, comparative sophistication and diversity of architecture and use of space (Sections 4.8 and 4.9) suggest that farming communities at Pitcarmick-type farms were not 'smallholders clinging to difficult land' (Carver *et al.* 2012: 195) or of lower status (Ralston and Armit 2003: 229). If reasonable, Carver *et al.*'s (2012) estimate of 20-24 cattle in byres at Pitcarmick would place farmers at Pitcarmick a long way up the social scale (Márkus 2017: 188). The way in which they appear to have appropriated the prehistoric ring-cairn at Lair (Section 4.2) has parallels with the behaviours of contemporary elites in the same region: the practice of laying claim, either in disputed territories or in areas where ownership was lax or vacant. One exquisite small find at Lair that suggests a well-connected community is the glass bead described in Section 3.8: and while Campbell sees this as suggestive that Lair was 'connected to a higher status lowland site', it may instead have been that it was the community at Lair that was of higher social status. The farmers at Lair were, perhaps, the 'farmer republics' of Fraser (2009: 348; Section 1.5). Fox (2012: 162-9) and Banham and Faith (2014: 248-250) emphasise the 'conscious choice' that Anglo-Saxon farmers in England had in selecting and defining moorland territories, and this ability to select localities to settle, at least in soil quality, has been shown for Pitcarmick buildings in Section 4.11. The measured spacing of Pitcarmick buildings in parts of the Perthshire Hills (Section 4.11) also suggests this. Nicolaisen (1997: 113) made the same point regarding the founders of *pett*-named lowland settlements. What this means for pre-Pictish settlement (Armit 1999; Halliday 2006; Maxwell 1987) needs to be explored further but in Section 4.11 it was suggested that there was little evidence for local power-centres or control of local land resources, despite the likelihood of an estate structure, and also then that there was little competition for land in the hills in the 7th century. Elsewhere in upland Perthshire, the Carn Dubh model of continuity in land use through the later Iron Age might have persisted (Tipping 1995a, 2013), but the maintenance of grazed pasture does not need a high human population or sedentism. If Pitcarmick buildings were byre-houses, as reconstructed at Pitcarmick by Carver *et al.* (2012) and for some of the buildings at Lair (Section 4.6), their introduction to hillsides in upland Pictland was at the forefront of agrarian technology in northern Europe (Hamerow 2012: 147; McKerracher 2018; Oosthuizen 2013; Rippon 2007; Rippon *et al.* 2015: 305; Wickham 2005: 292-3).

Place-name evidence can be used to explore social status further. House C1 at Pitcarmick (Carver *et al.* 2012) seems to have been occupied twice, the earlier at around AD 680-880 and the later at AD 1020-1180: abandonment was suggested between these periods. House E2 was also occupied in the high medieval period. The archaeological record at Pitcarmick can fruitfully be compared to the chronology of place-names because Pitcarmick is a *pett* place-name: 'Cormac's share' (Section 1.6). *Pett* place-names were formed after the later 9th century

AD (Broun 2015: 53; Woolf 2007: 325), most in the 10th century AD (Taylor 2011: 79) and all probably before the 11th century AD (Woolf 2007: 325). The name is likely to have been given to Pitcarmick in the 11th century AD reoccupation (McNiven: Section 1.6). *Pett* names have been given a new hierarchical significance by some historians. Woolf (2007) argued that *pett* meant "substantial farm or 'estate centre'" and represented (2007: 324) 'a household responsible for paying dues directly [to the king] rather than through an intermediate lord', part of an estate, though having considerable independence (see also Broun 2015: 53-55). Does this imply that the Pictish, pre-Gaelic settlement at Pitcarmick held a similar elevated significance to its later *pett* component? A case is made in Section 4.12 for Lair, and so for Pitcarmick buildings more generally, that 7th century AD colonisation was an innovative agrarian development. Pitcarmick buildings should not be seen as marginal. They emerged when 7th century AD climatic amelioration allowed the uplands to be used in new, precocious ways, with the introduction of byres (Carver *et al.* 2012). This environmental change might have been enough, given the economic and political significance of cattle, for lords to have encouraged colonisation, but in the remoteness of north-east Perthshire, this endeavour was pursued by what Loveluck (2013: 81) describes as 'free farming lineages'.

4.16 After the 'Pitcarmicks'

with a contribution from Łukasz Banaszek and David Cowley

Krus and Hamilton (Section 2.5) place the abandonment phases of Buildings 1, 2 and 3 at Lair at *AD 735-940*, *AD 850-980* and *AD 815-960* respectively. The alternative dating model would push this back to the late 8th to late 10th centuries AD. The pollen record is not so precisely dated, but the final recorded vegetation changes, interpreted to indicate a decline in some human activities on the hillside, occurred around AD 975-1025 (lpaz Lair 3b: Section 2.6). These two independently dated records are in good agreement, and of particular interest when considered alongside evidence suggesting late 10th century AD origins for Perth (Hall *et al.* 2005).

The grass heath continued to be maintained and grazed. A few birch trees are likely to have become re-established, suggesting reduced grazing, but they may have grown in relative abundance away from livestock in the gorge of the Allt Corra-lairige (Figure 1.12). Evidence for cereal cultivation at Lair ceased after AD 1030-1090 (Section 2.6). Why the arable land was abandoned is unknown but there is no evidence from which to infer 'failure' of the settlement (Cowley 1997: 167).

Abandonment is unlikely to have had a climatic cause: northern hemisphere temperatures rose after the end of the Oort solar minimum *c.* 1050 AD (McDermott *et al.* 2001), though at the latitude of Scotland, not necessarily by much (Mann *et al.* 2008). Soils became wetter (Proctor *et al.* 2002; Trouet *et al.* 2009), particularly in the summer growing season (Edwards *et al.* 2017), but soils at Lair that were likely to have supported crops were well-drained. There are no detailed upland pollen records for this time in the region to explore how widespread this change was. The lowland pollen record at Rae Loch (Edwards and Whittington 1998) has clear evidence for the pre-eminence in the lowlands of crop cultivation.

Perhaps socio-economic change meant the end of the Pitcarmick buildings and economies, possibly the imposition of hunting reserves (Dixon 2017: 244-5; RCAHMS 1990: 6-8): that at Clunie in lower Glen Shee is first recorded in AD 1161 but was visited prior to this by David I (r. 1124-1153) (Gilbert 1979: 21). A shift from dispersed to nucleated settlement in the late 1st millennium AD is identified in Scotland by Dixon (2017: 244), and McNiven (Section 1.6) has shown the number of post-*c.* 900 AD *bal*-names cluster around Lair. Dodgshon (2015: 181), with almost no understanding of its early chronology, has also sought the emergence of the nucleated 'fermtoun' (or township) in the 10th and 11th centuries AD. This begs the question as to how close the Pitcarmick-type farms were to early townships. Many Pitcarmicks do occur in clusters of buildings (RCAHMS 1990). Of the three excavated buildings at Lair that could be dated by Bayesian modelling, one interpretation suggests all were for a substantial time contemporary (Section 4.5) and there was considerable spatial organisation to the landscape (Section 4.8). There was arable ground as well as pasture, and the construction of byre-houses early in the development of these farms implies manuring of the arable (Section 4.12). What cannot, however, be demonstrated is the separation of a field continuously manured (infield) from one taken in occasionally (outfield), and the separation of these from common grazing, the core structure of townships. Field boundaries themselves cannot be identified, even from LiDAR survey (Banaszek and Cowley: Section 1.8) or cannot be distinguished from later boundaries: enclosed field-systems are mapped at Pitcarmick (Hooper 2002) but their role remains unexplored. And the township that was later to work the land at Lair, Corra-lairig, is markedly dislocated from the 1st millennium farms, as so many are in the region (below).

At some point between the 10th century, when Gaelic was spoken (Section 1.5), and the 16th century when Timothy Pont first records it, the name 'Lair' was given. It can mean either 'site of a building, vestige; ruin' or derive from the Gaelic for 'fork', probably referring to the meeting place of the Allt an Lair and Allt Corra-lairige burns (McNiven 2014). If the former, the Gaelic name could perhaps refer to the ring-cairn, the most

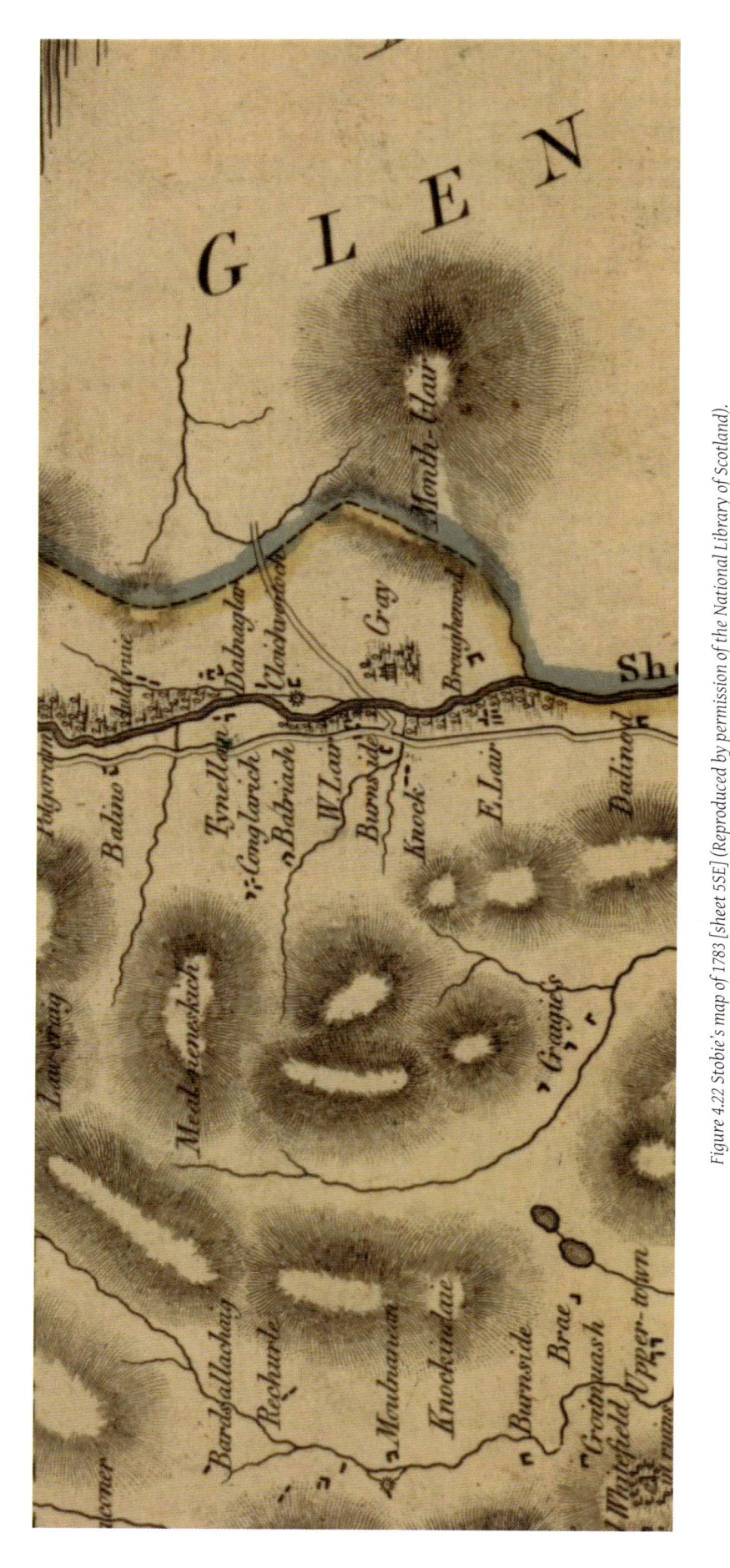

Figure 4.22 Stobie's map of 1783 [sheet 5SE] (Reproduced by permission of the National Library of Scotland).

noticeable 'ruin' in the area, or perhaps to the remains of the Pitcarmick buildings themselves.

Portable finds in House 8 at Carn Dubh were of 11-14th century AD date (Rideout 1995) and Building 6 at Lair produced a sherd of 13-15th century AD pottery (Sections 3.7 and 4.6). Much more substantive activity is seen at Pitcarmick where House C1 is thought to have been re-occupied from AD 1020-1180 and House E1 replaced by house E2 at AD 1020-1220 (Carver *et al.* 2012): land use contemporary with this development is not understood. On Ben Lawers, above Loch Tay, Atkinson (2016) excavated a complex sequence of turf and stone buildings at around 320 m OD, the earliest building abandoned and destroyed in the late 10th century AD, replaced in the 12th century and again at AD 1300-1440 (Atkinson 2016: 86). A likely shieling hut nearby is dated to AD 1395-1470, with another in use from the later 15th century AD. Building 6 at Lair, which yielded the piece of medieval pottery, may also have been a shieling (Section 4.6). It is likely that shieling remains are later than Pitcarmick buildings (Section 4.14) but how much later is not known. They may in the main have also occupied different environmental niches: in north-east Perthshire, shielings are few both below 400 m OD and above 500 m OD (RCAHMS 1990), higher than Pitcarmick buildings.

All the excavated early medieval buildings at Pitcarmick were disturbed by later ploughing, which could not be dated (Carver *et al.* 2012: 155). The mapping at Lair (Banaszek and Cowley: Section 1.8) demonstrates the disfigurement of the upland by very extensive cultivation traces. They are not dated but there are no grounds to suggest that the rig-system here is other than post-medieval in date. The more general context for its cultivation is probably as outfields expanded above the

4. Discussion

main valley, perhaps as population expanded prior to the reorganisation that created the pattern of modern farms. Elsewhere, this sort of expansion carried more permanent settlement onto shieling grounds, as seen in the place-names of deserted townships such as Cro na h-Airighe in the glen above the Spittal of Glen Shee (RCAHMS 1990: 119-20, no. 14). The presence of possible shieling huts at Lair is probably evidence of a similar history. At Lair, the process of expansion eventually 'leap-frogged' these outfields to found a new farmstead by AD 1700 at Corra-lairig (RCAHMS 1990, 151-2, no.16).

Building 11 at Lair (Section 4.6), with its more formally constructed rectangular enclosure is likely to be of 18th or even early 19th century date. The lade, fed by the Allt Corra-lairige and which runs north-east across the slopes at Lair (Figures 1.16 and 2.1) is also probably quite late, though quite where it supplied water to remains unclear. No mills are shown on this side of the glen on any of the county maps, and while roughly following the 350 m contour it could formerly have continued northwards several kilometres, and perhaps into the next catchment of the Allt Coire Leonard was a more likely destination. The only farmstead known here is the house and garden shown here on the 1st edition of the OS 6-inch map and named Tigh an Uillt, the 'house of the stream'. This does not appear on Stobie's 1783 map of Perth and Clackmannan (Figure 4.21), which is thought to record settlement prior to 'clearance' (RCAHMS 1990: 9). Townships were mapped high in the Allt Corra-lairige catchment, one called Corylarich, or Corra-lairig (RCAHMS 1990: 291.16-20), extraordinarily high at 440 m OD (Figure 1.8). The name may appear as yet another corruption as Conglack, in the parish of Kirkmichael: the Perthshire Hearth Tax (1691-1692) notes four "herths" taxed at £2 16 s, plus a further four 'herths' for Jon Spalding and the elder and younger Jacks, and a Kill (?kiln), also taxed at £2 16s (Margaret Borland-Stroyan, *pers comm*). Corra Lairig is recorded archaeologically to have had nine buildings, a corn-drying kiln, several small enclosures and numerous larger fields (ID29511), as large as some townships on the valley floor. It appears ruinous on the 1st edition OS 6" map of 1862-1863, ended by early 19th century depopulation.

Caulfeild's military road through Glen Shee was built 1748-1750 as part of a wider enhancement of the road system between Perth to Braemar, with 300 Welsh Fusiliers beginning work in Blairgowrie and 300 men of General Guise's regiment starting in Braemar with the aim of meeting at Spittal of Glenshee (Farquharson 2011: 21). The very well-preserved stretch of road at Lair (Figures 1.16, 2.1 and 4.23) is a rare survival as for the most part the 18th-century road is now the modern road. The impact of the first road with bridges cannot be underestimated, connecting the glen, the impressive bridge at Spittal of Glenshee a dramatic symbol of this new age.

Figure 4.23 The well-preserved stretch of military road at Lair, dating from c. 1750 (D. Strachan: 2012).

5. Conclusions

5.1 Introduction

This final chapter will begin by considering the threats to the remarkable and valuable archaeological remains at Lair and in the uplands of north-east Perth and Kinross more widely (Section 5.2). The project objectives (Section 1.10) are then reviewed (Section 5.3) and the impact of our results and interpretations assessed with regard to understanding Pitcarmick-type and Pitcarmick-related buildings, their economies and landscapes, and our understanding of their regional, national and international contexts. Some lessons learned are briefly considered in Section 5.4 before some of the many future research opportunities these rich landscapes offer are viewed (Section 5.5).

5.2 Threats to the resource

While the archaeological earthworks at Lair, as elsewhere, are gradually eroding through natural processes, the most immediate threats to the resource are from agricultural practices. At Lair these take the form of animal trampling at feeding points and erosion through increased vehicle access. Comparison of Figure 1.17 with Figures 1.15 and 1.16 confirms that while only a single-track ran through the site in 1978, by the start of the project in 2012 a series of dendritic routes had been added, some of which have track-depths of up to c. 0.5 m. Such an intrusive physical process can very quickly destroy both the shallow and fragile earthworks and buried archaeology confirmed through the excavations: Building 14 is bisected by a track, as is the enclosure of Buildings 7 and 8, while various parallel tracks run very close to Building 1 (Figure 1.16). Elsewhere on the hills, heather burning for grouse continues and, while this can reveal details of archaeological sites in plan, it is unquantified in terms of physical impact on the earthworks and buried remains. These issues could be addressed through increased legal protection as very few Pitcarmick buildings are designated as Scheduled Monuments: indeed none of the structures at Lair have any specific heritage designation.

5.3 The impact of the Glenshee Archaeology Project

In addition to the social, economic and educational benefits of the project, which are outwith the remit of this publication, the results of the project can be assessed against the research objectives set out in Section 1.10:

Define the chronology, phasing and sequence of the construction of the Pitcarmick-type buildings at Lair and establish any temporal relationship between them: are the multiple groups of buildings contemporary or do they represent a sequence of construction over time? Are they contemporary with the buildings at Pitcarmick (Carver et al. 2012)?

The project employed LiDAR technology (Section 1.8) and geophysical survey (Section 2.2) in re-visiting the archaeological field remains at Lair described by RCAHMS in 1990. Excavation of seven buildings and other archaeological features was undertaken in 34 trenches. Archaeology from the second half of the 1st millennium AD was targeted and the relation of the prehistoric ring-cairn to later Pitcarmick buildings was explored. Excavation (Section 2.3) and Bayesian-modelled ^{14}C dating (Section 2.5) successfully showed that Building 3 (and probably 4-5) at Lair were contemporary with the excavated early medieval buildings at Pitcarmick (Carver *et al.* 2012). Significantly, Bayesian modelling also showed that Buildings 1 and 2 at Lair were of early medieval date, albeit probably slightly later.

Define the nature and function of individual buildings; is difference in size and form indicative of function? Were they all dwellings, were some byres, or have specialist functions (e.g. for smithing or craft production)?

Excavation (Section 2.3) found that there was a dynamism of form and construction in the early medieval buildings at Lair, such that functions of particular buildings probably changed through time as the settlement evolved. Excavation and analysis of small finds (Chapter 3) defined spatial patterning of activities in some buildings. Several buildings were used at different times for different purposes but different activities may have occurred at the same time. Detailed analysis proved more problematic, partly the result of poor survival of floor deposits and partly because planned chemical and geo-archaeological analyses were not fulfilled (Section 2.4). However, the project has added weight to the interpretation of Pitcarmick buildings as byre-houses and, significantly, has argued that Pitcarmick buildings, probably with associated outbuildings, were well-planned, highly organised and well-resourced permanent farms (Sections 4.6-4.8; 4.11 and 4.12). The excavation has importantly argued specialist functions for the annexes of Pitcarmick buildings, a defining feature of the site-type previously unrecognised.

Define any evidence of reconstruction, maintenance and abandonment; were individual buildings rebuilt? Were they deliberately destroyed or were they abandoned?

Building 3 has been shown by excavation to have undergone at least one major rebuilding. While it was

5. Conclusions

not possible to identify regular maintenance or partial remodelling at other buildings, it is likely that Buildings 1 and 2 replaced an early structure. There was no sign of deliberate destruction of buildings or the settlement through burning, so abandonment is assumed. The farms were abandoned at the same time as crop cultivation, in the 11th century AD.

Define the relationship of the structures to their wider landscape context: are there nearby working areas, are they set within 'in-field'? Define the contemporary environmental character and extent of related agricultural practices and landholdings? Is it possible to identify contemporary field-systems, clearance cairns and land boundaries? Is there evidence for agriculture or horticulture in close proximity to the structures?

An argument was developed from the spatial organisation of the buildings at Lair (Section 4.8) that they represent individual farm units, separated by natural features like streams, though the kin and economic relations of the communities cannot be reconstructed in the absence of human bone. The uplands were farmed for both crops and livestock: the Pitcarmick buildings at Lair were not early medieval shielings (Sections 4.14 and 4.15). Though permanent farms, evidence for the structure of the contemporary agrarian regime was not forthcoming (Section 4.12), not even for field-boundaries, because the extensive visible cultivation remains (Section 1.8) are later than the early medieval period (Section 4.16).

What was the relationship of the Pitcarmick buildings to the remains of previous periods? Why were these sites chosen for re-occupation in the early medieval period? Is there any evidence for continuity of settlement at the site?

Pitcarmick buildings frequently occur close to prehistoric sites. While this is partly the result of the survival of monuments (Section 1.8), selection of previously occupied sites, with the best soils and already cleared of stones, is also a possible driver (Section 4.3). It is argued, however, that there was no settlement continuity between prehistory and the early medieval period at Lair, and that assumed settlement continuity in other studies is insecurely founded (Section 4.3). The re-structuring of the prehistoric ring-cairn at Lair is suggested as indicating that prehistoric remains were important to Pitcarmick-building communities in their laying claim to land, and in legitimising their occupation.

Finally, the wider research questions for the project were identified as follows:

When and how did the Pitcarmick building tradition emerge? Who built Pitcarmick-type buildings? How does this tradition of upland settlement relate to contemporary lowland settlement systems? How did they relate to wider political and socio-economic systems? Do the settlements represent a particular way of living or a cultural tradition which is distinct from other parts of Scotland in the 1st millennium AD, or is differential preservation in other regions biasing our perception of this tradition? When and why did the tradition end?

The evidence from the excavations at Pitcarmick and Lair strongly suggest that this building tradition emerged in the early-mid 7th century AD (Section 4.5 and *passim*). While the mechanisms behind this remain unclear, it is probable that the adoption of the elongated building form was influenced by external developments, particularly across the North Sea as part of a wider architectural trend in turf building construction across northern Europe (Section 4.10). Before the early-mid 7th century the upper hill pastures at places like Pitcarmick and Lair were thinly occupied, perhaps only visited by herders. At what date the estates and holdings incorporated into the parochial structure were established is unknown, although there is documentary evidence for estate structure, but no early medieval power-centre has been identified in either Glen Shee or Strathardle. We do not know whether re-population of the uplands was promoted or encouraged by the estates or was a movement independent of authority, though we favour the latter. The relation between the, probably more densely populated, lowlands and the uplands remains unclear and, without much more excavation and dating, cannot be satisfactorily modelled (Section 4.11). While arable farming was part of the economy at Lair it is improbable that upland farms had the same arable/pasture balance as those in the rich soils of Strathmore.

Colonisation occurred at a time of climatic amelioration, the end of the 'late antique little ice age' (Section 4.12). This association has led to the suggestion that, far from pushed by population pressure, key elements of the population saw opportunities being created by climate change, and were sufficiently independent, confident and innovative to take advantage of this change (Section 4.14). Choice was possible in where to set up Pitcarmick farms, though full demonstration of this, from environmental variables, is not yet possible (Sections 4.11 and 4.12). This population movement coincided with the local emergence of the Pitcarmick building tradition. Why is, perhaps, the most intriguing question.

It is an open question as to whether the Pitcarmick tradition was local to north-east Perth and Kinross and the wider region. To a considerable extent, the eastern watershed of the River Tay represents a boundary between different late prehistoric architectural elements, and the Cairngorm to the north represents a sharply different environment. Our interpretation is, however, that comparable buildings are found west of the Tay, and new potential examples, though unexcavated, have been cited. The 7th century AD climatic amelioration is suggested to have led to a previously unnoticed agrarian resurgence over most of Scotland (Section 4.13) but it is clear from other parts of Britain that the uplands saw a great diversity of building traditions.

As noted above, the end of the Pitcarmick tradition at Lair coincided with a decisive change in the agricultural economy, as local cereal cultivation ceased in the 11th century AD. If the value of byre-houses was more related to the concentration and transfer of manure to arable ground than to the need to over-winter livestock (Section 4.12), the synchroneity of these two changes is explained. Why crops were no longer grown at Lair is not known. Closer integration with the lowland agricultural economy may have driven this. Socio-political change with the emergence of hunting reserves may have led to de-population. It is unlikely that farming 'failed': abandonment has connotations which are inappropriate to this period and these farms.

5.4 Lessons learned

Turf building are increasingly recognised as a largely unexplored architectural feature in Scottish archaeology, and potentially filling many gaps in the settlement record. The recognition of turf-built Pitcarmick buildings in upland Perth and Kinross from traditional field survey techniques (RCAHMS 1990) was a remarkable achievement and a significant breakthrough. Martin Carver's interpretation and publication in 2012 of John Barrett's and Jane Downes' mid-1990s excavation at Pitcarmick, and the Glenshee Archaeology Project, have done much to further the understanding of these turf buildings.

However, turf buildings in Scotland have proved difficult to identify and excavate. The fragile nature of the construction material and processes of erosion often leads to only very ephemeral surface traces being present, and being ill-defined, often their extent and form can prove problematic for any quantitative classification (Section 4.9). Buried features can be equally problematic. The Glenshee Archaeology Project began with a pilot season to come to terms with the difficulties of excavating sites with little surviving stratigraphy, and this marked only by subtle changes in particle size and colour. The choice in excavation technique between open-areas or trenches, often a question of resource, is critical. Excavation of Building 1 at Lair, completed over years 1 and 2, opened too small an area to allow full interpretation. Though planned, the full gamut of geo-archaeological techniques (chemical mapping of floors and soil micromorphology) was not applied to the excavations: it is recommended that any future work must include these.

Systematic macro-botanical analyses of on-site contexts at Lair were not pursued, partly because of resource costs, but largely because the off-site pollen record was seen to successfully clarify the local agricultural base. Nevertheless, on-site and off-site analyses should go hand-in-hand: they are complementary. Pollen records must be sensitive to the archaeological record: careful consideration of basin size and pollen source area characterised the work at Lair, and this has paid off, but nevertheless the core for analysis was from the centre of a peat basin and not directly adjacent to the farmed mineral soils.

5.5 Potential for future research

At Lair and at other Pitcarmick buildings, excavation and dating of nearby prehistoric archaeological sites might inform discussion on the nature and extent of any prehistoric– early medieval–medieval settlement continuum. It is doubtful, given the short durations of most structures, however, whether continuity can ever be demonstrated. Arguably the exceptionally rich roundhouse archaeology in Glen Shee may prove a valuable contribution, with site-types such as the Dalrulzion form remaining very poorly understood. Such work might prove or disprove notions of a transition from the round to elongated form over the 'long' Iron Age. These are all areas to be considered in the light of the Perth and Kinross Archaeological Research Framework, currently being developed by Perth and Kinross Heritage Trust. However, in this regard it should be noted that while interpreted as later than the early medieval period on the basis of form, excavation of Building 7 failed to produce any definitive dating evidence, emphasising the difficulty of establishing chronology at some buildings. Pollen analysis remains the best way to establish continuity of land use, provided that the temporal resolution of analyses is sufficiently small, though it does not, of course, define continuity of settlement itself.

The exciting synchroneity of the Pitcarmick buildings at Lair and Pitcarmick has allowed the construction of the causal relations between environment and human activity detailed in Chapter 4. The chronological model needs to be tested: this almost goes without saying. One test would be the systematic ^{14}C dating and Bayesian modelling of more contexts at Pitcarmick: how synchronous were developments at the two farms? Another is by excavation of other Pitcarmick buildings or clusters: repeating and trying to replicate the data of the Glenshee Archaeology Project: it is probable that many of these sites are under similar threats to Lair. Equally, more careful analyses of contemporary land use around other Pitcarmick buildings are urgently needed. The extraordinary array of field-systems at Pitcarmick itself, for instance, remain uninvestigated. How typical of the uplands was the agricultural regime defined at Lair? There remains the nagging thought that Lair, being lower and warmer than most other Pitcarmick farms, was also slightly different.

References

Adam, R.J. (ed.) 1960. *John Home's Survey of Assynt* (Scottish Historical Society 3rd Series, vol. 52). Edinburgh: Scottish Historical Society.

Alcock, L. 1987. Pictish studies: Present and future, in A. Small (ed.) *The Picts: A new look at old problems*: 80-92. Dundee: University of Dundee Department of Geography.

Alcock, L. 2003. *Kings and Warriors, Craftsmen and Priests in Northern Britain AD 550-850*. Edinburgh: Society of Antiquaries of Scotland.

Alcock, L. and Alcock E.A. 1987. Reconnaissance excavations on Early Historic fortifications and other royal sites in Scotland, 1974-84: 2. Excavations at Dunollie Castle, Oban, Argyll, 1978. *Proceedings of the Society of Antiquaries of Scotland* 117: 119-147.

Alcock L., Alcock E. and Driscoll S.T. 1989. Reconnaissance excavations on Early Historic fortifications and other royal sites in Scotland, 1974–84: 3. Excavations at Dundurn, Strathearn, Perthshire, 1976–77. *Proceedings of the Society of Antiquaries of Scotland* 119: 189–226.

Allen N.G. 1979. Walling materials in the eighteenth century Highlands. *Scottish Vernacular Buildings Working Group* Newsletter 5: 1–7.

Andersen, C.B.H. and Olsen A.L.H. 2014. Medieval turf houses in Jutland, Denmark: a regional building practice?, in M.S. Kristiansen and K. Giles (eds) *Dwellings, Identities and Homes: European Housing Culture from the Viking Age to the Renaissance*. Hojbjerg, Denmark.

Andersen, S. Th. 1979. Identification of wild grasses and cereal pollen. *Danmarks Geologiske Undersögelse* Årbog 1978: 69-92.

Anderson, A.O. and Anderson, M.O. 1961. *Adomnan's Life of Columba*. Edinburgh.

Anderson, S. and Rees, A.R. 2006. The excavation of a large double-chambered souterrain at Ardownie Farm, Monifieth, Angus. *Tayside and Fife Archaeological Journal* 12: 14-60.

Anderson S. and Suddaby, I. forthcoming *An Upland Anglian Settlement at Kersons Cleugh, near Longformacus, Scottish Borders*. Edinburgh: Scottish Archaeological Internet Report.

Apted, M.R. 1963. Excavation at Kildrummy Castle, Aberdeenshire, 1952-62. *Proceedings of the Society of Antiquaries of Scotland* 96: 208-236.

Armit, I. 1999. The abandonment of souterrains: evolution, catastrophe or dislocation? *Proceedings of the Society of Antiquaries of Scotland* 129: 577-596.

Armit, I. 2002. Land and freedom: implications of Atlantic Scottish settlement patterns for Iron Age land-holding and social organisation, in B. Ballin Smith and I. Banks (eds) *In the Shadow of the Brochs: The Iron Age in Scotland*. Stroud: Tempus.

Armit, I. and McKenzie, J. 2013. *An Inherited Place: Broxmouth Hillfort and the South-East Scottish Iron Age*. Edinburgh: Society of Antiquaries of Scotland.

Armstrong, R.A. 1825. *A Gaelic Dictionary*. London: J. Moyes at the Temple Printing Office.

Ashmore, P.J. 1999. Radiocarbon dating: avoiding errors by avoiding mixed samples. *Antiquity* 73: 124-130.

Atkinson, J.A. 2016. *Ben Lawers: An Archaeological Landscape in Time. Results from the Ben Lawers Historic Landscape Project, 1996–2005*. Scottish Archaeological Internet Reports 62. DOI: 10.9750/issn.1473-3803.2016.62 (accessed 30.7.19).

Atkinson, J., Duffy, P. and MacGregor, G. 2003. Rannoch Archaeological Project 2001 Pilot Season. Unpublished data structure report.

Ayers, B. 2016. *The German Ocean: Medieval Europe around the North Sea*. Sheffield: Equinox Publishing.

Bailey, L. 2014. Excavation and survey in advance of the Griffin Wind Farm, Aberfeldy, Perth and Kinross. *Tayside and Fife Archaeological Journal* 19-20: 20-35.

Baker, A., Hellstrom, J.C., Kelly, B.F.G., Mariethos, G. and Trouet, V. 2015. A composite annual-resolution stalagmite record of North Atlantic climate over the last three millennia. *Scientific Reports* 5, 10307; DOI: 10.1038/srep10307 (accessed 30.7.19).

Baldwin Brown, G. 1915. Notes on a necklace of glass beads found in a cist in Dalmeny Park, South Queensferry. *Proceedings of the Society of Antiquaries of Scotland* 49: 332-338.

Banaszek, Ł., Cowley, D.C. and Middleton, M. 2018. Towards national archaeological mapping. Assessing source data and methodology—a case study from Scotland. *Geosciences* 8, 272: 1-17. DOI: 10.3390/geosciences8080272 (accessed 30.7.19).

Banham, D. and Faith, R. 2014. *Anglo-Saxon Farms and Farming*. Oxford: Oxford University Press.

Bantelmann, A. 1955. *Tofting, Eine Vorgeschichtliche Warft an Der Eidermündung*. Offa-Bücher 12.

Barber, J.W. 1981. Excavations on Iona, 1979. *Proceedings of the Society of Antiquaries of Scotland* 111: 282-380.

Barber, J. 1998. *The Archaeological Investigation of a Prehistoric Landscape: Excavations on Arran 1978-1981*. Edinburgh: Scottish Trust for Archaeological Research.

Barber, J.W. and Crone, B.A. 2001. The duration of structures, settlements and sites: some evidence from Scotland, in B. Raftery and J. Hickey (eds) *Recent Developments in Wetland Research* (Occasional Paper 14): 69-86. Dublin: WARP.

Barclay, G. 2001. The excavation of an early medieval enclosure at Upper Gothens, Meikleour, Perthshire. *Tayside and Fife Archaeological Journal* 7: 34-44.

Barclay, G.J. and Maxwell, G.S. 1998. *The Cleaven Dyke and Littleour. Monuments in the Neolithic of Tayside*. (Society of Antiquaries of Scotland Monograph Series 13). Edinburgh: Society of Antiquaries of Scotland.

Barrett, J.C. and Downes, J. 1993. North Pitcarmick (Kirkmichael parish). *Discovery and Excavation Scotland 1993*: 102-103.

Barrett, J.C. and Downes, J. 1994. North Pitcarmick (Kirkmichael parish). *Discovery and Excavation Scotland 1994*: 87-88.

Barrow, G.W.S. 1998. The uses of place-names and Scottish history – pointers and pitfalls, in S. Taylor (ed.) *The Uses of Place-Names*: 54-74. Edinburgh: Scottish Cultural.

Batey, C. and Freeman, C. 1986. Lavacroon, Orphir, Orkney. *Proceedings of the Society of Antiquaries of Scotland* 116: 285-300.

Bayley, J., Dungworth, D. and Paynter, S. 2001. *Archaeometallurgy*. Swindon: Centre for Archaeology Guidelines.

Bell, J.N.B. and Tallis, J.H. 1973. Biological flora of the British Isles. *Empetrum nigrum* L. *Journal of Ecology* 61: 289-305.

Bennett, K.D. 1989. A provisional map of forest types for the British Isles 5000 years ago. *Journal of Quaternary Science* 4: 141-144.

Bennett, K.D. 1994. *Annotated Catalogue of Pollen and Pteridophyte Spore Types of the British Isles*. Department of Plant Sciences, University of Cambridge.

Bennett, K.D. 1996. Late-Quaternary vegetation dynamics of the Cairngorms. *Botanical Journal of Scotland* 48: 51-64.

Beresford, G. 1979. Three deserted medieval settlements on Dartmoor: a report on the late E. Marie Minter's excavations. *Medieval Archaeology* 23: 98–158. doi.org/10.5284/1000320

Berson, B. 2002. A contribution to the study of the medieval Icelandic farm: the byres. *Archaeological Islandica* 2: 34-60.

Beug, H.J. 2004. *Leitfaden Der Pollenbestimmung Fur Mitteleuropa Und Angrenzende Gebiete (Manual for Classification of Western and Central European Pollen Floras)*. Munich: Verlag Friedrich Pfeil.

Bil, A. 1990. *The Shieling 1600-1840. The Case of the Central Scottish Highlands*. Edinburgh: John Donald.

Bil, A. 1992. Transhumance place-names in Perthshire. *Proceedings of the Society of Antiquaries of Scotland* 122: 382-402.

Birks, H.J.B. 1989. Holocene isochrone maps and patterns of tree-spreading in the British Isles. *Journal of Biogeography* 16: 503-540.

Black, S., Strachan, D. and Sneddon, D. 2017. *Glenshee Archaeology Project 2017*. Data Structure Report. Northlight Heritage Report 192 for Perth and Kinross Heritage Trust.

Blackford, J.J. and Chambers, F.M. 1991. Proxy records of climate from blanket mires: evidence for a Dark Age (1400 BP) climatic deterioration in the British Isles. *The Holocene* 1: 63-67.

Blackmore, S., Steinmann, J.A.J., Hoen, P.P. and Punt, W. 2003. The Northwest European pollen flora, 65: Betulaceae and Corylaceae. *Review of Palaeobotany and Palynology, (The Northwest European Pollen Flora, VIII,)* 123: 71-98.

Blair, J. 2018. *Building Anglo-Saxon England*. Princeton: Princeton University Press.

Blakelock, E.S. and McDonnell, G. 2007. A review of the metallographic analysis of Early Medieval knives. *Historical Metallurgy* 41(1): 40-56.

Bohncke, S. 1981. Pollen analysis of the Lochan Mor section, in J. Barber (ed.) Excavations on Iona, 1979. *Proceedings of the Society of Antiquaries of Scotland* 111: 368-370.

Bronk Ramsey, C. 1995. Radiocarbon calibration and analysis of stratigraphy: The OxCal program. *Radiocarbon* 37(2): 425-430.

Bronk Ramsey, C. 1998. Probability and dating. *Radiocarbon* 40(1): 461-474.

Bronk Ramsey, C. 2001. Development of the radiocarbon calibration program. *Radiocarbon* 43(2A): 355-363.

Bronk Ramsey, C. 2009a. Bayesian analysis of radiocarbon dates. *Radiocarbon* 51(1): 337-360.

Bronk Ramsey, C. 2009b. Dealing with outliers and offsets in radiocarbon dating. *Radiocarbon* 51(3): 1023-1045.

Bronk Ramsey, C. 2017. *OxCal v4.3.2*. Oxford: Oxford Radiocarbon Accelerator Unit.

Brooks, S.J. 1996. Three thousand years of environmental history in a Cairngorms lochan revealed by analysis of non-biting midges (Insecta: Diptera: Chironomidae). *Botanical Journal of Scotland* 48: 89-98.

Broström, A., Nielsen, A.B., Gaillard, M., Hjelle, K., Mazier, F., Binney, H. *et al*. 2008. Pollen productivity estimates of key European plant taxa for quantitative reconstruction of past vegetation: a review. *Vegetation History and Archaeobotany*, 17: 461-478.

Broun, D. 2015. Statehood and lordship in 'Scotland' before the mid-twelfth century. *Innes Review* 66 (1): 1-71.

Brown, D. 2012. The seven kingdoms in *De situ Albanie*: a record of Pictish political geography or imaginary map of ancient *Albanie*?, in E.J. Cowan and R.A. MacDonald (eds) *Alba. Celtic Scotland in the Middle Ages*: 24-42. East Linton: Tuckwell Press.

Brugmann, B. 2004. *Glass Beads from Early Anglo-Saxon Graves*. Oxford: Oxbow Books.

Buck, C.E., Cavanagh, W.G. and Litton, C.D. 1996. *Bayesian Approach to Interpreting Archaeological Data*. Chichester: Wiley.

Büntgen, U., Myglan, V.S., Ljungqvis, F.C., McCormick, M., Di Cosmo, N., Sigl, M., Jungclaus, J., Wagner, S., Krusic, P.J., Esper, J. Kaplan, O., de Vaan, M.A.C., Luterbacher, J., Wacker, L., Tegel, W. Kirdyanov, A.V. *et al.* 2016. Cooling and societal change during the Late Antique Little Ice Age from 536 to around 660 AD. *Nature Geoscience* 9: 231-236.

Bunting, M.J., Schofield, J.E. and Edwards, K.J. 2013. Estimates of relative pollen productivity (RPP) for selected taxa from southern Greenland: A pragmatic solution. *Review of Palaeobotany and Palynology* 190: 66-74.

Bunting, M.J. and Tipping, R. 2004. Complex hydroseral vegetation succession and 'dryland' pollen signals: a case study from north-west Scotland. *Holocene* 14: 53-63.

Campbell, E. 1991. Excavations of a wheelhouse and other Iron Age structures at Sollas, North Uist, by R J C Atkinson in 1957. *Proceedings of the Society of Antiquaries of Scotland* 121: 117–173.

Campbell, E. 1996. The archaeological evidence for external contacts: imports, trade and economy in Celtic Britain AD 400-800, in K.R. Dark (ed.) *External contacts and the economy of late Roman and Post-Roman Britain*: 83-96. Woodbridge: Boydell Press.

Campbell, E. 1998. The spearhead, in N. Sharples (ed.) *Scalloway. A Broch, Late Iron Age Settlement and Medieval Cemetery in Shetland*: Oxford: Oxbow.

Campbell, E. 2007. *Continental and Mediterranean imports to Atlantic Britain and Ireland, AD 400-800* (Council for British Archaeology Research Report No 157). York: Council for British Archaeology.

Campbell, E. 2009. Anglo-Saxon/Gaelic interaction in Scotland, in J. Graham-Campbell and M. Ryan (eds) *Anglo-Saxon Irish relations before the Vikings. Proceedings of the British Academy* 157: 253-263.

Canti, M.G. and Linford, N. 2000. The effects of fire on archaeological soils and sediments. *Proceedings of the Prehistoric Society* 66: 385-396.

Cappers, R.T.J., Bekker, R.M. and Jans, J.E.A. 2006. *Digital Seed Atlas of the Netherlands*. (Groningen Archaeological Studies 4). Eelde: Barkhuis Publishing.

Carter, S., Dalland, M. and Long, D. 2005. *Early Land-use and Landscape Development in Arisaig*. Edinburgh: Scottish Archaeological Internet Report 15.

Carter, S., Tipping, R., Davidson, D., Long, D. and Tyler, A. 1997. A multi-proxy approach to the function of post-medieval ridge-and-furrow cultivation in upland northern Britain. *Holocene*: 447-456.

Carver, M. 2008. *Portmahomack: Monastery of the Picts*. Edinburgh: Edinburgh University Press.

Carver, M. 2019. *Formative Britain: An Archaeology of Britain, Fifth to Eleventh Century AD*. Routledge Archaeology of Northern Europe. London and New York: Routledge.

Carver M., Barrett J., Downes J. and Hooper J. 2012. Pictish byre-houses at Pitcarmick and their landscape: investigations 1993–5. *Proceedings of the Society of Antiquaries of Scotland* 142: 145-199. doi.org/10.5284/1000184

Carver, M., Downes, J. and Barrett J. 2013. *Pitcarmick Excavations 1993-5* [data-set]. York: Archaeology Data Service [distributor] doi.org/10.5284/1021677

Carver, M., J. Garner-Lahire, and C. Spall. 2016. *Portmahomack on Tarbat Ness: Changing Ideologies in North-East Scotland, Sixth to Sixteenth Century AD*. Edinburgh: Society of Antiquaries of Scotland.

Carver, M. and Spall, C. 2004. An Iona of the East: the early medieval monastery at Portmahomack, Tarbat Ness. *Medieval Archaeology* 48: 1-30.

Caseldine, C.J. 1979. Early land clearance in south-east Perthshire. *Scottish Archaeological Forum* 9: 1-15.

Cavers, G. and Crone, A. 2017. *A lake dwelling in its landscape. Iron Age settlement at Cults Loch, Castle Kennedy, Dumfries and Galloway*. Oxford: Oxbow.

Chapelot, J. and Fossier, R. (transl Cleere, H.) 1985. *The Village & House in the Middle Ages*. London: Batsford.

Charman, D.J., Blundell, A., Chiverrell, R.C., Hendon, D. and Langdon, P.G. 2006. Compilation of non-annually resolved Holocene proxy climate records: stacked Holocene peatland palaeo-water table reconstructions from northern Britain. *Quaternary Science Reviews* 25: 336-350.

Cheape, H. 2014. 'Every timber in the forest for MacRae's house': Creel houses in the Highlands. *Vernacular Building* 37: 31-50.

Cheyette, F.L. 2008. The disappearance of the ancient landscape and the climatic anomaly of the early Middle Ages: a question to be pursued. *Early Medieval Europe* 16: 127-165.

Christie H. 2014. Got swag? Investigating beads and bead trade in Scotland in the first millennium AD. Unpublished M. Litt. thesis, University of Glasgow.

Clarke, D.V. 2007. Reading the multiple lives of Pictish symbol stones. *Medieval Archaeology* 51:1, 19-39, DOI: 10.1179/174581707x224642

Clarke, D., Blackwell, A. and Goldberg, M. 2012. *Early Medieval Scotland. Individuals, communities and ideas*. Edinburgh: National Museums Scotland.

Close-Brooks, J. 1986. Excavations at Clatchard Craig, Fife. *Proceedings of the Society of Antiquaries of Scotland* 116: 117-184.

Colchester Treasure Hunting & Metal Detecting. 2017. *Spindle-Whorls*. Viewed 17 February 2017: http://www.colchestertreasurehunting.co.uk/spindlewhorls.html

Coleman, R. and Hunter, F. 2002. The excavation of a souterrain at Shanzie Farm, Alyth, Perthshire. *Tayside and Fife Archaeological Journal* 8: 77-101.

Cook, M. 2013a. Paradigms, assumptions, enclosure and violence: the hillforts of Strathdon. *Journal of Conflict Archaeology* 8(2): 77-105.

Cook, M. 2013b. Open or enclosed: Settlement patterns and hillfort construction in Strathdon, Aberdeenshire, 1800 BC- AD1000. *Proceedings of the Prehistoric Society* 79: 327-352.

Cook, M. and Dunbar, L. 2008. *Rituals, Roundhouses and Romans: Excavations at Kintore, Aberdeenshire 2000–2006, Volume 1 Forest Road* (STAR Monograph 8). Edinburgh: Scottish Trust for Archaeological Research.

Cottam, M.B. and Small, A. 1974. The distribution of settlement in Pictland. *Medieval Archaeology* 18(1): 43-65.

Cowgill, J., Neergaard, M. and Griffiths, N. 1987. *Knives and Scabbards*. Medieval Finds from Excavations in London 1. London: Her Majesty's Stationery Office.

Cowley, D.C. 1997. Archaeological landscapes in Strathbraan, Perthshire. *Tayside and Fife Archaeological Journal* 3: 161-175.

Cowley, D.C. and Harrison, J. 2001. *'Well shelterd and watered': Menstrie Glen, a farming landscape near Stirling*. Edinburgh: RCAHMS.

Crawford, B.E. 1987. *Scandinavian Scotland*. Leicester: Leicester University Press.

Crew, P. 2006. Metalworking residues and processes, in L. Laing and D. Longley (eds) *The Mote of Mark: a Dark Age hillfort in south-west Scotland*: 36-39. Oxford: Oxbow Books.

Crone, A. and Campbell, E. 2005. *A crannog of the 1st millennium AD. Excavations by Jack Scott at Loch Glashan, Argyll, 1960*. Edinburgh: Society of Antiquaries of Scotland.

Crone, A. and Watson, F. 2003. Sufficiency to scarcity: Medieval Scotland, 500-1600, in T.C. Smout (ed), *People and Woods in Scotland. A History*: 60-81. Edinburgh: Edinburgh University Press.

Cruickshank, G.D.R. 2012. The battle of Dunnichen and the Aberlemno battle-scene, in E.J. Cowan and R.A. MacDonald (eds) *Alba. Celtic Scotland in the Middle Ages*: 69-88. East Linton: Tuckwell Press.

Cruickshanks, G. and McLaren, D. forthcoming. The vitrified material from Culduthel Farm phases 7 and 8, in C. Hatherley and R. Murray (eds) *Culduthel: An Iron Age Craft Centre in North-East Scotland*. Edinburgh: Society of Antiquaries of Scotland.

Crumlin-Pedersen, O. 2010. *Archaeology and the Sea in Scandinavia and Britain: A Personal Account*. Maritime Culture of the North 3 (first delivered as Rhind Lectures to the Society of Antiquaries of Scotland in 2008). Roskilde: The Viking Ship Museum.

Curle, C.L. 1982. *Pictish and Norse finds from the Brough of Birsay 1934-74* (Society of Antiquaries of Scotland Monograph Series No. 1). Edinburgh: Society of Antiquaries.

Dalgleish, C. 2012. Scotland's Medieval countryside: evidence, interpretation, perception, in N. Christie and P. Stamper (eds) *Medieval Rural Settlement. Britain and Ireland, AD800-1600*: 270-282. Oxford: Oxbow.

Daubney A. 2010. LIN-D92A22: *A Early Medieval Spindle Whorl*. Viewed 1 November 2016: https://finds.org.uk/database/artefacts/record/id/409249

Davies, F.M. 1997. Holocene Palaeoenvironmental Studies in the Oban Region, Western Scotland. Unpublished PhD thesis, Newcastle upon Tyne.

Davies, A.L. and Tipping, R. 2004. Sensing small-scale human activity in the palaeoecological record: fine spatial resolution pollen analyses from West Glen Affric, northern Scotland. *Holocene* 14: 233-245.

Dijkstra, H. 1996. De tuinwal op het eiland Texel. *Jaarboek Monumentenzorg*, no. Monumenten en bouwhistorie: 140–48.

Dijkstra, M.F.P. 2011. Rondom de Mondingen van Rijn & Maas: Landschap En Bewoning Tussen de 3e En 9e Eeuw in Zuid-Holland, in Het Bijzonder de Oude Rijnstreek. Academisch proefschrift, Leiden: Universiteit van Amsterdam.

Dixon, N. 2004. *The Crannogs of Scotland*. Stroud: Tempus.

Dixon, P. 2002. The medieval peasant building in Scotland: the beginning and end of crucks, in J. Klapste (ed.) *The Rural House from the Migration Period to the Oldest Standing Buildings*: 187-200. Prague: Ruralia IV, Pamatky Archeologicke.

Dixon, P. 2017. Rural settlement patterns on the ground, in K.J. Stringer and A.J.L. Winchester (eds) *Northern England and Southern Scotland in the Central Middle Ages*. Woodbridge: The Boydell Press.

Dixon, P. 2018. What do we really know about transhumance in Medieval Scotland, in C. Costello and E. Svensson (eds) *Historical Archaeologies of Transhumance across Europe*. London: Routledge (no page numbers: e-book consulted).

Dodgshon, R.A. 1998. *From Chiefs to Landlords. Social and Economic Change in the Western Highlands and Islands, c. 1493-1820*. Edinburgh: Edinburgh University Press.

Dodgshon, R.A. 2008. Bones, bows and byres: early dairying in the Scottish Highlands and Islands, in P. Rainbird (ed.) *Monuments in the Landscape*: 165-176. Stroud: Tempus.

Dodgshon, R.A. 2015. *No Stone Unturned. A history of Farming, Landscape and Environment in the Scottish Highlands and Islands*. Edinburgh: Edinburgh University Press.

Dobney, K. and Rielly, K. 1988. A method for recording archaeological animal bones. *Circaea* 5: 79–96.

Driscoll, S.T. 1997. Pictish settlement in North-East Fife: the Scottish Field School of Archaeology excavations at Easter Kinnear. *Tayside and Fife Archaeological Journal* 3: 74-118.

Driscoll, S. 1998. Formalising the mechanisms of state formation: early Scottish lordship from the ninth to the thirteenth centuries, in S. Foster, A. MacInnes and R. MacInnes (eds) *Scottish Power Centres: from the early middle ages to the 20th century*: 32-58. Glasgow: Cruithne.

Driscoll, S.T. 2011. Pictish archaeology: persistent problems and structural solutions, in S. Driscoll, J. Geddes and M. Hall (eds) *Pictish Progress: New Studies on Northern Britain in the Early Middle Ages*: 245-279. Leiden: Brill.

Driscoll, S., Brophy, K. and Noble, G. 2010. The Strathearn Environs and Royal Forteviot project (SERF). *Antiquity*, 84(323).

Dumayne, L. 1993a. Iron Age and Roman vegetation clearance in northern Britain: further evidence. *Botanical Journal of Scotland* 46: 385-392.

Dumayne, L. 1993b. Invader or native? - vegetation clearance in northern Britain during Romano-British time. *Vegetation History and Archaeobotany* 1993: 29-36.

Dumayne-Peaty, L. 1999a. Late Holocene human impact on the vegetation of southeastern Scotland: a pollen diagram from Dogden Moss, Berwickshire. *Review of Palaeobotany and Palynology* 105: 121-141.

Dumayne-Peaty, L. 1999b. Continuity or discontinuity? Vegetation change in the Hadrianic-Antonine frontier zone of northern Britain at the end of the Roman occupation. *Journal of Biogeography* 26: 643-655.

Dunbar, E., Cook, G.T., Naysmith, P., Tripney, B.G. and Xu, S. 2016. AMS 14C dating at the Scottish Universities Environmental Research Centre (SUERC) Radiocarbon Dating Laboratory. *Radiocarbon* 58(1): 9-23.

Duncan, A.A.M. 1975. *Scotland, The Making of the Kingdom*. Edinburgh: Oliver and Boyd.

Duncan, H.B. and Spearman, R.M. 1984. Small finds, in P. Yeoman. Excavation at Castlehill of Strachan, 1980-81: 354-360. *Proceedings of the Society of Antiquaries of Scotland* 114: 315-364.

Dungworth, D. and Wilkes, R. 2009. Understanding hammerscale: the use of high-speed film and electron microscopy. *Historical Metallurgy* 43.1: 33–46.

Dunwell, A. and Coles, G. 1998. Archaeological and palynological investigations on the Antonine Wall near Glasgow Bridge, Kirkintilloch. *Proceedings of the Society of Antiquaries of Scotland* 128: 461-480.

Durno, S.E. 1962. Pollen analysis of peat, in M.E.C. Stewart. The excavation of two circular enclosures at Dalnaglar, Perthshire: 154-158. *Proceedings of the Society of Antiquaries of Scotland* 95: 134-158.

Edmonds, M. 1995. *Stone Tools in Society: Working Stone in Neolithic and Bronze Age Britain*. London: Routledge.

Edvardsson, R., and McGovern. T.H. 2005. Archaeological Excavations at Vatnsfjörður 2003-2004. *Archaeologica Islandica* 4: 16–30.

Edwards, K.J. 1981. The separation of *Corylus* and *Myrica* pollen in modern and fossil samples. *Pollen et Spores* 23: 205-218.

Edwards, K.J. 1998. Detection of human impact on the environment: palynological views, in J. Bayley (ed.) *Science and Archaeology: An Agenda for the Future*: 69-88. London: English Heritage.

Edwards, K.J. and Whittington, G. 1998. The palaeoenvironmental background: pollen studies at Rae Loch, in G.J. Barclay and G.S. Maxwell (eds) *The Cleaven Dyke and Littleour. Monuments in the Neolithic of Tayside* (Society of Antiquaries of Scotland Monograph Series 13: 5-12. Edinburgh: Society of Antiquaries of Scotland.

Edwards, T.W.D., Hammarlund, D., Newton, B.W., Sjolte, J., Linderson, H. Sturm, C., St. Amour, J.A., Bailey, J.N-L. and Nilsson, A.L. 2017. Seasonal variability in Northern Hemisphere atmospheric circulation during the Medieval Climate Anomaly and the Little Ice Age. *Quaternary Science Reviews* 165: 102-110.

Egan, G. 2010. *The Medieval Household. Daily living c.1150-c.1450. Medieval finds from excavations in London Volume 6*. London: Boydell Press/Museum of London. 2nd Ed.

Egan, G. and Pritchard, F. 1991. *Dress Accessories c. 1150-1450. Medieval finds from excavations in London Volume 3*. London: Stationery Office/Museum of London.

Ellis, C. 2017. Monks, priests and farmers: a community research excavation at Baliscate, Isle of Mull. *Scottish Archaeological Internet Report* 68.

Evans, E.E. 1969. Sod and turf houses in Ireland, in J.G. Jenkins (ed.) *Studies in Folk Life - Essays in Honour of Iowerth C. Peate*: 80-90. London: Routledge & Kegan Paul.

Fairhurst, H. 1939. The galleried dun at Kildonan Bay, Kintyre. *Proceedings of the Society of Antiquaries of Scotland* 73: 185-228.

Farquharson, L. 2011. *General Wade's Legacy: the 18th century military road system in Perthshire*. Perth: Perth and Kinross Heritage Trust.

Favre, E., Escarguel, G., Suc, J., Thévenod, G. and Thévenod, L. 2008. A contribution to deciphering the meaning of AP/NAP with respect to vegetation cover. *Review of Palaeobotany and Palynology* 148: 13-35.

Fellows-Jensen, G. 1985. Scandinavian settlement in Cumbria and Dumfriesshire: The place-name evidence, in J.R. Baldwin and I.D. Whyte (eds) *The Scandinavians in Cumbria*: 65-82. Edinburgh: Scottish Society for Northern Studies.

Fenton, A. 1968. Alternating stone and turf - an obsolete building practice. *Folk Life* 6: 94-103.

Fenton, A. 1982. The longhouse in Northern Scotland, in B. Myhre, B. Stoklund and P. Gjærder (eds) *Vestnordisk Byggeskikk Gjennom to Tusen År: Tradisjon og Forandring fra Romertid til det 19. Århundre*: 231-240. Stavanger: Arkeologisk museum i Stavanger.

Fenton, A. and Walker, B. 1981. *The Rural Architecture of Scotland*. Edinburgh: John Donald.

Ferreiro, A., Mesones, J., Meynet, A., Muñoz, N., Palumbo, B., Radi, C. and Vázquez, G. 2014. *Construir con terrón: de la tierra a la experiencia (Building with turf: from the earth to the experience)*. Montevideo: MEC.

Finlayson, B. 1990. The examination of surface alteration, in C. R. Wickham-Jones (ed.), *Rhum, Mesolithic and later sites at Kinloch: Excavations 1982-86*: 53-54. Edinburgh: Edinburgh University Press.

Fitter, A.J. 1978. *An Atlas of the Wild Flowers of Britain and Northern Europe*. London: Collins.

Forbes, V., and Milek, K. 2014. Insects, activity areas and turf buildings' interiors: An ethno-archaeoentomological case study from 19th to Early 20th-Century Þverá, northeast Iceland'. *Quaternary*

International 341: 195–215. doi.org/10.1016/j.quaint.2013.10.014

Ford, B. 1987. The iron objects, in P. Holdsworth. *Excavations in the medieval burgh of Perth 1979-81*: 130-141. Edinburgh: Society of Antiquaries of Scotland.

Foreman, M. 1998. iv. Whorls (Graves 11, 17B, 142), in G. Drinkall, M. Foreman and M.G. Welch (eds) *The Anglo-Saxon Cemetery at Castledyke South, Barton-on-Humber*. London: Bloomsbury.

Forsyth, K. 1995. The Ogham-inscribed spindle-whorl from Buckquoy: evidence for the Irish language in Pre-Viking Orkney? *Proceedings of the Society of Antiquaries of Scotland* 125: 677-696.

Forsyth, K. 1996. The Ogham Inscriptions of Scotland: An Edited Corpus. Unpublished PhD thesis, Harvard University.

Forsyth, K. 2005. Origins: Scotland to 1100, in J. Wormald (ed.) *Scotland: A History*. Oxford: Oxford University Press.

Foster, S.M. 1989. Aspects of the late Iron Age, Vols I and II. Unpublished PhD thesis, University of Glasgow.

Foster, S.M. 1990. Pins, combs and the chronology of later Atlantic Iron Age settlement, in I. Armit (ed.) *Beyond the Brochs. Changing perspectives on the later Iron Age in Atlantic Scotland*: 143-174. Edinburgh: Edinburgh University Press.

Foster, S.M. 2004. *Picts, Gaels and Scots*. London: Batsford. 2nd Ed.

Fowler, P. 2002. *Farming in the First Millennium AD. British Agriculture between Julius Caesar and William the Conqueror*. Cambridge: Cambridge University Press.

Fox, H. 2012. *Dartmoor's Alluring Uplands*. Exeter: Exeter University Press.

Franklin, J. and Goodall, I. 2012. The iron, in *Perth High Street: Archaeological Excavation 1975-1977, The excavations at 75-95 High Street and 5-10 Mill Street, Fascicule 2- Ceramics, metalwork, religious and wooden object*: 123-188. Perth: Tayside and Fife Archaeological Committee.

Fraser, I.A. 1987. Pictish place-names – some toponymic evidence, in A. Small (ed.) *The Picts: A new look at old problems*: 68-72. Dundee: University of Dundee Department of Geography.

Fraser, I. and Halliday, S. 2007. The early Medieval landscape, in RCAHMS. *In the Shadow of Bennachie. A Field Archaeology of Donside, Aberdeenshire*: 115-135. Edinburgh: Society of Antiquaries of Scotland and RCAHMS.

Fraser, J.E. 2006. *The Pictish Conquest. The Battle of Dunnichen 685 and the Birth of Scotland*. Stroud: Tempus.

Fraser, J.E. 2009. *From Caledonia to Pictland: Scotland to 795*. Edinburgh: Edinburgh University Press.

Gailey, A. 1984. *Rural Houses of the North of Ireland*. Edinburgh: John Donald.

Gardiner, M. 2018. The changing character of transhumance in early and later Medieval England, in C. Costello and E. Svensson (eds) *Historical Archaeologies of Transhumance across Europe*. London: Routledge (no page numbers: e-book consulted).

Gilbert, J.M. 1979. *Hunting and Hunting Reserves in Medieval Scotland*. Edinburgh: John Donald.

Gimingham, C.H. 1995. Heaths and moorland: an overview of ecological change, in D.B.A. Thompson, A.J. Hester and M.B. Usher (eds) *Heaths and Moorland: Cultural Landscapes*: 9-20. Edinburgh: Her Majesty's Stationery Office.

Glenshee Archaeology Project: Exploring Early Medieval Turf Longhouses. Viewed 2 May 2017 http://www.socantscot.org/research-project/glenshee-archaeology-project-exploring-early-medieval-turf-longhouses/

Goodall, I.H. 1990. Knives, in M. Biddle (ed) *Winchester Studies. Artefacts from medieval Winchester. Part ii. Object and economy in medieval Winchester*: 835-860. Oxford: Clarendon Press.

Goodall, I.H. 2011. *Ironwork in medieval Britain. An archaeological study* (Society of Medieval Archaeology Monograph No. 31). London: Society of Medieval Archaeology.

Goslinga, M. 2017. Beelden van Armoede: Fotografie van de Plaggenhutten Op Het Aardscheveld En Lombok Bij Assen Tussen 1896 En 1933. *Nieuwe Drentse Volksalmanak* 2017: 1–44.

Govan, S. (ed.) 2003. *Medieval or Later Rural Settlement in Scotland: 10 Years On*. Edinburgh: Historic Scotland.

Graham-Campbell, J. and Batey, C.E. 1998. *Vikings in Scotland. An archaeological survey*. Edinburgh: Edinburgh University Press.

Grant, A. 1982. The use of tooth wear as a guide to the age of domestic ungulates, in B. Wilson, C. Grigson and S. Payne (eds) *Ageing and Sexing Animal Bones from Archaeological Sites* (British Archaeological Reports British Series 109): 91-107. Oxford: British Archaeological Reports.

Green, H. S. 1980. *The Flint Arrowheads of the British Isles: a detailed study of material from England and Wales with comparanda from Scotland and Ireland*. Oxford: Archaeopress.

Green, M. 2012. *The Celtic World*. London: Routledge.

Grimm, E.C. 1987. CONISS: a FORTRAN 77 program for stratigraphically constrained cluster analysis by the method of incremental sum of squares. *Computers and Geosciences* 13: 13-35.

Groenendijk, H.A. 2006. Dorfwurt Ulrum (De Marne, Prov. Groningen). Eine Fundbergung Im Jahre 1995 Als Anregung Zur Benutzung Hydrologischer Messdaten Bei Der Erhaltung von Grosswurten. *Palaeohistoria* 47/48. http://rjh.ub.rug.nl/Palaeohistoria/article/view/25150.

Guido, M. 1978. *The Glass Beads of the Prehistoric and Roman Periods in Britain and Ireland*. London: Society of Antiquaries of London.

Guido, M. 1999. *The Glass Beads of Anglo-Saxon England* c. AD 400-700. Woodbridge: Boydell Press.

Haggarty, G.R., Hall, D.W. and Chenery, S. 2011. Sourcing Scottish Redwares (MPRG Occasional Paper No 5).

Hall, D.W. 2012. Medieval pottery, in M. Carver, et al. Pictish Byre houses at Pitcarmick and their landscape: investigations 1993-5: 179-180. *Proceedings of the Society of Antiquaries of Scotland* 142: 145-199.

Hall, M., Hall, D and Cook, G. 2005. What's cooking? New radiocarbon dates from the earliest phases of the Perth High Street excavations and the question of Perth's early medieval origin. *Proceedings of the Society of Antiquaries of Scotland* 135: 273–285.

Hall, V.A. and Mauquoy, D. 2005. Tephra-dated climate- and human-impact studies during the last 1500 years from a raised bog in central Ireland. *Holocene* 15: 1086-1093.

Hallén, Y. 1994. The use of bone and antler at Foshigarry and Bac Mhic Connain, two Iron Age sites on North Uist, Western Isles. *Proceedings of the Society of Antiquaries of Scotland* 124: 189-231.

Halliday, S.P. 1993. Marginal agriculture in Scotland, in T.C. Smout (ed.) *Scotland Since Prehistory. Natural Change and Human Impact*: 64-78. Aberdeen: Scottish Cultural Press.

Halliday, S.P. 2001. Rig and Furrow in Scotland, in J. Barber. *Guidelines for the Preservation of Areas of Rig and Furrow in Scotland*: 10-20. Edinburgh: Scottish Trust for Archaeological Research.

Halliday, S. 2006. Into the dim light of history: More of the same or all change?, in A. Woolf (ed.) *Landscape and Environment in Dark Age Scotland* (St John's House Papers No. 11): 11-28. St Andrews: St John's House.

Halliday, S.P. 2007. Unenclosed round-houses in Scotland: occupation, abandonment and the character of settlement, in C. Burgess, P. Topping and F. Lynch (eds) *Beyond Stonehenge. Essays on the Bronze Age in honour of Colin Burgess*: 49-56. Oxford: Oxbow.

Hamerow, H. 1999. Anglo-Saxon timber buildings: the continental connection, in H. Sarfatij, W.J.H. Verwers and P.J. Woltering (eds) *In Discussion with the Past: Archaeological Studies Presented to W.A. van Es*, 119–28. Zwolle / Amersfoort: Spa Uitgevers / Rijksdienst voor het Oudheidkundig Bodemonderzoek (ROB).

Hamerow, H. 2012. *Rural Settlements and Society in Anglo-Saxon England*. Medieval History and Archaeology. Oxford: Oxford University Press.

Hamilton, J.R.C. 1956. *Excavations at Jarlshof, Shetland*. Edinburgh: Her Majesty's Stationary Office.

Hamilton, W.D. and Kenney, J. 2015. Multiple Bayesian modelling approaches to a suite of radiocarbon dates from ovens excavated at Ysgol yr Hendre, Caernarfon, North Wales. *Quaternary Geochronology* 25:75-82.

Harck, O., Kossack, G. and Reichstein, J. 1992. Frühe Bauern Auf Sylt, in M. Müller-Wille, Und D. Hoffman, (eds) *Der Vergangenheit Auf Der Spur: Archäologische Siedlungsforschung in Schleswig-Holstein*, 11–38. Karl Wachholtz Verlag Neumünster.

Harding, D.W. 2004. *The Iron Age in northern Britain: Celts and Romans, natives and invaders*. London and New York: Routledge.

Harding, D.W. 2009. *The Iron Age Round-House: Later Prehistoric Building in Britain and Beyond*. Oxford: Oxford University Press.

Harris, J. 1985. A preliminary survey of hut circles and field systems in SE Perthshire. *Proceedings of the Society of Antiquaries of Scotland* 114: 199-216.

Hatherley, C. and Murray, R. forthcoming. *Culduthel: An Iron Age Craft Centre in North-East Scotland*. Edinburgh: Society of Antiquaries of Scotland.

Haue, N. 2012. Jernalderens samfund i Nordjylland - belyst med udgangspunkt i byhøjen Nr. Tranders, Aalborg. Doctoral thesis, Institut for Kultur og Samfund, Afdeling for arkæologi, Moesgård: Aarhus University. https://www.academia.edu/12163529/Jernalderens_samfund_i_Nordjylland_-_belyst_med_udgangspunkt_i_byh%C3%B8jen_Nr._Tranders_Aalborg.

Heald, A. 2007. Jarlshof, Shetland (Dunrossness Parish), Stray Find. *Discovery Excavation Scotland* 8: 175.

Heald, A. 2011. The interpretation of non-ferrous metalworking in Early Historic Scotland, in S.T. Driscoll, J. Geddes and M.A. Hall (eds) *Pictish Progress. New studies on Northern Britain in the Early Middle Ages*: 221-241. Brill: Leiden/Boston.

Heald, A. and Hunter, F. 2008. Metal artefacts, in D. Abernethy. Bruach An Druimein, Poltalloch, Argll: excavations directed by the late Eric Cregeen, 1960-62: 43-50. Edinburgh: *Scottish Archaeological Internet Report* 27.

Heald, A. and McLaren, D. 2013. Metalworking at Burland and beyond, in H. Moore and G. Wilson (eds) *Ebbing Shores. Survey and Excavation of Coastal Archaeology in Shetland 1995-2008*: 259-64. Edinburgh: Historic Scotland.

Helama, S., Jones, P.D. and Briffa, K.R. 2017a. Limited Late Antique cooling. *Nature Geoscience* 10(4): 242-243.

Helama, S., Jones, P.D. and Briffa, K.R. 2017b. Dark Ages Cold Period: A literature review and directions for future research. *Holocene* 27(10): 1600-1606.

Henderson, G. and Henderson, I. 2004. *The Art of the Picts: sculpture and metalwork in early medieval Scotland*. London: Thames & Hudson.

Hermanns-Auðardóttir, M. 1989. *Islands Tidiga Bosättning: Studier med Utgångspunkt i Merovingertida-Vikingatida Gårdslämningar i Herjólfsdalur, Vestmannaeyar, Island* (Studia Archaeologica Universitatis Umensis 1). Umeå: Umeå Universitet Arkeologiska Institutionen.

Herschend, F. and Mikkelsen, D.K. 2003. The Main Building at Borg (I:1), in G.S. Munch, O.S. Johansen and E. Roesdahl (eds) *Borg in Lofoten: A Chieftan's Farm in North Norway.*, 41–76. Arkeologish Skriftserie

1. Trondheim/Lofote: Tapir Academic Press/Lofotr: The Viking Museum at Borg.

Hingley, R., Moore, H.L., Triscott, J.E. and Wilson, G. 1997. The excavation of two later Iron Age fortified homesteads at Aldclune, Blair Atholl, Perth & Kinross. *Proceedings of the Society of Antiquaries of Scotland* 127: 407-466.

Hinton, D.A. 2005. *Gold and Gilt, Pots and Pins: possessions and people in medieval Britain*. Oxford: Oxford University Press.

Hodgson, N., McKelvey, J. and Muncaster, W. 2012. *The Iron Age on the Northumberland Coastal Plain. Excavations in advance of development 2002-2010*. Tyne and Wear Archives & Museums Archaeological Monograph No. 3. Newcastle Upon Tyne: TWM Archaeology and the Arbeia Society.

Hoffmann, R.C. 2014. *An Environmental History of Medieval Europe*. Cambridge: Cambridge University Press.

Holden, T.G. 1998. *The Archaeology of Scottish Thatch* (Technical Advice Note 13). Historic Scotland: Edinburgh.

Holman, K. 1996. *Scandinavian Runic Inscriptions in the British Isles: Their Historical Context*. Trondheim: Tapic Academic Press.

Holmes, J. 2012. Animal bone, in M. Carver, J. Barrett, J. Downes and J. Hooper 2012. Pictish byre-houses at Pitcarmick and their landscape: investigations 1993–5. *Proceedings of the Society of Antiquaries of Scotland* 142: 145-199.

Hooper, J. 2002. A Landscape Given Meaning: An archaeological perspective on landscape history in highland Scotland. Unpublished PhD thesis, University of Glasgow.

Hope-Taylor, B. 1977. *Yeavering. An Anglo-British centre in Northumbria* (Department of Environment Archaeology Report No. 7). London: Her Majesty's Stationery Office.

Housley, R.A., Blockley S.P.E., Matthews I.P., MacLeod A., Lowe J.J., Ramsay S., Miller J.J. and Campbell E.N. 2010. Late Holocene vegetation and palaeoenvironmental history of the Dunadd area, Argyll, Scotland: chronology of events. *Journal of Archaeological Science* 37: 577-593.

Housley R.A., Campbell E.N., Miller J.J. and Ramsay, S. 2004. A high-resolution study of human impact and land use around the first millennium AD royal centre at Dunadd, Argyll, in R.A. Housley and G. Coles (eds) *Atlantic Connections and Adaptations*: 12-28. Oxford: Oxbow.

Huggett, J. 1988. Imported grave goods and the early Anglo-Saxon economy. *Medieval Archaeology* 32: 63-96.

Huijts, C.S.T.J. 1992. De voor-historische boerderijbouw in Drenthe: reconstructiemodellen van 1300 vóór tot 1300 na Chr. Doctoral thesis, Rijksuniversiteit Groningen.

Huisman, D.J. and Milek, K.B. 2017. Turf as Construction Material. *Archaeological Soil and Sediment Micromorphology* 1: 113–20.

Hunter, F. 2007. *Beyond the Edge of the Empire – Caledonians, Picts and Romans*. Rosemarkie: Groam House Museum.

Huntley, B. 1981. The past and present vegetation of the Caenlochan National Nature Reserve, Scotland. II. Palaeoecological investigations. *New Phytologist* 87: 189-222.

Huntley, B. 1994. Late Devensian and Holocene palaeoecology and palaeoenvironments of the Morrone Birkwoods, Aberdeenshire, Scotland. *Journal of Quaternary Science* 9: 311-336.

Huntley, B. and Birks, H.J.B. 1983. *An Atlas of Past and Present Pollen Maps for Europe: 0-13000 Years Ago*. Cambridge: Cambridge University Press.

Hutcheson, A. 1889. Notes on the stone circle near Kenmore and of some hill forts in the neighbourhood of Aberfeldy, Perthshire. *Proceedings of the Society of Antiquaries of Scotland* 23: 356-367.

Innes, J.B. and Shennan, I. 1991. Palynology of archaeological and mire sediments from Dod, Borders Region, Scotland. *Archaeological Journal* 148: 1-45.

Jesch, J. 1991. *Women in the Viking Age*. Suffolk: Boydell & Brewer.

Johansen, O.S. and Søbstad, T. 1978. De Nordnorske Tunanleggene Fra Jernalderen. *Viking: Tidsskrift for Norrøn Arkeologi* Bind XLI: 9–56.

Johnson, D. 2014. Ingleborough. Anglo-Saxons in the Dales. *Current Archaeology* 296: 14-20.

Jones, M.E. 1996. *The End of Roman Britain*. London: Cornell University Press.

Jones, R., Haggarty, G.R., Hall, D.W. and Will, R. 2006. Sourcing Scottish White Gritty ware. *Medieval Ceramics* 26-27: 45-84.

Kelly, F. 1998. *Early Irish Farming*. Dublin: Institute for Advanced Studies.

Kerr, T.R., Swindles, G.T. and Plunkett, J. 2009. Making hay while the sun shines? Socio-economic change and climatic deterioration in Early Medieval Ireland. *Journal of Archaeological Science* 36(12): 2868-2874.

King, J. and Nicholson, J.A. 1964. Grasslands of the forest and sub-alpine zones, in J.H. Burnett (ed.) *The Vegetation of Scotland*: 168-231. Edinburgh: Oliver & Boyd.

Kinnaird, T., Bolòs, J., Turner, A. and Turner, A. 2017. Optically-stimulated luminescence profiling and dating of historic agricultural terraces in Catalonia (Spain). *Journal of Archaeological Science* 78: 66-77.

Kok, M.S.M. 2005. 'What the Romans Did for Us: A Question of Identity in the Broekpolder', in D. Hofmann, J. Mills and A. Cochrane (eds.) *Elements of Being: Mentalities, Identities and Movements* (BAR International Series 1437): 71–76. Oxford: Archaeopress.

Kokalj, Ž., Zakšek, K. and Oštir, K. 2011. Application of sky-view factor for the visualization of historic landscape features in Lidar-Derived relief models. *Antiquity*, 85: 263-273. DOI: 10.1017/S0003598X00067594

Kuijt, I., Prentiss, W.C. and Pokotylo, D.L. 1995. Bipolar reduction: an experimental study of debitage variability. *Lithic Technology* 20(2): 116-127.

Kupiec, P., Milek, K., Gisladóttir, G.A. and Woollett, J. 2016. Elusive *sel* sites: the geoarchaeological quest for Icelandic shielings and the case of þorvaldstaoasel, in northeast Iceland, in J. Collis, M. Pearce and F. Nicolis (eds) *Summer Farms. Seasonal exploitation of the uplands from prehistory to the present*, 221-236. Sheffield: J.R. Collis Publications.

Lagerås, P. 2007. *The Ecology of Expansion and Abandonment. Medieval and post-Medieval land-use and settlement dynamics in a landscape perspective*. Stockholm: National Heritage Board.

Laing, L. 1975. *The archaeology of late Celtic Britain and Ireland c.400-1200 AD*. London.

Laing, L. 1993. *A catalogue of Celtic Ornamental Metalwork in the British Isles c. AD 400-1200*. Nottingham Monographs in Archaeology No.5. British Archaeological Reports British Series 229.

Laing, L. and Laing, J. 1993. *The Picts and the Scots*. Stroud: Alan Sutton.

Laing, L. and Longley, D. 2006. *The Mote of Mark: a Dark Age hillfort in south-west Scotland*. Oxford: Oxbow.

Lane, A. and Campbell, E. 2000. *Excavations at Dunadd: an early Dalriadic capital*. Oxford: Oxbow.

Little, R. 2016. Iceland Report: This Fragile Tradition. *Iceland NET 2016* (blog). Viewed 18 August 2016: http://archnetwork.org/iceland-report-becky-little/.

Little, R. and Morton, T. 2001. *Building with Earth in Scotland: Innovative Design and Sustainability*. Edinburgh: Scottish Executive Central Research Unit. http://www.gov.scot/Publications/2002/02/10646/File-1.

Lock, G. and Ralston, I. 2017. *Atlas of Hillforts of Britain and Ireland*. Earthstar Geographics CNES/Airbus D. Viewed 23 June 20-19: https://hillforts.arch.ox.ac.uk

Logan, N.A. 2017. "Wretched Huts" and "Despicable Hovels": The Pre-Improvement Farmhouse in the Western Lowlands of Scotland'. *Vernacular Building* 40: 1–22.

Logan, N.A. 2018. "Primitive Modes of Building": Farmhouses and Cottages in the Western Lowlands of Scotland 1620-1820. *Vernacular Building* 41.

Loveday, R. 2006. Where have all the neolithic houses gone? Turf – an invisible component. *Scottish Archaeological Journal* 28(2): 81–104. doi.org/10.3366/E1471576707000046

Loveluck, C. 2013. *Northwest Europe in the Early Middle Ages*. Cambridge: Cambridge University Press.

Lowe, C. 2006. *Excavations at Hoddom, Dumfriesshire. An Early ecclesiastical site in south west Scotland*. Edinburgh: Society of Antiquaries of Scotland.

Lowe, C. 2008. *Inchmarnock: An Early Historic Island Monastery and Its Archaeological Landscape*. Edinburgh: Society of Antiquaries of Scotland.

Lowe, J.J. 1982. Three Flandrian pollen profiles from the Teith Valley, Scotland. II. Analyses of deteriorated pollen. *New Phytologist* 90: 371-385.

Macdonald, A.D.S. and Laing, L.R. 1973. Early ecclesiastical sites in Scotland: a field survey, part II. *Proceedings of the Society of Antiquaries of Scotland* 102: 131-132.

MacDonald, A.D.S. and Laing, L.R. 1975. Excavations at Lochmaben Castle, Dumfriesshire. *Proceedings of the Society of Antiquaries of Scotland* 106: 124-157.

MacGregor, A. 1974. The Broch of Burrian, North Ronaldsay, Orkney. *Proceedings of the Society of Antiquaries of Scotland* 105: 63-118.

MacGregor, G. 2010. Legends, traditions or coincidences: remembrance of historic settlement in the Central Highlands of Scotland. *International Journal of Historical Archaeology* 14: 398–413.

MacLeod, M. and Mees, B. 2006. *Runic Amulets and Magic Objects*. Woodbridge: Boydell Press.

Mahler, D.L. 1993. Shielings and Their Role in the Viking-Age Economy, in C.E Batey, J. Jesch and C.D. Morris (eds) *The Viking Age in Caithness, Orkney and the North Atlantic: Select Papers from the Proceedings of the Eleventh Viking Congress, Thurso and Kirkwall, 22 August-1 September 1989*, 487–505. Edinburgh/Aberdeen/Glasgow: Edinburgh University Press/University of Aberdeen/University of Glasgow.

Mann, M.E. and Jones, P.D. 2003. Global surface temperatures over the past two millennia. *Geophysical Research Letters* 30: 1820-1824.

Mann, M.E., Zhang, Z., Hughes, M.K., Bradley, R.S., Miller, S.K., Rutherford, S. and Ni, F. 2008. Proxy-based reconstructions of hemispheric and global surface temperature variations over the past two millennia. *Proceedings of the National Academy of Sciences* 105(36): 13252-13257.

Manning, W.H. 1985. *Catalogue of the Romano-British iron tools, fittings and weapons in the British Museum*. London: British Museum Publications.

Márkus, G. 2017. *Conceiving a Nation: Scotland to AD 900*. Edinburgh: Edinburgh University Press.

Marshall, D.N. 1964. Report on the excavations at Little Dunagoil. *Transactions of the Buteshire Natural History Society* 16.

Mays, S. 1998. *The Archaeology of Human Bone*. London.

Maxwell, G. 1987. Settlement in southern Pictland: a new overview, in A. Small (ed.) *The Picts: A new look at old problems*: 31-44. Dundee: University of Dundee Department of Geography.

Mazier, F., Galop, D., Brun, C. and Buttler, A. 2006. Modern pollen assemblages from grazed vegetation in the western Pyrenees, France: a numerical tool for more precise reconstruction of past cultural landscapes. *Holocene* 16: 91-103.

Mazier, F., Galop, D., Gaillard, M., Rendu, C., Cugny, C., Legaz, A. *et al.* 2009. Multidisciplinary approach to reconstructing local pastoral activities: an example from the Pyrenean Mountains (Pays Basque). *Holocene* 19: 171-188.

McClatchey, J. 1996. Spatial and altitudinal gradients of climate in the Cairngorms - observations from climatological and automatic weather stations. *Botanical Journal of Scotland* 48: 31-50.

McCormick, F. 1998. Calf slaughter as a response to marginality, in C.M. Mills and G. Coles (eds) *Life on the Edge. Human Settlement and Marginality*: 49-53. Oxford: Oxbow.

McCormick, F., Kerr, T.R., McClatchie, M. and O'Sullivan, A. 2014. *Early Medieval Agriculture, Livestock and Cereal Production in Ireland, AD 400-1100* (British Archaeological Reports International Series 2647). Oxford: British Archaeological Reports.

McCormick, M., Büntgen, U., Cane, M.A. *et al.* 2012. Climate change during and after the Roman Empire: reconstructing the past from scientific and historical evidence. *Journal of Interdisciplinary History* 43: 169-220.

McDermott, F., Mattey, D.P. and Hawkesworth, C. 2001. Centennial-scale Holocene climate variability revealed by a high-resolution speleothem $\delta^{18}O$ record from SW Ireland. *Science* 294: 1328-1331.

McDonnell, G. 1994. The slag report, in B. Ballin-Smith (ed.) *Howe: Four Millennia of Orkney Prehistory. Excavations 1978-82* (Society of Antiquaries of Scotland Monograph Series 9): 228-34. Edinburgh: Society of Antiquaries.

McDonnell, J.G. 1986a. The iron and ironworking, in J.R. Hunter *Rescue Excavations on the Brough of Birsay 1974-82*: 198-203. Edinburgh, Society of Antiquaries of Scotland.

McDonnell, J.G. 1986b. Slag from Clachard Craig, in Close-Brooks, J. 1986. Excavations at Clatchard Craig, Fife. *Proceedings of the Society of Antiquaries of Scotland* 116: 117-178.

McDonnell, J.G. 1998. Irons in the fire – evidence of ironworking on broch sites, in R.A. Nicholson and S.J. Dockrill (eds) *Old Scatness Broch, Shetland: retrospect and prospect* (NABO Monograph No. 2): 150-62. Bradford: University of Bradford.

McDonnell, J.G. 2000. Ironworking and other residues, in A. Lane and E. Campbell (eds) *Excavations at Dunadd: an early Dalriadic capital*: 218-20. Oxford: Oxbow.

McGill, C. 2004. Excavations of cropmarks at Newbarns, near Inverkeilor, Angus. *Tayside and Fife Archaeological Journal* 10: 95-118.

McIntyre, A. 1998. Survey and excavation at Kilearnan Hill, Sutherland, 1982-3. *Proceedings of the Society of Antiquaries of Scotland* 128: 167-201.

McKerracher, M. 2018. *Farming Transformed in Anglo-Saxon England. Agriculture in the long Eight Century*. Oxford: Windgather Press.

McLaren, D. and Heald, A. 2006. The vitrified material, in I. Armit (ed.) *Anatomy of an Iron Age roundhouse. The Cnip wheelhouse excavations, Lewis*: 155-8. Edinburgh: Society of Antiquaries of Scotland.

McLaren, D. and Dungworth, D. forthcoming. The manufacture of iron at Culduthel: ferrous metalworking debris and iron metallurgy, in C. Hatherley and R. Murray (eds) *Culduthel: An Iron Age Craft Centre in North-East Scotland*. Edinburgh: Society of Antiquaries of Scotland.

McNiven, P.E. 2011. Gaelic Place-Names and the Social History of Gaelic-Speakers in Medieval Menteith. Unpublished PhD thesis, University of Glasgow.

McNiven, P. 2014. *The Place-names of Glenshee: a preliminary study for the Perth and Kinross Heritage Trust*. Unpublished report. Viewed 30.7.19: http://www.pkht.org.uk/files/4315/2537/5533/GAP_theplacenamesofglenshee_pmcniven.pdf

McNiven, P. 2017a. The Place Names of the Cateran Trail. Viewed 30.7.19: http://commonculture.org.uk/events-2/

McNiven, P. 2017b. Place-names of the Cateran Trail. Mini Trail. Viewed 30.7.19: http://commonculture.org.uk/wp-content/uploads/2017/02/CWWPlaceNameResearchMiniTrail_LR.pdf

McVean, D.N. 1964. The forest zone, in J. Burnett (ed.) *The Vegetation of Scotland*: 144-167. Edinburgh: Oliver & Boyd.

Meid, H. 1994. *Gaulish Inscriptions: Their interpretation in the light of archaeological evidence and their value as a source of linguistic and sociological information*. Budapest: Archaeolingua Alapituany. 2nd Ed.

Middleton, W.D. 2004. Identifying chemical activity residues on prehistoric house floors: a methodology and rationale for multi-elemental characterization of a mild acid extract of anthropogenic sediments. *Archaeometry* 46: 47-65.

Middleton, W.D. and Price, T.D. 1996. Identification of activity areas by multielement characterization of sediments from modern and archaeological house floors using inductively coupled plasma-atomic emission spectroscopy. *Journal of Archaeological Science* 23: 673-687.

Milek, K.B. 2007. Houses and Households in Early Icelandic Society: Geoarchaeology and the Interpretation of Social Space. PhD dissertation, University of Cambridge. https://www.repository.cam.ac.uk/handle/1810/245017.

Milek, K.B. 2012. The Roles of pit houses and gendered spaces on Viking-Age farmsteads in Iceland. *Medieval Archaeology* 56: 85-130.

Milek, K.B. and Roberts, H.M. 2013. Integrated geoarchaeological methods for the determination of site activity areas: a study of a Viking Age house in Reykjavik, Iceland. *Journal of Archaeological Science* 40(4): 1845–1865.

Miller, J. 2002. The Oakbank crannog: building a house of plants, in B. Ballin-Smith and I. Banks (eds) *In the*

Shadow of the Brochs - The Iron Age in Scotland: 35-43. Stroud: Tempus.

Miller, J. and Ramsay, S. 2001. *The Vegetation History of Kilmartin Glen over the last two millennia*. Glasgow: School of Archaeology.

Mímisson, K. 2016. Building Identities: The Architecture of the Persona. *International Journal of Historical Archaeology* 20(1): 207–27. doi.org/10.1007/s10761-015-0322-5

Mitchell, J. and Noble, G. 2017. The monumental cemeteries of northern Pictland. *Medieval Archaeology* 61: 1-40.

Mitchell, S., Anderson, S. and Johnson, M. 2010. The excavation of a multi-period site at Alloa, Clackmannanshire. *Tayside and Fife Archaeological Journal* 16: 30-47.

Moore, P.D., Webb, J.A. and Collinson, M.E. 1991. *Pollen Analysis*. Oxford: Blackwell. 2nd Ed.

Morris, F.M. 2015. Cross-North Sea contacts in the Roman period. *Oxford Journal of Archaeology* 34 (Issue 4, October): 415–438. doi.org/10.1111/ojoa.12067

Morton, T., and Little, R. 2015. *Experimental Earth Structures, Renders and Plasters*. Research Report. Edinburgh: Historic Scotland.

Munch, G.S., Johansen, O.S. and Roesdahl, E. (eds) 2003. *Borg in Lofoten: A Chieftan's Farm in North Norway*. Arkeologish Skriftserie 1. Trondheim/Lofoten: Tapir Academic Press/Lofotr: The Viking Museum at Borg.

Munro, R. 1882. *Ancient Scottish lake dwellings or Crannogs*. Edinburgh: David Douglas.

Murray J.C. 1982. *Excavations in the Medieval Burgh of Aberdeen 1973-81* (Society of Antiquaries of Scotland Monograph Series No 2). Edinburgh: Society of Antiquaries.

Myhre, B. 2000. Germanic kingdoms bordering on two empires, in E. Kramer *et al.* (eds) *Kings of the North Sea, AD 250-850*: 41–54. Leeuwarden / Nijmegen / Husum / Stavanger / Newcastle upon Tyne / Esbjerg: Fries Museum / Museum Het Valkhof / Nordfriesisches Museum Nissenhaus / Arkeoligisk Museum i Stavanger / Tyne and Wear Museums / Esbjerg Museum.

Myrdal, J. 2012. Scandinavia, in H. Kitsikopoulos (ed.) *Agrarian Change and Crisis in Europe, 1200-1500*: 204-249. London: Routledge.

Naysmith P., Cook G., Freeman S., Scott E.M., Anderson R., Dunbar E., Muir G., Dougans A., Wilcken K., Schnabel, Russell N., Ascough, P. and Maden, C. 2010. 14C AMS at SUERC: improving QA data from the 5 MV tandem AMS and 250 kV SSAMS. *Radiocarbon* 52(2): 263-271.

Nicholson, A. 1997. The iron, in P. Hill (ed.) *Whithorn and St Ninian. The excavation of a monastic town, 1984-91*: 404-433. Sutton: Whithorn Trust.

Nicolaisen, W.F.H. 1997. On Pictish rivers and their confluences, in D. Henry (ed.) *The Worm, the Germ and the Thorn*: 113-118. Balgavies: Pinkfoot Press.

Nicolaisen, W.F.H. 2001. *Scottish Place-names: Their Study and Significance*. London: Batsford.

Nicolay, J.A.W. 2014. *The Splendour of Power: Early Medieval Kingship and the Use of Gold and Silver in the Southern North Sea Area (5th to 7th Century AD)* (Groningen Archaeological Studies 28). Groningen/Eelde: University of Groningen Library/Barkhuis Publishing.

Nicolay, J.A.W. 2015. Kingship in Early-Medieval "Frisia": historical versus archaeological sources, in A. Willemsen and H. Kik (eds) *Golden Middle Ages in Europe*: 24–32. Turnhout: Brepols Publishers. doi.org/10.1484/M.STMH-EB.5.109452

Nicolay, J.A.W., and Postma, D. 2018. Woonstalhuizen uit de Late Middeleeuwen: Variatie in Landschap en Constructiewijze, in J.A.W. Nicolay (ed.) *Huisplaatsen in de Onlanden: De Geschiedenis van een Veeweidegebied* (Groningen Archaeological Studies 34): 254-293.. Eelde/Groningen: Barkhuis/Groningen University Library.

Nieuwhof, A. 2011. Discontinuity in the Northern-Netherlands coastal area at the end of the Roman period. *Neue Studien Zur Sachsenforschung* 3: 55–66.

Noble, G., Gondek, M., Campbell, E. and Cook, M. 2013. Between prehistory and history: the archaeological detection of social change among the Picts. *Antiquity* 87: 1136–1150.

Noble, R. 1984. Turf-walled houses of the Central Highlands. An experiment in reconstruction. *Folk Life* 22: 68-83.

Noble, R.R. 2000. Creel Houses of the Scottish Highlands, in T.M. Owen (ed.) *From Corrib to Cultra; Folklife Essays in Honour of Alan Gailey*: 82-94. Belfast: The Institute of Irish Studies.

Noble, R.R. 2003. Earth buildings in the Central Highlands: research and reconstruction, in S. Govan (ed.) *Medieval and Later Rural Settlement in Scotland: 10 Years On*: 45-52. Edinburgh: Historic Scotland.

O'Brien, C. 2002. The early Medieval shires of Yeavering, Breamish and Bamburgh. *Archaeologia Aeliana* 30: 53-74.

Oosthuizen, S. 2013. *Tradition and Transformation in Anglo-Saxon England. Archaeology, common rights and landscape*. London: Bloomsbury.

O'Sullivan, P.E. 1976. Pollen analysis and radiocarbon dating of a core from Loch Pityoulish, eastern Highlands of Scotland. *Journal of Biogeography* 3: 293-302.

Ottaway, P. 1992. *Anglo-Scandinavian ironwork from 16-22 Coppergate* (Archaeology of York Series 17/6). York: Archaeology of York.

Ottaway, P., Edwards, G., Jones, J., Starley, D. and Watson, J. 2009a. Knives, in D.H. Evans and C. Loveluck (eds) *Life and Economy at Early Medieval Flixborough, c. AD 600 – 1000. Excavations at Flixborough Volume 2*: 203-233. Oxford: Oxbow.

Ottaway, P., Wastling, L.M., Rogers, N., Foreman and Starley, D. 2009b. Domestic fittings and implements, in D.H. Evans and C. Loveluck (eds) *Life and Economy at Early Medieval Flixborough, c. AD 600 – 1000. Excavations at Flixborough Volume 2*: 165-243. Oxford: Oxbow.

Page, R.I. 1973. *An Introduction to English Runes*. Woodbridge: Boydell Press.

Parker Pearson, M. (ed.) 2012. *From Machair to Mountains*. Oxford: Oxbow.

Parkin, S.J. 2014. 'Valuing the Vernacular: Scotland's Earth-Built Heritage and the Impacts of Climate Change'. Doctoral thesis, Stirling: University of Stirling. Viewed 30.7.19: http://hdl.handle.net/1893/22126

Parkin, S.J., and Adderley, W.P. 2017. The past ubiquity and environment of the lost earth buildings of Scotland. *Human Ecology* 45(5): 569–583. doi.org/10.1007/s10745-017-9931-4

Paterson, D. 2011. The Holocene History of *Pinus sylvestris* woodland in the Mar Lodge Estate, Cairngorms, eastern Scotland. Unpublished PhD thesis, University of Stirling.

Payne, S. 1973. Kill-off patterns in sheep and goats – the mandibles from Aşvan Kale. *Journal of Anatolian Studies* 23: 281–303.

Peate, I.C. 1946. *The Welsh House: A Study in Folk Culture*. Liverpool: H. Evans & Sons, the Brython Press.

Peers, C. and Radford, C.A.R. 1943. The Saxon monastery of Whitby Abbey. *Archaeologica* 89: 27-88.

Peters, M.E. and Higuera, P.E. 2007. Quantifying the source area of macroscopic charcoal with a particle dispersal model. *Quaternary Research* 67: 304–310.

Piggott, S. 1953. Three metalwork hoards of the Roman Period from southern Scotland. *Proceedings of the Society of Antiquaries of Scotland* 87: 1-50.

PNF, Taylor, S. with Márkus, G. 2006-12. *Place-Names of Fife* Volumes 1-5. Donington: Shaun Tyas.

Postma, D. in prep. House Plan Analysis Hallum-Hellema (Friesland): A Reconsideration of the Early Medieval Turf and Timber Buildings (6. Archaeo Build Report). Lelystad/Madderty: Archaeo Build.

Postma, D. 2010. Salt Marsh Architecture: Catalogue, Technology and Typological Development of Early Medieval Turf Buildings in the Northern Coastal Area of the Netherlands. MA thesis, University of Groningen. Groningen. Viewed 30.7.19: http://arts.studenttheses.ub.rug.nl/11088/

Postma, D. 2015. *Het zodenhuis van Firdgum: middeleeuwse boerderijbouw in het Friese kustgebied tussen 400 en 1300*. Groningen / Eelde: Terpencentrum, Rijksuniversiteit Groningen / Barkhuis.

Proctor, C.J., Baker, A. and Barnes, W.L. 2002. A three thousand year record of North Atlantic climate. *Climate Dynamics* 19: 449-454.

Punt, W., Marks, A. and Hoen, P.P. 2002. The Northwest European pollen flora, 66, Myricaceae. *Review of Palaeobotany and Palynology (The Northwest European Pollen Flora, VIII)* 123: 99-105.

Ralston, I. 1987. Portknockie, promontory forts and Pictish settlement, in A. Small (ed.) *The Picts: A new look at old problems*: 15-26. Dundee: University of Dundee Department of Geography.

Ralston, I. 1997. Pictish homes, in D. Henry (ed.) *The Worm, the Germ and the Thorn. Pictish and Related Studies Presented to Isabel Henderson*: 19-34. Balgavies: Pinkfoot Press.

Ralston, I.B.M. and Armit, I. 2003. The Early Historic period: An archaeological perspective, in K.J. Edwards and I.B.M. Ralston (eds) *Scotland After the Ice Age. Environment, Archaeology and History, 8000 BC-AD 1000*: 217-240. Edinburgh: Edinburgh University Press.

Ramsay, S. 1995. Woodland clearance in west-central Scotland during the past 3000 years, Unpublished PhD thesis, University of Glasgow.

Ramm, H.G., McDowall, R.W. and Mercer, E. 1970. *Shielings and Bastles*. London: Her Majesty's Stationery Office.

RCAHMS. 1990. *North-east Perth: an archaeological landscape*. Edinburgh: Her Majesty's Stationery Office.

RCAHMS. 1994. *South-east Perth: an archaeological landscape*. Edinburgh: Her Majesty's Stationery Office.

RCAHMS. 2007. *Handlist of site finds and their records from the Brian Hope-Taylor archive in the RCAHMS record*. Edinburgh: Her Majesty's Stationery Office.

Rees, A. 2009. The excavation of an Iron Age unenclosed settlement and an Early Historic multiple burial and metalworking area at Hawkhill, Lunan Bay, Angus. *Tayside and Fife Archaeological Journal* 15: 22-72.

Reimer P.J., Bard E., Bayliss A., Beck J.W., Blackwell P.G., Bronk Ramsey C., Grootes P.M., Guilderson T.P., Haflidason H., Hajdas I., Hatte C., Heaton T.J., Hoffmann D.L., Hogg A.G., Hughen K.A., Kaiser K.F., Kromer B., Manning S.W., Niu M., Reimer R.W., Richards D.A., Scott E.M., Southon J.R., Staff R.A., Turney C.S.M. and van der Plicht J. 2013. IntCal13 and Marine13 radiocarbon age calibration curves 0-50,000 Years cal BP. *Radiocarbon* 55(4): 1869-1887.

Rhodes, A.N. 1995. Charcoal analysis of mor humus soils: a palaeoecological assessment of the utility of moorland soils for the reconstruction of extended fire histories, in D.B.A. Thompson, A.J. Hester and M.B. Usher (eds) *Heaths and Moorland: Cultural Landscapes*: 249-255. Edinburgh: Her Majesty's Stationery Office.

Rhys, G, 2015. Approaching the Pictish language: historiography, early evidence and the question of Pritenic, Unpublished PhD thesis, University of Glasgow.

Rideout, J.S. 1995. Carn Dubh, Moulin, Perthshire: survey and excavation of an archaeological landscape 1987-90. *Proceedings of the Society of Antiquaries of Scotland* 125: 139-195.

Rijksdienst voor het Cultureel Erfgoed (RCE). 2016. Nationale Onderzoeksagenda Archeologie

2.0. Archeologie in Nederland. 2016. https://archeologieinnederland.nl/bronnen-en-kaarten/nationale-onderzoeksagenda-archeologie-20.

Rippon, S. 2007. *Beyond the Medieval Village. The diversification of landscape character in southern Britain*. Oxford: Oxford University Press.

Rippon, S., Smart, C. and Pears, B. 2015. *The Fields of Britannia*. Oxford: Oxford University Press.

Ritchie, A. 1995. Meigle and lay patronage in the 9th and 10th centuries AD. *Tayside and Fife Archaeological Journal* 1: 1-10.

Ritchie, J.N.G.1967. Keil Cave, Southend, Argyll: a late Iron Age cave occupation in Kintyre. *Proceedings of the Society of Antiquaries of Scotland* 99: 104-110.

RMS Registrum Magni Sigilli Regum Scottorum, J. M. Thomson et al (eds). Edinburgh 1882-1914.

Robertson, N.M. 1997. The Early Medieval carved stones of Fortingall, in D. Henry *The Worm, the Germ and the Thorn: Pictish and Related Studies Presented to Isabel Henderson*: 137-140 . Balgavies: Pinkfoot Press.

Rogers, J.M. 1992. The Formation of the Parish Unit and Community in Perthshire. Unpublished PhD thesis, University of Edinburgh.

Rogers, N.S.H. 1993. *Anglian and other finds from Fishergate* (Archaeology of York Series 17/9). York: Archaeology of York.

Romankiewicz, T. 2011. *The Complex Roundhouses of the Scottish Iron Age: An architectural analysis of complex Atlantic roundhouses (brochs and galleried duns), with reference to wheelhouses and timber roundhouses* (British Archaeological Reports British Series, BAR 550, vol. I). Oxford: Archaeopress.

Romankiewicz, T. 2016. Building (ancient) lives: new perspectives on the past for a sustainable future. *The European Archaeologist* 48: 25–30.

Ross, A. 2006. The Dabhach in Moray: a new look at an old tub, in A. Woolf (ed.) *Landscape and Environment in Dark Age Scotland* (St John's House Papers No. 11): 57-74. St Andrews: St John's House.

Ross, A. 2011. *The Kings of Alba, c. 1000 – c. 1130*. Edinburgh: John Donald.

Ross, A. 2015. *Land Assessment and Lordship in Medieval Northern Scotland* (The Medieval Countryside 14). Turnhout: Brepols.

Ross, A. 2019. Medieval European land assessment, Fortriu, and the *dabhach*. in A.E. Blackwell (ed) *Scotland in Early Medieval Europe*. Leiden: Sidestone Press.

RRS v *Regesta Regum Scottorum* vol. v (*Acts of Robert I*), A. A. M. Duncan (ed.). Edinburgh 1988.

Rymer, L. 1976. The history and ethnobotany of bracken. *Botanical Journal of the Linnaean Society* 73: 151-176.

Sacher, E. 1938. *Die aus Grassoden und Holz gebauten Höfe und Kirchen in Island*. Würzburg.

Saeftel, F. 1967. Wohnhügel-leute im Nordseeküstenbereich und ihre Grassoden-Bauweise: eine haus- und siedlungskundliche Studie zur Geschichte des frühgeschichtlichen Nordseeraumes (Studien und Materialen 1). Bräist/Bredstedt: Nordfrisk Institut.

Samson, R. 1982. Finds from Urquhart Castle in the National Museum, Edinburgh. *Proceedings of the Society of Antiquaries of Scotland* 112: 465-476.

Sanderson, D.C.W. and Murphy, S. 2010. Using simple portable OSL measurements and laboratory characterisation to help understand complex and heterogeneous sediment sequences for luminescence dating. *Quaternary Geochronology* 5: 299-305.

ScARF. n.d. Scottish Archaeological Research Framework (ScARF). Info Page. The Scottish Archaeological Research Framework Website. Accessed 26 August 2017. http://www.scottishheritagehub.com/.

ScARF. 2012. Medieval Panel Report, in M. Hall and N. Price (eds) Scottish Archaeological Research Framework: Society of Antiquaries of Scotland. http://tinyurl.com/bogzn5w

Schliemann, H. 1875. *Troy and its Remains; A Narrative of Researches and Discoveries Made on the Site of Ilium, and in the Trojan Plain*. London: John Murray.

Schmid, P. 1994. Oldorf: Eine Frümittelalterliche Friesische Wurtsiedlung. *Germania* 72/1.

Schmidt, H. 1994. *Building Customs in Viking Age Denmark*. (trans.) J. Olsen. Copenhagen: Poul Kristensen.

Schweingruber, F.H. 1990. *Anatomy of European Woods*. Berne: Haupt.

Scott E.M. 2003. The Third International Radiocarbon Intercomparison (TIRI) and the Fourth International Radiocarbon Intercomparison (FIRI) 1990-2002: results, analysis, and conclusions. *Radiocarbon* 45(2): 135-408.

Scott E.M., Bryant C., Cook G.T. and Naysmith P. 2003. Is there a fifth International Radiocarbon Intercomparison (VIRI)? *Radiocarbon* 45: 493-495.

Scott E.M., Cook G.T., Naysmith P., Bryant C. and O'Donnell D. 2007. A report on phase 1 of the 5th International Radiocarbon Intercomparison (VIRI). *Radiocarbon* 49: 409-26.

Scott E.M., Cook G.T. and Naysmith P. 2010. A report on phase 2 of the Fifth International Radiocarbon Intercomparison (VIRI). *Radiocarbon* 52(3): 846-858.

Scott, I.G. and Ritchie, A. 2009. *Pictish and Viking-Age Carvings from Shetland*. Edinburgh: Royal Commission on the Ancient and Historical Monuments of Scotland.

Scottish Remote Sensing Portal 2018. Viewed 30 July 2018: https://remotesensingdata.gov.scot/collections

Segerström, U. and Emanuelsson, M. 2002. Extensive forest grazing and hay-making on mires – vegetation changes in south-central Sweden due to land use since Medieval times. *Vegetation History and Archaeobotany* 11: 181-190.

SERF. 2010. *Strathearn Environs & Royal Forteviot 2006-2009*. Perth: Perth and Kinross Heritage Trust.

Shabalova, M.V. and van Engelen, A.M.V. 2003. Evaluation of a reconstruction of winter and summer temperatures in the Low Countries, AD 764-1998. *Climatic Change* 58: 219-242.

Sheridan, A. 2012. Bronze Age pottery, in M. Carver et al. Pictish Byre Houses at Pitcarmick and their landscape: investigations 1993-5. *Proceedings of the Society of Antiquaries of Scotland* 142: 173-176.

Sherley-Price, L. 1968. *Bede. A History of the English Church and People*. London: Penguin.

Sherlock, S.J. 2012. *A Royal Anglo-Saxon Cemetery at Street House, Loftus, North-East Yorkshire*. Hartlepool: Tees Archaeology.

Sigl, M., Winstrup, M., McConnell, J.R., Welten, K.C., Plunkett, G., Ludlow, F., Büntgen, U., Caffee, M., Chellman, N., Dahl-Jensen, D., Fischer, H., Kipfstuhl, S., Kostick, C., Maselli, O.J., Mekhaldi, F., Mulvaney, R., Muscheler, R., Pasteris, D.R., Pilcher, J.R., Salzer, M., Schüpbach, S., Steffensen, J.P., Vinther, B.M. and Woodruff, T.E. 2015. Timing and climate forcing of volcanic eruptions for the past 2,500 years. *Nature* 523: 543-549.

Sigurðardóttir, S. 2008. *Building with Turf*. (Transl Brown, N.M.). Skagafjörður Heritage Museum Booklet, IX. Skagafjörður Heritage Museum. http://bit.ly/2aMfSS3.

Simpson, I. and Adderley, W.P. 2011. Activities and accumulations: micromorphological analyses of archaeological sediments from multi-room houses in Finnmark, Norway, in B. Olsen, P. Urbanczyk and C.P. Amundsen (eds.) *Hybrid Spaces: Medieval Finnmark and the Archaeology of Multi-Room Houses*: 267-286. Oslo: Instituttet for Sammenlignende Kulturforskning.

Sinclair, J. 1795. *The Statistical Account of Scotland*, Kirkmichael, Perth, Vol. 15. Edinburgh: William Creech, 1795, 506. University of Edinburgh, University of Glasgow. (1999) The Statistical Accounts of Scotland online service: https://stataccscot.edina.ac.uk:443/link/osa-vol15-p506-parish-perth-kirkmichael

Smith, A. 1995. The excavation of a Neolithic, Bronze Age and Early Historic features near Ratho, Edinburgh. *Proceedings of the Society of Antiquaries of Scotland* 29: 69-138.

Smith, C. in prep. Report on the animal bones from Phase 3, Sloc Sàbhaidh, Baile Sear, North Uist. Archive report for SCAPE Trust.

Smith, M.A. 1998. Holocene regional vegetation history of the Lairg area, in R.P.J. McCullagh and R. Tipping (eds) *The Lairg Project 1988-1996: The evolution of an archaeological Landscape in Northern Scotland*: 177-199. Edinburgh: Scottish Trust for Archaeological Research.

Smith, W. McCombie. 1895. Recent Antiquarian Research in Glenshee. *Proceedings of the Society of Antiquaries of Scotland* 29: 96-99.

Smout, T.C. 1969. *A History of the Scottish People 1560-1830*. London: Fontana Press. 2nd Ed.

Southesk, Earl of. 1895. An Ogham Inscription at Abernethy. *Proceedings of the Society of Antiquaries of Scotland* 29: 244-251.

Spearman, R.M. 1997. The smithy and metalworking debris from Mills Mount, in S.T. Driscoll and P.A. Yeoman (eds) *Excavations within Edinburgh Castle in 1988-91* (Society of Antiquaries of Scotland Monograph Series 12): 164-8. Edinburgh: Society of Antiquaries of Scotland.

Stace, C. 1991. *New Flora of the British Isles*. Cambridge: Cambridge University Press.

Stace, C. 1997. *New Flora of the British Isles*. Cambridge: Cambridge University Press. 2nd Ed.

Stampfer, L. 2018. Embracing the North. Doctoral Thesis, Vienna: Technical University Vienna.

Starley, D. 2000. Metalworking debris, in K. Buxton and C. Howard-Davis (eds) *Bremetenacum: Excavations at Roman Ribchester 1980, 1989-1990*: 337-47. Lancaster: Lancaster Imprints Series No. 9.

Steensberg, A. 1952. *Bondehuse Og Vanmøller i Danmark Gennem 2000 År*. Arkæologiske Landsbyundersøgelser, I. København: Kommission Hos Alfred G. Hassings Forlad.

Steinhilber, F., Beer, J. and Fröhlich, C. 2009. Total solar irradiance during the Holocene. *Geophysics Research Letters* 36: L19704.

Stevenson, A.C. and Rhodes, A.N. 2000. Palaeoenvironmental evaluation of the importance of fire as a cause for *Calluna* loss in the British Isles. *Palaeogeography, Palaeoclimatology, Palaeoecology* 164: 195-206.

Stevenson, J.B. 1975. Survival and destruction, in J.G. Evans, S. Limbrey and H. Cleere (eds) *The Effect of Man on the Landscape: the Highland Zone*: 104-107. York: Council for British Archaeology.

Stewart, M.E.C. 1962. The excavation of two circular enclosures at Dalnaglar, Perthshire. *Proceedings of the Society of Antiquaries of Scotland* 95: 134-158.

Stewart, M.E.C. 1969. The Ring Forts of Central Perthshire. *Proceedings and Transactions of the Perthshire Society for Natural Science* 12: 21-32.

Stewart M.E.C. and Feachem R.W. 1961. Kinloch Rannoch. *Discovery Excavation Scotland* 1961: 42.

Stobie, J. 1793. *The counties of Perth and Clackmannan*. London: Stobie.

Stones, J.A. 1989. The small finds: summary report, in J.A. Stones (ed.) *Three Scottish Carmelite friaries. Excavations at Aberdeen, Linlithgow and Perth, 1980-1986*: 147-63. Edinburgh: Society of Antiquaries of Scotland.

Strachan, D. 2011. Before the burgh: 15,000 years of crossing the Tay, in D. Strachan (ed.) *Perth: a Place in History*. Perth: Perth and Kinross Heritage Trust.

Strachan, D. 2013. *Excavations at the Black Spout, Pitlochry and the Iron Age Monumental Roundhouses of North West Perthshire*. Perth: Perth and Kinross Heritage Trust.

Strachan, D. 2017. King's Seat Hillfort, Dunkeld: Project Design 2017-20. Unpublished report. Perth: Perth and Kinross Heritage Trust.

Strachan, D. and Sneddon, D. 2012. Glenshee Archaeology Project: 2012 Excavation, Unpublished Data Structure Report.

Strachan, D. and Sneddon, D. 2013. Glenshee Archaeology Project: 2013 Excavation, Unpublished Data Structure Report.

Strachan, D. and Sneddon, D. 2014. Glenshee Archaeology Project: 2014 Excavation. Unpublished Data Structure Report.

Strachan, D. and Sneddon, D. 2015. Glenshee Archaeology Project 2015 Excavation. *Perth and Kinross Heritage Trust/Northlight Heritage, Project 120, Report 149.*

Stratigos, M.J. 2016. The lost lochs of Scotland: tracking land-use change and its effects on the archaeological record. *Journal of Wetland Archaeology*, 16:1, 33-51. DOI: 10.1080/14732971.2016.1248129

Stuart, J. 1866. Account of excavations in groups of cairns, stone circles, and hut circles on Balnabroch, Parish of Kirkmichael, Perthshire, and at West Persie, in that neighbourhood. *Proceedings of the Society of Antiquaries of Scotland* 6: 402-410.

Stuiver M. and Kra R.S. 1986. Editorial comment. *Radiocarbon* 28(2B): ii.

Stuiver M. and Polach H.A. 1977. Reporting of 14C data. *Radiocarbon* 19(3): 355-363.

Stuiver M. and Reimer P.J. 1986. A computer program for radiocarbon age calibration. *Radiocarbon* 28(2B): 1022-1030.

Stuiver M. and Reimer P.J. 1993. Extended 14C data base and revised CALIB 3.0 14C calibration program. *Radiocarbon* 35(1): 215-230.

Taylor, D.B. 1990. *Circular Homesteads in North West Perthshire* (Abertay Historical Society Publication no. 29). Dundee: Abertay Historical Society.

Taylor, S. 2011. Pictish place-names revisited, in S. Driscoll, J. Geddes and M. Hall (eds) *Pictish progress: New Studies on Northern Britain in the Early Middle Ages*: 67-118. Leiden: Brill.

Thoms, L. and Halliday, S.P. 2014. Survey and excavation at two prehistoric hut-circles in Tulloch Field, Enochdhu, Strathardle, Perthshire with an evaluation of their research and regional contexts. *Tayside and Fife Archaeological Journal* 19-20: 1-19.

Thorneycroft, W. 1933. Observations on hut-circles near the Eastern Border of Perthshire, North of Blairgowrie. *Proceedings of the Society of Antiquaries of Scotland* 67: 187-208.

Thorneycroft, W. 1946. Further Observations on Hut-Circles. *Proceedings of the Society of Antiquaries of Scotland* 80: 131-5.

Tipping, R. 1987. The origins of corroded pollen grains at five early postglacial pollen sites in western Scotland. *Review of Palaeobotany and Palynology* 53: 151-161.

Tipping, R. 1994. The form and fate of Scottish woodlands. *Proceedings of the Society of Antiquaries of Scotland* 124: 1-54.

Tipping, R. 1995a. Holocene landscape change at Carn Dubh, near Pitlochry, Perthshire. *Journal of Quaternary Science* 10: 59-75.

Tipping, R. 1995b. Holocene evolution of a lowland Scottish landscape: Kirkpatrick Fleming. II. Regional vegetation and land-use change. *Holocene* 5: 83-96.

Tipping, R. 1996. Microscopic charcoal records, inferred human activity and climate change in the mesolithic of northernmost Scotland, in A. Pollard and A. Morrison (eds) *The Early Prehistory of Scotland*: 39-61. Edinburgh: Edinburgh University Press.

Tipping, R. 1997. Pollen analysis, late Iron Age and Roman agriculture around Hadrian's Wall, in A. Gwilt and C. Haselgrove (eds) *Reconstructing Iron Age Societies*: 239-247. Oxford: Oxbow.

Tipping, R. 2002. Climatic variability and 'marginal' settlement in upland British landscapes: a re-evaluation. *Landscapes* 3: 10-28.

Tipping, R. 2008. Blanket peat in the Scottish Highlands: timing, cause, spread and the myth of environmental determinism. *Biodiversity and Conservation* 17: 2097-2113.

Tipping, R. 2010. *Bowmont. An Environmental History of the Bowmont Valley and the Northern Cheviot Hills. 1000 BC – AD 2000.* Edinburgh: Society of Antiquaries of Scotland.

Tipping, R. 2013. The environmental context, in D. Strachan (ed.) *Excavations at the Black Spout, Pitlochry, and the Iron Age monumental roundhouses of North West Perthshire*: 57-60. Perth: Perth and Kinross Heritage Trust.

Tipping, R. 2017. Towards an Environmental History of Argyll & Bute: A review of current data, their strengths and weaknesses and suggestions for future work, in B. Simpson and S. Webb (eds) *An Archaeological Research Framework for Argyll*: 29-64 http://www.scottishheritagehub.com/rarfa

Tipping, R., Bradley, R., McCulloch, R., Sanders, J. and Wilson, R. 2012. Moments of crisis: from coincidence to hypothesis testing in defining the impacts of abrupt climate change in Scottish prehistory. *Proceedings of the Society of Antiquaries of Scotland* 142: 1-17.

Tipping, R., Davies, A.L. and McCulloch, R. 2006. Introduced oak woodlands in northern Scotland: pollen-analytical evidence for early historic plantations, in A. Woolf (ed.) *Landscape and Environment in Dark Age Scotland*: 29-48. St Andrews: St Andrews University Press.

Trier, B. 1969. *Das Haus im Nordwesten der Germania Libera*. Münster: Veröffentlichungen der Altertumskomission im Provinzialinstitut für westfälische Landes- und Volkskunde IV.

Trouet, V., Esper, J., Graham, N.E., Baker, A., Scourse, J.D. and Frank, D.C. 2009. Persistent positive North

Atlantic Oscillation mode dominated the Medieval Climate Anomaly. *Science* 324: 78-80.

Turner, J. 1975. The evidence for land use by prehistoric farming communities: the use of three-dimensional pollen diagrams, in J.G. Evans, S. Limbrey and H. Cleere, H. (eds) *The Effect of Man on the Landscape: the Highland Zone* (Council for British Archaeology Research Report No. 11): 86-95. London: Council for British Archaeology.

Tweddle, J.C., Edwards, K.J. and Fieller, N.R.J. 2005. Multivariate statistical and other approaches for the separation of cereal from wild Poaceae pollen using a large Holocene dataset. *Vegetation History and Archaeobotany* 14: 15-30.

Urbańczyk, P. 1999. North Atlantic turf architecture as an example of environmental adaption. *Archaeologia Polona* 37: 119-133.

van Geel, B. 1978. A palaeoecological study of Holocene peat bog sections in Germany and The Netherlands, based on the analysis of pollen, spores, and macro- and micro-scopic remains of fungi, algae, cormophytes and animals. *Review of Palaeobotany and Palynology* 25: 1-120.

Van Geel, B. and Berglund, B.E. 2000. A causal link between a climatic deterioration around 850 cal BC and a subsequent rise in human population density in NW-Europe? *Terra Nostra* 2000: 126-130.

Van Giffen, A.E. 1940. Een systematisch onderzoek in één der Tuinster Wierden te Leens. *Jaarverslag van de Vereeniging voor Terpenonderzoek* 20–24 (1935–1940): 26–107.

Van Hoof, J. and Van Dijken, F. 2008. The historical turf farms of Iceland: architecture, building technology and the indoor environment. *Building and Environment* 43: 1023-1230.

Verhulst, A. 2002. *The Carolingian Economoy*. Cambridge: Cambridge University Press.

von den Driesch, A. 1976. *A Guide to the Measurement of Animal Bones from Archaeological Sites*. Harvard: Peabody Museum Bulletin No 1.

Vuorela, I. 1973. The indication of farming in pollen diagrams from southern Finland. *Acta Botanica Fennici* 87: 3-41.

Wainwright, F.T. 1962. *Archaeology and Place-names and History: An essay on problems of co-ordination*. London: Routledge.

Wainwright, F.T. 1963. *The souterrains of southern Pictland*. London: Routledge.

Walker, B. 2004. The Parallelogram Plan: Accident or Design? *Yorkshire Buildings* 32: 82–88.

Walker, B. 2006a. *Scottish Turf Construction*. Technical Advice Note (TAN 30). Edinburgh: Historic Scotland. http://issuu.com/hspubs/docs/tan-30---scottish-turf-construction--june-06--plu-?e=0.

Walker, B. 2006b. The buildings at Hoddom: a vernacular perspective, in *Excavations at Hoddom, Dumfriesshire: An Early Ecclesiastical Site in South-West Scotland*: 184–185. Edinburgh: Society of Antiquaries of Scotland. http://www.socantscot.org/wp-content/uploads/2015/02/Hoddom-Table-of-Contents.pdf.

Walker, B. 2008. The Celtic cuppill and its implications in building construction and design. *Transactions of the Ancient Monuments Society* 52: 71–106.

Walker, B. and McGregor, C. 1996. *The Hebridean Blackhouse; A Guide to Materials, Construction and Maintenance*. Technical Advice Note (TAN 5). Edinburgh: Historic Scotland.

Walker, B. McGregor, C., and Little R. 1996. *Earth Structures and Construction in Scotland: a guide to the recognition and conservation of earth technology in Scottish buildings*. Technical Advice Note (TAN 6). Edinburgh: Historic Scotland.

Walker, M.J.C. 1977. Corrydon: a late glacial profile from Glenshee, South-east Grampian Highlands, Scotland. *Pollen et Spores* 19: 391-406.

Ward G.K. and Wilson S.R. 1978. Procedures for comparing and combining radiocarbon age-determinations: a critique. *Archaeometry* 20(1): 19-31.

Waterbolk, H.T. 1979. Siedlungskontinuität im Küstengebiet der Nordsee zwischen Rhein und Elbe. *Probleme der Küstenforschung im südlichen Nordseegebiet* 13: 1-21.

Waterbolk, H.T. 2009. *Getimmerd Verleden: Sporen van Voor- En Vroeghistorische Houtbouw Op de Zand- En Kleigronden Tussen Eems En IJssel* (Groningen Archaeological Studies 10). Groningen/Eelde: University of Groningen/Archaeological Research & Consultancy/Barkhuis.

Watkins, T. 1980. Excavation of a settlement and souterrain at Newmill, near Bankfoot, Perthshire. *Proceedings of the Society of Antiquaries of Scotland* 110: 165-208.

Watson, W.J. 1913. The circular forts of North Perthshire. *Proceedings of the Society of Antiquaries of Scotland* 47: 30-60.

Watson, W.J. 1915. Circular forts in Lorn and North Perthshire; with a note of the excavation of one at Borenich, Loch Tummel. *Proceedings of the Society of Antiquaries of Scotland* 49: 17-32.

Watson, W.J. 1926. *The History of the Celtic Place-Names of Scotland*. Edinburgh and London reprinted with an introduction by Simon Taylor, Edinburgh 2004 and, with an extended Introduction, Edinburgh 2011.

Welander, R., Batey, C. and Cowie, T. 1987. A Viking burial from Kneep, Uig, Isle of Lewis. *Proceedings of the Society of Antiquaries of Scotland* 117: 149-174.

Wells, J.M., Mighall, T.M., Smith, D.E. and Dawson, A.G. 1999. Brighouse Bay, southwest Scotland: Holocene vegetational history and human impact at a small coastal valley mire, in P. Andrews and P. Banham (eds) *Late Cenozoic Environments and Hominid Evolution: A Tribute to Bill Bishop*: 217-233. London: Geological Society.

Welsch, R.L. 1967. *Sod Walls*. 1991 facsimile reprint. Lincoln: J & L Lee Co.

Westerdahl, C. 1992. The maritime cultural landscape. *International Journal of Nautical Archaeology* 21 (1): 5–14. doi.org/10.1111/j.1095-9270.1992.tb00336.x

Westerdahl, C. 2014. The Maritime Middle Ages — past, present, and future. Some ideas from a Scandinavian horizon. *European Journal of Archaeology* 17 (1): 120–138. doi.org/10.1179/1461957113Y.0000000046

Whaley, D. 2006. *A Dictionary of Lake District Place-Names*. Nottingham: English Place-Name Society.

Whittington, G. 1975. Place names and the settlement pattern of dark age Scotland. *Proceedings of the Society of Antiquaries of Scotland* 106: 99-110.

Whittington, G. and Edwards, K.J. 1993. *Ubi solitudinem faciunt pacem appellant*: the Romans in Scotland, a palaeoenvironmental contribution. *Britannia* 24: 13-25.

Whittington, G., Edwards, K.J. and Cundill, P.R. 1990. *Palaeoenvironmental Investigations at Black Loch, in the Ochil Hills of Fife, Scotland* (Monograph No. 22). Aberdeen: O'Dell.

Whittington, G. and Soulsby, J.A. 1968. A preliminary report on an investigation into *pit* place-names. *Scottish Geographical Magazine* 84(2): 117-125.

Whyte, I.D. 1985. Shielings and the upland pastoral economy of the Lake District in Medieval and early modern times, in J.R. Baldwin and I.D. Whyte (eds) *The Scandinavians in Cumbria*: 103-119. Edinburgh: Scottish Society for Northern Studies.

Wickham, C. 2005. *Farming the Early Middle Ages*. Oxford: Oxford University Press.

Wickham-Jones, C.R. and G.H. Collins. 1977. The sources of flint and chert in northern Britain. *Proceedings of the Society of Antiquaries of Scotland* 109: 7-21.

Wilkinson, B. 2009. A study of turf: historic rural settlements in Scotland and Iceland. *Architectural Heritage* 20(1): 15–31. https://doi.org/10.3366/E135075240900017X.

Wilson, A. 2000. The metalwork, in A. Crone. *The History of a Scottish Lowland Crannog: Excavations at Buiston, Ayrshire 1989-90*: 138-40. Edinburgh: Scottish Trust for Archaeological Research/Historic Scotland.

Winchester, A.J.L. 2000. *The Harvest of the Hills. Rural Life in Northern England and the Scottish Borders, 1400-1700*. Edinburgh: Edinburgh University Press.

Winchester, A.J.L. 2017. Shielings and common pastures, in J.J. Stringer and A.J.L. Winchester (eds) *Northern England and Southern Scotland in the Central Middle Ages*: 272-297. Woodbridge: The Boydell Press.

Winlow, S. 2010. Two new dates from two old investigations: a reconsideration of The Womens Knowe, Inchtuthil and Kingoodie long cist cemetery, Invergowrie. *Tayside and Fife Archaeological Journal* 16: 49-56.

Woodley, N.C. 2018. An Iron Age and Early Historic settlement and working site at Walton Road, Dyce. *Tayside and Fife Archaeological Journal* 24: 39-56.

Woltering, P.J. 1974. 2000 Jaar Wonen: Opgravingen Op Texel. *Spiegel Historiael* 9: 322–335.

Woltering, P.J. 1975. Occupation History of Texel, I: The Excavations at Den Burg: Preliminary Report. *Berichten van de Rijksdienst Voor Het Oudheidkundig Bodemonderzoek* 23: 7–36.

Woolf, A. 2006. Dún Nechtain, fortriu and the geography of the Picts. *Scottish Historical Review* 85: 182-201.

Woolf, A. 2007. *From Pictland to Alba 789-1070*. Edinburgh: Edinburgh University Press.

Wright, A.D. 2012. The Archaeology of Variation: A case study of repetition, difference and becoming in the Mesolithic of West Central Scotland. Unpublished PhD thesis, University of Glasgow.

Zakšek, K., Oštir, K., and Kokalj, Ž. 2011. Sky-View Factor as a Relief Visualization Technique. *Remote Sensing*, 3: 398-415. DOI: 10.3390/rs3020398

Zimmermann, W.H. 1988. Regelhafte Innengliederung prähistorischer Langhäuser in den Nordseeanrainerstaaten. *Germania* 66/2: 465–488.

Appendix A

Data-set for Figures 4.13 and 4.15a			
Canmore ID	Name	Distance (km) from B-A	Height (m) above strath
31105	Hill of Alyth	2.66	130
28777	Welton of Creuchies	3.63	142
28872	Marleehill	4.58	122
31112	Tullymurdoch	6.55	171
28839	Ranageig	8.42	244
29240	Hill of Ashmore	9.45	250
27373	Craigsheal Burn	11.88	146
29042	Knockali, Corrie Burn	12.8	115
29021	Knockali	13.33	73
29030	Knockali	13.61	72
29039	Whitehouse	14.75	85
29091	Balnabroich	14.8	117
27296	Balnabroich	15.65	95
27227	Pitcarmick Burn	16.24	89
29409	Glenkilrie	16.61	83
27251	Pitcarmick Loch	16.71	169
27339	Cultalonie	17.28	125
27217	Pitcarmick	17.47	144
29394	Dalnaglar	18.5	0
29437	Lair	18.67	33
29451	Ashintully	19.02	77
29364	Finegand	20.9	34
27564	Gleann Fernoch	22.87	40

Data-set for Figure 4.14		
Canmore ID	Name	Distance (km)
29394	Dalnaglar	0.12
29364	Finegand	0.2
27564	Gleann Fernoch	0.28
29437	Lair	0.34
29509	Lair	0.43
29513	Lair	0.54
29039	Whitehouse	0.65
27217	Pitcarmick	0.77
29030	Knockali	0.88
27296	Balnabroich	0.91
29410	Glenkilrie	0.93
29409	Glenkilrie	0.94
29021	Knockali	1.075
29446	Lair	1.17
29103	Balnabroich	1.32
29092	Balnabroich	1.57
29091	Balnabroich	1.65
28777	Welton of Creuchies	1.67
27339	Cultalonie	1.81
31105	Hill of Alyth	1.84
29042	Knockali, Corrie Burn	2.51
27227	Pitcarmick Burn	2.63
28872	Marleehill	2.65
27251	Pitcarmick Loch	3.27
29451	Ashintully	3.42
27373	Craigsheal Burn	3.87
29240	Hill of Ashmore	4.52
28839	Ranageig	5.43
31112	Tullymurdoch	5.84

APPENDIX A

Data-set for Figure 4.15b		
Canmore ID	Name	Height (m) above strath
29394	Dalnaglar	0
29509	Lair	29
29437	Lair	33
29364	Finegand	34
27564	Gleann Fernoch	40
29513	Lair	55
29446	Lair	64
27234	Pitcarmick	66
29030	Knockali	72
29021	Knockali	73
29451	Ashintully	77
29410	Glenkilrie	78
29038	Knockali	79
29409	Glenkilrie	83
29039	Whitehouse	85
27227	Pitcarmick Burn	89
27229	Pitcarmick Burn	90
27231	Pitcarmick Burn	90
29036	Knockali	91
27296	Balnabroich	95
27298	Pitcarmick	96
27228	Pitcarmick Burn	97
29103	Balnabroich	101
27322	Pitcarmick Burn	112
29042	Knockali, Corrie Burn	115
29091	Balnabroich	117
27220	Pitcarmick	117
27233	Pitcarmick	119
28872	Marleehill	122
29092	Balnabroich	125
27339	Cultalonie	125
27250	Pitcarmick	125
27219	Pitcarmick	126
27343	Pitcarmick Burn	129
31105	Hill of Alyth	130
27302	Pitcarmick Burn	130
27331	Pitcarmick Burn	131
27222	Pitcarmick	134
27320	Pitcarmick Burn	140
27327	Pitcarmick Burn	140
27344	Pitcarmick Burn	140

28777	Welton of Creuchies	142
27217	Pitcarmick	144
27373	Craigsheal Burn	146
27264	Pitcarmick Loch	147
27328	Pitcarmick Burn	154
27223	Pitcarmick	161
27225	Pitcarmick	161
27251	Pitcarmick Loch	169
27346	Pitcarmick Loch	170
31112	Tullymurdoch	171
27324	Pitcarmick Loch	177
27332	Pitcarmick Burn	180
27270	Pitcarmick Loch	180
27341	Pitcarmick Loch	181
27342	Pitcarmick Loch	183
27325	Pitcarmick Loch	216
28839	Ranageig	244
29240	Hill of Ashmore	250

Data-set for Figure 4.17		
Canmore ID	Name	Aspect
27251	Pitcarmick Loch	19
27328	Pitcarmick Burn	20
27341	Pitcarmick Loch	21
27332	Pitcarmick Burn	22
27331	Pitcarmick Burn	29
27346	Pitcarmick Loch	36
27327	Pitcarmick Burn	37
27344	Pitcarmick Burn	42
27217	Pitcarmick	47
27302	Pitcarmick Burn	56
29364	Finegand	60
27219	Pitcarmick	60
27342	Pitcarmick Loch	69
27222	Pitcarmick	82
27234	Pitcarmick	84
29513	Lair	90
27220	Pitcarmick	92
27298	Pitcarmick	97
28777	Welton of Creuchies	97
27225	Pitcarmick	103
29446	Lair	108

APPENDIX A

27250	Pitcarmick	108
29038	Knockali	111
27223	Pitcarmick	111
27343	Pitcarmick Burn	120
27228	Pitcarmick Burn	126
27320	Pitcarmick Burn	126
27231	Pitcarmick Burn	127
29509	Lair	128
29437	Lair	130
27229	Pitcarmick Burn	135
27233	Pitcarmick	142
29036	Knockali	146
27227	Pitcarmick Burn	146
29021	Knockali	162
27339	Cultalonie	169
29394	Dalnaglar	172
29451	Ashintully	173
27324	Pitcarmick Loch	176
27264	Pitcarmick Loch	180
27270	Pitcarmick Loch	182
29030	Knockali	183
27322	Pitcarmick Burn	184
31112	Tullymurdoch	192
28839	Ranageig	206
29240	Hill of Ashmore	207
29103	Balnabroich	214
29409	Glenkilrie	216
27564	Gleann Fernoch	221
29410	Glenkilrie	222
28872	Marleehill	225
31105	Hill of Alyth	228
27373	Craigsheal Burn	231
27296	Balnabroich	237
29091	Balnabroich	251
29042	Knockali, Corrie Burn	272
27325	Pitcarmick Loch	274
29092	Balnabroich	280
29039	Whitehouse	284

Data-set for Figure 4.18		
Canmore ID	Name	KW/m²/yr
29364	Finegand	737579
27341	Pitcarmick Loch	742180
27332	Pitcarmick Burn	755334
27217	Pitcarmick	762080
27331	Pitcarmick Burn	764022
27251	Pitcarmick Loch	765975
27327	Pitcarmick Burn	776265
27344	Pitcarmick Burn	780589
27328	Pitcarmick Burn	781376
27346	Pitcarmick Loch	782853
27219	Pitcarmick	783518
29039	Whitehouse	792978
27298	Pitcarmick	793986
29092	Balnabroich	794017
27234	Pitcarmick	794903
27222	Pitcarmick	796094
27342	Pitcarmick Loch	800652
28777	Welton of Creuchies	800711
27302	Pitcarmick Burn	801081
27325	Pitcarmick Loch	802200
29042	Knockali, Corrie Burn	803060
27220	Pitcarmick	807779
28872	Marleehill	809066
27231	Pitcarmick Burn	809208
27229	Pitcarmick Burn	812819
27250	Pitcarmick	814130
29394	Dalnaglar	814439
31105	Hill of Alyth	817514
29091	Balnabroich	820617
27225	Pitcarmick	821882
27296	Balnabroich	822446
29038	Knockali	823671
27227	Pitcarmick Burn	823712
27343	Pitcarmick Burn	823756
29103	Balnabroich	824295
27320	Pitcarmick Burn	824424
29509	Lair	826380
29446	Lair	826649
27339	Cultalonie	827620
27228	Pitcarmick Burn	829197
28839	Ranageig	831061

APPENDIX A

29030	Knockali	832541
27223	Pitcarmick	833260
29036	Knockali	833450
27373	Craigsheal Burn	834325
29021	Knockali	843676
27264	Pitcarmick Loch	847819
29240	Hill of Ashmore	848055
27564	Gleann Fernoch	851316
29437	Lair	855197
27322	Pitcarmick Burn	855845
31112	Tullymurdoch	857733
29410	Glenkilrie	859601
29513	Lair	859775
27233	Pitcarmick	864082
29409	Glenkilrie	865098
29451	Ashintully	871363
27270	Pitcarmick Loch	873148
27324	Pitcarmick Loch	881292

Index

A9, 5, 17
A93, 7, 17, 21, 22, 25, 28
aber-names, 134
Aberlemno, 14
Abernethy, 7, 13, 14, 87
Áed, 14
agrarian, 75, 107–108, 138–149
agriculture (*see also* agrarian) 11, 16, 22, 139, 151
Alba, 14–15, 141
Aldclune, 6, 109
Allt Corra-lairige, 16–24, 66, 114–132, 147–149
Allt an Lair, 16–19, 147
Allt Cosach, 124
Alyth, 4–6, 14–16, 133–134, 171–176
Anglo-Saxon, 3–4, 86–87, 94, 103, 104, 131, 141, 146
Angus, 1, 4, 7, 10, 14–15, 124, 132, 143, 145
animal bone, 104–106
annexe, 41–50, 78–84, 96–128, 144
anvil, 45–49, 79–84, 114
arable (*see also* cereals, crops), 15–23, 123, 140–152
artefacts, 6, 33, 78–104
Ashintully, 15, 171–177
Atholl, 13–16, 109, 124
Avena-Triticum, 74–75

Balhomish, 124
Balnabroich, 1–8, 123–133, 171–176
Balnaguard Burn, 124
Balvarran, 15
Bankfoot, 6
Bannock Hill, 124
Barley, 76–77, 139–140
barns, 122–127, 146
Barry Hill, Alyth, 4–8, 132
Basin 1, 66–69
Basin 2, 19, 66–74, 107–119, 139
Bayesian, 25–41, 56–65, 110–111, 124, 147–152
bead, 35, 103–104, 131, 146
Ben Lawers, 145–148
Bertha, 7
Black Spout, 6, 109, 124
Black Water, 7–16
blackhouses, 122
Blacklunans, 16

Blair Atholl, 109, 124
Blairgowrie, 1–7, 13–14, 17, 132, 136, 140, 149
bone, 36–49, 61, 78–124, 145–151
Borenich, 4
Bridei, 14
Bridge of Cally, 7–15, 133–136
Britons, 3
broad rig, 11
Bronze Age, 1–31, 62, 80–86, 102–108, 143
Broxmouth, 143
Bruceton Stone, 6
buckles, 2, 6, 33, 87–97, 111
Building 1, 25–42, 57–128, 145–152
Building 2, 25–66, 80–84, 97–120
Building 3, 24, 41–129, 144–150
Building 4, 24, 41–51
Building 5, 24, 41–51, 97, 112–119
Building 6, 25–30, 51–52, 114–123, 148
Building 7, 25–31, 52–61, 110–123, 152
Building 8, 52, 116–123, 142
Building 9, 123
Building 10, 123
Building 11, 25, 149
Building 12, 24, 122
Building 13, 24, 122
Building 14, 25, 56, 117–123, 150
Building 15, 122
Bunrannoch, 124–126
butchery, 105, 144
byres, 3–8, 27, 52, 106–132, 144–152
byre-houses, 8, 27, 114–132, 145–152

cairn-fields, 4, 24, 133
Cairngorm, 107, 135, 152
Cairnwell, 7
Caisteal Mac Tuathal, Kenmore, 6
calves, 15, 49, 105–114, 144
Carn Dubh, 4, 7, 12, 99, 107, 108–109, 132, 139, 141–142, 146, 148
Castle Dow, 6
Caterthuns, 132
cattle, 10–19, 49–61, 104–147
Caulfeild, 25–28, 149
cereals, 70–77, 124, 139

Cheviots, 138
Clatchard Craig, 13, 82, 98, 102
clearance, 4–28, 50–56, 108–110, 138–151
climate, 16, 107–110, 140–151
climate change, 107, 151
Cnoc Feanndaige, 16
coarse stone, 82
Cochrage, 15
colonisation, 3, 133–151
continent, 3–13, 86, 104, 132
Corra-lairig, 10–11, 23–25, 147–149
crannogs, 6-7, 92, 97, 110, 145
creel-houses, 122
cropmarks, 124–126, 143
crops, 139–152
crucks (*see* cuppills), 4–8, 111
cultivation, 7–51, 66–78, 108–109, 121, 133–152
cultivation ridges, 28
cuppills, 4, 121–131

dabhach, 16, 132
dabhaicheans, 132
Dál Riata, 14
Dalmunzie, 16
Dalnaglar, 12–16, 107–108, 128–137, 171–176
Dalnoid, 16
Dalrulzion, 1–16, 152
Denmark, 129–131
Doldy, 15
dress accessories, 87–98
Drumderg, ix
Drumfork, 15
Drummond Hill, 6
Drumturn, 15–23
Dull, 6
Dundurn, 6–14, 92–104, 140
Dunfallandy, 6
Dunkeld, 4–16, 124–132
Dunmay, 16
Dunnichen, 14, 145
Dunnottar, 14

early historic (*see* early medieval), 3, 124, 137
Early Iron Age, 4
early medieval, 3–35, 55–66, 87–152
Easter Bleaton, 10
Easter Kinnear, 98, 102, 128, 131, 142

Easter Raitts, 119
economy, 1, 27, 66, 106–108, 123, 137–152
Elphin, 14
emporia, 3
England, 3–14, 103–104, 122–146
entrance, 8, 24–54, 82–84, 110–128

farm, 6–27, 123, 144–151
Finavon, 132
Finegand, 137, 171–176
flint, 31–45, 78–80
fort, 4, 6, 89–102, 132–143
Forteviot, 7–14, 109
Fortingall, 6, 104
Fortriu, 6–14
Frisian, 131

Gaelic, 6–17, 132, 144–147
geology, 16–18, 137
geophysics, 28–33, 150
glass, 6, 35, 103–104, 131, 146
Glen Clova, 124
Glen Esk, 124
Glen Isla, 4–15
Glen Prosen, 124
Glen Shee, 1–25, 62–65, 85–87, 107, 124–152
Glenkilrie, 11–12, 133, 171–177
Gowrie, 14–16, 124–132
Grandtully, 6
grazing, 12–21, 74–76, 106–119, 138–147
grubenhauser, (*see also* sunken-featured buildings), 128
gully, 8–10, 39–59, 97, 111–120, 143

Haálfdan, 14
hammerscale, 47–49, 98–102, 114
Hawkhill, 143
hearth, 8, 37–62, 76–77, 91–127, 142–149
Highland Boundary Fault, 1–7
Hill of Ashmore, 135–136, 171–177
hillfort (*see* fort) 4, 6, 89–102, 132–143
Hordeum, 57, 70–77, 139
household equipment, 93
hut-circle, 22, 133

Iceland, 110, 117, 119, 120–122, 127, 128, 130, 145–146
Inchtuthil, 4, 124
Iron Age, 1–6, 22, 87–108, 129–152

ironworking, 99–102

Jutland, 129–131

Keillor Stone, 6
Kenmore, 6
Kenneth MacAlpin, 6, 10
Kettins, 6
Kincardineshire, 14, 124
King's Seat, Dunkeld, 4–6, 132
Kintore, 124–126, 143
Kirkmichael, 14, 132–136, 149
knives, 88, 111
Knockali, 128–133, 171–177

Lair, 1–153, 171–177
Lair Farm, 19
Lamh Dearg, 16
Lammermuir Hills, 141
lamp, 42, 81–84
land use, 21–23, 108, 140–153
Late Antique, 140–151
little ice age, 140–151
Late Bronze Age, 4, 62, 102–108, 143
Late Iron Age, 6, 89–108, 132–143
late medieval, 6, 119
later prehistoric, 8–12, 107–133, 146
Leens type, 129–131, 144
lithics, 78–80
Litigan, 4–6
Loch Beanie, 6–7
Loch Benachally, 123–133
Loch Earn, 6
Loch of Clunie, 6
Loch Rannoch, 124
loft, 112–115, 128–130
Logierait, 6
longhouse, 10, 107, 123–131

Mael Coluim, 14
Marleehill, 133–137, 171–176
Meall Easganan, 16–17
medieval, 1–35, 55–66, 82–152
Meigle, 6–14
metal-work, 87–88
metal-working, 2–6, 47, 97–109

Middle Bronze Age, 4, 22, 143
migration, 4, 132–134
military road, 25, 28, 149
Moncreiffe Hill, 14
monumental roundhouses, 4, 109, 124
moor, 10–11, 22, 66, 134, 137, 144, 146
morphology, 25, 52, 98, 117, 123–129, 131, 152
mortar, 42, 81–84
Mount Blair, 9–16, 108
Mounth, 14, 132, 145
Muir of Gormack, 133

Netherlands, 4, 127–131, 144
Neolithic, 7–22, 86, 107, 119
Newbarns, 130, 143
Newmill, Bankfoot, 6, 143
Norse, 3–15, 87, 102–103, 144–145
North-east Perthshire, 124–148
Norway, 86–87, 129–131
nutshells, 40

Oakbank Crannog, 145
oats, 15, 77
ogham, 86–87
Old Faskally, 6
Onuist, 14

padlocks, 6, 91–97
pasture (*see also* grazing), 13–21, 67, 140–151
paving, 47, 84, 112–123
peat, 12–28, 66–76, 107–119, 140, 152
peat-cutting, 67–70
Perth, 1–22, 87–108, 124–133, 147–152
Perth and Kinross, 1–22, 87–108, 124–133, 150–152
Perthshire, 2–16, 106, 124–149
pett-names, 15
Pict – (e.g. Pictland, Pictish, Pictavia), 1–17, 86–87, 109, 123–147
Pictish, 1–17, 86–87, 109, 123–147
pig, 49, 104
pins, 87–98
Pit-names, 15
Pitcarmick, 1–48, 61–70, 84–85, 102–153, 171–177
Pitcarmick building, 25, 70, 123, 142–151
Pitcarmick-type building (*see* Pitcarmick building), 1–8
Pitlochry, 4–15, 109, 124

pits, 8, 36–59, 99–124, 143
place-names, 14–23, 106, 132, 144–149
plough, 33, 122
pollen, 5–28, 66–76, 107–110, 122, 137–152
post-holes, 8, 36–60, 101–124, 143
porches, 128
Portmahomack, 102, 131–142
post-medieval, 8–25, 111–148
pottery, 31–42, 80, 102, 116–119, 148
power-centres, 1–13, 132, 146
pottery, 31–42, 80, 102, 116–119, 148
purlins, 121–122

Queen's View, 4–6
quern, 45, 82–84

radiocarbon dating, 28, 56–57, 101
Rae Loch, 13, 107–108, 147
Ragnall, 14
Ranageig, 134–135, 171–176
Ratho, 128
raths, 142–143
RCAHMS, 1–52, 104–152
Recession, 138–142
research agendas, 129
rig, 11–30, 51, 133, 148
ring-cairn, 1, 8–9, 22–26, 28, 30–31, 37, 40, 51–52, 59, 61, 70, 108–109, 112, 120, 122, 133, 144–147, 150–151
River Ericht, 7, 133
River Garry, 4, 6
River Isla, 6
River Tay, 1–13, 124, 151
Rochallie, 15
roof, 8, 35–46, 110–130
rotary grinders, 47–50, 81–85, 114
rotary querns, 45, 82–84
roundhouses, 1–31, 70, 108–142
roundwood, 31–33, 59–62, 95, 108–110
rye, 139

Scandinavia, 86, 117, 142–145
Scheduled Monuments, 1, 150
Scone, 7–14
Scottish Redware, 52, 102–103
Scottish White Gritty ware, 35, 103

Secale, 71
security equipment, 91–97
settlement, 1–27, 56–62, 87–152
Shanzie Farm, Alyth, 6
sheep, 10–19, 45–54, 87, 104–127, 145–146
shielings, 10–16, 106–107, 123–151
short-house, 3
Sidlaw Hills, 4
slag, 44–56, 80, 98–101
smithing, 1, 25, 27, 98–102, 106, 129–150
social status, 122, 146
souterrains, 6, 143
spindle whorl, 44, 80–87
spinning, 84–86
Spittal of Glenshee, 6–23, 149
St Andrews, 14
stake-hole, 46
stone, 1–61, 76–131, 144–148
stone carving, 1, 6–7, 86–87
stone tools, 80–85
stone wall, 52–61, 109–122
Stormont Loch, 6
Stewart, Margaret, 1–6, 124–128
Strath Tay, 6–8
Strathardle, 1–24, 106, 124–151
Strathbraan, 108, 124
Strathclyde, 142
Strathearn, 7–16, 140
Strathmore, 4–7, 133, 151
Struan, 6
Stuart, John, 1
sub-glacial, 16
sunken-featured buildings (*see also grubenhauser*), 3
Sweden, 131
symbol stones, 6–15, 132

tathing, 144
thanages, 3, 132
thatch, 111–122
The Middle Ages, 11–15, 117
Terminus Post Quem, TPQ, 33–37, 54–63 110–116
Thorneycroft, Wallace, 1–8
timber, 3–4, 35–36, 93–94, 108–132, 144
timber halls, 3
tools, 44, 80–102, 114, 127
Torr Lochaidh, 16, 19, 20–25, 28

transhumance (*see also* shielings), 16, 106, 144–145
trees, 12–19, 33, 49, 69–76, 107–122, 137–147
Tullymurdoch, 133–134, 171–177
turf, 1–8, 28–62, 78–152

uplands, 1–22, 74, 104–109, 125–153
Upper Gcthens, Blairgowrie, 6

Viking, 3–14, 117–127, 145
vitrified material, 98–101, 132

Welton of Creuchies, 123–128, 171–176
whetstone, 42–49, 80–85, 114
woodland, 12–21, 70–76, 107–122, 137–146
woodland clearance, 12, 138